P9-BYA-901

Multicultural Psychology
Understanding Our Diverse Communities
SECOND EDITION

JEFFERY SCOTT MIO
California State Polytechnic University, Pomona

LORI A. BARKER
California State Polytechnic University, Pomona

JAYDEE SANTOS TUMAMBING
Private Practice

 **Higher Education**

Boston   Burr Ridge, IL   Dubuque, IA   New York   San Francisco   St. Louis
Bangkok   Bogotá   Caracas   Kuala Lumpur   Lisbon   London   Madrid   Mexico City
Milan   Montreal   New Delhi   Santiago   Seoul   Singapore   Sydney   Taipei   Toronto

The McGraw-Hill Companies

Higher Education

A DIVISION OF THE McGRAW-HILL COMPANIES

Published by McGraw-Hill, an imprint of The McGraw-Hill Companies, Inc., 1221 Avenue of the Americas, New York, NY 10020. Copyright © 2009, 2006. All rights reserved. No part of this publication may be reproduced or distributed in any form or by any means, or stored in a database or retrieval system, without the prior written consent of The McGraw-Hill Companies, Inc., including, but not limited to, in any network or other electronic storage or transmission, or broadcast for distance learning.

This book is printed on acid-free paper.

1 2 3 4 5 6 7 8 9 0 FGR/FGR 0 9 8

ISBN: 978-0-07-338271-5
MHID: 0-07-338271-X

Editor in Chief: *Michael Ryan*
Publisher: *Beth Mejia*
Executive Editor: *Michael Sugarman*
Developmental Editor: *Marley Magaziner*
Editorial Coordinator: *Jillian Allison*
Executive Marketing Manager: *James Headley*
Marketing Specialist: *Rebecca Saidlower*
Production Editor: *Karol Jurado*
Production Service: *Matrix Productions Inc.*
Cover Designer: *Margarite Reynolds*
Cover Image: *Marlene Yamada*
Media Project Manager: *Jessalyn Clark*
Senior Production Supervisor: *Tandra Jorgensen*
Composition: *10/12 Sabon by ICC Macmillan Inc.*
Printer: *45# New Era Matte, Quebecor World, Inc.*

Credits: The credits section for this book begins on page 357 and is considered an extension of the copyright page.

Library of Congress Cataloging-in-Publication Data

Mio, Jeffery Scott.
    Multicultural psychology / Jeffery Scott Mio, Lori A. Barker,
Jaydee Tumambing. — 2nd ed.
        p. cm.
    Includes bibliographical references and index.
    ISBN-13: 978-0-07-338271-5 (alk. paper)
    ISBN-10: 0-07-338271-X (alk. paper)
    1. Multiculturalism. 2. Multiculturalism—Psychological aspects. 3. Multicultural education. 4. Mental health education. I. Barker, Lori A. II. Tumambing, Jaydee. III. Title.

    HM1271.M555 2009
    155.8—dc22

                                                                2008009215

The Internet addresses listed in the text were accurate at the time of publication. The inclusion of a Web site does not indicate an endorsement by the authors or McGraw-Hill, and McGraw-Hill does not guarantee the accuracy of the information presented at these sites.

www.mhhe.com

To my parents Ruby and George Mio, and to "Uncle Putt," who has a library of everything I have written professionally.

JSM

To all of my students, who continually inspire me.

LAB

To my grandparents, Candida, Crispulo, Leonardo, and Felisa. I hope that you all continue to guide our family, in spirit. Rest in Peace.

JST

Contents

CHAPTER 1
What Is Multicultural Psychology?   *1*

CHAPTER 2

Multicultural Issues Involving Research and Testing   33

1, 3, 6, 7, 9

CHAPTER 3

Differences in Worldviews   59

CHAPTER 4

Differences in Communication   89

CHAPTER 5

Immigrants, Refugees, and the Acculturation Process   119

CHAPTER 6

Stereotyping, Prejudice, Discrimination, and Racism   149

CHAPTER 7

Cultural Identity Development   185

CHAPTER 10

Where Do We Go From Here? Building Multicultural Competence   *279*

About the Authors

Dr. Jeffery Scott Mio is a professor in the Psychology and Sociology Department at California State Polytechnic University, Pomona (Cal Poly Pomona), where he also serves as the Director of the M.S. in Psychology Program. He received his Ph.D. from the University of Illinois, Chicago, in 1984. He taught at California State University, Fullerton, in the Counseling Department from 1984 to 1986, then taught at Washington State University in the Department of Psychology from 1986 to 1994, before accepting his current position at Cal Poly Pomona.

Dr. Mio has taught multicultural psychology since 1986. He is a Fellow in Division 2 (Society for the Teaching of Psychology) and Division 45 (Society for the Psychological Study of Ethnic Minority Issues) of the American Psychological Association as well as a Fellow of the Asian American Psychological Association and the Western Psychological Association. He was honored with the Outstanding Career Achievement for Teaching and Training from the American Psychological Association's Minority Fellowship Program, the Outstanding Teaching Award from the Western Psychological Association, and the Distinguished Contribution Award from the Asian American Psychological Association. His research interests are in the areas of teaching of multicultural issues, the development of allies in multicultural psychology, and how metaphors are used in political persuasion.

Dr. Lori A. Barker is a professor in the Department of Psychology and Sociology at California State Polytechnic University, Pomona (Cal Poly Pomona). Dr. Barker is a licensed clinical psychologist and also works part-time as the Administrative Director of the Cal Poly Pomona, Ennis W. Cosby, Child and Family Services Friendmobile, a program that offers counseling, psychological assessment, tutoring, and mentoring to children and families in inner-city Pomona. She also worked for 11 years as a part-time staff psychologist and clinical supervisor with Cal Poly Pomona Counseling and Psychological Services. Dr. Barker received her B.A. in psychology from Yale University and her Ph.D. in clinical psychology from UCLA. After receiving her degree, Dr. Barker spent one additional year at UCLA as a National Institute of Mental Health Postdoctoral Research Fellow.

Dr. Barker is the recipient of a number of teaching awards, including Outstanding Teaching Award, Western Psychological Association; Outstanding Advisor, Psi Chi Western Region; Outstanding Advisor, Office of Student Life, Cal Poly Pomona; Professor of the Year, Psi Chi, Cal Poly Pomona Chapter. Her primary areas of interest include multiculturalism, community psychology, and child/adolescent psychology. Her current research is on multicultural education and diversity training and the factors that influence the effectiveness of such programs. Dr. Barker regularly gives presentations, workshops, seminars, and keynote addresses for community and professional organizations on a variety of topics, including cultural diversity, ethnic identity, mental health, parenting, mentoring, and spirituality.

Jaydee Santos Tumambing graduated from California State Polytechnic University, Pomona (Cal Poly Pomona) in 2003 with her M.S. in Psychology, specializing in Marriage and Family Therapy. She also attained her Bachelor's degree in Psychology from Cal Poly Pomona in 2001. During her years at the university, Ms. Tumambing participated in such research studies as body image for women, men's crying behaviors, race and persuasion, and racial name-calling. Ms. Tumambing was an active member of the Psi Chi National Honor Society and participated in retreats, such as the yearly Cross-Cultural Retreat, both as a participant and as a facilitator, for two consecutive years. She is now in private practice in the Los Angeles area. She also works as a contracted therapist for Counseling 4 Kids, providing in-home therapy for foster children and their families.

Ms. Tumambing graduated as the most outstanding student in her graduate class, but the journey that involved immigrating to a new country, learning a new language, dealing with stereotypes, discrimination, and racism, and realizing the need to embrace her identity helped lead her toward the path of academic and personal fulfillment. Her struggles as a woman and mother of color were the motivating factors in pursuing multicultural issues. Her parents began the journey when they emigrated from the Philippines, and she continues to challenge this world's view of what she should look like, how she should behave, and what she should become. This is so that her multiethnic child can continue to carry the legacy and pride of her own identity and pass it on for generations to come.

Preface

Throughout the years that we have taught courses on multicultural psychology and attended conference presentations and workshops on this topic, what has stuck with us are the stories that people had to tell. In fact, the genesis of this book was a student's reaction paper that was so moving we felt it just *had* to be published. Thus, we planned this book around stories (anecdotes) that illustrate scientific studies and other professional writings in the field of multicultural psychology. The personal stories from our students have generally not been edited for grammar, although some markedly ungrammatical phrases and sentences were modified to make them a bit more grammatical. We did this to maintain the flavor of their stories from the heart that seemed to illustrate the academic points we are trying to make.

In general, science tells us that anecdotes are not sufficient evidence to prove one's point. Although we agree with that stance from a scientific perspective and do not substitute anecdotes for scientific investigation, we do use anecdotes as central points around which to build our case for multicultural issues based upon science. In addition, multicultural psychology emphasizes the value of integrating quantitative and qualitative methods to accurately capture the richness of diverse cultures and communities. Thus, rather than substituting for science, our anecdotes are prototypes for scientific investigation. For example, science tells us that there are differences in the way in which men and women communicate. We illustrate those differences by presenting some anecdotes highlighting the common experience women have of sometimes being shut out of conversations, particularly ones that are about "male" topics. Science tells us that there are various stages or statuses of racial identity, and we present some prototypical anecdotes that illustrate how those statuses of racial identity affect one's perceptions and life experiences. Science tells us that ethnic minority clients may have very different reactions to White therapists, and we present an anecdote that conveys a typical reaction to a White therapist who did not approach an ethnic minority family in a culturally sensitive manner. Again, these stories are not meant to replace science but to enrich science—to add texture to the clean lines of science.

ORGANIZATION OF THE BOOK

This book is organized around the emphasis that we have in our undergraduate multicultural courses and arose out of a perceived need we saw in the field. The initial books on multicultural psychology were written for graduate students, because organizations governing graduate curricula required that such courses be taught. As multicultural psychology began to become a popular course at the undergraduate level, several genres of undergraduate texts were developed. One genre adapted the basic structure of graduate texts to the undergraduate level. The result was a focus on therapy with specific ethnic minority populations. The more advanced texts in this genre also had one or two chapters that dealt with other populations of diversity, such as women, lesbian, gay, and bisexual populations, and people with disabilities. Another genre of undergraduate texts was infused with international issues in psychology. Finally, other texts had more specific foci, such as multicultural communication or issues of racism. Our undergraduate courses focus more on many issues covered in other books (e.g., differences in worldviews, differences in communication, issues of racism, racial/cultural identity development, and immigration) than on therapy with specific ethnic minority populations or on international issues in psychology. We also have chosen to integrate issues specific to populations of diversity throughout our chapters rather than to cover such issues in separate chapters.

In chapter 1, we define relevant terms and discuss the overall importance of multicultural psychology and how it came into prominence. Historically, many in the field have identified three forces in psychology: psychoanalysis, behaviorism, and humanism. Some feel that multicultural psychology is the fourth force in our field. Moreover, an understanding of the cultural context is essential as we view behavior from the biopsychosocial perspective. Initially, the field of psychology attempted to describe general issues of human behavior and treated all individuals as if they were the same. Because the field was overwhelmingly White, those in communities of diversity saw these "general issues" as being imposed upon them and at times irrelevant to their lives. Thus, they began to define themselves, and from their varied definitions emerged a deeper understanding of human behavior.

Chapter 2 explores issues involving research and testing. We build upon the notion that the history of psychology was dominated by a White standard by explaining that sometimes the White standard is not relevant to communities of diversity or can even be damaging to them. For example, if we were to find that some groups diverge from a White standard, we might describe those groups as "deviant," "deprived," or "deficient." In one historical case described in this chapter, the researcher was interested in the differences between African Americans who performed well academically and those who did not perform well. That study was rejected by reviewers because it did not compare the African Americans with White students. The researcher wondered why one needed a White comparison group when the entire purpose of the study was to examine African Americans. There is also a preference for quantitative analysis in science, because it is believed that qualitative studies introduce too much bias or are not generalizable enough. However, bias can be introduced in quantitative analyses as well, through the choice of what to study, through the way in which one's measures are converted into numerical responses, through the interpretation of those results, and so on. Therefore, we discuss qualitative analyses, particularly as they apply to communities of diversity. Finally, we apply issues of research methodology to our understanding of psychological testing.

In chapter 3, we discuss various kinds of worldviews. First, we discuss issues of etic versus emic perspectives. In multicultural psychology, the etic perspective attempts to develop theory by finding similarities across different cultures, whereas the emic perspective emphasizes meaningful concepts within cultures that may not translate across cultures. Among the most important distinctions in the multicultural literature is the distinction between individualism and collectivism. That is because these perspectives are infused in societies, so one's cultural context may be from an individualistic society or from a collectivistic society. Different cultural groups may also have different values, such as the importance of the past, present, or future. Again, we discuss how diverse communities can have very different worldviews from those of their White majority counterparts.

Chapter 4 examines differences in communication. We first present rules of conversation that have been identified by linguists and psycholinguists. There are some regularities in conversations within various groups, but there are many examples of differences among groups. For example, people in some groups feel more comfortable standing closer to their conversational partners than do people in other groups. Another key distinction in multicultural communication is the one between high- and low-context communication groups. In high-context groups, less is said because the context carries with it much of the communication, whereas in low-context groups, more must be said because there may be different rules governing contextual communication that may be applied to the situation. We explore differences in communication that have been identified in diverse communities. We pay particular attention to gender differences in communication: men tend to use more direct methods of communication, and women tend to use more indirect methods; women also use "softening" methods so that their opinions do not seem so harsh. We finish this chapter by discussing bilingual communication, including both cognitive and social consequences.

In chapter 5 we discuss issues involving immigrants and refugees. Quite often, people do not make a distinction between these two populations. However, there can be some very important differences psychologically. For example, immigrants choose to come to the United States, and they prepare for that transition by studying this country and its traditions, learning English, deciding where to settle, and so on. In contrast, refugees come against their will. They often must escape from their countries of origin to save their lives, don't know where they will ultimately settle (often going from country to country until a final host country can be found), and encounter many hardships and even trauma in their transition. However, beyond those initial differences, immigrants and refugees can encounter many similar issues, such as language barriers, changing family roles, and problems with employment. We conclude this chapter by discussing models of acculturation, some of which may also apply to American-born individuals such as some American-Indian populations.

Chapter 6 focuses on issues involving racism. First, social psychologists make a distinction among stereotypes, prejudice, discrimination, and racism. All of these are forms of group categorization, but stereotypes relate to similarities we perceive within the categorized group, prejudice relates to our feelings about the categorized group, discrimination relates to our behaviors toward the categorized group, and racism relates to our institutional practices against the categorized group. Racism is also related to other "isms" (e.g., sexism, heterosexism, ableism) in that they all involve institutional practices that systematically disadvantage those on the downside of power. Although overt racism is largely a thing of the past, modern forms of racism still exist. One way to overcome racism and other "isms" is to understand issues of White privilege and other privileges of power. In so doing, one can become an advocate or ally for those unfairly disadvantaged by institutional practices.

Chapter 7 looks at issues of identity. People who are familiar with developmental psychology know that this is one of the central questions that arise in adolescence. In multicultural psychology, one must explore not only issues of who one is and what aspirations one has but also how those issues relate to one's racial/cultural identity. We discuss models of identity development, beginning with African-American identity development, then White identity development, and a general racial/cultural identity development model. This final model also includes other forms of identity, such as multiracial identity development and homosexual identity development. We conclude this chapter by discussing issues of multiple identities. For example, an African-American heterosexual woman who is a mother and a professor has a racial identity (African American), a sexual identity (heterosexual), a gender identity (woman), a parental identity (mother), and an occupational identity (professor). These are only a subset of potential identities; other identities include but are not limited to religion, ability, region, and marital status. At different times, one or a subset of these identities may come to the fore, and we need to understand how we can balance these different demands. Moreover, being secure within all our multiple identities means that when we emphasize one identity over another, we are not less of the other but rather are emphasizing the one identity in response to contextual demands.

In chapter 8, we discuss health issues. Health and health behaviors are related to one's worldview and the context within which one develops. For example, different ethnic minority groups encounter differential care in a health care system whose policies and behaviors are still affected by remnants of racism. Much of that may be due to poverty, since people with better health insurance are treated better than are those who are compelled to use public assistance programs. To the extent that there remain differences in socioeconomic status among different groups in this country, there remain differences in health care opportunities. However, even with the barrier of poverty removed, structural barriers remain, such as language and access. Change can occur if we increase the number of ethnic minority health care providers and address structural barriers in the health care system. We finish this chapter with the example of sickle cell anemia, a disorder that affects primarily African Americans in this country and that is relatively ignored by the health care system. Thus, there still appears to be racism within the system.

Chapter 9 deals with issues involving mental health, both diagnostically and therapeutically. We point out that the main classificatory system in the mental health field—*The Diagnostic and Statistical Manual of Mental Disorders*—tends to ignore issues of culture. That is because this document is based upon a medical model that emphasizes disorders existing within an individual as opposed to those in the environment. We describe how many large-scale studies that have examined mental disorders have underrepresented ethnic minority populations. Thus, although we can come to some conclusions about the prevalence and course of disorders in ethnic minority communities, at this point those conclusions must remain tentative. Also, some disorders may be specific to some cultures. These are called "culture-bound syndromes" and may be fundamentally different disorders or different expressions of similar disorders across cultural groups. An example of culture-bound syndromes that may be unique to the United States (and White women in particular) is eating disorders. In therapy, many ethnic minority groups either underutilize mental health services or may terminate treatment prematurely because of discomfort with their therapists. Their discomfort may be due to various barriers to treatment, such as cultural (value) differences, class differences, and language problems. To overcome those barriers, we need to develop culturally sensitive approaches to treatment. Development of such approaches has begun with the publication of the multicultural competencies by the American Psychological Association in 2003. We conclude by discussing the effectiveness of cultural matching between the therapist and the client and other forms of culture-specific therapies that have been developed over the years.

Finally, in chapter 10 we discuss general issues in increasing our multicultural competence. We must be aware of our cultural attitudes and understand how they may be different from attitudes of other cultures. In coming to understand our difference, we may encounter what we are calling the "Five D's of Difference": distancing, denial, defensiveness, devaluing, and discovery. The first four D's of Difference involve negative reactions we might experience in an effort to hold on to our own more secure patterns of behavior. However, the fifth D of Difference involves a positive reaction that we may experience by understanding how the difference expressed by the other culture may enrich our lives. Part of the reason for the four negative reactions to difference may be what we call the "Three S's of Similarity," which are simple, safe, and sane. When we prefer our own more secure patterns of behavior to the different ones we might encounter in another culture, our secure patterns feel more simple, make us feel safe, and keep us sane as opposed to confused. We offer suggestions to help you improve your multicultural competence, such as learning about other cultures before you encounter them, knowing about basic values, beliefs, and practices, not being afraid to ask questions, traveling to other places, becoming an ally, and making a decision to develop an attitude of discovery and courage.

We hope that you enjoy this book and learn a little bit more about yourself and others. We have certainly learned a little about ourselves in writing this book and became excited about that discovery. The field of multicultural psychology is relatively new, and it will undoubtedly change with the demographics of our country and the emergence of new and important issues. We intended to give you the tools to address and understand these emerging issues. The rest is up to you.

NEW TO THE SECOND EDITION

While there have not been any major new theories in the multicultural area since our last edition, the field continues to grow and new events in the world lead to new applications of our understandings. We have cited over 50 new publications since we completed our examination of the field for the first edition of our book, and we have cited some older publications to support some new sections of the current edition. While these new publications are in no way exhaustive, they are representative of some of the new literature in the field.

We have also added nearly 60 new reactions from our students. Some of these have replaced some of our former reactions, but most are additional illustrations of points we are trying to make. As we mentioned in our first edition, we have been struck by our students' stories over the years, and we feel that this narrative approach to supplement our academic discourse adds greatly to student understanding of the material. Moreover, nearly all of these reactions are in response to our first edition or lectures based on the first edition. Therefore, these reactions will help students identify even more with the material we present.

Most of the material in our chapter 8 on Health Psychology is the same, but we decided to conduct a major reorganization of this chapter. We feel that this new organization makes the chapter flow more smoothly.

Finally, we have replaced or added some sections to this book. Besides some relatively minor rewrites of numerous sections, we replaced our old section on cultural matching in therapy in chapter 9. In this replaced section, we examine what the literature on cultural matching has concluded thus far. While there is some evidence that matching the ethnicity of the client with the ethnicity of the therapist leads to improved treatment, there is other evidence that this kind of matching has not led to measurable differences in treatment. We examine why there may be these conflicting findings. A major section we have added is an analysis of the response to Hurricane Katrina in August 2005. Some have evaluated this response in terms of subtle racism. We have presented this response in terms of covert, unintentional racism. Those in charge were probably not consciously aware of some hidden racist ideas that they may have held, and to be consciously aware of these ideas would be aversive and painful. However, if one were to examine the delayed and confused response in the aftermath of Hurricane Katrina (which still exists, today), it might be concluded that racism has something to do with this response.

We hope that you find the changes we have made to be helpful and more illuminating. If we all understand the issues in this area, it will make communication with one another better and richer. Perhaps then we can come together to find solutions to what sometimes can be a cultural divide when we interact with those who are of different cultures from us.

ACKNOWLEDGMENTS

A book of this sort cannot be completed without the help of many people. First and foremost, we would like to thank students, family members, friends, and colleagues for helping to provide us with stories and anecdotes that illustrated theoretical and research points we made throughout the book. As we mentioned at the beginning of this Preface, the genesis of this book was one such personal story, so we are grateful to those whom we have quoted. We would also like to thank the following reviewers for their helpful comments: Gerardo D. Canul, University of California, Irvine; Chi-Ah Chun, California State University, Long Beach; Shreya Patel Hessler, Towson University; and Marc Weinstein, Troy University. Thank you also to those mentors and colleagues—particularly those active in Division 45 of the American Psychological Association—who helped shape our ideas throughout the years. Thanks also to Jenni Kolsky Goldman for her generosity in assigning her photography class to take most of the pictures in this book. Thanks to Tom Zasadzinski for numerous additional photographs in this second edition. Finally, thanks to Marlene Yamada for allowing us to use her art for the cover of this book.

JEFFERY SCOTT MIO
LORI A. BARKER
JAYDEE SANTOS TUMAMBING

CHAPTER 1

What Is Multicultural Psychology?

Gender Differences
Lesbian, Gay, and Bisexual Issues
THE RISE OF MULTICULTURALISM
SUMMARY

My whole life is a multicultural experience. I first learned to love and appreciate different cultures from my parents, who immigrated to the United States from the island of Barbados in the West Indies. I believe their openness to people from all walks of life came from their experiences as immigrants to this country, and they passed that on to me, my brother, and my sister.

Growing up with parents from a different country automatically made me aware that there are different cultures. Although I couldn't hear it, other people often commented that my parents spoke with an accent. I noticed that we ate different food. The differences were also apparent in the various groups with which we socialized. For example, we lived in a predominantly White neighborhood, but on the weekends we drove across town to the Black neighborhood to attend a Black church. Every weekend our house was full of people. My parents often invited their West Indian friends over to eat, play games, and tell stories. They also often befriended immigrant students from the local university they knew were far away from their families. We entertained students from all over—Latin America, Asia, Africa—and everybody was treated the same.

I also learned to love and appreciate different cultures from our family vacations. My parents took us on trips to different countries. Of course, they took us back to Barbados to learn about our West Indian roots, as well as to other Caribbean islands. We also traveled to Canada and Mexico. Again, in all our travels, I never saw my parents look down on or belittle anything or anybody in another culture. It was always seen as an adventure, an opportunity to see, do, and learn something new. And that has stayed with me for life. When I was old enough, I started traveling on my own.

My next primary multicultural experience was in high school. I attended a small, private, parochial school. The population was predominantly White (60%), but 40% other. By "other" I mean Cubans, Filipinos, Samoans, Koreans, Chinese, East Indians . . . you name it, we had it. In my closest circle of friends, one girlfriend was African American, one Cuban, one Bolivian, one Filipina, and one Chinese from Singapore. Talk about a United Nations! We all hung out together and everybody dated everybody else, no matter the background.

The utopia truly ended after high school. Some of the White people who were my friends throughout high school slowly distanced themselves from me and started hanging out only with other White people. I guess they saw that the rest of the world was not like our little oasis and succumbed to the pressure of the dominant outside culture, adopting its racist, prejudiced attitudes. I ended up feeling hurt and betrayed by them. Deep down, I learned not to trust White people. The innocence of youth was gone. But those few negative experiences did not outweigh the positives. I still feel most comfortable in a diverse environment, and my circle of friends, family, and colleagues continues to be very diverse. I notice that the similarities are not necessarily in the color of our skin but in our attitudes. I tend to associate with people who also value and respect cultural differences.

And now my love for other cultures has turned into a life mission. In my work as a teacher, researcher, and clinician, I try to teach others the value of learning about and interacting with people from different cultures. (LAB)

This story relates some of the life experiences of one of the authors of this book, Lori A. Barker (LAB). The experiences of the other two authors—Jeffery Scott Mio (JSM) and Jaydee Tumambing (JT)—also reflect their multicultural backgrounds. JSM is from a family whose grandparents immigrated to the United States from Japan, and JT is a biracial immigrant from the Philippines.

Throughout this book you will read many unique stories of people whom we identify by pseudonyms. Motivated by these and other personal stories shared with us over the years by students, colleagues, and friends, we have woven this material as illustrations into the fabric of theories, concepts, and research findings to create a textbook that uses a new approach to multicultural psychology. The book's topics include, among others, worldviews, communication, immigration, acculturation, racism, identity, and physical and mental health. We hope you enjoy the personal touch we have used in our approach.

WHAT IS MULTICULTURAL PSYCHOLOGY?

In the story that opens this chapter, LAB describes how her experiences interacting with people from many different backgrounds eventually led her to a career in multicultural psychology. Her story might give you some indication as to what the field of multicultural psychology is all about, but let us get more specific. In this chapter we introduce you to the field of multicultural psychology and to concepts that will be discussed in more detail in the following chapters.

Let us begin with a basic definition of the term **multicultural psychology.** First, let us define *psychology*. Most likely you already have had a class in introductory or general psychology where *psychology* was defined as the systematic study of behavior, cognition, and affect. In other words, psychologists are interested in how people act, think, and feel and in all the factors that influence those human processes. Therefore, you can probably guess that *multicultural psychology* involves examining in some way the effect of culture on the way people act, think, and feel. On one hand, culture is an external factor because it influences the events that occur around us and our interactions with other people, but on the

multicultural psychology—the systematic study of behavior, cognition, and affect in settings where people of different backgrounds interact.

other hand, culture also influences our internal processes, such as how we interpret the things going on around us.

The prefix *multi-* means "many," and the suffix *-al* means "of" or "pertaining to." Therefore, the term *multicultural* means pertaining to many cultures. If we put this together with *psychology,* we can conclude that *multicultural psychology* concerns the systematic study of behavior, cognition, and affect in many cultures.

That is a good place to start, but the term is really a little more complicated. What about the final component? We still have not defined *culture.*

> *I moved to Florida to take a position as a district manager for a grocery store chain. It was a bit of culture shock for me. I'm not used to all the different cultures. In California we have Mexicans and Vietnamese and Japanese, but in Florida they have Cubans and Haitians. I have one store in an area where it's all Cubans and everybody speaks Spanish. Then, you drive a few blocks and turn the corner and everybody is Haitian and speaks French. And the different groups don't get along. I'm not used to that. Even if I spoke Spanish fluently it wouldn't help, because people from the different countries speak Spanish differently, like people from Cuba versus people from Venezuela. They don't even understand each other. I have a lady friend I spend time with, and we often hang out with her friends from different countries. One night we went to a Greek restaurant and everyone in there was speaking their language, listening to their music, and just doing their thing. I felt very uncomfortable because I didn't understand any of it. The other night at her place an old man from Puerto Rico was visiting. It was very interesting because he was like a walking encyclopedia. He talked about the history of all the different cultural groups, why they look the way they do, how they ended up living in different regions. He went on and on for hours. I learned a lot from listening to him.*

> PETER, 40+-YEAR-OLD WHITE MAN

Culture is a complex term. Defining it is difficult, because although we use it all the time, we use it in so many ways. For example, in describing his experiences when moving from California to Florida, Peter used "culture" to refer to countries, languages, food, and music; he also referred to the influence of history and traditions. Those are some of the many ways we use the term *culture.*

You may also note that we describe Peter as "White." At times, we will identify those whose ancestors came from Europe as White, and at times we will refer to such individuals as European American. Those terms may be seen as interchangeable in most cases. Our experience has been that when we refer to White students as European American, many say, "I am not from Europe." They do not make the connection that when we refer to those whose ancestors originated in Asia, we label them as Asian Americans even if they were born in the United States. For those of us who teach and research topics in the multicultural domain, the term "European American" is more common, but we recognize that for most people, "White" is the more common term.

When someone asks you what culture you are from, how do you reply? Do you tell them your nationality (e.g., Chinese, El Salvadoran)? Do you tell them where your ancestors were from (e.g., "I'm Polish on my dad's side, but Swedish on my mother's")? Do you refer to your racial group (e.g., "I'm Black"), or do you use a specific ethnic label (e.g., "I'm African American")? If you answer in one of these ways, you are like most people, who, when asked about culture, reply by stating their race, ethnicity, or country of origin (Matsumoto et al., 1997).

Sometimes we use the word *culture* to mean various types of music, art, and dance. For example, when people refer to the cultural life of a city, they usually have in mind artistic opportunities, such as access to a good museum and a good symphony orchestra, and the quality of the plays that come to town. Other times we use the term *culture* to refer to such things as food, clothing, history, and traditions. For example, American Indian[1] culture is associated with powwows, sweat lodges, talking circles, and the like. These activities represent traditions that tribes have passed down from generation to generation and are ways in which the people connect with their cultural heritage, purify themselves, and express ideas and solve problems. Yet other times we use the term *culture* in reference to the regular or expected behaviors of a particular group. We might say "teen culture" to refer to the particular way adolescents act, talk, and dress. It signifies that adolescents behave differently from people of other age groups.

David Matsumoto and his colleagues (Matsumoto et al., 1997) conducted a study in which they asked university undergraduates to define *culture*, and they received a wide variety of responses, which the researchers coded and summarized into 18 categories. Three categories were used most often—Expressions, History, and Beliefs—but other categories included Race, Religion, Family, and Hobbies.

Kroeber and Kluckhohn (1952) and Berry and associates (1992) described six uses of "culture" in everyday language: (a) *descriptive*, the specific behaviors and activities associated with a culture; (b) *historical*, a group's heritage and traditions; (c) *normative*, the rules that govern the behavior of a group; (d) *psychological*, which emphasizes behavioral processes, such as learning and problem-solving; (e) *structural*, which reflects the organizational elements of a culture; and (f) *genetic*, which refers to the origins of that culture.

---

1. Various terms have been used to categorize indigenous peoples of the Americas. Common terms are "Native Americans," "American Indians," "Native American Indians," and "Aboriginals." The two most common terms are "Native Americans" and "American Indians." We have chosen to use "American Indians." That is because some White people who want to resist classification based upon racio-ethnic grounds have said, "I was born here in America, so I am Native American, too." Moreover, those of Mexican descent may also validly use the term "Native American" because many of their ancestors lived in the Western regions of the United States when those regions were still part of Mexico. According to our friend and colleague Joseph E. Trimble, the term "American Indian" is the least confusing and most accurate, so we have adopted that convention. However, we recognize that many American Indians still prefer the term "Native American." We are merely using "American Indian" as a convention for this book.

Let us use Mexican culture as an example. To talk about Spanish as the primary language is a descriptive use of "culture." To talk about the holidays the people celebrate, such as Cinco de Mayo and El Día de los Muertos, is a historical use. To talk about traditional gender roles and machismo is a normative use. To talk about the process of learning a new language or adjusting to a new culture is a psychological use. To talk about the importance of the extended family is a structural use. Finally, to talk about the combined influence of indigenous and Spanish (European) people on Mexican physical appearance is a genetic use.

So far, our discussion covers the ways in which we use the term *culture* in our everyday language. How do psychologists define *culture*? Psychologists have struggled to develop a concise definition of *culture*. Atkinson (2004) sums up the debate by saying that culture "consists of values and behaviors that are learned and transmitted within an identifiable community . . . and also includes the symbols, artifacts, and products of that community" (p. 10). In other words, culture usually refers to a particular group of people and includes their values, or guiding beliefs and principles, and behaviors, or typical activities. Those values and behaviors are symbolized in the things that the group of people produces, such as art, music, food, and language. All of those things are passed down from generation to generation. In summary, we could define **culture** as the values, beliefs, and practices of a group of people, shared through symbols and passed down from generation to generation.

culture—the values, beliefs, and practices of a group of people, shared through symbols, and passed down from generation to generation.

Narrow and Broad Definitions of Culture

The field of multicultural psychology distinguishes between narrow and broad definitions of culture. A narrow definition of culture is limited to race, ethnicity, and/or nationality. This use of the term is probably the more common one.

In contrast, a broad definition of culture includes "any and all potentially salient ethnographic, demographic, status, or affiliation identities" (Pedersen, 1999, p. 3). In other words, any of the important or meaningful ways in which we identify ourselves can be viewed as a culture. Sue, Ivey, and Pedersen (1996) give the following broad definition of culture: "any group that shares a theme or issue(s)" (p. 16). Therefore, language, gender, ethnicity/race, spirituality, sexual preference, age, physical issues, socioeconomic status, and survival after trauma all define "cultures." Under this broad definition, we can have simultaneous membership in more than one culture.

Some psychologists argue that a broad definition of culture isn't particularly helpful. Should something such as gender be included? Do men and women really have separate and distinct cultures? If this definition is taken to its extreme, anything could be considered a culture. Let us use the Deaf Community as an example.

If we define a culture as a distinct group of people characterized by shared customs, behaviors, and values, would the Deaf Community fit that definition? Backenroth (1998) thinks so. She argues that deaf people share a common language (sign language); have their own schools, churches, and social organizations; have common experiences and a common way of interacting with one another

PICTURE 1.1   What is culture? *Photograph by Tom Zasadzinski*

and with hearing people; and therefore have a distinct culture. Following is a description of Deaf culture by a deaf person:

> *Deaf culture for me is about the complexity of deafness. Life as a deaf person, life stories, and destinies. Deaf culture for me is not theatre, art and so on per se. These ways of expression are not particular for deaf people. However, the content in these different ways of expression can illustrate the Deaf culture, deaf people's lives. For example, the American artist Harry Williams, now deceased. He was painting violins without chords, separated violins, like two worlds. This example is a clear expression of the Deaf culture, not art per se but the content in art. The particular traits that deaf people in comparison to hearing people in society, for example the language, music, the pictures and so on, are typical deaf cultural expression . . . well, o dear it is so difficult to describe this in words but easy to experience.*

(ANONYMOUS RESEARCH PARTICIPANT, QUOTED IN BACKENROTH, 1998).

Do you agree with a broad or a narrow definition of culture? As we stated earlier, although some psychologists disagree, most multicultural psychologists subscribe to a broad definition of culture that includes statuses and affiliations such as gender, physical ability, religion, and sexual orientation. This broad definition of culture includes a wide range of **diversity** that encompasses differences beyond race, ethnicity, and nationality.

Culture and Worldview

Sue (1977) defines a **worldview** as "the way in which people perceive their relationship to nature, institutions, other people, and things. Worldview constitutes

diversity— differences beyond race, ethnicity, and nationality, such as sexual orientations, religions, and abilities.

worldview— a psychological perception of the environment that determines how we think, behave, and feel.

our psychological orientation in life and can determine how we think, behave, make decisions, and define events" (p. 458). In other words, different cultural groups perceive, define, and interact with their environment in different ways, on the basis of their past learning experiences (Sue, Ivey, & Pedersen, 1996). People from different cultures may see or experience the same thing but interpret it in drastically different ways. An example of this is seen in the differing ways the European-American and African-American communities reacted when, after his criminal trial, O. J. Simpson was acquitted of the murders of his ex-wife, Nicole Brown Simpson, and her friend Ronald Goldman.

> Time Magazine *calls October 3, 1995, one of "Eighty Days That Changed the World" (Poniewozik, 2003). At 10:00 a.m. that day the world paused to watch the verdicts in the O. J. Simpson criminal trial. O. J., a former NFL football star and popular celebrity in both the White and Black communities, was accused of brutally murdering his ex-wife, Nicole Brown Simpson, and her friend, Ron Goldman. The world was captivated by the case, and many watched the daily courtroom drama. When it came time for the jury forewoman to read the verdicts, some networks went to a split screen where on one side they showed crowds gathered at various spots in the African-American community, and on the other half showed groups gathered at popular spots in the European-American community. When the "not guilty" verdict was read African Americans jumped, shouted, and cheered as if they'd won the Superbowl, while European Americans looked shocked and stunned. Some cried while others expressed outrage.*
>
> *The media commented on the differing reactions of the two communities in the weeks and months following the verdict, including a documentary on CBS called "O. J. in Black and White" (CBS News, 1996). Many struggled to explain the drastically different reactions. Reactions to the O. J. verdict for both African Americans and European Americans go all the way back to slavery. In the south, black slaves far outnumbered white slave owners. Therefore, white slave owners used violence, fear, and intimidation to keep black slaves in line. Once slavery was abolished, whites, fearing for their safety, developed new tactics to keep large numbers of ex-slaves in line. The Ku Klux Klan accomplished this task through the continued use of violence, fear, and intimidation, but the justice system did as well. African Americans were often falsely accused and convicted of crimes for which they were not guilty, or given harsher sentences when they were. Even today, statistics indicate that African Americans are more likely to be arrested, imprisoned, and continue to receive harsher sentences for equivalent crimes when compared to European Americans, including the death penalty (Legal Services for Prisoners with Children, n.d.).*
>
> *Back track to 1992 and the verdicts in another famous trial of four European-American police officers accused of beating Rodney King, an African American. The beating was caught on videotape and aired on*

television over and over in the following weeks. African Americans hoped that for once the system would work in their favor. After all, hadn't everybody seen the videotape? When a majority European-American jury found the four European-American officers "not guilty" all hope was lost. African Americans reacted, not just to the verdict, but to centuries of unjust treatment. The Rodney King beating verdict was simply the straw that broke the camel's back; the match to the gasoline. African Americans (and others) in Los Angeles and other communities expressed their hurt, disappointment, pain, and rage by rioting for three days.

In 1995, when O. J. was acquitted, with the help of an African-American defense lawyer and a predominantly African-American jury, many African Americans said, "Finally! We beat them at their own game!" Hope was restored. On the other hand, when the system they invented no longer worked in their favor, European Americans cried foul and said the system was flawed.

ADAPTED FROM BARKER-HACKETT, 1995

The drastically different responses of the African-American and European-American communities to the verdicts in the O. J. Simpson trial illustrate the different worldviews of these two communities. Remember, worldviews are shaped by past experiences. The jubilation of the African-American community and the outrage of the European-American community can truly be understood only in the historical context of centuries of unjust treatment of African Americans by European Americans, particularly within the justice system. (Worldview will be discussed in more detail in chapter 3.)

What Is Race?

Previously we said that most people use the word *culture* to refer to their race, ethnicity, or nationality. The terms *culture, race,* and *ethnicity* are often used interchangeably, but technically their meanings are distinctly different. Their usage is often confusing. Atkinson (2004) calls them "three of the most misunderstood and misused words in the English language" (p. 5). Since they are vital to a discussion of multicultural psychology, we must try to define them and clear up some of the confusion. Let us begin by defining *race*.

The term *race* is used in two main ways—as a **biological concept** and as a **sociocultural concept.** Zuckerman (1990) says, "to the biologist, a race, or subspecies, is an inbreeding, geographically isolated population that differs in distinguishable physical traits from other members of the species" (p. 1297). Biologically speaking, a race is a group of people who share a specific combination of physical, genetically inherited characteristics that distinguish them from other groups (Casas, 1984). From this biological perspective, human beings are divided into three main racial groups—Negroid, Caucasoid, and Mongoloid. These three groups are distinguished from one another by phenotype, or noticeable physical features, such as skin color, texture of hair, shape and color of eyes, and thickness of nose and lips.

biological concept of race—the perspective that a race is a group of people who share a specific combination of physical, genetically inherited characteristics that distinguish them from other groups.

sociocultural concept of race—the perspective that characteristics, values, and behaviors that have been associated with groups of different physical characteristics serve the social purpose of providing a way for outsiders to view another group and for members of a group to perceive themselves.

Results of genetic studies indicate that the physiological differences among racial groups are superficial and that as human beings we have far more genetic similarities than differences (Latter, 1980; Zuckerman, 1990). Variation within different racial groups is far greater than is variation among the groups (American Anthropological Association, 1999). Estimates indicate that 88 to 90 percent of genetic variation occurs within local populations, while only 10 to 12 percent is between populations (Angier, 2000). Most respected scholars currently acknowledge that human beings came from the same beginnings in Africa and that genetic differences among groups can be explained by patterns of migration and adaptation as groups moved farther and farther away from that point of origin (Angier, 2000; Begley, 1995; Diamond, 1997). The American Anthropological Association (AAA) concluded that "race is not a legitimate biological or genetic contract; rather, it is an ideology used to justify the domination of one identifiable group of people by another" (AAA, 1999, as cited in Miller & Garvan, 2008, p. 15). In other words, there really is only one biological race . . . the human race (Atkinson, 2004; Fish, 2002).

Although a biological definition of race has little evidence to support it, once the broad categories were drawn and the idea of significant genetic differences among groups was propagated, the term took on sociocultural significance. "The concept of race has taken on important social meaning in terms of how outsiders view members of a 'racial' group and how individuals within a 'racial' group view themselves, members of their group, and members of other 'racial' groups. . . . Thus, the term *race* survives despite the lack of a scientific basis because it continues to serve one purpose or another for those who use it" (Atkinson, 2004, p. 8). Helms (1990) calls such purposes the psychological implications of racial group membership.

The sociocultural meaning of the term *race* resulted from the geographic isolation of groups sharing similar physical characteristics. Once those groups migrated to different parts of the globe, they also developed their own unique set of values, beliefs, and practices. The term also gained sociocultural significance because some groups used physical differences to justify the oppression of other groups. For example, White Europeans selected Black Africans for enslavement in part because of the drastic differences in physical appearance. It was easy to identify a Black African slave and distinguish him or her from a White European slave owner. Once Europeans enslaved Africans, a system of values and beliefs developed to justify the inhumane practice. Europeans propagated the ideas that Africans were primitive, savage, and inferior, even stating that slavery was good for "civilizing" them. Such beliefs were widely spread and passed down from generation to generation so that even today African Americans continue to combat stereotypes about their racial inferiority.

Thus race, rather than being a biological fact, is a sociocultural concept. This means that the term exists because it has become useful in our interpersonal, group, and societal relationships. Atkinson (2004) says that the sociocultural use of the term *race* continues because it provides people a way of organizing the world and reducing complexity, and for some groups it provides a vehicle for identity and empowerment. Because of confusion between the two definitions of

PICTURES 1.2   To some, the concept of race is biological, whereas to others, it is a social construction. *Photographs by Jersson Rivera*

the term *race*, there has been much debate in the psychological literature about the appropriateness of its use (e.g., Helms & Talleyrand, 1997; Yee, Fairchild, Weizmann, & Wyatt, 1993; Zuckerman, 1990).

The term **ethnicity** is often used interchangeably with race and culture. Technically, ethnicity refers to the combination of race and culture, for ethnicity is determined by both physical and cultural characteristics (Atkinson, 2004; Phinney, 1996). Individuals may be from the same racial group but come from different cultures, leading to their particular ethnicity. For example, Black people are all of African descent but now live all over the world in various cultures. Racially they are "Black," but depending on what part of the world they grew up in, they are from different cultures, leading to separate and distinct ethnic groups. Thus we have Afro-Cubans, Afro-Brazilians, and African Americans. That is why racial categories can be confusing. If a Black person from Cuba is filling out a survey in the United States and is asked to check off his or her race, which one does he or she check—African American or Latino? He or she is both. To select just one is misleading and inaccurate. The following story illustrates this dilemma.

ethnicity— a combination of race and culture.

> *For myself being half Thai and half Chinese, I know a lot of people don't consider that being biracial because they both fall under Asian, but the two different cultures still have an effect on me . . . I usually just tell people I'm Thai. I'm not really denying my Chinese side, it's just that my parents raised me with the Thai culture. Speaking Thai, eating Thai foods, learning the proper Thai etiquettes, etc. My parents never really put any of the Chinese part of me into my lifestyle. That is a big reason why I chose to be more Thai. It's more familiar to me than the Chinese culture. Now that I'm older I am exploring more Chinese culture and I learned that Thai and Chinese cultures are very different. I'm still more biased toward my Thai side, though. Probably because I can relate more since I grew up that way.*

Ning, 20+-year-old Biethnic (Thai/Chinese) Woman

Multicultural Psychology versus Cross-Cultural Psychology

Our goal has been to define *multicultural psychology*. So far, we have broken the term down into its components, stating that *psychology* is the systematic study of behavior, cognition, and affect; *multi-* and *-al* mean pertaining to many; and *culture* refers to the values, beliefs, and practices of a particular group of people that are shared through symbols and passed down from generation to generation. If we put all that together, we can define *multicultural psychology* as the systematic study of all aspects of human behavior as it occurs in settings where people of different backgrounds encounter one another. Multicultural psychologists are concerned with "the psychological reactions of individuals and groups caught up in culturally heterogeneous settings" including the "behaviors, perceptions, feelings, beliefs, and attitudes" that result from living in such conditions (Bochner, 1999, p. 21).

Our definition of multicultural psychology states that the field is interested in what happens when people of different backgrounds interact with one another. Bochner (1999) defines **culture contact** as "critical incidents where people from different cultural, ethnic, or linguistic backgrounds come into social contact with each other" (p. 22) and describes two broad categories of contacts: (1) contacts that occur between members of a culturally diverse society, or between people of many different backgrounds who live and work together on a daily basis; and (2) contacts that occur when people from one society visit another country, for purposes such as business, tourism, study, or assistance (e.g., Peace Corps). Multicultural psychology is interested in both types of cultural contact, although it emphasizes the first type.

Besides multicultural psychology, terms used in the literature include cross-cultural psychology, cultural psychology, and ethnic minority psychology. Sometimes these terms all refer to the same thing, and they often reflect historical developments in the field (i.e., different terms were used at different times), but sometimes there are some clear distinctions. For example, **cross-cultural psychology** is often concerned with comparisons across cultures, not, as multicultural psychology is, with comparisons of many cultures coexisting within one society. Although some might argue with that conclusion, in a broad sense multicultural psychology can be seen as the broad umbrella under which these other areas fall.

culture contact–critical incidents in which people from different cultures come into social contact with one another either (a) by living and working with one another on a daily basis, or (b) through visiting other countries on a temporary basis, such as for business, tourism, or study.

cross-cultural psychology–the study of comparisons across cultures or countries, as opposed to comparisons of groups within one society.

WHY DO WE NEED THE FIELD OF MULTICULTURAL PSYCHOLOGY?

We need multicultural psychology because, quite simply, the United States is a multicultural society. It is in fact a setting where people of different backgrounds encounter one another. According to the Census Bureau (Grieco & Cassidy, 2001; http://www.census.gov/prod/cen2000/dpi/2kh00.pdf), the population of the United States is currently 69.1% non-Hispanic White, 12.5% Hispanic, 12.3% Black, 3.7% Asian and Pacific Islander, and 0.9% American Indian. Census projections indicate that the European-American population will decline while each of the other racial groups will grow. Therefore, although European Americans currently make up the majority, U.S. Census projections suggest that sometime in this century the United States will become a "majority minority" country (National Population Projections, 2002). In other words, all ethnic minority groups combined will be larger than the European-American population.

This increasing diversification is due to two primary forces—immigration rates and differential birthrates (Sue & Sue, 1999). Ever since the Pilgrims arrived at Plymouth Rock, the population of the United States has been greatly influenced by immigration. Census 2000 data indicate that foreign-born and first-generation residents now make up one-fifth of the entire U.S. population, and that number is likely to keep growing (Schmidley, 2001). Currently, the largest numbers of immigrants into the United States come from countries in Asia (25%) and Latin America (51%). Unlike the early immigrants to this country, who were mostly White Europeans and were easily assimilated into mainstream culture, current immigrants are from more visible racial and ethnic groups that are not as easily assimilated (Atkinson, 2004).

In addition, ethnic minority groups continue to have higher birthrates. The average number of children per mother for European Americans is 1.7, whereas it is 2.4 for African Americans, 2.9 for Mexican Americans, and 3.4 for Vietnamese (Sue & Sue, 1999). The number of children born to foreign-born women has also been increasing. In 1980, 1 birth in 20 in the United States was to a foreign-born woman, whereas in 2000 the number increased to 1 in 5 (Schmidley, 2001). Those numbers indicate that ethnic minority groups are growing at a faster rate than are European Americans and help explain what Rodriguez (2002) refers to as the "browning" of America.

MULTICULTURALISM AS THE FOURTH FORCE

Paul Pedersen (1990, 1991), a leading multicultural psychologist, proposed the idea that multiculturalism is the **"fourth force"** in psychology. What does he mean? In psychology, the term *force* is used to describe a theory that has a huge influence on the field and precipitates a **paradigm shift,** or major change, in the way people think about human behavior.

The notion that multiculturalism is the fourth force suggests that this perspective will have just as big an impact on the field of psychology as the first three forces—psychoanalysis, behaviorism, and humanism (Table 1.1). Pedersen (1990, 1991) does not see multiculturalism as replacing the other three theories but, rather, as adding a fourth dimension to psychology to supplement and, ideally, to strengthen the other three. He says that labeling multiculturalism as the fourth

multiculturalism as the fourth force— the idea that multicultural psychology is so important that it will fundamentally change the direction of the field of psychology, as psychoanalysis, behaviorism, and humanism have.

paradigm shift— a major change in the way people think about a field.

TABLE 1.1　Multicultural Psychology as a Fourth Force

Force	Name of Theory	Key Theorists
First Force	Psychoanalysis	Freud
Second Force	Behaviorism	Pavlov, Thorndike, Watson, Skinner
Third Force	Humanism	Rogers
Fourth Force	Multiculturalism	Sue, Pedersen, White, Ivey, Bernal, Trimble

force "explores the possibility that we are moving toward a generic theory of multiculturalism that recognizes the psychological consequences of each cultural context, where each behavior has been learned and is displayed . . . and calls attention to the way in which a culture-centered perspective has changed the way we look at psychology across fields and theories" (Pedersen, 1999, p. xxii).

In other words, calling multiculturalism the "fourth force" challenges us to acknowledge that (a) all behavior is learned and occurs in a cultural context; (b) until recently, this fact has virtually been ignored by the field; and (c) once we understand the nature and contribution of culture, this understanding will dramatically alter and expand the way we study and understand behavior. Pedersen and other multicultural psychologists believe it is no longer possible for psychologists to ignore their own culture or the cultures of their clients and research participants. A multicultural perspective makes our understanding of human behavior more clear and meaningful, rather than more obscure and awkward. "The main goal of [multicultural psychology] is to convince general psychology that culture is an important contributor to the development of human behavior, and to our understanding and study of it" (Pedersen, 1999, p. 6). Thus, identifying multiculturalism as the "fourth force" in psychology attempts to place it at the center of the field.

UNDERSTANDING THE CULTURAL CONTEXT OF BEHAVIOR: THE BIOPSYCHOSOCIAL MODEL

One of the major tenets of multicultural psychology is that all behavior is learned and exhibited in a cultural context. Therefore, to fully understand human behavior, we must understand its cultural context. Culture influences everything.

Biopsychosocial Model—a model of human behavior that takes into consideration biological, cognitive-affective, social interpersonal, social institutional, and cultural factors.

The **Biopsychosocial Model** helps explain the effect of culture on behavior. This model grew out of behavioral medicine and health psychology and focuses on an understanding of the psychological, social, and biological factors that contribute to illness and that can be utilized in the treatment and prevention of illness and the promotion of wellness (Engel, 1977; Schwartz, 1982). Although the model originally focused on an understanding of physical illnesses, it is also very useful in understanding psychological ones. Let us take a closer look at this model.

On the morning of May 5, 2004, David Reimer retrieved a shotgun from his home while his wife, Jane, was at work, took it into the garage, and sawed off the barrel. He then drove to the nearby parking lot of a grocery store, parked, raised the gun, and shot himself. He was 38 years old. What led David to such despair that he decided to end his own life?

Press reports cited an array of reasons for his despair: bad investments, marital problems, his twin brother's death two years earlier. Surprisingly little emphasis was given to the extraordinary circumstances of his upbringing. This was unfortunate, because to truly understand David's suicide you first need to know his anguished history, chronicled in the book, *As Nature Made Him: The Boy Who Was Raised as A Girl*, by John Colapinto (2000).

David Reimer was one of the most famous patients in medical history. He was 8 months old when a doctor doing a routine circumcision accidentally removed his entire penis. David's parents were referred to a leading expert on gender identity, psychologist Dr. John Money, who recommended a surgical sex change from male to female and the administration of female hormones to further feminize his body. David became the ultimate experiment to prove that nurture, not nature, determines gender identity and sexual orientation. His twin brother, Brian, provided a perfect matched control.

Dr. Money continued to treat David and, according to his published reports through the 1970s, the experiment was a success. David, who'd been renamed Brenda, was portrayed as a happy little girl. The reality was far more complicated. "Brenda" angrily tore off dresses, refused to play with dolls, beat up her twin brother, and seized his toy cars and guns. In school she was relentlessly teased for her masculine gait, tastes, and behaviors. The other children wouldn't let her use either the boys' or the girls' restroom, so she had to go in the back alley. She complained to her parents and teachers that she felt like a boy. Brenda was also traumatized by her yearly visits to Dr. Money, who used pictures of naked adults to "reinforce" Brenda's gender identity and who pressed her to have further surgery on her "vagina." Meanwhile, Brenda's guilt-ridden mother attempted suicide; her father lapsed into alcoholism; and the neglected twin brother, Brian, eventually descended into drug use, petty crime, and clinical depression.

When Brenda was 14, a local psychiatrist finally convinced the parents to tell Brenda/David the truth. David later said about the revelation: "Suddenly it all made sense why I felt the way I did. I wasn't some sort of weirdo. I wasn't crazy."

David went through the painful process of converting back to his biological sex, yet was still very troubled and attempted suicide twice in his 20s. He eventually married, but he was not easy to live with, given his explosive anger, fears of abandonment, feelings of sexual inadequacy, and continued depressive episodes. At about the age of 30 David received help from a rival psychologist of Dr. Money, Dr. Milton Diamond at the University of Hawaii, but he continued to have difficulties. In the spring of 2002, his twin brother died of an overdose of antidepressant medication. Then, in the fall of 2003, David was cheated out of $65,000 by an alleged con man. The last straw seemed to come on May 2, 2004, when after 14 years of a difficult marriage, David's wife told him she wanted a separation. Two days later, David ended his own suffering.

(Adapted from Colapinto (2004), and "David Reimer," [2004])

Many factors contributed to David Reimer's suicide. The Biopsychosocial Model helps put those factors into perspective. The Biopsychosocial Model says that behavior can be understood on many levels (see Figure 1.1). The first is the *biological level*. At the most basic level, our behavior is influenced by our

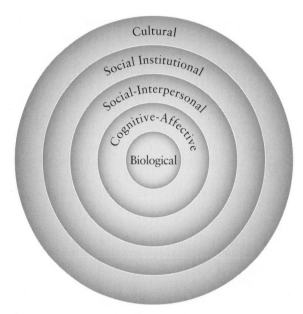

FIGURE 1.1 The Biopsychosocial Model. *Adapted from Engle (1977) and Myers (1986)*

physiological and genetic makeup. When we lack certain nutrients, our body sends us signals that something is out of balance and needs to be corrected. For example, if we do not have enough fluids in our body, we feel thirsty and are motivated to drink. If our body lacks fuel, we feel hungry and we eat. The behaviors of eating and drinking are linked to basic biological needs. Our behavior is also influenced by our genetic makeup.

There was evidently a strong genetic component to David Reimer's depression. His mother and brother suffered from depression, and his father may have as well. It is possible that his father was self-medicating his depression through alcohol abuse. Research clearly indicates that depressive disorders tend to run in families (Keller et al., 1986). Perhaps David Reimer inherited a biological predisposition to depression from one or both of his parents. His unusual life circumstances brought it out for him as well as for his brother.

The second level of the Biopsychosocial Model is the *cognitive-affective level*. Cognitions, in general, refer to our thoughts but include all our basic mental processes, such as memories, perceptions, and beliefs. *Affect* refers to feelings or emotions. This level examines the effect our thoughts and feelings have on our behavior. The connection between one's mental or psychological state and physical health has long been established. For example, we know that when we are stressed, our immune system is weakened and we are more likely to get sick. You have probably had the experience of coming down with a cold during or immediately after a particularly stressful week at school.

The cognitive-affective level is the level at which most people understand and think about mental disorder, because most of what we know and study in the field of psychology occurs at this level. Currently, the most popular theory of depression is the Cognitive Theory, proposed by Aaron Beck (1967a, 1970). Beck proposed that depression is associated with and maintained by negative thinking patterns. Beck noticed that depressed people exhibited what he labeled the **Negative Cognitive Triad,** or a negative view of the self, the world, and the future. He also noticed that depressed people made a number of *cognitive errors,* or distortions of reality. One example of a cognitive error is *overgeneralization,* wherein the person draws global conclusions about his or her worth, ability, or performance on the basis of a single fact.

Negative Cognitive Triad—Beck's label for the negative view depressed individuals tend to have of themselves, the world, and the future.

For instance, David Reimer may have concluded that because he did not have a penis, he was less of a man and would never be able to have a normal, happy, satisfying married life. According to Beck, these negative and distorted thoughts lead to negative or depressed feelings. Once people get caught in this negative cycle, it is very hard to get them out. Even after David met and married his wife, Jane, he was still plagued by feelings of low self-esteem and sexual inadequacy.

The third level of the Biopsychosocial Model is the *social-interpersonal level,* which focuses on the impact of social relationships on our behavior. For example, the various approaches to marriage and family therapy all emphasize that the problems of individual family members are the result of the interpersonal dynamics of the entire family system, or the unique pattern of interactions among family members. There was an interpersonal component to David Reimer's depression. His family relationships probably influenced his depression as he interacted with his alcohol-abusing father, his guilt-ridden mother, and his neglected brother. In addition, David received relentless teasing and cruelty from his peers, which probably also had an effect on the development of his depression.

The fourth level of the Biopsychosocial Model is the *social institutional level.* Social institutions are large, complex, relatively stable clusters of social relationships that involve people working together to address some basic human or societal need (Sullivan & Thompson, 1994). Examples of social institutions include the military, the government, the educational system, and large corporations. At this level of analysis we try to understand how behavior is influenced by our interactions with these large organizations. For example, a man may become depressed because his company is downsizing and he loses his job. A businesswoman may become depressed because she is juggling the demands of both career and family.

David Reimer's case was influenced by the family's interactions with the health care system, first with the botched circumcision and then with the referral to and advice of Dr. Money. At the time of the accident, David's parents were described as "teenagers barely off the farm" (Colapinto, 2004). It is not hard to imagine their fear and confusion and the influence that a powerful authority figure such as Dr. Money, with the backing of the medical establishment, had on their decision making. Any of you who have had a serious medical problem and have had to navigate the health care system can attest to how stressful this can be.

The final level of the Biopsychosocial Model is the *cultural level.* At last! You may have been wondering when culture would factor into this model. As we have discussed, culture reflects the values, beliefs, and practices of a group of people, and all behavior occurs in a cultural context. Let us go back to our previous example of the depressed businessman and let us say he is African American. He may feel that he was let go because of racism, a belief about the inferiority of African Americans that continues to pervade our society. What about the businesswoman? Although our cultural beliefs about the role of women have changed to incorporate the idea that women can have careers outside the home, we have not entirely abandoned the belief that women should be the primary caretakers of children. Women in America are caught in a bind between these two sets of beliefs.

David Reimer's case was influenced by the cultural attitudes of the time. In the 1960s and 1970s, when David was growing up, fairly traditional gender roles still predominated in our society. The belief was that David had to be either male or female and that this could be dictated by his genitals and how he was treated. However, when Brenda/David did not fit into the traditional ideas of how a girl ought to behave—wearing dresses, playing with dolls, walking and talking a certain way—he was ridiculed by his friends. As an adult, David equated masculinity, or being a "real man," with having a penis and being able to sexually satisfy his wife. Where did his ideas about masculinity and the proper husband role come from? They came from the larger society. What would have happened to David if he had been born into a different culture? Do you think his circumstances would have been different? What do you think would happen to him if he were born today?

Figure 1.1 depicts the Biopsychosocial Model as concentric circles, with the biological level in the center and each level a larger ring until the last and largest is the cultural level. The biological level is the most basic at which we can analyze and understand behavior, and the levels become larger and more complex as we go out, with each level influencing the other. As the last level, culture influences them all. Thus, the Biopsychosocial Model reminds us that all behavior occurs within a cultural context. A complete analysis of David Reimer's suicide must consider all the levels, from his biological predisposition to depression, to his negative thinking patterns, to his family dynamics and treatment by peers, to the health care system and cultural beliefs about gender roles. All of these worked together, seemingly against David, to lead him to that moment when he raised a shotgun and took his own life.

THE BASIC TENETS OF MULTICULTURAL THEORY

One of the major premises of multicultural psychology is that all behavior is learned and occurs in a cultural context. What are some of the other major ideas that shape the field?

The field of multicultural psychology evolved primarily out of the areas of clinical and counseling psychology and work that was done on conducting counseling and psychotherapy with diverse populations. Sue, Ivey, and Pedersen (1996) outline the basic tenets of a theory of multicultural counseling and therapy (MCT). Although some aspects are specific to treatment, the theory includes general principles that are the foundation of multicultural psychology.

TABLE 1.2   The Basic Assumptions of a Theory of Multicultural Counseling and Therapy (MCT) (Sue, Ivey, and Pedersen, 1996)

PROPOSITION 1	MCT is a metatheory of counseling and psychotherapy.
PROPOSITION 2	Both counselor and client identities are formed and embedded in multiple levels of experiences (individual, group, and universal) and contexts (individual, family, and cultural milieus). The totality and interrelationships of experiences and contexts must be the focus of treatment.
PROPOSITION 3	Development of cultural identity is a major determinant of counselor and client attitudes toward the self, others of the same group, others of a different group, and the dominant group. These attitudes are strongly influenced not only by cultural variables but also by the dynamics of a dominant-subordinate relationship among culturally different groups.
PROPOSITION 4	The effectiveness of MCT theory is most likely enhanced when the counselor uses modalities and defines goals consistent with the life experiences and cultural values of the client.
PROPOSITION 5	MCT theory stresses the importance of multiple helping roles developed by many culturally different groups and societies. Besides the one-on-one encounter aimed at remediation in the individual, these roles often involve larger social units, systems intervention, and prevention.
PROPOSITION 6	The liberation of consciousness is a basic goal of MCT theory. MCT theory emphasizes the importance of expanding personal, family, group, and organization consciousness of the place of self-in-relation, family-in-relation, and organization-in-relation. This emphasis results in therapy that not only is ultimately contextual in orientation but also draws on traditional methods of healing from many cultures.

Sue et al. (1996) lay out six basic assumptions of MCT. These are summarized in Table 1.2. The first proposition says that MCT theory is a "metatheory" of counseling and psychotherapy. This means that it is a generic theory that provides a framework for understanding all other therapeutic approaches, both the traditional ones (i.e., psychoanalytic, behavioral, humanistic) and the nontraditional ones, such as indigenous forms of healing. No one approach is viewed as inherently good or bad; each simply represents a different worldview.

The second proposition says that both client and counselor have multiple identities, at the individual, family, group, and cultural levels. These identities are dynamic, and the salience of one over the others varies across situations and across time. For example, LAB is an African-American, female, Christian, heterosexual individual. Those are four of her primary identities, and they are listed in their most typical order of importance. However, in some situations, the order switches, and one of the other identities becomes more salient; for example, when she is with only African Americans, her gender may become more important. To fully understand a person, we must understand all layers of his or her personal identity. (The concept of multiple identities is discussed further in chapter 7.)

The third proposition of MCT theory says that cultural identity plays a major role in one's attitudes toward the self, others in the same group, others in different groups, and the dominant group. One's cultural identity is shaped by a variety of forces, and it typically develops as one progresses through a series of stages, moving from a lack of awareness of culture and its impact, to encountering cultural issues and reflecting on oneself as a cultural being, to some form of internalization and integration of multiple cultural perspectives. (We discuss issues of cultural identity in detail in chapter 7.)

The fourth proposition says that therapy is most effective when the therapist takes into account the culture of the client when defining issues, setting goals, and developing treatment strategies. One of the main goals of multicultural training is to help therapists expand their repertoire of helping skills so they can find the best match between the client's culture, the client's presenting problems, and the interventions.

Proposition 5 expands on this idea by saying that therapists need to go beyond the traditional helping role of one-on-one therapy and be willing to integrate other things, such as indigenous forms of helping and community resources. Going to therapy carries a great stigma in some cultures; therefore, many people who need help do not seek services. Many people are more comfortable going to their pastor or priest. Perhaps psychologists could coordinate with clergy in making referrals, provide training for clergy to enhance their counseling skills, or provide counseling in church settings where individuals feel more comfortable. Or consider a Chinese person who comes to a Western therapist for help but who is also seeing a traditional Chinese herbalist. By opening up the lines of communication and cooperation, the therapist and the herbalist could work together to coordinate the client's treatment. (The issue of culture and mental health treatment is discussed further in chapter 9.)

Finally, Proposition 6 of MCT theory discusses the "liberation of consciousness." MCT emphasizes that psychologists need to break out of the traditional mode of thinking, open their minds, and expand beyond a Western, individualistic perspective to incorporate aspects of the family, group, organizations, and society. That means placing the person in context and understanding self in relation to all these other groups. These ideas should sound familiar, since they were discussed in connection with the Biopsychosocial Model.

Some aspects of MCT theory are specific to counseling and psychotherapy. Nonetheless, it also includes general principles that form the basis of multicultural psychology. One is the idea that culture provides the context for all behavior. Another is that each person has a cultural identity that is made up of many dimensions and layers. This cultural identity is shaped by larger cultural forces and by interactions with other groups, particularly the dominant group, and influences an individual's attitudes, feelings, and behaviors. We must expand our minds beyond traditional Western ways of thinking and try to understand and

PICTURE 1.3 Breaking away from traditional Western ways of doing things may give one insight into treating clients from other cultures. *Photograph by Carl Kriesant*

incorporate non-Western concepts and ideas (Picture 1.3). These premises are the meat and potatoes of multicultural psychology. The following quotation captures the essence of multicultural psychology:

> Indeed, cross-cultural and multicultural literature consistently indicates that all people are multicultural beings, that all interactions are cross-cultural, and that all of our life experiences are perceived and shaped from within our own cultural perspectives. (APA, 2003)

HISTORICAL BACKGROUND

In this section we highlight some of the historical events that had an effect on the field of multicultural psychology. This is not a comprehensive historical review but simply the description of a few key events to give you a sense of the way the field developed and the primary areas of theory, research, and practice in multicultural psychology. This section will give you a background for topics covered in more depth in the rest of the book.

Dubious Beginnings

The birth of psychology as a scientific field of study is traditionally regarded as having occurred in 1879 with the founding of the first psychological laboratory in Leipzig, Germany, by Wilhelm Wundt (Goldstein, 2005). Wundt's laboratory soon became a magnet for individuals wanting to become psychologists. Individuals who studied there went on to establish their own laboratories in countries around the world, including the United States. Wundt and his colleagues studied psychophysiological processes they called **structuralism.** Through a process called **introspection,** research participants reported on their own mental experiences. The researchers measured things such as sensation, perception, reaction times, imagery, and attention (Wade & Tavris, 2003).

structuralism—the first formal approach to psychology that attempted to examine the contents of people's minds.

The intense examination of individual differences and quest for heritable traits leading to greater survival of the species eventually led to research on racial group differences. Early names for this area of research included "ethnical psychology" and "racial psychology" (Guthrie, 1998). Haddon (1910) defined **ethnical psychology** as "the study of the minds of other races and peoples, of which, among the more backward races, glimpses can be obtained only by living by means of observation and experiment" (p. 6). Robert Guthrie (1998), in his book *Even the Rat Was White,* argues that this research was highly influenced by the popular notion of racial superiority and an underlying desire by White Europeans to lend scientific credibility to such beliefs. Early studies compared racial groups not only on psychophysiological measures but on intelligence and personality as well.

introspection—the method that structuralists used to examine the contents of people's minds.

ethnical psychology—the study of the minds of "other races and peoples."

Guthrie (1998) describes an early joint expedition by anthropologists and experimental psychologists sponsored by the Cambridge Anthropological Society to the Torres Straits in the South Pacific in 1889. Wundtian methods of psychophysics were used to examine hearing, vision, taste, tactile acuity, pain, motor speed and accuracy, fatigue, and memory in native peoples of that region. The researchers concluded that the inhabitants were far less intelligent than their examiners. Guthrie also describes another early psychophysiological study that took place at the World's Congress of Races, which convened at the St. Louis World's Fair in 1904. A number of prominent psychologists in attendance tested approximately 1,100 individuals from 22 different groups. Again, the conclusion was that some of the racial groups made many errors and took a long time to perform the tasks and looked similar to mentally deficient people. Guthrie cites other early studies that drew similar conclusions about the racial inferiority of certain groups.

Alfred Binet and Theophile Simon are credited with the development of the first standardized intelligence test in France in 1904. The most famous revision of Binet-Simon test was done in the United States in 1916 by Lewis Terman of Stanford University. Although it has been revised several times since then, the Stanford-Binet is still one of the most widely used intelligence tests, and Terman is considered one of the leading and most influential early psychologists. Terman standardized his intelligence test on a sample of about 1,000 children and 400 adults. All the children were White native Californians. Nonetheless, that did not stop him from drawing negative conclusions about the mental ability of Blacks, such as that they are not capable of abstract thinking and should be placed in special education classes (Terman, 1916). Based on his later testing of a sample of Mexican and American-Indian children, Terman concluded that individuals from these cultures were genetically inferior (Cohen & Swerdlik, 2002).

Guthrie (1998) claimed that Terman's test was biased in favor of White, middle-class culture. Test takers were asked to interpret middle-class proverbs such as "One swallow does not make a summer"; to repeat sentences based on the ability to speak the English language, such as "The early settlers had little idea of the great changes that were to take place in this country"; and to discriminate between "prettiness" and "ugliness." It is not difficult to imagine ethnic minority children struggling with such tasks. Terman's conclusions were not unusual for the time. Other studies comparing the mental abilities of Whites and members of minority groups reached similar conclusions (Guthrie, 1998). Standardized testing of ethnic minorities continues to be a controversial issue today and is discussed in more detail in chapter 2.

Results of such studies were used to support popular notions of racial inferiority and to support ideas and policies such as limitation of education and occupational opportunities for ethnic minorities. For example, Terman recommended that Blacks be placed in special education classes and trained for manual labor. Arguments of racial inferiority, buffered by questionable research practices, also fueled the **eugenics** movement (Guthrie, 1998), which believed that certain groups should not be allowed to procreate because they would pass on negative or deficient genes.

eugenics—
a movement that maintains that only "good genes" should be passed from generation to generation and that "undesirable" groups should be dissuaded from reproducing.

Ethnic minority psychologists were virtually nonexistent until the 1930s, when the first Black students began to enter graduate programs. These students protested the negative image of Blacks portrayed in the psychological literature and frequently dedicated their theses and dissertation research to refuting beliefs about Black mental inferiority. Examples of dissertation titles during this period include "Analysis of Test Results from Third Grade Children Selected on the Basis of Socio-Economic Status" by Howard Hale Long (PhD, 1933, Harvard University), "Non-Academic Development of Negro Children in Mixed and Segregated Schools" by Inez Beverly Prosser (PhD, 1933, University of Cincinnati), and "A Socio-Psychological Study of Negro Children of Superior Intelligence" by Martin David Jenkins (PhD, 1935, Northwestern University; all cited in Guthrie, 1998). Thus, the work of early psychologists on racial group differences and the response of ethnic minority psychologists to their racist conclusions can be considered the early roots of multicultural psychology. (For a more detailed history on issues of race, culture, and ethnicity in psychology, see Duckitt, 1992; Freedheim, 2003; Holliday & Holmes, 2003).

We Begin to Define Ourselves

Research among ethnic minority psychologists soon turned to the effects of forces such as racism, discrimination, and poverty on individuals from ethnic minority backgrounds. A landmark study in this area was conducted by Kenneth and Mamie Clark in 1939. The Clarks, a husband-and-wife team, conducted a study in which they showed a sample of African-American and European-American children Black and White dolls, or pictures of Black and White children, and asked a series of questions such as "Which doll is prettiest?" "Which doll is the smartest?" "Which doll is ugly?" "Which doll is dirty?" The Clarks found that African-American children tended to attribute more positive characteristics to the White dolls or pictures. They concluded that such responses indicated the low self-esteem of African-American children and that those negative self-perceptions were the result of racism and discrimination. Their results played a key role in the Supreme Court Decision in *Brown v. the Board of Education* in 1954 that resulted in the desegregation of schools. Guthrie (1998) states that this demonstrated the role that psychology could play in producing significant social change and that "there is no doubt of the impact of the Clarks' work for the betterment of American society" (p. 152). (To see a modern-day replication of the Clarks' doll study conducted by high school student Kiri Davis, go to www.mediathatmattersfest.org/6/index.php?id=2)

The Clarks' work also had a significant effect within the field of psychology in that it sparked further research in the area, most notably research on racial and ethnic identity, which continues to be one of the most dominant topics in the multicultural literature today (Parham, 2001). In 1970 Joseph White published the first article on African-American psychology in *Ebony* magazine, and in 1971 William Cross published a model on "nigrescence" or the "Negro-to-Black conversion experience" in which he described five stages that African Americans go through in the development of their racial identity. Cross proposed that African Americans begin in a stage where they identify primarily with White culture and see their Blackness as negative. Their progression through the stages is sparked by some significant, moving, or startling event that makes it impossible for them to avoid issues of race. Following that event, Cross believed, many Blacks enter a stage where they immerse themselves in their Blackness and devalue anything that is White. The final stage is one of acceptance and comfort both with one's own culture and with the dominant culture.

Cross's article sparked a long line of work on ethnic identity. Most notable in the group are Thomas Parham and Janet Helms (1981), who operationalized Cross's stages into the Racial Identity Attitude Scale, one of the most widely used and cited measures of racial identity. This scale has been adapted for use with a wide range of other populations, including Whites (e.g., Helms, 1995b), and gays and lesbians (e.g., Walters & Simone, 1993). The work of these individuals also influenced the development of other models of racial and ethnic identity. We have dedicated an entire chapter to this topic, so you will read much more about it in chapter 7.

Gender Differences

Once upon a time in psychology there was no such thing as gender differences. That might seem unthinkable to you, since today some people are making millions of dollars from the idea that men and women are from different planets, but there was a time when gender differences were not discussed in the field of psychology. If they were, women usually ended up with the short end of the stick.

In the early 1970s, during the resurgence of the women's movement in the United States, Carol Gilligan was a graduate student at Harvard University working with Lawrence Kohlberg. Kohlberg (1968, 1976) proposed six stages of moral reasoning based on research he conducted over a span of 12 years with 75 boys who ranged in age from 10 to 16 years old when the study began. Kohlberg used stories to test the boys' reasoning on a number of moral concepts. He was more interested in the reasoning behind his participants' answers than in what they would actually do. On the basis of his findings, Kohlberg concluded that children's moral reasoning changes with age and maturity, following his six stages in progressive order.

Gilligan (1993) found that men tended to base their moral choices on abstract principles, such as justice and fairness, whereas women tended to base theirs on principles of compassion and care. In other words, women tended to be more relationship oriented than men. According to Kohlberg's stages, this meant that women looked "less moral" than men because their responses did not fall into Kohlberg's higher levels of moral reasoning. Rather than concluding that women were not as moral as men, Gilligan suggested that women think and speak differently about relationships (Picture 1.4). Gilligan does not make strong claims about the cause of the differences but acknowledges that they "arise in a context where factors of social status and power combine with reproductive biology to shape the experience of males and females and the relations between the sexes" (Gilligan, 1993, p. 2). In other words, factors at the biological, social-interpersonal, and cultural levels interact to result in the differing reactions of men and women to moral dilemmas.

Gilligan (1993) criticized psychology for the "repeated exclusion of women from the critical theory-building studies of psychological research" (p. 1). Thanks in no small part to Gilligan and other leading women psychologists, research

PICTURE 1.4 Women may have different ways of moral reasoning than men do. *Photograph by Andrea Poltorak*

standards have changed. Women must now be included in studies, and gender differences must be examined in order for research to be considered good science. Another influence of Gilligan and others is that the psychology of women is a respected and growing field. We know that to truly understand the human condition, we must include humans from all backgrounds in our research samples. That was not always the case.

Lesbian, Gay, and Bisexual Issues

Lesbian, gay, and bisexual (LGB) issues were at first studied by the dominant culture to examine the extent to which homosexuality was a psychological disorder (Hancock, 2003). According to Hancock, this was the first generation of research on LGB issues. The second generation was a reaction to the first, as researchers set out to depathologize homosexuality. The current and third generation of research focuses more on the similarities and differences with respect to heterosexual populations and on some unique issues within the LGB community.

Currently, many researchers are examining gender differences within the LGB community (Blumstein & Schwartz, 1983; Dempsey, Hillier, & Harrison, 2001; Gonsiorek, 1993; Kurdek, 1995; Peplau, 1991). For example, Dempsey and associates have found that lesbians tend to have a more flexible sexual identity than do their gay male counterparts. Other current topics include racial and ethnic differences among LGBs (Chan, 1989, 1992; Croom, 2000; Greene, 1997), bisexuality (Dworkin, 2000, 2001; Fox, 1996; Ochs, 1996), and relationship, families, and parenting issues (Ben-Ari, 1995; Blumstein & Schwartz, 1983; Green, Bettinger, & Zacks, 1996; Mathews & Lease, 2000; Patterson, 1996).

PICTURE 1.5 Lesbian, gay, and bisexual individuals are beginning to define themselves rather than allowing the dominant culture to define them. *Photograph by Alyssa Harter*

THE RISE OF MULTICULTURALISM

As we have seen, the field of psychology has traditionally been a White-male-dominated field, in theory, research, and practice. Members of minority groups, such as African Americans, women, and the LGB community, have traditionally been left out or viewed as inferior. The same can be said for other diverse groups, such as people with disabilities and those of diverse religious backgrounds. The broader climate of social change, which addressed the issues of underrepresented, oppressed, and disadvantaged groups during the 1950s, 1960s, and 1970s (e.g., the civil rights movement, the War on Poverty), also affected the field of psychology. Over time, psychology and psychologists have been pushed to become more inclusive. Following are some examples of those efforts.

One way to examine how the field of psychology has dealt with multicultural issues is to look at the history of its primary professional organization, the American Psychological Association (APA). With a membership of over 150,000, APA is a large and powerful organization that sets the standards for the practice of psychology and represents the field in society at large. Historically, APA has the reputation among minority groups of having to be pushed to acknowledge and address their needs. (For a more detailed account of APA's handling of ethnic minority issues, see Comas-Diaz, 1990). One response to this was for groups to break away from APA and form their own organizations.

Various historical influences convinced Black psychologists to make such a move. These historical influences included the assassination of Senator Robert F. Kennedy and the civil unrest in many major cities in the United States in the mid-1960s. Moreover, very few African Americans were being trained in the top psychology programs in the country. Between 1920 and 1966, the 10 most prestigious psychology departments in the United States had awarded only 8 PhDs to African Americans out of a total of 3,767 doctorates; 6 of those 10 departments had not awarded a single PhD to an African American (Albee, 2003, in Freedheim, 2003). The following is a firsthand account of the inception of the Association of Black Psychologists (ABPsi) at the APA National Convention in 1968 by Dr. Joseph White, the "father" of Black Psychology.

Blacks were being called "dumb," and "stupid," and "inferior." Now they were talkin' about my mama and them, so I had some personal feelings about that. We all did. So it was a personal thing. We held a meeting to talk about how we didn't like what was going on in psychology. People started givin' sermons, and testifyin', and hootin' and hollerin'. As the "Black Grapevine" went into effect and folks heard about what was going on, more people started to come. Estimates range from 80 to about 200 Black psychologists and their allies who participated in those first meetings.

As the meetings grew bigger we realized we needed a bigger space, so we approached the person in charge of logistics for the conference to ask for a meeting room. At first we were told no. Well you know White folks don't plan anything without having a contingency plan, so we knew they had to have a room, so folks started gettin' upset. Then we were told we'd have to wait in line to get a room. Well Black folks reacted like we'd been waitin' 400 years and The Man acted like we'd been waitin' 5 minutes. Then folks got angry and we had what you call a communication breakdown. People started cursing. Someone called the man a mother f—and that we were gonna kick some a—. It got really heated so we had to take a break. We were told to come back in 5 minutes. In 5 minutes they had a meeting room for us on the first floor of the Hyatt Regency with cokes and refreshments and everything.

On the final day of the APA conference, members of our newly formed ABPsi executive council had a meeting with the executive council of APA. The members of ABPsi presented APA with a "challenge to change" that outlined a series of issues that demanded APA's immediate attention, including increased efforts to recruit African-American students in psychology, greater representation of African-American psychologists in APA, development of a means to provide mental health services to the African-American community, and recognition of the Black power and identity movement as a credible tool for fighting racism. . . . So, we made demands on APA, they responded, and we formed ABPsi, and ABPsi has been goin' ever since.

JOSEPH L. WHITE, PERSONAL COMMUNICATION, JULY 25, 2004

After the founding of ABPsi in 1968, other minority groups followed suit and formed their own organizations. Examples of other special-interest professional associations include the Association of Women in Psychology, the Asian American Psychological Association, the National Latino Psychological Association, and the Society of Indian Psychologists. When these groups began forming their own professional associations, APA recognized that it needed to become a more inclusive organization.

APA has also dealt with multicultural issues through its organizational structure. In 1979 APA established the Office of Ethnic Minority Affairs (OEMA) to handle issues related to cultural diversity, such as expanding the roles of ethnic minority psychologists (Holliday & Holmes, 2003). APA is organized into various divisions, each representing a particular area of interest. Currently, there are 53 divisions in APA, several of which deal with issues of diversity. Some of those divisions address specific cultural groups (e.g., Division 35, Society for the Psychology of Women). Others reflect broader areas of interest but have a history of paying significant attention to minority-related issues (e.g., Division 9, Society for the Psychological Study of Social Issues). See Table 1.3 for a listing of these divisions.

Division 45, The Society for the Psychological Study of Ethnic Minority Issues, founded in 1987, is the main division for psychologists interested in multiculturalism. Division 45 publishes its own journal, *Cultural Diversity and Ethnic Minority Psychology* (Educational Publishing Foundation), as do many of the other divisions. APA also deals with multicultural issues through the Office of

TABLE 1.3 Divisions of the American Psychological Association (APA) Concerned with Diversity Issues

Division 9	Society for the Psychological Study of Social Issues
Division 17	Society of Counseling Psychology
Division 27	Society for Community Research and Action: Division of Community Psychology
Division 35	Society for the Psychology of Women
Division 36	Psychology of Religion
Division 44	Society for the Psychological Study of Lesbian, Gay, and Bisexual Issues
Division 45	Society for the Psychological Study of Ethnic Minority Issues
Division 48	Society for the Study of Peace, Conflict, and Violence: Peace Psychology Division
Division 51	Society for the Psychological Study of Men and Masculinity

Information on each of these divisions can be obtained by visiting the APA Web site at www.apa.org.

Ethnic Minority Affairs and the Board for the Advancement of the Public Interest in Psychology.

Evidence for the rise of multiculturalism in psychology is also seen in the various documents and policies adopted by APA. The Ethical Principles of Psychologists and Code of Conduct (APA, 2002) is the main document guiding the profession of psychology. It defines the boundaries and responsibilities of the profession. The document is divided into two parts. The General Principles describe aspirational goals for the profession, and the Ethical Standards lay out specific dos and don'ts. Statements regarding the need for psychologists to pay attention to culture were first included in the document in 1992. In the current version, General Principle E, "Respect for People's Rights and Dignity" states:

> Psychologists are aware of and respect cultural, individual, and role differences, including those based on age, gender, gender identity, race, ethnicity, culture, national origin, religion, sexual orientation, disability, language, and socioeconomic status, and consider these factors when working with members of such groups. Psychologists try to eliminate the effect on their work of biases based on those factors, and they do not knowingly participate in or condone activities of others based upon such prejudices. (APA, 2002, p. 1063)

The Code also states that psychologists need to obtain training, experience, consultation, or supervision to ensure the provision of competent services to diverse populations, and that the specific characteristics of the individual, such as linguistic or cultural differences, should be taken into account when psychologists are interpreting the results of psychological tests. This is especially important when critical decisions are made on the basis of those results, such as placement in educational programs. The Code did not always include such statements. The fact that they are now included indicates that multiculturalism is supported, at least in principle, from the top down in the field of psychology.

A policy that illustrates the rise of multiculturalism in the field of psychology is the adoption of the multicultural competencies by APA in 2003. As mentioned earlier, the social climate of the 1960s and 1970s drew attention to the failure of psychology to address issues of diversity. In particular, the need to provide culturally sensitive forms of psychotherapy was highlighted, and the focus quickly turned to how to train psychologists to work with individuals from diverse cultural backgrounds.

In 1973 at an APA conference on training in psychology in Vail, Colorado, APA made a landmark decision that graduate training programs (Korman, 1974) must include courses on multicultural issues. However, implementation of that policy was slow. It was not until 2003, 30 years after the APA Vail Conference mandate, and after much hard work by leading multicultural psychologists across the country, that APA finally adopted a set of multicultural guidelines (APA, 2003), which were based in large part on the multicultural competencies proposed by many psychologists in the interim (e.g., Sue, Arredondo, & McDavis, 1992; Sue et al., 1998). The document is titled "Guidelines on Multicultural Education Training, Research, Practice, and Organizational Change for Psychologists" and reflects the knowledge and skills needed by psychologists in all areas of the field to work in our diverse and rapidly changing society. (See Table 1.4 for a summary of the guidelines.) By publishing these guidelines, APA took a greater step in formally acknowledging the importance of culture and set the standard for training psychologists to work with and study diverse populations.

The following is a story that illustrates the struggles faced in implementing multicultural training standards. One of the authors (JSM) had proposed including multicultural psychology as a "major area" of study for comprehensive examinations but was voted down by the clinical faculty.

> Stunned, the DCT [Director of Clinical Training] and I met, wondering what happened. Weeks later, he suggested that I try to make the proposal again, giving my colleagues the benefit of the doubt that perhaps they misunderstood my request. I stated my case even more clearly and passionately than before, also emphasizing APA's commitment to this area and its requirement that cross-cultural/multicultural content be infused into all graduate programs in psychology. This time, I thought for sure, my colleagues would understand and pass the proposal. However, to my surprise, the response was even more heated than before. I heard comments like these: "Cross-cultural psychology is too limited an area to be considered a major topic area for prelims." "There is nothing to cross-cultural psychology." "We allowed it to be a required course—what more do you want?" "Cross-cultural psychology is unimportant." "Haven't we already dealt with this? No means no!"
>
> You might think that this happened in the 1970s when the idea was still relatively new to those teaching in the profession. Or that those professors were "old fogies" who were trained under an antiquated

TABLE 1.4 Guidelines on Multicultural Education, Training, Research, Practice, and Organizational Change for Psychologists (APA, 2003)

Commitment to Cultural Awareness and Knowledge of Self and Others

Guideline 1	Psychologists are encouraged to recognize that, as cultural beings, they may hold attitudes and beliefs that can detrimentally influence their perceptions of and interactions with individuals who are ethnically and racially different from them.
Guideline 2	Psychologists are encouraged to recognize the importance of multicultural sensitivity/responsiveness to, knowledge of, and understanding about ethnically and racially different individuals.

Education

Guideline 3	As educators, psychologists are encouraged to employ the constructs of multiculturalism and diversity in psychological education.

Research

Guideline 4	Culturally sensitive psychological researchers are encouraged to recognize the importance of conducting culture-centered and ethical psychological research among people from ethnic, linguistic, and racial minority backgrounds.

Practice

Guideline 5	Psychologists are encouraged to apply culturally appropriate skills in clinical and other applied psychological practices.

Organizational Change and Policy Development

Guideline 6	Psychologists are encouraged to use organizational change processes to support culturally informed organizational (policy) development and practices.

system, anyway, so of course they would be against new ideas. What would you say if I told you that this happened to me in 1989? The surprising thing was that two of the most vocal opponents to the proposal were relatively new and young professors, so even the old-fogies excuse cannot be applied. This incident convinced me that I should be looking elsewhere for employment, and even though I received tenure from the university later, I gave it up to leave such an environment. (Adapted from Mio & Awakuni, 2000, pp. 1-2).

As that story and others like it illustrate, the multicultural movement has met serious resistance. Several authors cite various reasons for resistance to multiculturalism. Sue and associates (1998) identify what they call "the seven deadly resistances" (p. 28). These are arguments raised by the power structure against integrating multiculturalism into training programs, such as the contentions that current theories are generalizable to all populations and that conceptually sound multicultural standards do not exist. Mio and Awakuni (2000) wrote a book titled *Resistance to Multiculturalism: Issues and Interventions,* in which their main premise is that resistance to multicultural issues is rooted in various forms of racism. But they do not leave us without hope. They also outline what they think are effective ways of addressing such resistance, such as self-awareness, openness, and self-examination; knowledge and understanding of White privilege; and knowledge and understanding of ethnic identity models.

SUMMARY

Multicultural psychology is the systematic study of all aspects of human behavior as it occurs in settings where people of different backgrounds encounter one another. Essential to an understanding of multicultural psychology are such terms as *race, ethnicity,* and *culture,* as well as issues and controversies related to those terms.

A brief historical perspective shows that racism permeated the field from its early beginnings in research on individual and racial group differences and in the response by ethnic minority psychologists and women to bias in that research. Some psychologists suggest that multiculturalism is the "fourth force" in psychology, meaning that it will have as big an effect on our understanding of human behavior as did psychoanalysis, behaviorism, and humanism.

The main premise of multicultural theory is that all behavior occurs in a cultural context. Multicultural issues have gained greater acknowledgment and inclusion in the field of psychology over time, but not without resistance and struggle, as evidenced in the various policies and practices of the American Psychological Association.

Food for Thought

Whether or not multiculturalism truly is the fourth force in psychology remains to be seen. You are free to draw your own conclusions about that. We cannot deny, however, that culture is a critical factor in the way human beings think, feel, act, and interact. The field of multicultural psychology seeks to study that factor, with the ultimate goal of increasing our understanding of ourselves. We hope this chapter has whetted your appetite, for in the following chapters we introduce you to more specific areas of theory, research, and practice in the field of multicultural psychology.

Critical Thinking Questions

What were your early experiences with racial and ethnic differences? What were your early experiences with other aspects of difference? How have those early experiences shaped you into the person you are now?

Have you ever been to foreign countries and felt out of place? Have you ever been to other regions of the country and felt out of place? Have you ever been to different areas of your own city that have made you feel out of place? How have you handled those situations?

CHAPTER 2

Multicultural Issues Involving Research and Testing

RESEARCH METHODS IN PSYCHOLOGY
The General Research Model
The White Standard
Internal versus External Validity
QUANTITATIVE VERSUS QUALITATIVE RESEARCH
Quantitative Approaches
Qualitative Approaches

Korchin (1980) noted that researchers tend to question the generality of findings only when the research involves ethnic minority populations. Korchin mentioned that once he and his colleague had conducted research on why some African-American youths had made extraordinary achievements. A paper from the research was submitted for publication and rejected. One reviewer had indicated that the research was grievously flawed because it lacked a White control group. Why was a White control group necessary if the interest was in African Americans? More critically, Korchin asked why we do not require studies of Whites to have an African-American control group. In other words, we ask that ethnic minority research show its pertinence to other groups or more general phenomena, but we fail to make the same requests when the research involves White populations.

S. SUE (1999), P. 1072

As this quotation from Stanley Sue suggests, the scientific study of psychology is only as good as those who apply and interpret it. The field of psychology tries to apply scientific methods in the attempt to be "objective" in its discovery. As most researchers in the multicultural arena would agree, however, whereas our methods may strive for objectivity, our results and interpretations are laden with subjective values. In this chapter we examine multicultural issues relating to the different ways in which psychological research has been conducted and to psychological testing.

RESEARCH METHODS IN PSYCHOLOGY

The General Research Model

The standard way of applying science to psychology is to have a pool of potential research participants and to assign each participant to either a control group or an experimental group. Each individual is given an equal chance to be in the control or the experimental group. The control group either is not given any treatment at all or is given a typical kind of treatment, whereas the experimental group is given a regime that is designed to make some significant difference

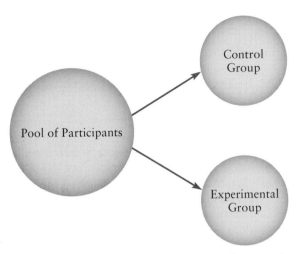

FIGURE 2.1   Assignment of research participants to control or experimental group.

(Figure 2.1). This difference is determined by comparing the results from the experimental group with the results from the control group.

To apply this general method to a concrete example, let us say that we are interested in finding out if a new medication will relieve the symptoms of depression. The control group in this instance is given a placebo—typically a sugar pill—and the experimental group is given the experimental medication. No one knows if he or she is receiving the sugar pill or the medication, and each individual has an equal chance of being in the control or the experimental group. After a period of time, we compare the groups to see if those who received the medication are measurably less depressed.

Although medical examples are the clearest form of experiments with people, let us explore an example more relevant to psychology. Suppose we are interested in finding out if a new method of teaching history will result in students learning the subject better. This new method asks students to act out historical events. The control group comprises the students learning history in the standard way, and the experimental group consists of the students acting out historical events. At the end of the academic year, students are tested about their knowledge of history, and we compare the scores from the two groups. If the new method is more effective in teaching history, the students in the experimental group will have higher scores on the history test than will the students in the control group. If the new method is less effective, the experimental group will have lower scores. If the new method does not make a difference one way or the other, the students in the two groups will have equal scores.

Now, what if we are interested in finding out if ethnic minority students learn as much as their White counterparts when both learn with the new method? We can compare the scores of ethnic minority students with those of White students and see if their scores are higher, lower, or the same. That seems to be an easy comparison. However, a wealth of evidence from the modeling literature suggests that children learn more if they can identify with models displaying the behaviors

(Bandura, 1977, 1986, 1997; Eron, 2000; Eron et al., 1996; Eron, Walder, & Lefkowitz, 1971). Therefore, to the extent that history learned in America is dominated by White European events, what can we conclude if we find that White children have higher scores than their ethnic minority counterparts? After all, the children will be portraying the White explorers, conquerors, and settlers in American history.

The White Standard

Jones (1993) discussed how the dominant research paradigm in American psychology is to see Whites as the standard against which all others are measured. Thus, if ethnic minorities are measured as different from the White standard, that difference is seen as deviant or deficient. You may recall that when researchers were studying children from inner city environments a number of years ago, they characterized the children as coming from "culturally deprived" environments. Interestingly, that phrase came from White liberals who were trying to empathize with these children, and they did not realize that they were perpetuating the notion that a White middle-class background was the "correct" environment, and anything less than that environment was "culturally deprived." More subtly, Derald Wing Sue had originally given his very influential book the title *Counseling the Culturally Different* (Sue, 1981; Sue & Sue, 1990, 1999). However, "different" implies that those who were not in the majority were different from the standard in society, so by 2003 the title of this book became *Counseling the Culturally Diverse* (Sue & Sue, 2003, 2008). As Sue and Sue (2003) put it,

> the phrase "culturally different" begs the question: "Different from what?" In almost all cases the comparison standard is related to White Euro-American norms and has the unintended consequence of creating a hierarchy among different groups (race, culture, ethnicity, etc.) in our society. (p. xv)

In other words, those diverse groups that are closer to the White Euro-American standard are deemed to be higher up in the hierarchy of groups and more acceptable to the majority, whereas those who are farther away from the norm are deemed less acceptable. In contrast, "diverse" implies that there are multiple perspectives or norms, with none being necessarily better or more desirable.

Internal versus External Validity

We began this chapter with a quotation from one of Stanley Sue's articles (Sue, 1999). The purpose of that article was to discuss the tension between internal and external validity. *Internal validity* refers to causal inference. In the experimental studies we discussed earlier, the procedures are designed to help us make an inference that a change in our procedure leads to a change in behavior. In the drug study, for example, a change in the medication (placebo versus medication) led to a change in depression; in the teaching study, a change in the method of teaching (standard teaching method versus students acting out history scenarios) led to a change in student learning. In other words, internal validity suggests that our changes make a difference.

The reason we randomly assign potential research participants to the experimental and control groups is to have more confidence that the changes in our procedures "cause" differences in behaviors. Suppose that we allow students to choose if they want to act out history or to learn history the usual way? If we find differences in learning, can we really infer that they result from the differences in teaching methods? Probably not. That is because those who choose to learn by acting out history may be more extraverted, so we may be measuring differences between extraverts and introverts, not between acting out history and standard teaching models. A great deal of effort is generally expended to ensure that studies are internally valid. If one cannot make any inference that one's changes lead to differences, the study will be useless, no matter how interesting or important the topic is.

On the other hand, *external validity* refers to the generalizabilty of the results we obtain. If we conclude from one study that our methods are effective, do those methods generalize to others? In many psychological studies, introductory psychology students participate in studies, and researchers conclude that "people" behave in similar manners. Is that inference justified? Sometimes yes and sometimes no. For example, if we were to study attraction and dating behavior, introductory psychology students might be very good research participants because they are at the age when such issues are very important if not dominant. However, if we were interested in poverty or grief, introductory psychology students might not be the best population to study.

External validity may be—and often is—at odds with internal validity. As Campbell and Stanley (1963) indicated in their classic publication:

> Both types of criteria are obviously important, even though they are frequently at odds in that features increasing one may jeopardize the other. While internal validity is the sine qua non, and while the question of external validity, like the question of inductive inference, is never completely answerable, the selection of designs strong in both types of validity is obviously our ideal. (p. 5)

As Sue (1999) indicated, even though psychology has recognized that both internal and external validity are important, the notions that internal validity is indispensible in experimental design and that external validity is "never completely answerable" have influenced the field to markedly favor internal validity over external validity. Sue calls this "selective enforcement of scientific principles." As Sue so eloquently put it:

> The phenomenon of selective enforcement of scientific criteria is apparent. We criticize research for problems in internal validity. Yet, we pay relatively little attention to external validity. Whether in research papers submitted for publication or research grant proposals submitted for funding, ethnic minority research is primarily scrutinized for internal validity problems. This is appropriate. Yet much of research, whether or not it is focused on ethnics, is not criticized for external validity problems. In experimental studies, the discrepancies between internal and external validity are brought into bold relief. Rigorous and sometimes elegant experimental designs allow us to make causal inferences. However,

because of their rigor and need to control for extraneous variables, they frequently involve small numbers of participants, foregoing issues of sampling and representativeness. (p. 1073)

Thus, when a researcher submits a study examining the effectiveness of a psychological treatment for depression, anxiety, or other forms of psychopathology, the study is typically reviewed for threats to internal validity and the proper application of statistical procedures, not for the degree to which the treatment can be generalized to all populations. Yet if you were in therapy for the treatment of one of those disorders, it would probably be more important for you to know if the treatment will work for you than to know if the study was conducted correctly. Scientifically, it is important that studies are conducted correctly, but practically, people want to know if things will work.

QUANTITATIVE VERSUS QUALITATIVE RESEARCH

Suppose you were given the following set of questions and were told to answer each one according to your preference:

At a party do you
   a. interact with many people, including strangers?
   b. interact with only a few close friends?

Do you
   a. initiate conversations?
   b. wait for others to begin talking to you?

Do you prefer to have
   a. many friends but only a little bit of time for each one?
   b. a few friends but have more time to spend with each one?

Do you find it
   a. easy to speak with strangers?
   b. difficult to speak with strangers?

Are you
   a. easily approachable?
   b. somewhat reserved?

Note that all "a" answers are extraverted forms of answers and all "b" answers are introverted forms. If you were to answer 20 such questions, we would be able to calculate how introverted or extraverted you are. Thus, if you had 5 "a" answers, you would have an extraverted score of 5, and if someone else had 12 "a" answers, he or she would have an extraverted score of 12. From those scores, we could conclude that you are more introverted and the other person is more extraverted.

Quantitative Approaches

The example on extraversion illustrates how a question can be turned into a meaningful number. You may have taken various tests that ask you to circle a number to indicate what your preference is or what characterizes you best, such as:

Did you like this movie?

1	2	3	4	5	6	7

I did not like it at all   I liked it a lot

Do you consider yourself to be creative?

1	2	3	4	5	6	7

I am not at all creative   I am very creative

Research that involves turning questions into meaningful numbers that can be compared with other numbers is called a quantitative study. Our entire system of statistics is based upon comparing numbers to make inferences about differences between groups or individuals.

Thus, in our earlier example involving the effectiveness of an antidepressant medication, we can ask the individuals to rate on a scale from 1 to 10 how depressed they are after treatment, with "1" meaning not depressed at all and "10" meaning deeply depressed. If the medication (experimental) group yields an average score of 3.7 and the placebo (control) group yields an average score of 6.2, we can conclude that the medication was effective in relieving the depression. This general approach is known in science as **Logical Positivism** (Georgaca, 2001; Hoshmand, 1994; Morrow, Rakhsha, & Castañeda, 2001; Unger, 1995).

Students are very much aware of such techniques of evaluation. Most professors assign a given number of points for tests, projects, papers, participation, and the like, and students who accumulate a higher number of points receive higher grades in the courses. Although this method is generally accepted and yields fairly accurate comparisons, there can sometimes be injustices or inaccuracies in this system. At some point in your life, someone else has probably received a higher grade in a course than you did. You may have felt that you understood more of the material than the other person did, so you may have felt that you suffered an injustice. On the other hand, you may have also benefited from this system, because you may have received a higher grade than another person who may have understood more in a particular course than you did.

Even more interesting is a situation in which two people both receive "A" grades, yet one individual just barely received the A and perhaps received it only because of extra-credit work or luck, whereas the other individual knew enough of the material to be able to teach the course. If both receive point accumulations of 95 out of 100 or both receive A grades, we will lose the subtleties of meaning behind those numbers or grades. To understand such subtleties, we need to employ qualitative research methods.

Qualitative Approaches

When people are asked if they prefer to interact with many people at parties or just a few close friends, they often say, "Well, it depends on the party." If you looked at those extraversion–introversion questions at the beginning of this chapter, you

Logical Positivism— a scientific approach that attempts to measure "truth" or real phenomena through methods of numbers and statistical analyses.

probably felt that your answer was dependent on the situation. If the party was lively, with lots of interesting people, you would probably be more interested in meeting a number of people. However, if there were many people to whom you could not relate, you probably would stick pretty closely to your friends. If you were standing in a line and some strangers were engaged in a conversation about a topic that was of interest to you, it would probably be easier for you to be drawn into the conversation. If you were sitting in an airport in front of the gate and people were reading books around you, it would be difficult for you to talk to strangers.

These examples suggest that collecting only numerical data may result in the loss of some important information and/or may ignore contextual variables that may affect how we respond. Qualitative approaches to research can be employed when a researcher determines that the gathering of strictly numerical answers to questions results in the loss of some essential information (Denzin & Lincoln, 2007a, 2007b; Elliott, 2005; Grbich, 2007; Hill, Thompson, & Williams, 1997; Liamputtong & Ezzy, 2005; Maxwell, 2004; Morrow, Rakhsha, & Castañeda, 2001; Phillon, He, & Connelly, 2005; Rissman, 2007; Seale et al., 2004; Silverman, 2004; Silverman & Marvasti, 2008; Yin, 2004). There are different kinds of qualitative data collection, such as case studies, structured interviews with open-ended questions, focus groups, and analyzing discourse (texts or narratives). Some people have used qualitative research to generate ideas for quantitative research, whereas others have used qualitative research as the goal of the research to give people an in-depth understanding of the phenomenon being examined. Our use of narratives in this book is a kind of qualitative application, because we are trying to convince you of some underlying truths or themes experienced by various people who have been touched by multicultural issues.

For example, Constantine, Kindaichi, Okazaki, Gainor, and Baden (2007) applied qualitative methods to examine how Asian international women adjusted to the United States and college. Through these methods, they were able to determine six prominent domains from their research participants: living in the United States, differences between their original cultures and the United States, English language issues, discrimination experienced, peer and family networks, and strategies for cultural coping. Without this qualitative procedure, one might assume that issues such as academics (since these were international students in college), individualism versus collectivism, and homesickness might have been prominent themes. The researchers might have then developed measures examining these themes. While these issues did come up, they were embedded within the larger themes that Constantine et al. identified. Thus, the Constantine et al. study provided us with a richer understanding of the issues with which these women dealt.

The examples at the beginning of this section showed how context can play a part in people's responses to research questions. However, contextual variables are not the only things that are lost in quantitative methods. If the choice is between preferring to interact with many people at a party and preferring to interact with just a few, if *on the whole* you prefer interacting with many people, your answer would be classified as extraverted. You may know someone who *always* prefers to interact with many people ("the life of the party"), and that person's response would also be classified as an extraverted answer. Is it really fair to give both of you one point on this question? Qualitative research methods can help us understand the degree to which a question is applicable to someone, or they can give us a sense of the profound differences between two respondents.

Finally, qualitative methods are often used when it is difficult to convert a question into a numerical response. Aesthetic questions are difficult to convert into numerical responses, particularly when respondents are asked to compare objects that are markedly different. For example, how would you convert to a number the joy you experience when you see a very close friend for the first time in years? How does that joy compare with the joy you experience when you finish a lengthy project that had many frustrations and obstacles along the way to completion? Certainly, you may try to quantify those experiences, but are the numbers resulting from that conversion really meaningful?

Research examining ethnic minority communities has employed qualitative techniques more and more. This is not to say that quantitative techniques have been discarded, but a trend is evident in the use of qualitative techniques. As Mio (2002) stated:

> As those of us in the multicultural arena know, measures on scales have helped us to understand elements of culture reasonably well, but this methodological approach has limited our understanding of culture, or at least the questions we can ask, for these questions must be reduced to quantifiable responses. Thus, in recent years, many multicultural researchers have drifted away from the logical positivistic methodology of numerical values that are statistically manipulated and analyzed and toward the more ethnographic and qualitative research methodologies used by our anthropology cousins. (p. 506)

One reason qualitative methods have not been widely employed is, frankly, that they are much more difficult than quantitative methods to employ. They typically use many fewer research participants and require more time to gather information because of the interview format of data collection. As noted in the section on quantitative approaches, our entire system of statistical inference is based upon quantitative, logical positivistic methods of inquiry. If we interview one or just a few individuals from a community, can we confidently generalize our results to the entire community or social group? How representative is that one individual or one community? A response from those who employ qualitative methods may be that we should not be confined only to those questions that can be answered in numerical form. Moreover, how representative are the research participants in quantitative studies? We can never be certain about the representativeness of our samples unless the samples cover the entire populations about which we are attempting to make inferences.

Another reason qualitative methods have not been widely employed is that we do not have an agreement on the best ways to interpret the information we receive. For example, as we will see in the next chapter, meanings of words, phrases, concepts, and so on may change from culture to culture or even subgroup to subgroup. Triandis and associates (1986) and Triandis and colleagues (1988) discussed the difficulty in measuring "self-reliance" across cultures. In individualistic cultures, self-reliance is related to the pursuit of one's own goals and has a flavor of being in competition with others. In collectivistic cultures, self-reliance is related to not burdening others and there is no sense of competition. (We also discuss individualism and collectivism in the next chapter.) Those different meanings clearly pose a difficulty in quantitative methods of inquiry, for what does a "6" on a 10-point scale mean when respondents rate themselves on a scale measuring self-reliance in a collectivistic culture as opposed to self-reliance in an individualistic culture? On the other hand, if we interview individuals in both cultures about the term and come up with a sense of how each culture can be characterized with respect to self-reliance, are we really examining the same concept? Again, we discuss these issues in more depth in the next chapter.

Equivalence of Measures

Many researchers have discussed the problem of equivalence between measures developed in one culture and their translations to another culture (Brislin, 1986; Brislin, Lonner, & Thorndike, 1973; Cheung, 1985; Lonner, 1979; Sue & Sue, 2000). These issues involve the concepts of *functional equivalence, conceptual equivalence, linguistic equivalence,* and *metric equivalence.* **Functional equivalence** refers to items that can be functionally instead of literally equated. For example, if we were to inquire about a child's knowledge of and conclusions about fairy tales, we might select *Beauty and the Beast* in this country, whereas we might select a well-known fairy tale for a child from the culture we are testing.

Conceptual equivalence refers to terms or phrases whose meanings are culturally equivalent. For example, Marsella (1980) found that the term *depression* does not exist in some cultures, but if one were to describe a condition wherein the individual experiences fatigue and slowness of thought, those symptoms could be identified by those cultures. Thus, although the *term* "depression" does not exist in those cultures, the *condition of* depression does.

Linguistic equivalence refers to how the test items are translated. Most people have accepted the standard that measures need to be back-translated instead of merely translated. *Back translation* is a procedure whereby the measure is translated into the target language, then translated back to the original language. If the back translation is the same or very nearly the same as the original, then the translation is acceptable for study. However, sometimes the back translation comes back very different from the original phrasing, so a different translation must be sought. There is an old joke from the cold war about a computer that was designed to read every book in Russian to see if any secret codes were being transmitted by the text. To test the computer, the American scientists had the computer translate "The spirit was willing but the flesh was weak." The computer whirred

functional equivalence—the equating of items on a test or a survey functionally as opposed to literally.

conceptual equivalence—refers to a term or phrase that is a culturally meaningful equivalent of the term being examined.

linguistic equivalence—the translation of a term from one language to another that carries with it similar meaning.

and translated the item into Russian, then back to English, and the result was "The vodka was good but the meat was rotten."

Finally, **metric equivalence** refers to numerical scores between different cultures. Some cultures may be "risk-averse" and not select the extremes of the possible answers. For example, in a culture that tends to be risk-averse, research participants presented with a 7-point scale may select 6 as the highest score, so the researcher may have to make 6 in that culture the equivalent of 7 in a culture that uses the full range of the scale.

metric equivalence— numeric scores that are generally equivalent from one culture to another.

Even with these precautions, one's work may not be done. Fernandez, Boccaccini, and Noland (2007) indicated that 10 percent of the U.S. population over the age of five speaks Spanish at home, and of these individuals, nearly half indicate that their English proficiency is not very good. Therefore, quite a number of individuals may need special accommodations in the testing situation. The authors proposed a four-step approach to selecting appropriate tests, including identifying translated tests, identifying research using these translated tests, confirming that the research applies to the client at hand, and determining the level of research support for using the translated test with the particular client. Acevedo-Polakovich et al. (2007) further indicated that the clinical interview portion of the testing situation should determine the person's immigration history, contact with other cultural groups, acculturative status, acculturative stress, socioeconomic status, and language abilities, and that attention needed to be paid to measure selection and assessment planning, and translation and the use of interpreters. Thus, mere translation of items is not enough. How many of you have been asked these kinds of questions before taking a test, such as an intelligence test?

Qualitative Approaches and Gender

Qualitative approaches to inquiry are not limited to multicultural issues. In fact, for years, research from the feminist literature has included qualitative methods. In her groundbreaking work, Carol Gilligan (1982/1993) discussed the differences between boys and girls based upon interviews with them about their reasoning through moral dilemmas. Here is one such interpretation:

> Most striking among these differences is the imagery of violence in the boy's response, depicting a world of dangerous confrontation and explosive connection, where [the girl] sees a world of care and protection, a life lived with others whom "you may love as much or even more than you love yourself." Since the conception of morality reflects the understanding of social relationships, this difference in the imagery of relationships gives rise to a change in the moral injunction itself. To Jake, responsibility means not doing what he wants because he is thinking of others; to Amy, it means doing what others are counting on her to do regardless of what she herself wants. Both children are concerned with avoiding hurt but construe the problem in different ways—he seeing hurt to arise from the expression of aggression, she from a failure of response. (p. 38)

Clearly, much more depth can be derived from this analysis than can be obtained from an interpretation of quantitative differences in choices among

PICTURE 2.1   Men and women can respond to research questions differently from each other. *Photograph taken by Lil Abellon*

alternative courses of action when children are given moral dilemmas to evaluate. Gilligan not only posits the reasoning behind the choices the children make in their course of action but also asserts what their different forms of imagery (or worldviews) are in guiding their choices. Of course, one might disagree with Gilligan's interpretations, but one would have to come up with an alternative set of interpretations of the meanings of children's worldviews, which again would require more depth of interpretation than can be derived from an analysis of different numerical averages. Other researchers have provided us with guidance on using qualitative methods in examining issues of gender (Hesse-Biber & Leavy, 2003; Hesse-Biber & Yaiser, 2003; Seale et al., 2004; ten Have, 2004).

Qualitative Approaches and Older Populations

Because of greater life experiences, older populations are more aware of contextual variables when considering questions. Hayes (1996) has developed a model of inquiry with older ethnic minority individuals that she calls *ADRESSING*. This acronym stands for (a) Age and generational influences, (b) Disability, (c) Religion, (d) Ethnicity, (e) Social status, (f) Sexual orientation, (g) Indigenous heritage, (h) National origin, and (i) Gender. Thus, when developing research programs designed to measure older populations, researchers should include or at least consider all those variables. For example, many researchers lump all Asians together when conducting research comparing different ethnic minority populations with one another or with Whites. However, Asians from Hong Kong may respond quite differently from Asians from the Philippines.

> *I was serving on a jury, and it was striking how much the individuals on the opposite side of the issue actually seemed to hate each other. I thought that farmers tried to help other farmers where they could, but this wasn't happening in this case. The suit that each was pressing against the other seemed rather trivial, but they were determined to make the other pay or at least suffer. Then it struck me—one of the guys was from Belgium and the other was from Germany. The Belgian was obviously not over World War II and wanted to extract all that he could out of this German farmer.*

SAM, 40+-YEAR-OLD JAPANESE-AMERICAN MAN

As this quotation indicates, the Hayes model is not restricted to studying ethnic minority populations. Here, national origin is an obviously important factor along with generational influences, in view of the fact that many older Belgians still harbor resentments toward Germans. It is hard to imagine that 50 years from now, older Belgians will still harbor those feelings, since their generation will have had a markedly different experience with people of German origin. Similarly, many older Koreans might still harbor resentments toward those of Japanese origin because of the hardships caused by World War II (Kim, 1997; Sung, 1991),

PICTURE 2.2 Older individuals may prefer data collection forms different from those preferred by young individuals.

whereas it is doubtful that Korean-American adults will harbor such resentments toward Japanese Americans 50 years from now.

Iwamasa and her colleagues (Chin, Mio, & Iwamasa, 2006; Hilliard & Iwamasa, 2001; Iwamasa & Sorocco, 2002) have indicated that elderly individuals, particularly Asian elderly individuals, may feel more comfortable with qualitative studies than with quantitative studies. When elderly research participants filled out items with numerical responses, they failed to see the relevance of those items and also wondered why they had to answer them three times (pretest, test, and posttest). On the other hand, they seemed to enjoy the focus-group study in which they participated because they were able to share stories with their contemporaries, and their fellow participants seemed to stimulate their memories by questions being asked. When Iwamasa and her colleagues gave elderly Asian-American participants open-ended questions, they found that the answers were more extensive when the questions were asked and answered orally than when the questions were asked in written form and required responses in writing. Thus, part of the advantage of these qualitative techniques of data gathering seems to lie in the communal interaction in which the participants were able to engage.

EXPERIMENTAL DESIGNS

Two common research designs are cross-sectional and longitudinal designs. *Cross-sectional designs* gather data across different age groups. For example, if we wanted to know if people become more conservative as they grow older, we might collect data from those in their 20s, 30s, 40s, 50s, 60s, and 70s and see if the participant responses are more conservative in later age groups than in earlier age groups. One problem with this kind of research is that it may not accurately characterize the progression of political thought. Younger people may feel more liberal about some current issues, and older people may feel more conservative about them.

The *longitudinal design* follows a certain set of individuals over a period of time. Thus, to find out about liberal and conservative attitudes, we might want to collect data on 20-year-old individuals, then follow them for 60 years to see if their attitudes do in fact become more conservative over time. Obviously, a disadvantage of this research design is the length of time it takes to collect the data and analyze it. A researcher has to have the vision to design this study when she or he is very young, the funding to sustain the research, and the patience to wait 60 years for the results. Along the way, some individuals may pass away, and the researcher may also pass away. Another disadvantage of this research is that the particular cohort of individuals may be unusual. For example, individuals who grew up during the Great Depression may have an entirely different worldview from that of individuals who grew up during the civil rights movement.

Research in aging has long advocated sequential designs in studying elderly populations (Nesselroade & Labouvie, 1985). The *sequential design* is a combination of the cross-sectional and longitudinal designs. Researchers collect data on multiple cohorts of individuals and follow them over a period of time so that by the end of the study, all age groups may be represented. For example, we might

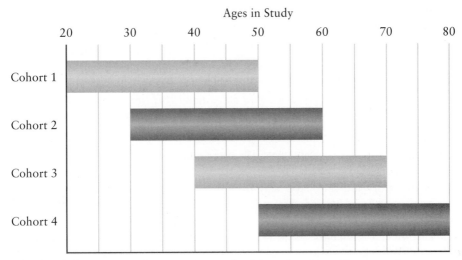

FIGURE 2.2 Overlap of age ranges in each of the cohorts in a 30-year study.

design a study collecting data on individuals in their 20s, 30s, 40s, and 50s and follow those four cohorts for 30 years (Figure 2.2). Thus, individuals in the first group will ultimately represent ages from 20 to 49 (assuming that some individuals were 19 years old when they first began the study), individuals in the second group will represent ages from 30 to 59, individuals in the third group will represent ages from 40 to 69, and individuals in the fourth group will represent ages from 50 to 79. Although this design still requires the researcher to actively collect data for a long period of time, it requires much less time (30 years) than a strict longitudinal design (60 years) in this example.

In the sequential design, the researcher will be able to compare data from multiple groups at similar ages. For example, if we want to see how liberal or conservative individuals are at age 45, we can look at three groups: the cohort whose data was collected in their 20s, and 20 years later, many of these individuals (about half) will have become 45 years old; the cohort whose data was collected in their 30s, all of whom will have become 45 years old 20 years later; and the cohort whose data was collected in their 40s, which will have many individuals (about half) whose data at age 45 will be available. If a cohort is unusual, the data collected from it will be different from the data from other cohorts. However, if the data is more a function of age than of cohort, the results will be similar across the different cohorts.

PSYCHOLOGICAL TESTING

Psychologists have long been engaged in various types of testing, including intelligence testing, personality testing, and diagnostic testing. Multicultural issues and challenges arise in all these types of tests. Today more than ever before, psychologists need to be aware of these issues.

Intelligence Testing

When I was young, I remember being called to the school counselor's office. Someone I had never met began giving me a test that I later recognized was an intelligence test. One of the items was "What is the Vatican?" I didn't know what it was. After the test, I asked the examiner what it was, and she told me. Since I was raised Buddhist and I was only a child, how was I supposed to know what the Vatican was? I remember thinking that the item was really unfair.

JEREMY, 40+-YEAR-OLD JAPANESE-AMERICAN MAN

As this story indicates, the way in which we measure intelligence can be a reflection of cultural knowledge, not what Spearman (1904, 1927) would call "general intelligence" or *g*. Many standardized intelligence tests, such as the Stanford-Binet Intelligence Scale (Thorndike, Hagen, & Sattler, 1986) and the Wechsler Intelligence Scales for Children (Wechsler, 1991), use cultural knowledge as a part of the overall measurement of intelligence. This practice is based upon Alfred Binet's long-held belief that such information was a direct measure of intelligence (Binet & Simon, 1905). This so-called direct measure contrasted with a movement headed by Sir Francis Galton to measure intelligence indirectly through sensory acuity (Galton, 1883). Galton measured intelligence by examining things such as visual acuity, how high a pitch people could hear, and how accurately people could detect different weights. Although the cultural knowledge method of measuring intelligence has proven to be much more successful and meaningful than the sensory acuity method, it is still vulnerable to subjective assessments of what is important to know and what is not.

Measuring intelligence has been a psychological pursuit at least since the time of Binet and Galton. We all have encountered people who we feel are smarter than or not as smart as we are, so this question seems to have some inherent interest. The problem is that historically it seems that some people may have biases or assumptions about issues of intellect that influence the science they conduct. A famous case is that of Cyril Burt. Burt contended that Blacks were intellectually inferior to Whites as determined by his scientific investigations. Burt, who was a prominent figure in educational psychology, was quite influential in his day, and people accepted his findings without question. Part of the reason for that unquestioning acceptance may have been that his findings were consistent with the general racism of the time. Years later, however, many researchers have determined that Burt based his findings on his own assumptions and the genetic theory of intelligence that he was supporting, not on actual data analysis (Dorfman, 1978; Gillie, 1977; Kamin, 1974).

More recently, Hernstein and Murray (1994) published a controversial book titled *The Bell Curve: Intelligence and Class Structure in American Life*. One of their central theses was not controversial: smart people generally do better than those who are not as smart. However, their other central thesis was controversial: ethnic minority individuals are not as smart as White individuals, so ethnic minorities should be trained for more service-oriented and physical-labor occupations, whereas Whites should be trained to do more intellectually challenging work. The authors go on to state that an appeasing "custodial state" should be created so that those less intellectually able will not rise up in opposition to being suppressed:

> In short, by *custodial state*, we have in mind a high-tech and more lavish version of the Indian reservation for some substantial minority of the nation's population, while the rest of America tries to go about its business. In its less benign forms, the solutions will become more and more totalitarian. Benign or otherwise, "going about its business" in the old sense will not be possible. It is difficult to imagine the United States preserving its heritage of individualism, equal rights before the law, free people running their own lives, once it is accepted that a significant part of the population must be made permanent wards of the state. (p. 526)

Although many have attacked Hernstein and Murray for their apparently racist stance (e.g., Gould, 1996; Samuda, 1998), what Hernstein and Murray really seem to ignore is that they take our measures of intelligence as unquestioned. As the story at the beginning of this section indicates, there may be some systematic reasons why some individuals do not score as highly on intelligence tests as do others. If a group of individuals not in the mainstream are asked about items that are common in the mainstream, should we be surprised that they do not score as highly as those who are exposed to those items? The solution to this problem is *not* to simply add questions that are common to this subgroup and not to the mainstream but to try to find measures that truly get at some essence of intelligence. This pursuit is very difficult, however, because nearly every set of items is layered with cultural influence.

In addition to the relevance of specific items, another issue in measuring intelligence is that different cultures may value different contributions to what is called intelligence. Okagaki and Sternberg (1991) interviewed White American parents, Mexican-American parents, and Asian immigrant parents about what they felt contributed to their children's intelligence. Asian parents reported that noncognitive factors, such as motivation and social skills, were more important than cognitive skills, such as problem solving and creativity; Mexican-American parents valued cognitive and noncognitive skills equally; and White parents valued cognitive skills more. Armour-Thomas (2003) posited:

> Although not ruling out other explanations, it is possible that the observed ethnic differences in intellectual performance may be attributed to different cultural values about what it means to be intelligent. If this is the case, an intelligence measure may be assessing different notions of valued intellectual abilities in different racial and ethnic groups and, in so doing, invalidating its results for these groups. (p. 363)

As the Hernstein and Murray quotation about a custodial state indicates, a great deal is at stake when measuring intelligence. In fact, intelligence tests, aptitude tests, achievement tests, and other forms of placement tests have been referred to as "high stakes testing" because the results of the tests have some very real implications for getting into schools, applying for jobs, setting the tone for how people respond to you, and so forth. For example, most college students have had to take college entrance exams such as the SAT. If students receive high scores on these exams, their chances of getting into their colleges of choice are enhanced. If they receive low scores, their chances are diminished. Thus, the stakes are high for students taking these tests.

> *High stakes testing is more common than most people stop to reflect on. Looking back on life I realize this testing started when I was just a little girl and tested to get into the GATE program in elementary school. The tests continued throughout my schooling and even outside of school, such as testing for my driver's permit and, ultimately, my driver's license. The tests continued throughout high school, including the exit exam, the SAT test, and the placement tests once I was admitted to college. Even in regards to jobs these tests have been prevalent, such as the drug tests and background tests.*
>
> *Thinking about high stakes testing reminds me of when immigrants had to take difficult literacy tests to enter into the United States so many years ago. I remember learning in my high school class that the creators of these tests were the elite and that the tests often contained elaborate language that even many Americans wouldn't fully comprehend. Even if it is not to that past extent, there are still literacy tests that are in favor of [native] English speakers.*
>
> KAYLENE, 20+-YEAR-OLD BIRACIAL (LATINA/WHITE) WOMAN

How did you feel when you took these tests and when you received your results? Intelligence tests have considerable impact. If you score quite high on intelligence tests, your teachers may give you more opportunities to succeed or may interpret some of your failures as a function of your not trying hard enough or of other factors getting in the way of your success. If you score low on intelligence tests, your teachers may assume that you do not know the answers, anyway, so why spend time on you? They may attribute your failures to your low abilities instead of to other factors getting in your way. If you experience a lifetime of these kinds of assessments, you will tend to succeed or fail depending upon expectations (Rosenthal, 1991, 1994; Rosenthal & Jacobson, 1968). Chapter 6 begins with a story related to teacher expectations.

Intelligence, Context, and Older Adults

In considering intelligence and aging, Labouvie-Vief (1985) discussed how our Western view of mature intelligence resides outside context and observed that we regard consideration of contextual variables to be less mature or less intelligent. "According to such deficit interpretations, one might argue, of course, that the concrete bias of the uneducated and/or the old reflects an inherent restriction on abstract thinking" (p. 516). However, she cited an interaction reported by Luria (1976) to question the degree to which we cling to our own (or at least Luria's) conceptions of intelligence and ignore cultural and contextual variables:

> subjects often assimilate the information presented in the problem to their own ways of conceptualizing reality; they construct new premises and correctly operate upon those. The following excerpt from Luria's

study will serve as a good example. Three subjects were first shown a picture of a saw, an ax, and a hammer and then asked if a "log" belonged to the same category (i.e., tools).

Experimenter (E): Would you say these things are tools? All three subjects (S-1, S-2, S-3): Yes.

E: What about a log?

S-1: It also belongs with these. We make all sort of things out of logs—handles, doors, and the handles of tools.

S-2: We say a log is a tool because it works with tools to make things.

E: But one man said a log isn't a tool since it can't saw or chop.

S-3: Yes you can—you can make handles out of it! . . .

E: Name all the tools used to produce things . . .

S-1: We have a saying: take a look in the fields and you'll see tools. (Luria, 1976, pp. 94-95)

If presented with the same task, city-educated subjects will almost inevitably exclude "log" from the category of tools, and from this fact Luria argues that the uneducated display a deficit in classificatory behavior. Yet one also senses here a different dimension; these Uzbekistan peasants appear engaged in a bantering argument about the proper definition of "tool," rejecting any one concrete definition and arguing for a more flexible and perhaps even creative stance. And indeed, although the experimenter attempts to guide the subjects towards a "correct" definition of tools, one is hard put to judge who is more "rigid" or "concrete"—the subjects or the experimenter! (p. 517)

In other words, the experimenter had a particular conception of intelligence and was trying to measure that conception through a predetermined metric. When the elderly research participants brought their experience to bear on the situation, showing flexibility in their thinking, the experimenter rejected this flexibility in favor of an "objective" definition of "tool." Which person is displaying more intelligence?

Alternative Conceptions of Intelligence

Sternberg (2002) related a research project by Cole, Gay, Glick, and Sharp (1971), who studied the Kpelle tribe in Africa. They were trying to sort objects conceptually:

In Western culture, when adults are given a sorting task on an intelligence test, more intelligent people typically will sort hierarchically. For example, they may sort names of different kinds of fish together, and then place the word "fish" over that, with the name "animal" over "fish" and over "birds," and so on. Less intelligent people will typically sort functionally. They may sort "fish" with "eat," for example, because we eat fish, or they may sort "clothes" with "wear" because we wear clothes. The Kpelle sorted functionally—even after investigators unsuccessfully tried to get the Kpelle spontaneously to sort hierarchically.

Finally, in desperation, one of the experimenters (Glick) asked a Kpelle to sort as a foolish person would sort. In response, the Kpelle quickly and easily sorted hierarchically. The Kpelle had been able to sort this way all along; they just hadn't done it because they viewed it as foolish–and probably considered the questioners rather unintelligent for asking such stupid questions. (pp. 503-504)

As you can see, our limitations in measuring intelligence may be the limitations of both how we measure intelligence and how we understand intelligence.

The son of one of our regular customers came fishing with his father. His father was bragging about how intelligent his son was. He was going to MIT and was in the process of developing his own math system or something like that. I watched his son hook his hook onto one of the eyes of his fishing pole and go to get some bait out of the bait tank. While he was away, the wind had blown his hook off of the eye, and his hook was flapping in the wind. When he came back, he looked at the eye where his hook should have been, and when it wasn't there, he started looking at every eye, wondering where his hook was. Any idiot should have known that his hook was flapping in the wind, but this so-called genius didn't seem to have any common sense.

ANTHONY, 20+-YEAR-OLD JAPANESE-AMERICAN MAN

As the story indicates, there are different ways of being intelligent. The "genius" did not seem to be able to figure out a simple problem, and he thus appeared to be of less than average intelligence to Anthony.

Most of how we have measured intelligence in the past has been what Sternberg and his colleagues would call "analytic intelligence" (Sternberg, 1985, 1988, 1995, 1997, 1999, 2002, 2003; Sternberg et al., 1996; Sternberg et al., 1999). Sternberg's general model suggests that intelligence is not made up of a single factor *g* as Spearman (1904) had suggested. Instead, it is made up of at least three components: analytic intelligence, creative intelligence, and practical intelligence. Intelligence tests and academic achievement tests have measured primarily analytic intelligence because it is the easiest component to measure. It depends heavily upon memorization and calculations based upon learned formulas. Thus, those who excel in creative and practical forms of intelligence are not identified by our standard measures (Wagner, 2000).

When I was a student in high school, I was always interested in comparing scores on tests, especially on important tests. My older brother scored in the 1500 range on the SATs, while I didn't quite [do] as well with only a 1060. I always wondered how this was possible because we attended the same schools growing up, and had pretty much the same teachers. Where he had the ability to read a book and memorize the information, I had to study material for hours and use

different types of methods in order to get the information to stay long
enough to remember it for an upcoming test. At the time I just thought
that he was smarter than me, but now I know that he excelled in
analytic intelligence, which tests like the SATs measure above creative
and practical intelligence. This is mainly because analytic intelligence is
the easiest to measure.

MONICA, 20+-YEAR-OLD EUROPEAN-AMERICAN WOMAN

As a test of this triarchic theory of intelligence, Sternberg and his colleagues (Sternberg et al., 1996; Sternberg et al., 1999) measured children who excelled only in analytic intelligence, only in creative intelligence, only in practical intelligence, in all three, or in none of the three. They then gave these children matching or mismatched instructions for performing a task. For example, children who excelled only in analytic intelligence performed better when given analytic instructions than when given practical instructions; children who excelled in practical intelligence performed better than did children who excelled in analytic intelligence when given practical instructions; and so forth. These results confirmed that differing forms of intelligence produce measurably different performances in different contexts.

A different conception of intelligence was proposed by Gardner (1983, 1993, 1999). Whereas standard intelligence tests generally measured a verbal component (with mathematical abilities subsumed under this verbal component) and a

PICTURE 2.3   Creativity may be seen as a type of intelligence. *Photograph by Tom Zasadzinski*

TABLE 2.1   Gardner's Eight Types of Intelligence

Type of Intelligence	Examples of Intelligence
Linguistic intelligence	Reading and understanding a book; understanding oral presentations; writing term papers for a class
Logical-mathematical intelligence	Solving mathematical problems; understanding advanced calculus; logical reasoning processes
Spatial intelligence	Developing a cognitive map of a route; doing mental rotations; estimating if objects will fit into certain spaces
Musical intelligence	Playing a musical instrument; composing music; appreciating the construction of music
Bodily-kinesthetic intelligence	Playing athletic events; learning new dance steps; being able to control one's bodily movements
Interpersonal intelligence	Being able to talk easily with others; detecting changes in emotional states of others; understanding others' motives
Intrapersonal intelligence	Being attuned to our own emotional states; understanding our own abilities; knowing how to change ourselves
Naturalist intelligence	Understanding patterns of nature; being able to survive in naturalistic settings

nonverbal component of intelligence, Gardner proposed that intelligence comprises seven intelligences: (1) linguistic, (2) logical-mathematical, (3) spatial, (4) musical, (5) bodily-kinesthetic, (6) interpersonal, and (7) intrapersonal. He later added an eighth intelligence: naturalistic intelligence (Gardner, 1999) (Table 2.1). The following is an example of one of Gardner's forms of intelligence:

> *I went to a Stevie Wonder concert last night. Man, that guy is a genius! During one part of the concert, he just came out by himself with his guitar and asked people to shout out their names and occupations. Right then and there, he composed songs using these people's names and jobs. I've never been so impressed by anyone in my life!*
>
> DAVE, 20+-YEAR-OLD WHITE MAN

Although intelligence test purists might identify Gardner's linguistic and logical-mathematical intelligences as the only true measures of intelligence, classifying the other forms of intelligence as merely learned abilities, Gardner would hold fast to the notion that these are true forms of intelligence. Dave would certainly agree that he was in the presence of genius when he saw Stevie Wonder.

> *Overall, I have found through Sternberg and Gardner that I don't have to [have] analytical intelligence to be intelligent; that I can be*

PICTURES 2.4a-b   Some see bodily-kinesthetic and musical abilities as distinct forms of intelligence. *Photographs by Tom Zasadzinski*

> *intelligent in other ways. Reflecting on the approaches that these two psychologists have come up with has made me feel more secure about myself, more intelligent, and has made me appreciate other approaches about intelligence more. I believe when it comes to defining who is and who is not intelligent that we as a whole society need to redefine it, because so many people are left feeling unintelligent because they were not able to pass or do well on a test and this is unfair, sad, and a tragedy.*

CARRIE, 20+-YEAR-OLD BIRACIAL (LATINA/WHITE) WOMAN

Personality and Diagnostic Testing

Much of personality and diagnostic testing is subject to the same problems of general study discussed earlier in this chapter. If we were to use a test to determine the personality characteristics of an individual or the level of depression that an individual is experiencing, then we would have to make sure that the test is measuring the same or very similar characteristics. The measuring instrument should have functional, conceptual, linguistic, and metric equivalence. Because so many personality and clinical tests are developed in the United States, the most amount of energy expended in addressing equivalence issues has been devoted to linguistic equivalence, particularly Spanish. Thus, many instruments such as the Minnesota Multiphasic Personality Inventory (MMPI; Hathaway & McKinley, 1967; MMPI-2; Butcher et al., 1989) have been translated into Spanish (Dana, 1993; Montgomery, Arnold, & Orozco, 1990; Velasquez, Callahan, & Young, 1993; Whitworth, 1988).

In examining the literature on the MMPI applied to various ethnic minority groups, Zalewski and Greene (1996) found that although there were very few group differences, it was premature to suggest that single norms could be applied to all cultural groups. However, they did find that factors such as socioeconomic status, education, acculturation, and intelligence were more important in determining different MMPI profiles than was cultural group membership. Ultimately, if differences *were* found based on one's identification with one's group membership, then a separate group membership test would have to be administered to give meaning to any interpretation of the MMPI profile.

Moreland (1996) identified one of the central questions regarding personality testing and ethnic minority populations: Do we look at group personalities to characterize a set of people (such as nations or specific ethnic minority groups), or do we pay attention only to individual personalities that we measure? Certainly, some countries or groups value certain characteristics, and those characteristics may be distinguished from characteristics valued by other countries or groups. For example, countries can be classified as generally more collectivistic or generally more individualistic (Hofstede, 1980; Triandis, 1995). However, when we characterize a country or a group, we may be confirming certain stereotypes about individuals from those countries or groups and not appreciating the rich variation within those groups. On the other hand, since most personality assessment tools have been developed in the United States and other Western countries, how much do these assessment tools really apply to those from other cultures?

Perhaps the most difficult question to address when applying tests and other measures to ethnic minority populations is the problem of bias. We have been discussing the difficulties in making these instruments as equivalent as possible, to eliminate as much bias from the tests as possible. However, there are at least two other kinds of bias: *bias of the user* and *bias in the usage* (Helms, 1995a). **Bias of the user** refers to the introduction of bias into the interpretation of the test by the user of the test. If the user has a predetermined assessment of a group of individuals, then the test results may be interpreted to confirm that bias. For example, Adembimpe (1981) found that African Americans were more likely to be diagnosed with schizophrenia when presenting the same symptoms as their White counterparts, who were more likely to be diagnosed with bipolar disorder. In the clinical psychology realm, schizophrenia is considered to be the more severe diagnosis with a worse prognosis for recovery. Paniagua (2001) indicated that ethnic minority populations are seen by the majority group as being more pathological because the majority group does not value the lifestyles and norms of the ethnic minority groups as much as they value their own.

In contrast, **bias in the usage** of a test refers to how a test is used. For example, if a teacher uses a test of verbal fluency—which may be a good test for native English speakers—to determine who in a first-grade class will be section leader, the use of that test may be biased if the test is administered in an area with many children whose parents are monolingual in a different language. Eventually, these children may become as fluent in English as their White counterparts, but at this very early age, most of them will not be as fluent in English. Thus, they will lose out on an early experience in leadership not because they lack leadership ability but because of another factor. Sometimes bias in the usage of a test is unconscious; sometimes, however, the bias is intentional and conscious.

bias of the user— a bias in the interpretation of a test when the test user has a particular perspective or bias that may disadvantage a person or group.

bias in the usage— a bias introduced when a test is used in an inappropriate manner, such as being administered in a language in which the test taker is not fluent.

SUMMARY

Psychologists have conducted research with ethnic minority populations in many ways, and challenges can arise in these research studies. Traditionally, multicultural studies were conducted by measuring differences between White populations and ethnic minority comparison groups. Such a comparison may not make any sense if the target of study is the ethnic minority group being studied. For example, if we want to know why some American Indians maintain a strong tie to their tribal reservation and others do not, there is no need to have a White comparison group. However, in the past, many mainstream researchers insisted on White comparison groups when the topic of study concerned ethnic minority groups.

Important differences exist between quantitative data and qualitative data. Quantitative data is data that can be transformed into numbers so that averages of one group can be compared with averages of another group. Qualitative data is more difficult to collect and to interpret. However, qualitative data may be more meaningful in studies of ethnic minority groups, comparisons between women and men, and studies of elderly populations.

One problem in studying different groups is the issue of equivalence. This problem is particularly important when the material in a study needs to be translated into a different language. There are at least four problems of equivalence: functional, conceptual, linguistic, and metric equivalences.

Research projects have differing designs. The two most common designs are cross-sectional and longitudinal designs. The cross-sectional design collects data all at once across different age groups, and the longitudinal design collects data at one point in time and follows the original group across time to collect data across all age groups. A combination of these two designs is the sequential design, which collects data across different age groups and follows the research participants over a period of time. Since some of the research participants are older than others, data that is the equivalent of data from a longitudinal design can be collected in a much shorter period of time.

Finally, multicultural issues arise in psychological testing. Intelligence testing, personality testing, and clinical assessment are subject to the same kinds of difficulties and challenges as other kinds of studies. Even if these tests are constructed carefully, the use of them can be biased. An added challenge is that sometimes these tests involve what is called "high stakes testing": the results of the tests may have a major impact upon the individuals' lives, so particular care should be taken when using such tests.

Food for Thought

Most students have taken tests such as SATs to get into college, so you probably know the importance of high stakes testing whether you were consciously aware of the term for this kind of test or not. You got into the college or university where you are because of the SAT score you received and/or you *did not* get into another college or university because your score was not high enough. As you can see, tests

continued

of this nature can have a major impact on your life and can even be life-changing events. Think about how you might feel if you were to go to a different country and be given a test that would affect your status in that country. You might gain some insight into the importance of psychological assessment.

Critical Thinking Questions

Have you ever been certain about something? If so, how did you know it was true? How did you go about "proving" its truth?

Have you ever been associated with a group that was the object of a research study (such as your gender, your ethnicity, your religious group)? If so, what did you think about the conclusions of the research? Did they apply to you or not?

Have you ever been compared unfavorably with someone or with a group that had an advantage over you? How did that make you feel? Can you construct a study that is more fair?

Did you ever perform poorly on a test and feel that if your teacher had just interviewed you, he or she would have come away with a much better picture of your abilities?

Have you ever felt that you were being measured against someone else's standards?

CHAPTER 3

Differences in Worldviews

WORLDVIEW OF WOMEN
WORLDVIEW OF LESBIAN, GAY, AND BISEXUAL INDIVIDUALS
SUMMARY

I was teaching a course in multicultural psychology. When I discussed differences in perceptions based upon cultural perspectives (the emic distinction), a student related a story about her missionary work in Uganda. She said that the Ugandan people would receive welfare checks at the beginning of the month, and they would immediately spend it on as many supplies as they could. Quite often, their supplies would run out before the end of the month, and they would nearly starve until they received their check the next month. "This drove me crazy," the student said. "I finally said, 'Don't you understand why you are running out of supplies? You are spending all of your money at the beginning of the month! All you have to do is save some money, and near the end of the month, you could buy more supplies.' They replied, 'No, it is you who do not understand. There is hyperinflation in this country, and our money buys much more at the beginning of the month than it does at the end of the month. The most logical thing we can do is to spend all of our money at the beginning of the month.' Right then and there, I learned the importance of understanding a culture before you try to change it."

JEREMY, 40+-YEAR-OLD JAPANESE-AMERICAN MAN

Different people with different experiences often see the world in quite disparate manners. Those who live in cold climates may see the world quite differently from those who live in warm climates; those who live in crowded cities may see the world differently from those who live in rural environments; those who are of one ethnicity may see the world differently from those of another ethnicity. This chapter will examine some of the ways in which people have what are called different **worldviews,** which reflect the ways in which the world is filtered through one's experiences and teachings.

worldview—
a psychological perception of the world that determines how we think, behave, and feel.

etic perspective—
an attempt to build theories of human behavior by examining commonalities across many cultures.

emic perspective—
an attempt to derive meaningful concepts within one culture.

DIFFERENT PERSPECTIVES FOR LOOKING AT CULTURES

The chapter-opening story illustrates a major topic in the multicultural arena—the distinction between the *etic* and the *emic* perspectives on cultures. These terms derive from the linguistic terms "phonetic" and "phonemic" (Pike, 1967). The **etic** approach attempts to find commonalities across cultures. It examines cultures from the outside to build theories that develop universal aspects of human behavior. The **emic** approach examines only one culture from within that culture. This approach attempts to derive what is meaningful among group members (Berry et al., 1992; Brislin, 1980; Jahoda, 1982; Mestenhauser, 1983; Reynolds, 1999). Kim and his colleagues (Kim & Berry, 1993; Kim & Park, 2006; Kim, Yang, & Hwang, 2006) call the emic approach the "indigenous and cultural psychology" approach to investigation. Sue and Sue (2003) call the etic approach a culturally universal perspective, whereas the emic approach is a culturally specific perspective.

Imposing a Worldview

Although both of these approaches are necessary, Berry (1969) cautions against **imposed etics,** by which he means the imposition of an outsider's worldview on a different culture. Sometimes observers assume that some behaviors or concepts are universal or have the same meaning they do in the observers' culture. For example, the student described by Jeremy in the opening story demonstrated imposed etics when she tried to impose on the Ugandan people her own value of saving money for use later on. She believed that saving money was an obviously universal value and that the Ugandan villagers needed to learn it to survive. When the problem of hyperinflation was pointed out to her, she immediately understood that she was imposing her own worldview on these villagers.

> **imposed etics**—the imposition of one culture's worldview on another culture, assuming that one's own worldviews are universal.

Mischel's (1958, 1961) studies represent a historical example of imposed etics. Mischel was interested in studying **delay of gratification.** He set up studies wherein children had a choice between a less desirable reward that they could have immediately (such as a small piece of candy) and a more desirable reward that they could have if they waited until the next day (such as a large piece of candy). He found that White children at the Stanford Day Care Center predominantly chose to wait for the more desirable reward, whereas African-American children in the inner city of Oakland chose to take the less desirable reward immediately. Mischel concluded that African-American children in the inner city did not know how to delay gratification, but that if we could teach them to delay gratification, they could work themselves out of the inner city.

> **delay of gratification**—the ability to wait for a more desirable reward instead of taking a less desirable reward immediately.

However, alternative interpretations to this conclusion would suggest that the African-American children were actually behaving adaptively for a number of reasons based upon their experiences: The experimenter could have been lying to them and would not show up the next day; the children may have been hungry, so the small piece of candy was more meaningful to them immediately; the experimenter could be robbed the next day; the experimenter's car could break down, so he might not show up; and so forth (Mio & Awakuni, 2000; Mio & Iwamasa, 1993; Mio & Morris, 1990). Therefore, even though Mischel's studies were well intentioned, they were still an example of imposed etics: Mischel thought he was studying delay of gratification (or lack thereof), whereas the more meaningful concept for the children was adaptive behavior.

A former student wrote about his frustrations with some of his colleagues when doing a group project. He felt that students were more interested in getting A grades instead of learning something useful. He previously talked about how frustrating it was when people who thought they were doing more work than their share would take it upon themselves to tell professors about those students who were not pulling their weight. He framed his interpretation in terms of imposed etics:

> *Because our society as a whole is more individualistic, we impose etics*
> *on those who may not be motivated the same way. In the group setting,*

we assume that everyone wants to get an "A" on a project. And if you want to get an "A" then you will participate. If you aren't participating, then you obviously do not care about your grade. As a member of the group, I will make sure that you are not rewarded and, more importantly, I will not be punished.

JAMAAL, 20+-YEAR-OLD AFRICAN-AMERICAN MAN

Even when there is some overlap or connection between ideas from different cultures, there may be cultural variations. A colleague told us of the connection between Freud's Oedipal complex and a Japanese variant of this story:

There was an old article (1980s?) about the Ajase complex. It told of a Japanese psychiatrist in the 1920s or '30s who was pondering Freud's Oedipal complex. He concluded that the Oedipal complex was based on a Western family structure, and so, came up with the Ajase complex. Ajase is a mythical character as was Oedipal. The story of Ajase speaks to the close Mother–Son relationship in an Asian family (especially a Japanese family?). In fact, the myth does not even mention Ajase's father explicitly, just Ajase resolving his relationship with his mother (his mother did not have Ajase out of love for Ajase, but out of love for her husband and family duty as well—Ajase was torn apart when he realized this truth). This Japanese psychiatrist went to Vienna to present his thesis to Freud, himself. As I recall Freud's reaction, he found this cross-cultural variation of the Oedipal complex fascinating and read the thesis.

I think the Ajase complex speaks to the need for culture specific assessment of Freudian theory and of Ericksonian theory as well (Kohlberg could also be included).

YASUE, 60+-YEAR-OLD JAPANESE-AMERICAN MAN

At first blush, this Ajase complex seems to be very similar to the Oedipus complex. However, the Ajase story does not include a jealousy of one's father, a fear that the father would cut off the boy's penis, nor an underlying sexual connection between Ajase and his mother. Instead, the story seems to underscore the cultural value of not sticking out or being too prideful. Ajase thought he was special and thought he was central to the family structure, so he was devastated to discover that he was conceived due to family obligations.

Understanding Differences from Within

As discussed in chapter 2, "self-reliance" is a good example of how different countries can conceptualize terms differently. Triandis and associates (1986, 1988) found that individualistic countries conceive of self-reliance as related to the pursuit of one's own goals, whereas collectivistic countries conceive of it as related to not burdening others. We will be discussing individualism and collectivism much more extensively later in this chapter, but, briefly stated, individualistic cultures tend to place individual rights over the rights of the collective, whereas collectivistic cultures tend to place collective rights over the rights of the individual. Of course, each culture has some elements of the other (i.e., individualistic cultures have some elements of collectivism and collectivistic cultures have some elements of individualism), but on balance, there are identifiable tendencies in most cultures (see Triandis, 1995). The emic definitions of self-reliance give completely different flavors to the term and an insight into the countries defining the term.

Sue and Sue (2000) give another example of emic differences between individualistic and collectivistic societies in defining a term:

> For example, one aspect of good decision making in the Western [individualistic] cultures may be typified by an ability to make a personal decision without being unduly influenced by others, whereas good decision making may be understood in Asian [collectivistic] cultures as an ability to make a decision that is best for the group. (p. 3)

Again, we see that the individualistic definition of the term (good decision making) involves a reflection of individualism: independence; the collectivistic definition of the term involves a collectivist value: paying attention to others.

A former student wrote about how homosexuality was understood in the Philippines before Western religious concepts took over the country:

> *I believe also that lesbians, gays, and bisexuals have a connection with religion and spirituality. Beyond the privileges discussed in class, early shamans of almost every tribe and nation were almost always homosexual (though I have read that some were bisexual). In ancient Greece and Rome, many priests dressed in matron's gowns and paraded as women in certain festivals, and priestesses of certain deities wore belts that had a phallus shape in front for certain rites. The notion is that these are people who are in between norms of usual interaction or in between genders; they can be both. Thus, they were perceived also as being able to traverse in between the normal and paranormal worlds. In the Philippines, they were once called* babaylan *(priests; most likely gay men or wounded warriors and sickly men) and* catalonan *(priestesses; most likely lesbians or infertile women). It was not until the arrival of Christianity that these people were demonized and labeled as sinful. In many early societies, homosexuals are delegated the positions of spiritual leaders primarily for two things: one, because they cannot or will not aid in the propagation of the tribe; and two, because they are seen to be not one, not another, yet both. This is a mysterious quality that was attributed to and associated with special abilities. In modern day India, a special class of eunuchs who dress in feminine garb are believed to be able to curse or bless people because of this very reason. Thus, homosexuality has a long and intriguing yet hidden history.*

TREVOR, 20+-YEAR-OLD CHINESE-FILIPINO MAN

Male and Female Perspectives

One might apply the emic/etic distinction to how men and women interpret certain terms. A former student discussed how she perceives safety and noted that many men in her life do not see it the way she does and call her paranoid:

> *Many times at night, when I am walking to my car, I carry my keys in my hand and keep looking around making sure nobody is too close to me. I get a sort of nervous feeling when I am by myself at night and it never really dawned on me until we went over women's worldviews that very few men if any have ever done that. I have been known to carry a bottle of pepper spray on me and every once in awhile I get teased for being over cautious by some of my male friends but I know it's because they have never really experienced how it feels to be a relatively small defenseless person.*
>
> *I am currently writing a report about the effects of society blaming the victim on victims of sexual assault. It's upsetting to me that so many people can blame female victims of sexual assault by saying that they were either out where they shouldn't be or dressed inappropriately or in some way shape or form had it coming to them. Now I am not saying that every man feels this way or even most men, but for any man who has ever thought that just disgusts me. I mean what right does a man*

PICTURE 3.1 "Denim Day" has become a symbol protesting violence against women. *Photograph by Tom Zasadzinski*

*have to blame a female for sexual assault when he has never known
how it feels to be as defenseless as a woman feels on a day to day basis.*

KERRY, 20+-YEAR-OLD EUROPEAN-AMERICAN WOMAN

As one can see, the emic perspective involves differences between cultures in interpreting concepts and terms. On the other hand, the etic perspective attempts to find commonalities across cultures. Landrine, Klonoff, and Brown-Collins (1995) stated, "'Truth' is understood as both the emic and the etic data, or as the emic data alone, but not as the etic data alone" (p. 62).

Connecting the distinction between the emic and etic perspectives with Berry's (1980) notion of imposed etics, students are encouraged to think of times when they felt misunderstood by someone else. Such a situation can be conceptualized as imposed etics in that one person probably felt that the other person's behavior was based on one sort of motivation, whereas it was based on another sort of motivation. Have you ever been misunderstood by someone and then found, when you talked it over with that person, that the misunderstanding was just a matter of the two of you interpreting the situation differently?

Well-Meaning Clashes

Of course, emics and etics refer to larger societies or at least subcultures as opposed to individual differences in interpretation. However, our collective individual

PICTURE 3.2   How much do men understand women's worldview regarding safety?
Photograph by Tom Zasadzinski

interpretations can lead to greater societal differences. Brislin (2000) pointed out that in some cultures (e.g., the United States), belching after eating is considered to be rude, whereas in other cultures, belching is a compliment to the chef on the excellent food. In Japan, people are expected to sip their tea very loudly to indicate to the host that the tea is very delicious, whereas in the United States, people are supposed to sip their tea or coffee quietly.

Much of our adaptation to other countries involves learning the emic rules of conduct. Brislin (2000) talked about "well-meaning clashes," which are cultural differences in interpretation that are not meant to harm others but that cause problems because there are different emic interpretations of situations or concepts. Cushner and Brislin (1996) developed a number of such scenarios. Here is one of them:

> After a year in the United States, Fumio, from Japan, seemed to be adjusting well to his graduate-level studies. He had cordial relations with his professors, interacted frequently with other graduate students at midday coffee breaks, and was content with his housing arrangements in the graduate student dormitory. Fumio's statistical knowledge was so good that professors recommended that certain American students should consult him for help in this area. He seemed to be excluded, however, from at least one type of activity in which many other of the American graduate students participated. This was the informal gathering of students at the local pub (bar) at about 5:00 on Friday afternoons. People did not stop and invite him to these gatherings. Since he was not invited, Fumio felt uncomfortable about simply showing up at the pub. Fumio wondered if the lack of an invitation should be interpreted as a sign that he was offending the American students in some way. (p. 202)

As one can see, Fumio was acting according to his own cultural perspective, which demanded that one be invited to a social gathering, whereas the American cultural perspective was that since this was an informal gathering, anyone could show up. Because he was not invited, Fumio wondered if he was being purposely excluded from the event.

After hearing this story, a former student wrote in her reaction paper:

> *My boyfriend, Carl, told me a story about a foreign exchange student from Japan. She was in one of his classes. She had only been in the United States for a couple of months and did not have very much confidence in the way that she spoke English. She came to class every day, sitting quietly in the back of the classroom for most of the quarter. Carl saw her every day looking sad and sitting alone. After a few weeks of class had passed, he decided to say hello to her. He had been watching a Japanese television program on his satellite and had learned how to speak certain words in Japanese. He said hello to her in Japanese, and as soon as the words came out of his mouth her face lit up and she smiled and said hello back to him. Every day for the rest of the quarter Carl said hello to her in Japanese and every day she returned the greeting by saying hello and with a smile. At the end of the quarter, she told him how appreciative she was*

*that he took the time to say hello to her every day. He was the only friend
that she had in America at the time. Throughout the quarter he
introduced her to more people. She now has several friends and no longer
sits in the back of the classroom alone.*

AMY, 20+-YEAR-OLD WHITE WOMAN

INDIVIDUALISM VERSUS COLLECTIVISM

We touched upon the concepts of **individualism** and **collectivism** in chapter 2 and earlier in this chapter. In this section, we will discuss these concepts in more detail. Perhaps the most respected name in this area is Harry Triandis (Triandis, 1989, 1995). As the basis for understanding these terms, Triandis (1995) wrote:

> *Collectivism* may be initially defined as a social pattern consisting of closely linked individuals who see themselves as parts of one or more collectives (family, co-workers, tribe, nation); are primarily motivated by the norms of, and duties imposed by, those collectives; are willing to give priority to the goals of these collectives over their own personal goals; and emphasize their connectedness to members of these collectives. A preliminary definition of *individualism* is a social pattern that consists of loosely linked individuals who view themselves as independent of collectives; are primarily motivated by their own preferences, needs, rights, and the contracts they have established with others; give priority to their personal goals over the goals of others; and emphasize rational analyses of the advantages and disadvantages to associating with others. (p. 2)

As a way of measuring individualism and collectivism, Triandis asked people to rate the degree to which they agree with various statements that relate to the terms, such as:

a. One should live one's life independently of others.
b. It is important to me that I do my job better than others would do it.
c. My happiness depends very much on the happiness of those around me.
d. I would sacrifice an activity that I enjoy very much if my family did not approve of it.

If you agree with the first two statements, then you hold an individualistic perspective; if you agree with the second two statements, then you hold a collectivistic perspective.

An immigrant from Ghana expressed her frustration regarding how stuck she felt between her collectivistic culture of origin and her newly adopted individualistic country of the United States. She never feels fully accepted here, but she is teased by her friends back home in Ghana for acquiring values such as personal space and a "time is money" mentality.

> *We immigrants never feel like we have a home. I always miss home and
> have idealistic and romantic views of it and cannot wait to go home
> especially when people keep asking me when I would go back for good. It*

individualism— a social pattern in which individuals tend to be motivated by their own preferences, needs, and rights when they come into conflict with those of a group or collective in which the individual is a member.

collectivism— a social pattern in which individuals tend to be motivated by the group's or collective's preferences, needs, and rights when they come into conflict with those of the individual.

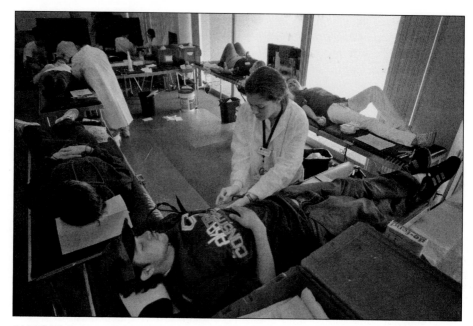

PICTURE 3.3   Collective behavior can help all. *Photograph by Tom Zasadzinski*

is like "Hello, this is home!" I eventually decided maybe this is not home, then when I go back home I feel so awkward because I notice too quickly how my people have no boundaries. They will visit you without any announcement and stay forever. They tell me how "Americanized" I have become and even say I have an American accent and American values. Then I feel restless and miss [my U.S.] home. Sometimes I have to bribe my way out of everything. I remember I once planned to meet some friends at the park at 2 pm. I was at the park exactly at 2 pm and they showed up at 5 pm when I was leaving. I was so angry that they were late and they laughed at me for a long time and called me an "Uptight American Lady." They laughed at how quickly I have forgotten the African "time." They laughed so hard I wanted to take the next plane back to the U.S. I said to myself, I can't believe how they did not respect me! But that was not the issue. They did not mean to disrespect me. I just have to remember that it is a different culture. I have to remember to switch my roles quickly. Recently I was mulling over this and was wondering where do I really fit? I realized I honestly do not fit anywhere. Americans quickly notice I have an accent and ask me when I am going back to where I came from and Ghanaians can tell that I have acquired some American tastes and values. I must say it is very difficult for me to relax at either place. The only place I can truly call my home is when I sit alone with myself and my thoughts, in my room all alone.

ADJOA, 40+-YEAR-OLD GHANA IMMIGRANT WOMAN

The Individual and Society

Triandis also made a distinction between *idiocentrism* and *allocentrism*. He believed that individualism and collectivism were ways of characterizing the dominant perspectives of societies, whereas idiocentrism and allocentrism were ways of characterizing individuals. Thus, if an individual is **idiocentric** in an individualistic society, then his or her perspective will be in concert with society's perspective. However, if an individual is **allocentric** in an individualistic society, then his or her perspective will be at odds with society's perspective.

Because individualism and collectivism reflect a society's dominant modes of interaction, most people in societies are consistent with the society's perspective (i.e., individualistic societies have more idiocentric individuals in their respective societies, and collectivistic societies have more allocentric individuals in their respective societies). However, a certain percentage of people find themselves mismatched with respect to their society's perspective. Triandis calls these people **countercultural** individuals.

> Thus, in collectivist societies there are *idiocentrics,* who look for the earliest opportunity to escape the "oppression" of their ingroups, and in individualistic societies there are *allocentrics,* who reject individual pursuits and join gangs, clubs, communes, and other collectives. The idiocentrics reject conformity to the ingroup and are most likely to leave their culture and seek membership in individualistic cultures. They are also very likely to criticize and object to their culture. (p. 36)

A former international student from Hong Kong agrees with the notion of idiocentrism and allocentrism:

> *I have found the concept of idiocentrism and allocentrism to be interesting because it directly relates to my experience here in the United States. . . . It is interesting because that is exactly how I feel after coming here to study. I was considered a more individualistic person in Hong Kong; though I lived with my parents, I was independent and responsible. I took care of myself and I had my own personal life and my parents did not have to worry about me. Quite often I kept in touch with my siblings and we had family gatherings from time to time.*
>
> *However, living in the States for more than five years, I have found that though I have not changed, compared to my friends' life styles here I am a collective person. I think that as an individual, I have the freedom to make my own decisions and have my own life, and I have to be responsible for my life. For my family, even though I do not have to take care of them, at least basic things like keeping in touch with them have to be done. However, my friends who live here seem to not feel this way. They say they have a busy schedule and they do not have time to do that. For those who live with their parents, they say they usually go home late, so they have their dinner alone or eat out with friends before going back home. It is amazing when I have found that most of*

idiocentrism— individualistic tendencies that reside within an individual. Individualism refers to the society, whereas idiocentrism refers to an individual.

allocentrism— collectivistic tendencies that reside within an individual. Collectivism refers to the society, whereas allocentrism refers to an individual.

countercultural individuals— idiocentric individuals residing in a collectivistic culture, or allocentric individuals residing in an individualistic culture.

my friends who live with parents have their own television in their bedrooms, they watch TV in the bedroom and would not think of watching TV in the living room with their siblings and parents.

VERONICA, 20+-YEAR-OLD HONG KONG IMMIGRANT WOMAN

In a widely cited study, Hofstede (1980) examined individualism and collectivism across 39 countries. The United States ranked as the highest country in individualism, with Australia, England, Canada, the Netherlands, and New Zealand rounding out the top 6 countries. As the reader will note, these countries are typically classified as "Western" countries. In fact, 15 of the most individualistic countries are what we would consider Western countries, since all are in Europe or are predominantly White former British colonies (United States, Canada, Australia, and New Zealand). South Africa ranked 16th in individualism followed by two more European countries, then Israel, then Spain. The highest-ranking individualistic Asian country was India at 21. Of the 19 lowest-ranking individualistic countries (i.e., the countries that scored in the collectivistic direction), only 3 were European countries (Turkey, Greece, and Portugal), with all other countries coming from Asia, Latin America, and the Middle East.

masculine-feminine dimension— a continuum of authority from hierarchical (masculine) to egalitarian (feminine).

Hofstede also categorized countries according to what he termed a **masculine-feminine dimension,** depending upon what he felt were power distances. A country in which there was a great deal of power between those high in authority and those not in authority was labeled a masculine country; a country in which there was less power between these two points in the authority hierarchy was labeled a feminine country. Triandis (1995) later renamed this dimension a horizontal-vertical dimension. Figure 3.1 depicts this dimension.

At the beginning of this section (p. 67) we noted four statements from the scale Triandis devised to measure the degree to which people are horizontally individualistic ("One should live one's life independently of others"), vertically individualistic ("It is important to me that I do my job better than others would do it"), horizontally collectivistic ("My happiness depends very much on the

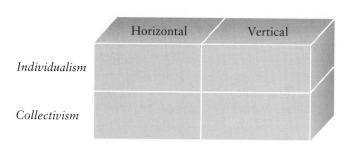

FIGURE 3.1 Triandis's Individualism–Collectivism and Horizontal–Vertical Dimensions.

happiness of those around me"), and vertically collectivistic ("I would sacrifice an activity that I enjoy very much if my family did not approve of it"). In other words, the horizontal dimension places everyone at or near the same level, so the horizontally individualistic statement sees everyone as being equal and having an equal opportunity to live independently of others, whereas the horizontally collectivistic statement sees one person's happiness as being a shared (collective) experience. The vertical dimension deals with hierarchical structures of societies, so the vertically individualistic statement reflects competition, with each one trying to outdo others, whereas the vertically collectivistic statement reflects the requirement that the individual accede to the collective's desires and the belief that family is more important than the individual.

Many of our students are intrigued by the vertical dimension. Although it applies to their lives, they have never had a word to categorize their experiences. The following are some of the reactions we have received from students in the past.

> *Over the weekend I had something really funny happen between two of my friends. My friend, Ralph, who is White, was talking about his family and how not close they were to each other and how he did not love his father. My other friend, Tammy, who is Asian, was there also. She did not understand how someone could say that kind of stuff about their own family. I guess she and her family are very close and they do not disrespect each other even when they are not around. She was not upset, I think it just showed the differences of the cultures. . . . I have always seen the Asian culture as a collectivistic culture and this backs up my beliefs.*
>
> Connie, 20+-year-old White Woman

> *I am from a Filipino background where everything is centered on the family. For example a family member's achievement in work, school, etc. can be looked at as the family's accomplishment. In other words, successes and failures from each family member are representative of the family as a whole. One way that I see this as an advantage is that because the family works together, each member encourages, supports and helps the others. So in this type of family there is great social support. The disadvantage to this is that when one member of the family fails at something, the family as a whole is also seen as a failure as well. So there is increased pressure to do well and accomplish goals. And this in turn may put a strain on the relationship between parent and child.*
>
> *A second advantage (vertical collectivism) is the fact that when parents become older and their own children grow up, their children take them into their homes and care for them, compared to other families where the parents are set up in retirement homes or their own homes (where they care for themselves) or convalescent homes (where other people care for them). The disadvantage to this is that when*

parents are living in the homes of the children boundaries are unclear. The relationship changes from parent/child to parent/adult child. And when the transition isn't smooth there could also be a strain on their relationship.

ANN MARIE, 20+-YEAR-OLD FILIPINA-AMERICAN WOMAN

As Ann Marie indicated, there can be disadvantages to the collectivistic perspective, particularly the vertical collectivistic perspective. Because part of this orientation involves respect for one's elders and those in authority, one may feel as a victim to the desires of those in authority. The following student talked about the break–up she had with her boyfriend because his mother did not believe that it was appropriate for him to have a girlfriend before he became established and was on a financially good footing:

Most Chinese parents do not allow their children to have girlfriends or boyfriends until their children reach specific ages. I heard from my friends that some of their parents allowed them to have girlfriends or boyfriends when they go to college, but some allow them only when they graduate from college. Different Chinese parents set different ages, but I think for most of the European American and African American parents I know of, they do not have this kind of requirement for their children. European Americans and African Americans can have girlfriends or boyfriends when they are in high school.

In my personal story, my parents allow me to engage in relationships in college. Therefore, I had a boyfriend because I got permission from my parents. The bad thing was my ex-boyfriend's mother did not allow her children to have a girlfriend. She thought her son can get married when he was 28 so he can engage into a relationship by 26 or 27. The reason was when her son is 26, he should finish his graduate school and start to make a living. When he makes money, he is able to support a family by himself. For example, he is able to afford family expenses such as a home mortgage. Therefore, his mother asked us to break up. But my ex-boyfriend and I really liked each other so we did not want to obey her. However, she successfully forced us to break up because she was aggressive about this. She contacted me and talked to me in a very disrespectful way. Therefore, I got greatly hurt by her. I had a horrible time with her and experienced a lot of pressure from her. . . .

I know that this experience can apply to most of the Chinese parents I know because I heard a lot of similar stories from my Chinese friends.

LI-CHIANG, 20+-YEAR-OLD HONG KONG IMMIGRANT WOMAN

As one can see, Li-Chiang was already becoming "Americanized" and wanted to continue her relationship without regard to the wishes of her boyfriend's parents. However, her boyfriend was more traditional in his beliefs and could not disregard his mother's wishes. Sue and Morishima (1982) presented a clinical case that reflected the situation that Li-Chiang faced. A Chinese-American woman married a man born in Hong Kong. Everything was going well in their marriage until her husband's parents immigrated to the United States and lived with them. No matter what she did, her parents-in-law (particularly her mother-in-law) criticized her efforts. She wanted her husband to ask his parents to back off, but he did not feel that he could confront them. This situation nearly led to their divorce. When we present this case to our classes and ask students how they might handle the situation, many have said things like, "I'd tell my mother-in-law to mind her own business," "I'd tell my mother-in-law that if she didn't like how I did things, she could do them herself," and "I would kick them out of my house." These "solutions" would definitely have led to a divorce in this particular case. We will discuss how the therapist resolved this dilemma in our next chapter, because it relates to issues of communication. However, for purposes of this chapter, this case illustrates how influential vertical collectivism is in guiding lives. As a hint to how the case was resolved, the therapist used vertical collectivism in her intervention.

Guilt versus Shame

In individualistic societies, **guilt** is a prominent negative emotion. In fact, psychoanalytic theory places guilt as one of the fundamental ways of punishing us for violations of cultural expectations (Brenner, 1982). According to psychoanalytic theory, our behaviors are a result of what is called the "compromise formation." In this formula, the id wants to express a drive (sexual or aggressive), the ego employs a defense mechanism to express that drive, and the superego evaluates the defense mechanism. If the defense mechanism expresses the drive in a socially appropriate manner, then we feel good and fulfilled; if the drive is expressed in a socially inappropriate manner, then we are punished through depression or anxiety. Guilt is at the core of both depression and anxiety.

On the other hand, collectivistic (particularly Asian) societies tend to place more emphasis on **shame** as a motivating negative emotion (Shon & Ja, 1982; Sue, Mak, & Sue, 1998; Sue & Sue, 2003; Yeh & Huang, 1996). Whereas guilt is more of an individualistic notion wherein someone does something wrong and feels guilty about it, shame is a more collectivistic concept wherein the offending behavior is a reflection of one's upbringing or community. As Shon and Ja put it, "Shame and shaming are the mechanisms that traditionally help reinforce societal expectations and proper behavior. The East Asian concept of *tiu lien* (loss of face) embodies the social concept of shame" (p. 214). This distinction between guilt and shame seems to resonate with many of our Asian students.

> *Thinking about the concept of shame, I remember that we have a phrase that is similar to "shame on you," but the pronoun "you" is replaced with "people." It applies in situations where one has made a mistake. This phrase clearly indicates the notion that the mistake not only aroused guilty feelings but also brings shame to the family, and it is*

guilt–a prominent negative emotion in individualistic cultures that involves an individual's sense of personal regret for having engaged in a negative behavior.

shame–a prominent negative emotion in collectivistic cultures that involves an individual's sense of regret for having engaged in a negative behavior that reflects badly upon his or her family and/or upbringing.

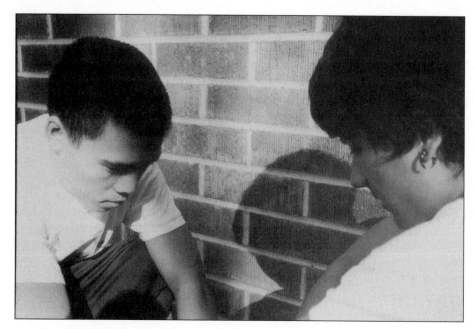

PICTURE 3.4 Western cultures emphasize guilt, whereas Eastern cultures emphasize shame. *Photograph by Janice Leung*

commonly used for children so as to let them know they should not make mistakes again and should prevent "loss of face" in the family.

VERONICA, 20+-YEAR-OLD HONG KONG IMMIGRANT WOMAN

Face Giving and Social Support

loss of face/face saving—loss of face involves being publicly revealed for negative behavior; face saving involves being able to protect one's public persona.

face giving/giving face—extolling the virtues of another person in public. It would be considered boastful and individualistic if the individual did this himself/herself.

As the preceding discussion indicates, shame is related to the concept of loss of face. An important social skill in collectivistic/Asian societies is the ability to help those with whom one is interacting to save face if they make a social mistake (Leong, 1998; Redding & Ng, 1982; Sue, Mak, & Sue, 1998). Most people are aware of the notion of **loss of face/saving face.** One strategy to avoid losing face is to not stick out from the collective or otherwise leave oneself open to criticism from the group (Kitayama & Markus, 1999; Kitayama et al., 1997; Kitayama et al., 2004; Kitayama & Uchida, 2003; Markus & Kitayama, 1991). However, most people are not aware of the notion of **face giving/giving face** (Lim, 1994; Ting-Toomey & Cocroft, 1994). Face giving is extolling the virtues of another in public. In collectivistic societies, it is generally inappropriate or deemed to be overly drawing attention to oneself to talk about one's accomplishments. It is much more culturally appropriate to be humble about one's accomplishments and allow someone else to let others know about them. This allows one's self-esteem to be uplifted without seeming to toot one's own horn. For example, let's say that you have won a very prestigious award but you are in a setting where most people do not know about this award. In the United States, you might say something

PICTURE 3.5   Face giving is a common practice in Asian cultures.

like, "I was honored and humbled to win this award." Even though you say that in a very demure manner, Asian groups still see it as inappropriate bragging. In Asian groups, it is much more appropriate to say nothing about your award, but since some people may know about it, someone else is expected to announce to the group that you have won the award. You can then express your humility about receiving it. This other person is engaging in face giving.

Notice that in face giving, your collective still knows about your award, and your esteem is raised in the group and your own self-esteem is increased. However, there is an appropriate way to do this and an inappropriate way to do this. Kitayama and Markus (2000) have discussed this in terms of how one gains happiness and subjective well-being through one's social relations. They suggest that in individualistic societies, good feelings are "owned" by individuals, and people connect with others by discussing their good feelings with one another. This is seen as a personal property that the two interacting individuals may share with each other. In East Asian cultures, happiness and good feelings are the property of the interpersonal atmosphere, so the feelings are in the relationship between the two interacting individuals, not within each individual. Thus, one can see the importance of face giving in collectivistic societies. If one brags about one's own accomplishments, there is a bad feeling in the air; if one gives face to another, there is a good feeling in the air, and the two are drawn closer together through the process of empathy.

time focus—an orientation that values a particular time perspective. Some cultures value the past, some value the present, and some value the future. Although all cultures value all three, some cultures value one of these perspectives more than do other cultures.

human activity—the distinction among being, being & in becoming, and doing. Being refers to an individual's being accepted just as he or she is. Being & in becoming refers to an individual's evolving into something different and presumably better. Doing refers to an individual's being valued for the activity in which he or she is engaged.

social relations—the distinction among lineal, collateral, and individualistic. Lineal orientation is a respect for the hierarchy within one's family. Collateral orientation is essentially the same as collectivism. Individualistic orientation is the same as individualism.

people/nature relationship—how people relate to nature, be it subjugated to nature, in harmony with nature, or mastery over nature.

VALUE ORIENTATION AND WORLDVIEWS

Kluckhohn and Strodtbeck's Value Orientation Model

As Sue and Sue (2003) have pointed out, Kluckhohn and Strodtbeck (1961) presented a model of worldview based upon value orientation. They identified four dimensions and examined how different groups responded to those dimensions. Table 3.1 presents these dimensions and value orientations.

Past, present, and future **time focus** are self-evident. However, the other value orientations probably need explanation. In the **human activity** dimension, "being" refers to being what you are, which is fine. "Being & in becoming" means that you are motivated to become something more than what you are right now; you need to nurture your "inner self" to realize your potential. "Doing" refers to the value of activity. If you work hard, you will eventually be rewarded.

In the **social relations** dimension, "lineal" is related to our earlier discussion of a vertical relationship, in which there is a hierarchy of authority. "Collateral" suggests that we should respect the opinions of our family and our friends when encountering problems, so this term is related to our earlier discussion of collectivism. "Individualistic" is what we discussed earlier about individualism.

Finally, **people/nature relationship** refers to how people relate to nature. "Subjugation to nature" refers to one's subjugation to external forces, such as God, fate, and biology. "Harmony with nature" suggests that people should try to be in harmony with nature, allowing nature to be dominant in some circumstances and trying to overcome nature in other circumstances. "Mastery over nature" refers to trying to conquer and control nature.

Clearly, these dimensions can differ across different racial/ethnic groups, as Kluckhohn and Strodtbeck demonstrated. In a bit more explicit comparison among differing racial/ethnic groups, Ho (1987) examined the values (worldviews) of the dominant groups typically discussed in the United States. See Table 3.2.

In examining Ho's table, one can see that there seems to be much more similarity among worldviews of ethnic minority populations than there is between any one of those groups and the middle-class White American worldview. One might speculate that the ethnic minorities' somewhat common worldviews are at least partially influenced by their experience of racism within the United States.

TABLE 3.1   Kluckhohn and Strodtbeck's Value Orientation Model

Dimensions	Value Orientations		
1. Time Focus	Past	Present	Future
2. Human Activity	Being	Being & In Becoming	Doing
3. Social Relations	Lineal	Collateral	Individualistic
4. People/Nature Relationship	Subjugation to Nature	Harmony with Nature	Mastery over Nature

TABLE 3.2   Ho's Depiction of Value Orientation Comparison among Racial/Ethnic Groups

Area of Relationships	Middle-Class White Americans	Asian Americans	American Indians	Black Americans	Hispanic Americans
People to Nature/ Environment	Mastery over Future	Harmony with Past–Present	Harmony with Present	Harmony with Present	Harmony with Present
Time Orientation	Future	Past–Present	Present	Present	Past–Present
People Relationships	Individual	Collateral	Collateral	Collateral	Collateral
Preferred Mode of Activity	Doing	Doing	Being-in-Becoming	Doing	Being-in-Becoming
Nature of Man	Good & Bad	Good	Good	Good & Bad	Good

In a wonderful example of American Indian value orientation, Trimble (2003) discussed a classroom exercise in which he asks students to engage. This exercise demonstrates to students how attachment to personally valued items is ephemeral for many American Indians, particularly in the Pacific Northwest. It also demonstrates how one might feel when left out of a collective activity. Because of the ephemeral (or permanent) nature of our attachment to objects, the exercise helps to demonstrate the time orientation dimension discussed in the Kluckhohn and Strodtbeck (1961) study.

> To demonstrate the value of sharing–and the nature of the Potlatch system of the northwest coast tribes in Canada and the United States– I ask students to bring something of value to the next class meeting and inform them that they may have to give it to someone else. At the beginning of that class, I arrange the students in a circle, and one by one I have them place their valued possession in the circle's center. Students then are asked to pick out their valued possession and give it to someone else in the circle, someone whom they respect and wish to honor for their value to the group (the instructor does not participate in the distribution process). Outcomes differ from class to another. On some occasions, a few students do not receive recognition or gifts, and discussion can become spirited as they attempt to deal with being overlooked. Discussions invariably gravitate to the difference between the reciprocity norm and sharing one's possessions without expecting to receive anything in return. (Trimble, 2003, p. 230)

Can you imagine giving someone else one of your prized possessions? Can you imagine doing this and not receiving anything in return?

Derald Wing Sue's Worldview Model

Derald Wing Sue has been one of the most prolific and influential authors in the multicultural arena. In fact, he and his two brothers (Stanley and David) have all contributed heavily to this literature. Awhile back, Derald Wing Sue (1978)

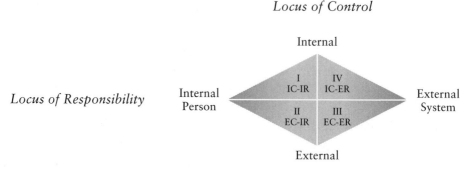

FIGURE 3.2   Derald Wing Sue's (1978) Worldview Model.

locus of control—
the focus of control over outcomes of one's life, be it internal or external control.

locus of responsibility—the focus of responsibility for one's position in life, be it internal feelings of responsibility or external, societal responsibility.

marginal man—
Stonequist's concept of how one feels when one is caught between two worlds.

proposed a model of a person's worldview that examined the intersection of **locus of control** and **locus of responsibility**. Both of these dimensions vary along an internal–external continuum. Thus, a person can have an internal locus of control, an external locus of control, an internal locus of responsibility, and an external locus of responsibility. When crossed, these two dimensions yield four forms of worldview.

People with an *internal locus of control* and an *internal locus of responsibility* (IC–IR) worldview, or Quadrant I in the model, believe that they have control over their lives and that their position in life is based on their own attributes. This is the dominant view in the United States. All of us can control our own lives because of our own abilities. The "American Dream" is based upon this worldview, and those who fail may fall victim to problems such as depression and guilt because they believe that they have no one to blame but themselves for their failures.

People with an *external locus of control* and an *internal locus of responsibility* (EC–IR) worldview, or Quadrant II in the model, have little control over their lives yet accept the dominant society's view that they are responsible for their position. Sue and Sue (2003) cite Stonequist's (1937) concept of the **marginal man** (person) to describe these individuals. They feel caught between two worlds, yet they do not see racism as having any relevance to their position in life.

People with an *external locus of control* and an *external locus of responsibility* (EC–ER) worldview, or Quadrant III in the model, have little control over their lives and also feel that the dominant societal system is against them. As one can see, this is a recipe for disaster, and individuals often give up trying to succeed. Seligman's (1982) notion of learned helplessness is often associated with this quadrant. This concept suggests that people can become depressed because they have learned that no matter what they do, something bad will happen or that they cannot predict their environment, so life seems meaningless. When a system of racism constantly assaults people, they often give up and develop a worldview in which they are powerless to change anything.

Finally, people with an *internal locus of control* and an *external locus of responsibility* (IC–ER) worldview, or Quadrant IV in the model, believe that they have high personal abilities and could control their lives if the system of oppression and racism were not preventing them from realizing their full potential. Sue and Sue suggest that these individuals take pride in their ethnicities and strongly identify with their own ethnicity and others who see the injustices in the world.

Nagata and Takeshita (1998), in their examination of Japanese Americans who were interned during World War II, reported the reactions of some of their Nisei (children of Japanese immigrant parents) research participants:

> It [the internment] affected me, my self-esteem, that they would think that of me. . . . You feel like "I'll show you that you're wrong!" That's part of what drove me to do what I did. (p. 599)

What this participant did was to volunteer for the United States Army to fight in the war effort. Thus, his feeling of disempowerment from a racist system drove him to prove that he had some degree of control over his life. One's experience with racism determined if one developed an EC–ER worldview or an IC–ER worldview. Nagata and Takeshita's discussion continued:

> "Seeing the evacuation notice, I couldn't believe it, you know," recalled an interviewee. "They can't do that to me. I'm an American! That was a natural response of most of us Nisei." However, as a disempowered ethnic minority group who experienced consistent and significant stressors related to discrimination from before the war, Japanese Americans had already drawn upon their cultural strengths and values in times of need. Such previous exposure to past discrimination helped some Nisei to cope. One interviewee noted that he was not entirely surprised by the internment decision, given the level of prejudice that existed at the time, and pointed out that well before the war, Japanese Americans in his community were treated as second-class citizens, restricted to the back-row seating in movie theatres, and barred from certain barber shops, swimming pools, and churches. Perloff (1983) found that individuals who felt least vulnerable prior to being victimized expressed the most difficulty in coping with negative life events, while those who felt most vulnerable had the least difficulty coping with their victimization. Based on this finding, one might hypothesize that for some Nisei, an already established sense of vulnerability may have interacted with Japanese cultural values to enhance coping ability. (pp. 599-600)

Thus, many of those with little exposure to racism seemed to take the internment experience very hard and developed an EC–ER worldview. Those with this worldview had the most difficult time adjusting to internment and may have even developed depression or other forms of difficulties at the time of removal from their homes. On the other hand, many of those who had actively experienced the racism around them seemed to understand that this was an oppressive system against which they had to resist, and they seemed to develop an IC–ER worldview, knowing that they had their own abilities and that those abilities must be used to fight the system of oppression or to prove to the oppressors their worth.

ETHNIC MINORITY WORLDVIEW

We discuss issues of racism and related terms more extensively in chapter 6, but here we address the issue of ethnic minority status in the development of an individual's worldview. As the Sue (1978) model suggests, this issue is very important in shaping one's view of the world.

As Janet Helms and her colleagues have indicated, those major groups we consider to be ethnic minority groups in the United States are identifiably different from the White Anglo-Saxon Protestant (WASP) majority (Cook & Helms, 1988; Helms, 1992, 2001; Helms & Cook, 1999). They refer to the dominant ethnic minority groups as **ALANA**s (African Americans, Latinas/Latinos, Asian Americans, and Native Americans) or **VREG**s (Visible Racial/Ethnic Groups). This is to avoid the term "minority," because that term implies "an inescapable psychological reminder of the disempowered status of individuals who are not White" (Helms & Cook, 1999, p. 28). Moreover, "minority" is an inaccurate term in areas where ALANAs are the numerical majority. Similarly, "majority" is used to describe Whites whether or not they are a numerical majority group. Thus, ALANA and VREG are terms that can be used in contrast to WASP but on equal footing.

ALANA—Helms's acronym for African Americans, Latinos, Asian Americans, and Native Americans.

VREG—Helms's acronym for those who are Visible Racial/Ethnic Groups.

Some individuals are referred to as "White ethnics." These are individuals whose families have either recently emigrated from Europe or have held on to their country-of-origin identification. A good example of the latter use of the term can be seen in celebrations of St. Patrick's Day in the United States. Those of Irish background "put on their Irish hats" and engage in more Irish activities and mannerisms than they normally display. What distinguishes White ethnics from ALANAs or VREGs is that White ethnics can blend into society and be indistinguishable from Whites who have been in this country for a number of generations. However, ALANAs cannot do this, since they have physical features (e.g., skin color, hair texture, shape of eyes) that distinguish them from the White population. Therefore, ALANAs may experience racism or even just be thought of as different from the "norm," which, in turn, can have a profound influence on their worldviews.

In a benign example of different worldviews, an African-American colleague talked about her daughter's closest friend in her daycare school:

> It's interesting . . . Allie's best friend at her daycare is Rebecca. Allie is the only African-American child in the daycare, and Rebecca is the only Asian-American girl, and somehow they seem to know that they are the most different from the other children, so they have become close.
> I don't know if the other children or the daycare workers actually treat them differently, but they just seem to know that they are different.

LINDA, 30+-YEAR-OLD AFRICAN-AMERICAN WOMAN

This feeling of being different is learned quickly. Vasquez (2001) recounted her first day in elementary school:

> When I first entered elementary school in the first grade, I cried daily for weeks and weeks. My mother was very distressed, assuming

separation anxiety. She had not expected this, since during the first 6 years of my life, I had been versatile in staying with any number of extended relatives; my parents had assumed that entering school would be an easy adjustment. Although what I felt may have been partly "separation anxiety," the experience of entering a White majority school, with not a single teacher or administrator of color, led to my world feeling suddenly unsafe. It was not the color difference but the attitudes of those with power toward those of us of color (primarily Hispanic, since there were very few Asian students, and Black students attended a segregated school). The subtle and not-so-subtle negative attitudes were clear. We were ignored, spoken to more curtly and harshly than the White children, and some of the children of color (mostly boys, as I recall) were treated harshly (e.g., knocked down on the playground) and called racial epithets. I remember feeling incredible empathy for Latino children who were abused on the playground and felt an immediate identification with and protection of those like me. I remember feeling the pain of loss of positive regard at both a personal and a group level but had no words to describe the loss and sadness and lack of safety and resulting anxiety that emerged. (pp. 66-67)

With experiences like those, ALANAs learn very quickly that the world is different for them than it is for Whites. These differences are reinforced by media presentations of the world (Cortés, 2000). We once witnessed an exchange in a predominantly White area of the country that illustrated the different worldviews of Whites and ALANAs:

WHITE WOMAN: *How was your spring break?*

LATINO MAN: *It was nice. I was able to hang out with my friends. However, we were stopped by the police, which kind of bummed me out.*

WHITE WOMAN: *Why were you stopped?*

LATINO MAN: *The usual reasons.*

WHITE WOMAN: *What do you mean by that?*

LATINO MAN: *The cops just stopped us because we were Mexican. Everytime my friends and I drive around together, we get stopped. We weren't doing anything except driving and laughing and talking together, but we got hassled.*

WHITE WOMAN: *But they can't do that! Police are not supposed to stop people for no reason.*

LATINO MAN: *We always get stopped for no reason. They see our dark color and they stop us.*

WHITE WOMAN: *But that can't happen! That's not fair!*

LATINO MAN: *But it is my world.*

However, Castellanos and Gloria (2007) have used cultural worldviews to help Latino students succeed in college. This effective use of strength-based worldviews will be revisited in our chapter on culture and mental health.

WORLDVIEW OF WOMEN

As we discussed earlier, women's worldview is different from men's, especially regarding the issue of safety. We discuss sexism a bit more in chapter 6, but for now, let us examine how issues of sexism and other kinds of societal expectations can color a woman's worldview.

I remember at a very young age being taught that men came first and the needs of women came last. I was told that what women had to say really had no importance compared to what the men had to say, but as they instill this value onto me I always believed that this was not fair and as I grew up I learned that not everyone holds this to be true. I became very independent and tried to succeed in everything and yet I knew in my heart that there were still disadvantages for women that were not out in the open but kept under lock and key. I still believed that we were moving in the right direction for change. When something like this [an experience of sexism she encountered] happens I am able to understand a little more clearly why women fought so hard to earn their rights to be equal. It is such a sadness to know we have come a long way, but to realize there are some people not willing to change is a greater sadness.

BONNIE, 20+-YEAR-OLD MEXICAN-AMERICAN WOMAN

Women are often shaped by society's standards of beauty, which are applied to women and not to men. This is particularly true for girls and women of color.

Unfortunately, I've seen black children who try to make their skin white by painting their skin with white paint. In addition, I've heard black children say that they wanted "white girl" hair because they are tired of their "monkey braids." I don't think that this negative socialization is affecting only black children. I think that this negative socialization is affecting all minority children. When my sister was younger (we are biracial; half Mexican and half white), she asked our dad why he didn't marry a white woman. My sister added that she wished he had married a white woman because my sister wanted blonde hair and blue eyes; she wanted to look like Barbie. It is this way of thinking that creates general "beauty" rules/guidelines in our society. Children are growing up thinking that white is beautiful. It is extremely depressing.

LOIS, BIRACIAL (MEXICAN-AMERICAN/WHITE) WOMAN

Other issues help to shape women's worlds. Iwamasa and Bangi (2003) discussed various mental health issues related to women, including a higher incidence of depression, postpartum depression, and eating disorders. Eating disorders affect women more than men because thinness is considered an important component of

PICTURE 3.6   Women's and men's worldviews often differ. *Photograph by Andrea Poltorak*

femine beauty. Woodside and Kennedy (1995) indicated that eating disorders are relatively rare among men, so this is predominantly a women's issue. Halpern, Benbow, Geary, Gur, Hyde, and Gernsbacher (2007) examined why science and mathematics fields are often not in women's worldviews. Mio and associates (2003) discussed the impact violence can have on women's views of the world. Interestingly, violence against men is more often perpetrated by strangers, and violence against women is more often perpetrated by their partners. Thus, women encounter violence in settings where they would expect to find the most love and protection. Imagine how that can change one's worldview. Moreover, women encounter sexual harassment in the workplace much more than men do. As Koss and associates (1994) would say, there is no safe haven for women, since violence against them can occur at home, in the workplace, and in the community. Kerry's story near the beginning of this chapter illustrates that men often have no concept of the feelings of vulnerability in women's lives.

WORLDVIEW OF LESBIAN, GAY, AND BISEXUAL INDIVIDUALS

The worldview of lesbian, gay, and bisexual (LGB) individuals still contains a large element of fear and danger (Herek, 1995, 2000). Because of heterosexism (discrimination by heterosexuals against nonheterosexuals), LGB individuals do not feel safe in the present environment.

PICTURE 3.7   Many lesbian, gay, and bisexual individuals congregate in groups to feel safer. *Photograph by Alyssa Harter*

> *I can't have a picture of my partner on my desk without people wondering who it is or grilling me about my relationship with her. I can't walk hand-in-hand with my partner without fear of someone yelling obscenities at me or even beating me up or worse. It is hard to explain how much fear I have just being myself because I can't control what someone else might do or how someone else might react.*

LONNIE, 30+-YEAR-OLD WHITE LESBIAN WOMAN

Some LGB individuals also feel that they are always on display or are sources of curiosity. Therefore, they can never feel completely at ease around straight individuals. A lesbian woman on our campus talked about how uncomfortable she was participating in an exercise involving targeted and nontargeted individuals at a campus-sponsored cross-cultural retreat. In this exercise, everyone stands on one side of the room, and when one is in a targeted group (e.g., women, ethnic minorities, LGBs, individuals coming from a lower SES background) identified by the moderator, one has to go to the other side of the room. After each targeted group is identified, its members are reunited with the main group. The purpose of this exercise is to give everyone the experience of being in a targeted group so that they can empathize with people who are in targeted groups (Barker-Hackett & Mio, 2000). As a woman in a discussion group said:

> When I had to go to the opposite side of the room when [the moderator] said that all LGB individuals had to be targeted, it was

really irritating to look back at the main group. I saw how people were craning their necks to see who was gay on campus. When I was in other targeted groups, people didn't seem nearly as curious as to who was on the opposite side. It only happened when the issue of gayness came up.

FAWN, 30+-YEAR-OLD WHITE LESBIAN WOMAN

Some LGB individuals know that they are living in the context of a straight world. However, they wish that their straight friends could understand a worldview from the LGB perspective:

I am going to start off by saying that I love, care, and cherish my close friends; they are a multicultural blend that I would do anything for. They range from European American to Asian American as well as a mixture of straight and gay individuals, but for the most part my close friends are straight. Yes, they all know that I am gay and they fully accept me for who I am, then again, I am not the type of person that would shove my sexuality down someone's throat or make them feel uncomfortable around me. So, why do I bring them up?

I firmly believe that they need to mix things up when it comes to going clubbing or just to hang out, meaning gay clubs or hangouts. It seems that all we do is hang out at straight clubs the majority of the time, which is not a problem for me. However, I would like for them to at least go to gay clubs once in awhile just so I can mingle or be around people that I can relate to or have an interest within.

I did mention my thoughts and feelings on this matter, adding that I enjoy their company, although I would like to see them take an interest in my "gay culture" just as I have taken an interest in being part of [their] straight community. I explained that it is important for me to retain them as close friends as well as it is important for me to remain true to myself.

MIGUEL, 30+-YEAR-OLD BIRACIAL (MEXICAN/GERMAN) GAY MAN

Many LGB individuals report that others feel that their sexual orientation is their entire identity. It is easy to imagine that an African-American woman might have an identity as a woman separate from her African-American identity (and separate from her combined African-American woman identity), but LGB individuals often are seen only through the prism of their sexuality.

When I first joined this organization and people found out I was gay, they introduced me to [names of three other gay men]. At our next meeting, I got introduced to them, again. Year after year, I got introduced to the same three guys, as if people were saying, You gay guys hang out over here and don't bother the rest of us. No one would bother asking me about what my other interests were and that I might have something in common with them instead of these three guys. Yes, these guys were nice and I enjoyed interacting with them, but I would have liked it if someone were to take some interest in me other than simply knowing that I was gay.

VAN, 40+-YEAR-OLD AMERICAN-INDIAN MAN

Finally, some LGB individuals must operate in an environment where they do not know if they will be accepted or rejected by their families (Hancock, 2003). If they are rejected by their families of origin, think of the worldviews that may result. The people whom they love and trust the most rejected them, so they may end up not trusting anyone or at least having a very difficult time trusting people in the world.

SUMMARY

Worldviews come in many forms. The world looks quite different depending on whether a person is looking at behavior and concepts from within a culture or from without. The emic perspective is the perspective from within a culture, and this perspective seems to be more important than the etic perspective, or the perspective from outside the culture being examined. Although both of these perspectives are important in advancing our scientific knowledge of cultures, quite often those who view the culture from without impose their own worldviews on the behaviors of the culture being observed. This can lead to wildly different (and wrong) interpretations of the behaviors.

Perhaps one of the most important distinctions between cultures is the individualism-collectivism dimension. Individualistic societies place more importance on individual rights, whereas collective societies place more value on the desires of the collective. This dimension also exists in conjunction with the horizontal-vertical distinction. Thus, a society can be horizontally individualistic, vertically individualistic, horizontally collectivistic, or vertically collectivistic, depending on the degree to which it is hierarchically structured. The individualism-collectivism distinction has important implications for how one experiences some negative emotions. Individualistic societies tend to place more importance on guilt, whereas collectivistic societies place more importance on shame. Collectivistic societies also tend to place more emphasis on face saving and face giving.

Kluckhohn and Strodtbeck (1961) presented a model that examines various dimensions of viewing the world. In combination, cultures, groups, or subgroups can be understood in terms of these value orientations. According to the Kluckhohn and Strodtbeck model, racial/ethnic groups in the United States seem to have worldviews that are much more similar to one another than they are to the White middle-class American worldview. This situation is perhaps due to similar experiences with racism. The Derald Wing Sue (1978) model of worldview seems to combine the Kluckhohn and Strodtbeck model with racism. As Helms and her colleagues indicate, the issue of racism is very important in the development of the worldviews of ALANAs, because these views are identifiably different from those around whom this society was developed. Women and men develop differing worldviews because of their experience with sexism and other issues that affect women more than men. Finally, LGB individuals may have differing worldviews, particularly about issues of safety, given the current situation in the United States.

Food for Thought

When one of the authors (JSM) was at a conference for deaf people, he felt uncomfortable and out of place. All around him, people were using American Sign Language (ASL), and although he knew some signs and phrases in ASL, the deaf people were signing so fast that he could not keep up with them. As he described this situation, "The silence was deafening." Obviously, these people had no intention of harming him—they were merely communicating with one another. Still, he felt out of place and even a little frightened, because his worldview was so different from that of the people around him, or, rather, the dominant worldview was so different from his own. In thinking about the issues raised in this chapter, recall a situation in which you had a markedly different view of the world from those around you. You probably felt a little uncomfortable or afraid. That is a normal feeling until one begins to understand and appreciate the dominant worldview. If you did some reading about this situation or the people in it, you probably felt a little more comfortable and less afraid the next time you encountered it. Did you gain some insight into someone who has entered your world?

Critical Thinking Questions

Have your actions ever been misconstrued by another person or a group of people because they had different assumptions from yours? If so, how did that make you feel? What steps did you take to correct their misconception?

Have you ever misperceived someone else's actions because you applied your own assumptions, which were different from the other person's? If so, how did you resolve the problem?

Would you characterize yourself and your family as allocentric (collectivistic) or as idiocentric (individualistic)? Do you fulfill society's expectation regarding this dimension?

What advantages and disadvantages does your worldview on collectivism and individualism have when you interact with the society at large?

Have you ever engaged in face giving? Has anyone ever given you face? What kind of connection did you feel with that person after the face giving?

If you are a Person of Color, do you feel you stand out because of your ethnicity/race in certain situations? If you are White, do you tend to notice when a Person of Color is around? How do you feel about this dynamic?

If you are a woman, to what extent is your view of the world markedly different from that of men? If you are a man, to what extent is your view of the world markedly different from that of women?

If you are an individual who is LGB, how does your worldview differ from that of those who are straight? If you are straight, how does your worldview differ from that of LGB individuals?

CHAPTER 4

Differences in Communication

I was talking with a guy who is pretty "Americanized." His mother was still very influenced by Japanese traditions. He was telling me that his mother was worried that his brother was not going to come to the wedding of a family friend. He wasn't even going to send a wedding gift. This guy said, "Mom kept saying, 'I don't know what I'm going to do,' and I kept saying, 'Well, that's how he is. You know how he is, so don't worry about it.' However, she kept saying, 'I don't know what I'm going to do.' Why do you think my mom wouldn't give it up?"
I said, "Well, if she is very traditionally Japanese, she was telling you indirectly that she wanted you to tell your brother that he should send a wedding gift." This guy said, "Oh, is that *what she was saying?! Now it makes sense. No wonder why she kept repeating herself."*

JEREMY, 40+-YEAR-OLD JAPANESE-AMERICAN MAN

As this story indicates, there are different ways of communicating, and it seems that in the United States, overt, direct communication is required. Although most people can understand or interpret implications and other forms of indirect communication, some contexts or some people require direct communication. In this chapter we discuss issues of communication that can differ across cultural groups and genders.

CONVERSATIONAL RULES

Grice (1975) proposed a set of conversational rules that guide people's conversations. (See Table 4.1.) Grice suggested that we all engage in what is called the **cooperative principle**; that is, we strive to communicate with one another sincerely and effectively. He proposed four maxims that guide such conversations: *quality, quantity, relevance,* and *manner*.

The maxim of **quality** suggests that whenever we engage in a conversation, we strive to be truthful. Since you and I are engaged in a cooperative conversational relationship, you are expecting me to tell you the truth or to give you my honest opinion on the topic we are discussing. If you can never be certain that I am telling you the truth, you may choose to break off our conversation. Alternatively, if you do not know that I am telling you a lie, we are not engaged in a cooperative relationship—I am manipulating you.

The maxim of **quantity** suggests that each of us should contribute an appropriate amount to our conversation. In normal conversations, two speakers are generally expected to contribute equally. Have you ever tried to talk with a partner who dominated the conversation, never allowing you to contribute? Did that irritate you? If so, you were irritated because your conversational partner violated

cooperative principle—a psycholinguistic term that assumes that we strive to communicate with one another sincerely and effectively when we engage in a conversation.

quality—the maxim that suggests that we tell each other the truth when we engage in a conversation.

quantity—the maxim that suggests that we contribute an appropriate amount of talk when we engage in a conversation.

TABLE 4.1   Grice's Conversational Maxims with Rummelhart's Additions

Maxim	Brief Definition
Quality	Tell the truth.
Quantity	Say about as much as is appropriate for the situation.
Relevance	Stick to the topic.
Manner	Speak to your partner in an appropriate manner.
Relations with Conversational Partner	Take advantage of your past relationship with your conversational partner; fill in others who may not be privy to your mutual understandings.
Rule Violations	Identify when you are breaking one of the conversational maxims.

the maxim of quantity. However, in some contexts, it is appropriate for one person to dominate the conversation. For example, on talk shows or in television interviews, it is appropriate for the interviewee to contribute more to the conversation than the host or interviewer, who asks only brief questions to move the conversation forward. This is also true in therapy, where the client is expected to contribute more to the conversation than the therapist, who mostly listens. What other contexts can you think of in which one partner is supposed to dominate the discussion?

The maxim of **relevance** suggests that we strive to remain "on-topic." If we suddenly start talking about baseball during a discussion of multicultural psychology, we are violating the maxim of relevance, because our utterance does not relate to the topic, even though it may be truthful and of an appropriate length. Some people may go into long digressions when talking, and you may wonder if they are being relevant. Quite often these people get back on track and say something that ends up being relevant to the topic, but by the time they get there, they have violated the maxim of quantity.

relevance—the maxim that suggests that our discussion is relevant to the conversation.

Finally, the maxim of **manner** suggests that people should be clear in their communication and pay attention to normal standards of conduct. This is the broadest maxim and can include a wide range of issues. For example, you would not discuss quantum mechanics with a 3-year-old, nor would you speak in a disrespectful manner to someone in a position of authority. You would not talk in an intentionally obscure manner, nor would you shout to someone standing two feet in front of you. In the United States, the appropriate distance between two people engaging in a typical conversation is about 1½ feet. It would violate the maxim of manner to stand 6 inches from that person's face, and it would also be a violation if you were to stand 10 feet away. A former colleague described an interesting formality when he made a presentation in Germany:

manner—the maxim that suggests that we are clear in our language and that we pay attention to normal standards of conversation, such as not shouting at someone who is right in front of us.

I went to Germany the summer after I served as the interim department chair. After my talk, there was a question-answer period. The director of the institute began this period by asking me a question. This guy and very few others asked me questions. After a while, I noticed that some of the other professors were passing notes down the aisle, but they never asked me any questions. When my talk was over, I asked the director of the institute why it was that the other professors were not engaged in the question-answer period. He told me that they actually were engaged, but in Germany, only people at the same level or higher could ask questions, and since I was the director of my institute, only he and a few other directors could ask me questions. The younger professors were writing questions they wanted asked, and they passed these questions down to those who could address me.

JAMES, 40+-YEAR-OLD WHITE MAN

Such a formal system may not exist in the United States, but we often have informal rules similar to the one described by James. If you work in a large corporation, you may have been told that you must take any questions to your supervisor because the manager or director of the organization cannot be bothered by every question from every employee. In the United States, however, there is more of an egalitarian tradition. People are considered equal to one another, so we do not have to worry about violating the maxim of manner when we ask people of different status hierarchies questions.

Norman and Rummelhart (1975) added two maxims to Grice's conversational rules: *relations with conversational partner* and *rule violations*. The maxim of **relations with conversational partner** suggests that we should rely on our previous experience with our partners in our conversations. If we were talking to you about multicultural psychology, we would know that you know something about the topic, so we could talk about something within the area knowing that you would be able to follow what we are saying. However, if we were talking with someone who knew nothing about multicultural psychology, we might have to give a brief sketch of the area before we could discuss a specific topic. If you had an inside joke with a friend, you could use telegraphic language to refer to the inside joke and apply it to the present situation, but if you were with people unfamiliar with the inside joke, you should fill them in before making the comments or let them know later why the situation was so funny.

The maxim of **rule violations** suggests that whenever one is violating one of the other maxims, one needs to signal that violation. For example, if we want someone to interpret an utterance as ironic, or the opposite of what the literal utterance means, we need to signal it with a voice inflection or some other means. We are sure that you all have been in a boring lecture or at a boring party where someone has said, "This is *real* interesting." The emphasis on "real" done with a voice inflection or stress signals that you should not interpret the utterance literally but ironically. Some people draw quotation marks in the air when they want others to interpret an utterance ironically instead of literally or to disregard the utterance. For example, someone might say "The 'experts' say you should do

relations with conversational partner—the maxim that suggests that we use our previous relationship with our conversational partner so that we do not have to repeat shared experiences.

rule violations—the maxim that suggests that we signal our conversational partners when we are about to engage in a violation of one of the other maxims.

this . . ." and draw quotation marks in the air with their fingers when she says "experts," which means that you should disregard the advice that the experts are giving.

As one can imagine, different cultures can have different conversational rules, but they most likely have similar general maxims that guide their behaviors. Where the greatest variation occurs is in the maxim of manner, since there are different rules governing what is an appropriate or an inappropriate manner. We turn next to these nonverbal aspects of language.

NONVERBAL ASPECTS OF LANGUAGE

One of the greatest differences among cultures is the way in which nonverbal communication is used. Sue and Sue (2003) categorize nonverbal communication into *proxemics, kinesics, paralanguage,* and *high- and low-context communication.* Because high–low context communication is such an important issue in the multicultural literature, we present it in the next section.

Proxemics

Proxemics deals with personal space. When people interact with one another, they keep a standard range of distance between them. The range of distance varies depending on the context, such as a close, intimate relationship or a public lecture (Hall, 1966, 1976). As we saw earlier, in normal conversations the distance between two conversational partners is usually about 1½ feet. According to Hall, the acceptable distance is 1½ to 4 feet. However, numerous studies have found that conversational partners in other cultures tend to stand or sit closer to each other when interacting than do those in the United States and other Western countries (Dolphin, 1999; Matsumoto, 2000). Goldman (1980) found that individuals in the United States feel more uncomfortable when someone stands too close than when he or she stands too far away.

> **proxemics**—personal space in conversations.

Remland, Jones, and Brinkman (1991) studied three European countries (the Netherlands, France, and England). Although some differences were found for pair interaction, such as distance (more distance between Dutch participants, less distance between French pairs, even less distance between English pairs in declining distance) and body orientation (French participants more directly across from each other than Dutch or English participants), no differences were detected when gender and age were examined. In other words, culture was the dominant influence in proxemics in these countries. Some early studies questioned the importance of culture in influencing proxemics (Fortson & Larson, 1968; Mazur, 1977; Shuter, 1977), but more recent studies have confirmed this importance (Mindess, 1999; Sussman & Rosenfeld, 1982; Wolfgang, 1985).

Sue and Sue (2003) have given a very practical reason why proxemics is an important topic in multicultural studies. When an individual from a culture that prefers smaller distances between speakers comes in contact with an individual from a culture that prefers larger distances, the first individual might misinterpret the second one's warmth, sincerity, or motive. Imagine a person from a close culture trying to stand closer to a person from a distant culture, who keeps

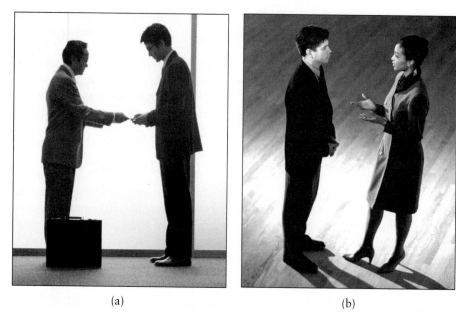

(a)   (b)

PICTURES 4.1a-b Asians tend to stand farther away from each other while talking than their American counterparts. When talking with someone from a different culture, a person can find it difficult to determine a comfortable talking distance.

moving away. The person from the close culture may feel that the other is not a very warm person or is trying to hide something, whereas the person from the distant culture may feel that the other is trying to become overly personal or invasive. JSM once greeted an African-American friend whom he had not seen in a while. When JSM reached out to shake his hand, he pulled him closer and gave him a hug, saying, "Come over here like you really know me!" The friendship was close enough that he felt comfortable telling JSM why he was hugging him, and JSM felt comfortable enough to give him a hug back, but imagine how it would have seemed if he had tried to give JSM a hug and JSM had pulled away.

Kinesics

kinesics—bodily movements in conversations, including hand gestures, facial expressions, and eye contact.

Sue and Sue (2003) define **kinesics** as aspects of communication that deal with bodily movements. This is a wide-ranging category that includes "facial expressions, body movements, gestures, and conversational regulators" (Andersen, 1999, p. 245). One kinesics aspect that has been studied extensively is eye contact or gaze duration. Matsumoto (2000) reported that eye contact can be an indication of either aggression or nurturance, depending on the context. He cites the animal literature as a suggestion of a genetic, animalistic basis for the relation between gaze duration and dominance. Certainly, most of us can remember being told as children that it was impolite to stare at someone else. However, equally embedded in our minds are phrases such as "gazing lovingly into someone's eyes" or "casting a loving glance," which indicate that eye contact or gazes can also indicate affection or care.

As one might expect, different cultures seem to engage in different levels of eye contact. Some early studies have found that people from Arabic cultures tend to gaze longer and more directly than do people from the United States (Hall, 1963; Watson & Graves, 1966). Within the United States, African Americans gaze less directly than their European-American (White) counterparts (LaFrance & Mayo, 1976). American Indians tend to have even less eye contact (Richardson, 1981) and prefer a side-by-side orientation to an eye-to-eye orientation. A friend and colleague of ours, Joseph Trimble, once told us:

> *When I am interacting with my White colleagues, I sit or stand across from them and interact with them in a manner that is comfortable for them. However, when I visit my friends on the Lakota reservation, I find myself standing side-by-side with them, looking at my feet and kicking at the ground. We rarely look at each other, but we have very good and deep conversations.*
>
> JOSEPH TRIMBLE (PERSONAL COMMUNICATION, JANUARY 1999)

Sue and Sue (2003) discuss smiling as an important part of kinesics. In general, smiling is an indication of happiness, liking, and other positive feelings. However, Asian cultures may also use smiling as a way of discharging uncomfortable feelings. Ekman (1972) conducted a series of experiments in which he showed American and Japanese students highly stressful videotapes (e.g., of a surgical operation) and secretly videotaped their facial expressions. Half of the time the research participants watched the videotapes alone, and half of the time they watched the videotape with an older, high-status experimenter. The American participants showed facial expressions of disgust, fear, and other negative affects when they watched the film alone or with the experimenter. However, the Japanese participants displayed these negative expressions when watching the videotape alone, but they smiled in the presence of the high-status experimenter. That was because they did not want to offend the experimenter by seeming to disapprove of the task the experimenter was asking them to perform. Thus, although facial expressions of emotion may have some universal application, as evidenced by the similar expressions of the American and Japanese participants when viewing the videotapes alone, the social setting may be an important determinant of the kinesics displayed in a particular situation. Sue and Sue connected this tendency for Asians to smile when discharging negative emotions with a misunderstanding that arose in the aftermath of the Rodney King verdict during a confrontation between African Americans and Korean grocery store owners.

> African Americans confronted their Korean-American counterparts about exploitation of Black neighborhoods. During one particularly heated exchange, African Americans became incensed when many Korean-American store owners had a constant "smile" on their faces. They interpreted the facial expression as arrogance, taunting, and lack of compassion for the concerns of Blacks. Little did they realize that a smile

in this situation more rightly indicated extreme embarrassment and apprehension. (p. 128)

Kinesics may be determined by the general influences of individualism and collectivism. They tend to be more synchronized in collectivistic cultures (Andersen, 1999; Argyle, 1975), whereas in individualistic cultures, people are allowed to "do their own thing" and not coordinate their movements with others as much. Matsumoto (1991) speculates that "collective cultures will foster emotional displays of their members that maintain and facilitate group cohesion, harmony, or cooperation, to a greater degree than individualistic cultures" (p. 132).

Paralanguage

paralanguage—
nonverbal vocal cues in conversation, such as loudness of voice, silences, and rates of speech.

Sue and Sue (2003) refer to **paralanguage** as a category that involves the use of nonverbal vocal cues in communication, such as loudness of voice, silences, and rate of speech. Perhaps the aspect of paralanguage that lends itself to the most cultural variation of meaning is silence. In the United States, silences are often signals for the receiver of a message to contribute to the conversation. When silences last too long, people in the United States often become uncomfortable and want to fill in the silence. Many of you have probably heard the expression "pregnant pause," which indicates the discomfort one feels when the conversation has come to a halt and there is an extended period during which neither conversational partner contributes to the conversation.

However, Hall (1966, 1976) has found that silences mean quite different things in different cultures. For example, some cultures (Russian, Spanish) view silences as agreement among the conversational partners. Asian cultures view silence as a sign of respect for elders. For American Indians, silences are a way of gathering one's thoughts, so to break the silence merely disrupts their train of thought. As Richardson (1981) advised when seeing American Indians in a therapy situation:

> Do not lean toward the client and commence giving the "third degree" or studying him or her with piercing eyes. Do not be upset with long pauses, but, on the other hand, do not try "seating out the client" to see who can be the winner. A loud and overbearing manner is exceedingly irritating and makes Indians feel subservient, and this will cause them to shut you out as they clam up and remain quiet. (p. 236)

The forms of nonverbal communication we have mentioned are important contributors to conversations between partners, but one of the most important but underappreciated aspects of nonverbal communication is the distinction between high- and low-context communication, which we will now examine.

HIGH- VERSUS LOW-CONTEXT COMMUNICATION

A daughter from a higher-class family [in Malaysia] fell in love with the son of a lower-class family. The son approached his parents and told them that he wanted to marry the girl from a higher-class family. His mother said she would approach the girl's family to see if it were acceptable to them. She made an appointment with the girl's mother and went to the home on the proper day. She was greeted by the mother and was shown into the sitting room. Refreshments were brought in consisting of tea and bananas. The two mothers talked about the weather and other things, but they never mentioned their children. After a period of time the boy's mother thanked her hostess politely and left. Upon returning home she told her son that the marriage was unacceptable and, therefore, not possible. (Shon & Ja, 1982, p. 216)

How did the mother from the lower-class family know that the mother from the higher-class family disapproved of the marriage? It is because she used the context of the situation to understand the other mother's wishes. In Malaysia, tea and bananas do not go together, so the mother from the higher-class family was giving the other mother the message that their children should not go together. Hall (1976, 1999) would call this **high-context communication** (HC), which means that much of the communication is carried either by the context of the situation or by societal rules that are internalized. Conversely, **low-context communication** (LC) is language-dependent: The language itself is the crucial aspect of the communication, and context does not carry as much meaning. As Hall (1999) put it:

> A high-context (HC) communication or message is one in which most of the information is either in the physical context or internalized in the person, while very little is in the coded, explicit, transmitted part of the message. A low-context (LC) communication is just the opposite; i.e., the mass of the information is vested in the explicit code. (p. 47)

Although no culture is exclusively HC or LC, cultures are on a continuum between high and low context. Communication in the United States tends to be at the low-context end of this continuum (German-Swiss, Germans, and Scandinavians are at the lowest end according to Hall), and many Asian countries tend to be at the high end. Hall connects the Asian dependence upon context to the Chinese written language, which is over 3,500 years old and which has not changed much in the past 3,000 years. Thus, other countries whose written languages are derivations of the Chinese language (e.g., Japan, Korea) are HC countries.

One advantage of HC is that it allows individuals to avoid confrontations. In the example of the Malaysian mothers, notice how the mother from the higher class does not have to directly state her wish that their two children not marry. Also, the mother from the lower class does not have to be embarrassed by being told to her face that her son is not acceptable to the other family. Although we in the United States might prefer this clarity, direct questioning in HC countries is considered to be a sign of immaturity, because it causes both parties to lose face (Andersen, 1999). Incidentally, although we do not know how this situation was ultimately resolved, it is possible that in the long run, the mother from the upper-class family gave her consent to the marriage. As Elliot and associates (1982) found, those who talked less and allowed context to communicate more were seen as more attractive in collectivistic cultures. Thus, if these mothers had additional contact in the future, the mother from the upper-class family may have come to

high-context communication— communication in which the context conveys much of the meaning.

low-context communication— language-dependent communication, in which the words carry most of the meaning and context plays a lesser role.

see the mother from the lower-class family as more attractive because she could read contextual cues. For those of you who are romantics, there is still hope that love conquered all in this case.

As indicated earlier, HC helps one to save face. What is saving face? According to Ting-Toomey (1994), "Face involves the claimed sense of self-respect or self-dignity in an interactive situation" (p. 3). Thus, saving face is preserving one's dignity when interacting with another person or when being viewed or evaluated in a public context. The topic of HC communication helping to save face elicited the following reaction from one of our students when direct communication embarrassed her and made her lose face:

> *I went to Australia when I was 15 years old. It was my first time leaving my own place [Hong Kong], and I had no experience of talking with people from different cultures. In Australia, people talk to each other in a very direct way just like Americans do. I did not feel comfortable when they talked that way. For example, I lived with a host family when I first arrived in Australia. My host family usually went to bed very early. One day, I took a shower around ten, and I did not know it was very noisy when I took the shower. The next day my host family told me not to take showers so late. They could not fall asleep because of the noise the shower made. I felt they talked to me in a very direct way, and they made me feel embarrassed. I also felt they were rude because I thought they could tell me this in a more gentle, unobvious, and subtle way. However, I still kept saying sorry to them. Moreover, I thought that they were angry with me. I finally realized it was not true after years of contact with people from low-context societies. It is their culture that leads them to communicate in a very direct way. I feel uncomfortable because I was raised in a collective culture, and we never communicate in such a direct way. People who communicate directly in my culture would be labeled as impolite and not well raised. I think the major reason is they do not save others' faces. Therefore, people in my culture do not like such direct people. I finally understand there are two types of communication, and this concept will help me a lot in my real life when I communicate with Americans.*
>
> LI-CHIANG, 20+-YEAR-OLD HONG KONG IMMIGRANT WOMAN

With respect to HC communication, a joke among Japanese Americans is that when they visit non-Japanese families for dinner, they go home hungry. That is because of the Japanese concept of *enryo*. This term means to hold back or to suppress one's desires. Thus, in Japanese-American families influenced by *enryo*, if one is hungry and is offered more food, one must say no. The food must then be offered again, and again the answer must be no. If the food is offered a third time, it is appropriate to accept the food while also complimenting the cook on how tasty the food is. However, when Japanese Americans visit the homes of people from other cultures and are offered food, when they refuse the food the first time, the food is taken away, even though the visitor may still be hungry.

A co-author of this book (LAB) is an African-American woman whose brother is married to a Japanese-American woman. She used to get irritated when her sister-in-law continued to offer her food even when LAB had said she was full and did not want any more to eat. LAB's thought was, "I just said no—why are you offering me food again?" However, after some time, she came to realize that her sister-in-law was just following the Japanese tradition of offering the food multiple times just in case she (LAB) was holding back and being polite in the Japanese tradition. Thus, LAB has now learned how to be definitive in saying no the first time she refuses the food.

As you may recall, in chapter 3 we discussed a family-therapy case presented by Sue and Morishima (1982) that involved a mother-in-law from Hong Kong who was unreasonably critical of her daughter-in-law's efforts. Her attitude caused extreme marital distress for the daughter-in-law and her husband and nearly precipitated a divorce. The husband would not intervene on his wife's behalf because he did not want to show disrespect to his own mother. As promised, we will now discuss the therapeutic intervention that was chosen and that seemed to resolve this conflict. The therapist discovered that the mother-in-law had an older brother whom she respected and who lived about 50 miles away. The therapist suggested that the daughter-in-law contact this uncle and explain the situation to him. He recognized the seriousness of the situation, so they planned a dinner in which he was invited to eat with the family. After the dinner, the uncle told his sister that the daughter-in-law looked tired and unhappy and wondered if she was working too hard. His sister (the mother-in-law) immediately recognized that he was criticizing her and that she needed to back off her daughter-in-law. To signal to her brother that she had received the message, she acknowledged that her daughter-in-law was doing her chores well. Later, the daughter-in-law reported that her mother-in-law had noticeably reduced her criticisms, had begun praising the daughter-in-law's work, and had even begun helping with the household chores.

Notice how this intervention took advantage of HC communication. Neither the uncle nor the mother-in-law had to directly confront the other about the situation. That allowed the mother-in-law to save face and also understand what a serious effect her criticisms were having. Interestingly, by praising her daughter-in-law, the mother-in-law was also able to maintain her higher status in the relationship, but she came to realize that this status also came with the responsibility to be fair and to give positive feedback with the negative feedback. Finally, this example demonstrates the importance of vertical collectivism, since the mother-in-law did not challenge her older brother's authority.

When I presented this case to one of my classes, it resonated with a student from the Philippines, who said that his family has been engaging in family therapy all along without knowing it. He said that when family conflicts arise, a respected intermediary intervenes. Being older is not the important factor here. Rather, the family recognizes certain individuals for having strengths in various areas. When a dispute arises, they turn to the individual with strength in that particular area and follow his or her counsel.

Direct versus Indirect Communication

direct communication—blunt communication that is literal and to the point.

indirect communication—communication that relies upon context and the receiver's ability to draw inferences.

Related to high- versus low-context communication is *direct versus indirect communication*. Most people know that **direct communication** is literal and assertive communication. It is related to low-context communication in that the message is contained in the language used. **Indirect communication** relies on both context and the receiver's powers of inference. To illustrate the difference between these two forms of communication, let us say that someone wants a window closed. Direct speech would say, "Close the window." Indirect speech would say, "Are you cold?" Brown and Levinson (1978) indicated that indirect speech acts are used because they convey a degree of politeness in communication. As such, they are universal.

A student of ours resonated to both indirect communication and high-context communication. She related this rather amusing anecdote to us:

> *I come from a culture that values indirectness. I remember when I was getting married; it is customary for the bride to look sad and depressed. She should let her family feel that she is not happy leaving home. If a bride smiles and shows that she is happy it is an indirect way of saying she does not value her family and she would forget them if she leaves home. I cried and acted so sad. My younger sister however took it a step further; she ran away from home the night before her wedding. I remember my father huffing and puffing and screaming, "If she does not want to marry we would just cancel it—nobody is forcing her." I laughed so hard secretly because I knew she wanted so badly to get married but she was trying to show that she was a "good girl." I always resented the indirect way of doing things because we always have to refuse things and gifts when it is offered to us for the first time and luckily people would continue to insist. God knows how difficult it was for me when I migrated to the USA. I kept insisting my friends eat more or take something I offered them when they said no. They resented it and thought I had no boundaries.*
>
> ADJOA, 40+-YEAR-OLD GHANA IMMIGRANT WOMAN

Yum (1999) acknowledges that indirect communication may be a universal component of all languages. However, she cites wide cultural variations in preference for direct or indirect communication styles. As we discussed before, many Asian countries are concerned with saving and giving face. Therefore, it should not be surprising to find that indirect speech is prevalent in Asian countries (Katriel, 1986; Lebra, 1976). Lebra (1976) indicated that this level of indirect communication can be extremely subtle. Lebra reported that a woman communicated discord with her mother-in-law based on slight irregularities found in the mother-in-law's flower arrangement. Table 4.2 summarizes Yum's comparison of North American and East Asian forms of communication (p. 83).

TABLE 4.2 Comparison between the North American and the East Asian Orientations to Communication Patterns

East-Asian Orientations	North-American Orientations
1. Process orientation	Outcome orientation
Communication is perceived as a process of infinite interpretation	Communication is perceived as the transference of messages
2. Differentiated linguistic codes	Less differentiated linguistic codes
Different linguistic codes are used depending upon persons involved and situations	Linguistic codes are not as extensively differentiated as in East Asia
3. Indirect communication emphasis	Direct communication emphasis
The use of indirect communication is prevalent and accepted as normative	Direct communication is a norm despite the extensive use of indirect communication
4. Receiver centered	Sender centered
Meaning is in the interpretation	Meaning is in the messages created by the sender
Emphasis is on listening, sensitivity, and removal of preconception	Emphasis is on how to formulate the best messages, how to improve source credibility, and how to improve delivery skills

Ethnic Minority Patterns of Communication

A great deal of research has been conducted comparing Asian and East-Asian forms of communication with Western forms of communication because of the general interest in collectivistic versus individualistic cultures. Most of the foregoing information deals with this comparison. A few other studies have examined differences in communication patterns among other ethnic minority populations in the United States. As you know, sometimes generalizations cannot be applied to all people in a group, but the following are general trends identified by some researchers.

African Americans

Ribeau, Baldwin, and Hecht (1999) identified seven issues of importance when their African-American participants interacted with White Americans: (1) negative stereotyping, (2) acceptance, (3) personal expressiveness, (4) authenticity, (5) understanding, (6) goal attainment, and (7) power dynamics. Note that these issues are not different from those of other groups. However, they are more important when White Americans interact with African Americans and serve as the context within which the communication occurs.

Ribeau and associates found that African Americans are particularly attuned to issues of negative stereotyping. They identified two types of **negative stereotyping**: (1) typical kinds of stereotyping, which cast African Americans in a negative light,

negative stereotyping—stereotyping that casts African Americans in a negative light, or that limits discussion to "African-American topics" such as athletics and music. ("Negative stereotyping" can be applied to any group, but Ribeau and associate refer specifically to African Americans here.)

PICTURES 4.2 Conversational dynamics can differ when African Americans speak with other African Americans as opposed to White individuals. *Photographs by Jonathan De Leon*

acceptance—the feeling that one is accepted as an equal in the conversation.

personal expressiveness—speaking from the heart and not the head.

authenticity—being truthful and not trying to be merely "politically correct."

understanding—the sense that a conversational partner has enough experience to truly understand the African-American experience.

goal attainment—the goal of mutual understanding between two conversational partners.

and (2) indirect stereotyping, which limits discussion to "African-American topics" such as music or athletics. Related to negative stereotyping is **acceptance.** Some African-American participants indicated that they did not feel accepted by their White conversational partners.

Many African Americans prefer to speak from the heart and not the head, which Ribeau and colleagues call **personal expressiveness.** Because of the history of African Americans in the United States, many African Americans do not show this open expression to their White conversational partners until a sense of trust has been established. Connected with this issue is **authenticity.** One of Ribeau and associates' research participants expressed his frustration about "so many phony conversations—White people trying to impress African Americans with their liberalness" (p. 150). Orbe (1999) suggested that one of the difficulties is in trying to figure out what is authentic or sincere and what is merely politically correct. Orbe reported one research participant struggling with this problem: "I guess that I have found it very difficult to distinguish when they [Whites] are sincere versus when they are trying to be politically correct. . . . I struggle with that" (p. 231).

Understanding is also important to many African Americans. Quite often a barrier to understanding is one's lack of experience with racism or even with other African Americans. If an African-American conversational partner does not feel that his or her White partner has had sufficient experience with African Americans, he or she may feel that understanding cannot take place. As one of Ribeau and associates' participants indicated, "If people don't share the same life experiences, they can't be expected to truly understand each other. If Whites haven't been exposed to Blacks, there will be a 'fear of the unknown'" (p. 150).

Goal attainment is the sixth issue identified by Ribeau and associates. This is the goal of mutual understanding between the two conversational partners. Part of the problem in communication may be that the two partners have different emic definitions of concepts discussed. I remember seeing an 11-year-old African-American boy in therapy many years ago. He told me that sometimes he makes money by "hustling." When I asked him what he meant by that, he told me that hustling was the term used for standing around in grocery store parking lots and offering to help older people put their groceries into their car trunks. Sometimes the boy would get tips for this assistance. (I was relieved when I heard this definition.)

Finally, **power dynamics** are in effect when interacting with African Americans. This category is divided into two subcategories: powerlessness and assertiveness. Powerlessness is the feeling of being trapped or manipulated by one's conversational partner or otherwise unable to express oneself freely. To overcome feelings of powerlessness, some African Americans engage in overly assertive verbiage, "code switching," or "doing the dozens." Code switching is switching from "the Queen's English" to Black English or other forms of African-American coded language. It is something of a game in which the speaker says things that his or her White conversational partner either does not understand or misinterprets; the speaker then knows internally that he or she has control of the conversation. This is what Johnson (1995) and Orbe (1999) would refer to as "playing the part" or "SNAP! culture," in which a person changes in a snap (with a snap of the finger indicating this instant transformation). "Doing the dozens" is a game in which some African Americans (particularly males) engage. In this game, they attempt to one-up their conversational partners by putting them down or making fun of them. Ribeau and associates emphasize that this is by no means universal among African Americans, but it is popular among many and most African Americans at least understand the game being played.

Latinos/as

There have been relatively few studies examining communication styles among Latinos/as as different from those of their White counterparts. Of the few such studies, Hall's (1966) found that Latinos/as tend to be from a "contact" culture, whereby they tend to touch their conversational partners more (see also Andersen, 1999, and Dolphin, 1999). Hall's classification has been reaffirmed by others (Jones, 1994; Patterson, 1983). Related to contact is emotional expressiveness, with contact cultures expressing more interpersonal warmth and low-contact cultures being more interpersonally "cool" (Andersen, 1999).

> When I was first getting to know my (Latino) friend, he would invite me to his home for large family barbeques and parties and what not, and I remember it caught me off guard when each one of his relatives hugged me or kissed me on the cheek when I was introduced to them. These were people I was meeting for the first time and they were hugging me; I remember feeling very uncomfortable, like they were invading my personal space. It took me quite awhile to get used to greeting his family in that manner; I don't remember exactly how long, but ten years later now, I think nothing of it.
>
> The reverse was also interesting, when my friend and I were first starting to hang out, I would invite him to my home for our family get-togethers, which are much smaller by comparison. I remember how shocked he was that my family was so small and that I only had one

power dynamics— powerlessness and assertiveness in conversations with African Americans. Sometimes, African Americans can feel powerless when conversing with White conversational partners. In response, they may "code switch"; that is, they may switch from the mutual conversational rules to African-American rules, such as Black English or other such verbiage. In code switching, African Americans can regain a sense of control over the conversation.

PICTURE 4.3 Latino people tend to touch each other while talking more than do people in other cultures.

cousin. I also remember him thinking that my family disliked him because as I introduced him to everyone they would simply shake his hand. No hugging or kissing on the cheek. It took me a long time to convince him that my family didn't dislike him and that it was simply a cultural thing. I had to explain to him that that was just the way my family greets new people they are meeting for the first time and that it was nothing personal, they greeted everyone new like that.

SHELLY, 20+-YEAR-OLD EUROPEAN-AMERICAN WOMAN

One interesting aspect of Latino—particularly Mexican and Mexican-American—communication is the use of proverbs, sayings, and metaphors (Aranda, 1977; Campa, 1947; Castellanos & Gloria, 2007; Sellers, 1994; Zormeier & Samovar, 1999). These proverbs, or *dichos,* are used to transmit important cultural values. Sellers (1994) identified some prototypical proverbs used to transmit the values of collectivism, fatalism, present-time orientation, being orientation, and family:

Collectivism

Better to be a fool with the crowd than wise by oneself.

A solitary soul neither sings nor cries.

He who divides and shares is left with the best share.

Fatalism

God gives it and God takes it away.

He who is born to suffer will start from the cradle.

Submit to pain because it is inevitable.

Present-Time Orientation

Don't move the water; the river is already flooding.

There is more time than life.

Don't do today what you can put off until tomorrow.

Being Orientation

He who lives a hurried life will soon die.

He who gets drenched at dawn has the rest of the day to dry out.

He who wants everything will lose everything.

Family Values

A tree that grows crooked cannot be straightened.

Better to die on your feet than to live on your knees.

A man is king in his home.

Castellanos and Gloria (2007) have used this notion of *dichos* to help Latina/o students to succeed in higher education. These *dichos* include:

Higher Education

Where there's food for one, there's food for many. (encouraging students to help one another)

A person who's close to a good tree receives good shade. (encouraging students to seek a good mentor)

What one learns well will never be lost. (encouraging students to pursue research opportunities and professional development)

Vasquez (2000) indicated that these proverbs, sayings, or *dichos* are very powerful when used properly in therapy. They are so ingrained in many Mexican-American minds that when they are relevant either to what is preventing clients from acting or to what an appropriate perspective can be for a situation, therapy can move rapidly.

As everyone congratulated my friends on their new business venture, the President of the Hispanic Chamber of Commerce Association made a comment; he said, "Dime con quein andas y te dire quien eres" which translates [to], "Tell me who you associate with and I'll tell you who you are." As he said this everyone nodded in agreement. He went on to say in Spanish "we want associates who want to invest in a future, people who want to succeed, not those who make excuses. We consider this a family of contacts where like-minded people may do business together." At the end of his speech, everyone cheered and clapped and they systematically went around the room and introduced themselves and their businesses to my friends. In a way, it reminded me of an induction ceremony and the Dicho *was sort of creed everyone followed.*

ALICIA, 20+-YEAR-OLD ECUADORIAN-AMERICAN WOMAN

American Indians

As we discussed earlier, an important aspect of American-Indian communication is silence (Richardson, 1981). Another thing to keep in mind when interacting with American Indians is that quite often time is considered in terms of eras instead of chronology. The Kluckhohn and Strodtbeck (1961) notion of present-time orientation does not really capture the significance of this value. In American-Indian terms, the present time can be years, decades, or even centuries, because the current time can signify a phase in the development or progress of their people. In therapy, this concept of time can clash with the chronologically governed time of a therapy session. Quite often, Western-trained therapists see being late to a session as a form of resistance (Greenson, 1967). However, to the American-Indian client, getting to the therapy session around the time of the scheduled appointment is within the present time when he or she is seeking help. Finally, as we have previously discussed, American Indians tend to engage in less eye contact, and direct eye contact with someone who is an elder is considered to be a sign of disrespect (Garwick & Auger, 2000; Sue & Sue, 2003).

Communication Patterns of the Elderly

There have not been many studies examining how elderly individuals differ from nonelderly individuals in communication styles. Most of the studies conducted have concentrated on how grandparents interact with their grandchildren. Much of the interest in this area has been stimulated by the relatively recent increase in grandparents taking responsibility for much of the care of their grandchildren because of child abuse or neglect in the parents' home, divorce, and/or working parents (Jendrek, 1994; McKay, 1989, 1993, 1999; McKay & Caverly, 1995). The major motivation of grandparent–grandchild interaction is the desire by the grandparents to transmit knowledge based upon their lives and family history (Nussbaum & Bettini, 1994). This is in keeping with Erik Erikson's (Erikson, 1950, 1964) notion that a life-stage motivation in older ages is to pass on

PICTURE 4.4   Elderly individuals enjoy interacting with their grandchildren and passing on information. *Photograph by Tom Zasadzinski*

wisdom to subsequent generations. Nussbaum and Bettini also note that grandchildren are quite interested in this kind of knowledge as well. McKay (1999) stated that it is very important for elderly individuals to be able to share their family histories: "These individuals have a lifetime of wisdom and experience to impart; to be unable to do so is a loss not only to the listener, but to the teller as well" (p. 179).

Many of our students relate to the notion of the importance placed on communication from grandparent to grandchild and vice versa:

My grandfather would often use the term "Pobre pero honesto"—he took pride in being an honest man. He would repeatedly say, I don't have much but I have my dignity. My grandfather just turned 92 and he still is poor but honest. I love my grandfather for all the sacrifices he made for his family and for the values that he instilled in all of us. It's his selflessness that inspires me to better myself as an individual. I want to pass on the torch of knowledge to my nieces and nephew so that they can be even better than me.

SARAH, 20+-YEAR-OLD MEXICAN-AMERICAN WOMAN

My family moved here from the Philippines when I was only 6 months old, so I was pretty much raised here. It is a Filipino tradition to take care of our grandparents and great-grandparents when they get older so when our family moved here my great-grandparents moved in with me, my mom, and my dad. They lived with us until they passed away a few years ago. I'm sad to say that even though I was taught to always respect my elders there were many times growing up when I began to see them as more of a hassle. I know that this is very sad to say because I loved them both very much, but because I was raised in an American culture I felt like I did not really relate to them. I am somewhat disappointed in myself for feeling this way because I constantly took it out on my great-grandparents, especially my great-grandmother. I felt that when she would ask me about my day, or what I had done that weekend, or even if I was hungry that she was just trying to control me and get into my business. Now I know that she was just interested in what was going on in my life because she was old and didn't have much going on in her life so her family was everything to her. I should have treated her better because she took care of me from the day I was born, and I feel like the way I repaid her was by being mean. The sad thing is, is that the only time I realized how great she is was when she was already gone. I know that this is so cliché, but it is true. You really never appreciate the people you love until they are gone. I want to get back to my roots of respecting my elders so I am going to start spending more time with my grandmother. She is getting old, and to that stage where she's beginning to become lonely and she has feelings of being useless. My great-grandmother went through this stage and I didn't realize it because I was too busy being a high school student.

CELESTE, 20+-YEAR-OLD FILIPINA-AMERICAN WOMAN

GENDER DIFFERENCES IN COMMUNICATION

Sometimes I'll go to parties and I'll be in a conversation with a group of people, and I've noticed that men will not only dominate the conversation, but they will also look at you like you're stupid if you have an opinion on a "male" topic. I know that I've had it happen to me many times when the topic was related to sports or cars. I may not be an "expert" on these topics, but I believe that my opinions are not stupid.

SYLVIA, 20+-YEAR-OLD FILIPINA-AMERICAN WOMAN

Women's communication occurs within a context of sexism. Sylvia's experience should not be surprising. How many times do you find yourself in a class in which the first question or comment is made by a White male student? In a classic experiment, Broverman and associates (1970) asked both male and female mental health professionals to check off the personality characteristics of mentally healthy adult women, mentally healthy adult men, and mentally healthy adults.

The characteristics listed were bipolar, such as "very subjective–very objective," "very submissive–very dominant," and "feelings easily hurt–feelings not easily hurt." Male and female mental health professionals agreed markedly on their ratings. Broverman and colleagues found that the characteristics for mentally healthy men and mentally healthy adults were in almost perfect agreement, whereas the characteristics for mentally healthy women and mentally healthy adults were in disagreement. Thus, women could not be perceived to be both mentally healthy women and mentally healthy adults. For example, when asked what mentally healthy women should be, the research participants checked off that women should be submissive, whereas when asked what mentally healthy adults should be, the participants checked off that people should be dominant.

The Broverman (1970) study of characteristics associated with men and women has been replicated in a worldwide study by Williams and Best (1982, 1994). They sampled college students (as opposed to mental health professionals) and found that there was amazing agreement among the 30 countries they studied. Men were characterized as active, aggressive, individualistic, loud, rational, and tough, whereas women were characterized as affectionate, dependent, gentle, sensitive, submissive, and weak. Interestingly, assessments of these characteristics varied from country to country. Thus, whereas the Broverman study suggested that adult male characteristics were seen as more mentally healthy than adult female characteristics, respondents in other countries varied in the assessment of the desirability of these characteristics.

PICTURE 4.5 Men and women have different communication styles. *Photograph by Andrea Poltorak*

tag questions–
questions added to
a statement of
assertion, such as
"This is good, don't
you think?"

Lakoff (1975) found that women used **"tag questions"** more often than their male counterparts. Tag questions are questions added to a statement of assertion. An example of a tag question would be "This class is interesting, don't you think?" The tag question ("don't you think?") allows the conversational partner to agree or disagree with the assertion ("This class is interesting"). Traditionally, tag questions have been interpreted as an indication of weakness or passivity on the part of the speaker (Paludi, 1998). However, Paludi indicates that another interpretation of tag questions is that they connote warmth by inviting the other individual to engage in a conversation. Another form of communication more commonly used by women than by men is **qualifiers** (Carli, 1990; Wood, 1994, 1999). Qualifiers are words or phrases that soften statements, such as "I may be wrong, but I think this class is interesting." The phrase "I may be wrong" is a qualifier. Again, one interpretation of this usage is that women are less confident about their topics of discussion or are otherwise passive, but another interpretation is that they are using these styles of communication to convey warmth and politeness.

qualifiers–words or
phrases that soften
statements, such
as "I may be wrong,
but . . ."

Wood (1994, 1999) has written extensively about gender differences in communication. Table 4.3 summarizes her findings and the findings of others who have examined this area.

These findings are about general differences between men and women, and they do not apply to *every* man and woman. We presented this table in one of our classes as a point of discussion, and a woman in the class said that she and her husband engaged in behavior exactly opposite to what the table suggested. However, most students agree with these observations. One of our students observed male–female differences in communication on the television show "The Apprentice":

> In "The Apprentice," contestants are put into two competing groups, which most of the time is usually a male and a female group. You can see right away how different the males and females interacted within their own group. After being given a task, the male group took no time to socialize; instead they were more assertive and task oriented. Their communication was direct and often involved a lot of argument and interruption between sharing of ideas. On the other hand, female groups tried to include all the members' thoughts and opinions on pending decisions. However, whenever conflict rose within the group, the females hesitated on being straightforward about their problems. It seems like dealing with the problems was by spreading gossip behind each other's back. Somehow in the end the male group always won.
>
> Given the fact that males are socialized to be more direct and aggressive, I wonder if this is what fuels their power and success? Because of this, I sometimes feel that men act a bit too arrogant, especially in conversations with women. I have seen men act as if they are the ones who know better, and perhaps this attitude, whether conscious or unconscious, can sometimes make them feel superior to women.

VALERIE, 20+-YEAR-OLD CHINESE-AMERICAN WOMAN

TABLE 4.3   Wood's Presentation of Differences Between Feminine and Masculine Speech Communities

Feminine Talk	Masculine Talk
1. Use talk to build and sustain rapport with others.	1. Use talk to assert yourself and your ideas.
2. Share yourself and learn about others through disclosing.	2. Personal disclosures can make you vulnerable.
3. Use talk to create symmetry or equality between people.	3. Use talk to establish your status and power.
4. Matching experiences with others shows understanding and empathy ("I know how you feel").	4. Matching experiences is a competitive strategy to command attention ("I can top that").
5. To support others, express understanding of their feelings.	5. To support others, do something helpful—give advice or solve a problem for them.
6. Include others in conversation by asking their opinions and encouraging them to elaborate. Wait your turn to speak so others can participate.	6. Don't share the talk stage with others, wrest it from them with communication. Interrupt others to make your own points.
7. Keep the conversation going by asking questions and showing interest in others' ideas.	7. Each person is on her or his own; it's not your job to help others join in.
8. Be responsive. Let others know you hear and care about what they say.	8. Use responses to make your own points and to outshine others.
9. Be tentative so that others feel free to add their ideas.	9. Be assertive so others perceive you as confident and in command.
10. Talking is a human relationship in which details and interesting side comments enhance depth of connection.	10. Talking is a linear sequence that should convey information and accomplish goals. Extraneous details get in the way and achieve nothing.

Another student resonated to the point that men will often equate disclosure with vulnerability:

I am one for details when I talk to someone. I need detailed directions, I want details when someone is describing something to me, and I love it when someone tells me details from a movie or a conversation that they had had with someone. My husband thinks that details are trivial and it drives him crazy when I ask him to try and remember the details of a conversation or something else. He is the type that believes one should just get to the point of the conversation, and that's it, nothing more. . . .

I had a friend share with me things that she had been experiencing and we talked for almost an hour or two. It brings us closer together when we share those experiences with one another and we can help each other out with problems. Her husband said he doesn't understand how women could stay on a phone for so long and talk about what he called "nothing." I asked her to ask him what he talks to his friends about when he talks and he told her to tell me that they just talk about what things have happened to them that they have either done better than someone else or they usually compare experiences, but the conversation doesn't last for an hour. He also complained that his wife discloses too much information; something my husband has told me that I do, too. He seems to feel that people shouldn't know too much about you and your life because you never know when they can use it against you. That idea kind of goes along with the masculine talk idea that personal disclosure can make one vulnerable.

ABIGAIL, 30+-YEAR-OLD EUROPEAN-AMERICAN WOMAN

Wood (1999) emphasizes that gender differences in communication are more a product of socialization than of biology. There seem to be two sources of such socialization: family communication and communication between playmates. Paludi (1998) suggests that this socialization occurs very early, as parents respond measurably differently to boys and girls. Will, Self, and Datan (1976) found that differences in socialization happened even when people only *thought* they were interacting with a boy or a girl. They dressed an infant in pink and referred to it as "Beth," and dressed the same infant in blue and referred to it as "Adam." They found that the research participants played with this infant measurably differently—for example, offering "Beth" a doll and "Adam" a toy train.

BILINGUAL COMMUNICATION

At a very young age of 5, my father sent my brother and me to Mexico to learn how to speak "proper" Spanish. I attended kindergarten through third grade in a private school that taught only in Spanish. At the age of 9, my father sent for us, and we continued school here in Southern California in classes which were taught in all English. It was a difficult transition due to the fact that I hardly knew the English language, but after a year I managed to grasp the most important words to be able to communicate with my peers at school. At home, where I was able to speak Spanish with my parents, I felt a lot more comfortable because I didn't have to struggle to get a point across.

PENNY, 20+-YEAR-OLD MEXICAN-AMERICAN WOMAN

Most people in the world are bilingual or multilingual (Matsumoto, 2000; Snow, 1993; Whitney, 1998). There are various ways in which people can become bilingual. Some people grow up in societies in which two or more languages are pervasive and in which one must know multiple languages to survive (e.g., Switzerland and Quebec); some are bilingual because their native language is not the official language of the country (e.g., Zulu speakers in South Africa who needed to learn English and Lithuanian speakers who needed to learn Russian before the fall of the Soviet Union); some are bilingual because they immigrated to a country that speaks a different language (e.g., Spanish or Cantonese speakers who immigrate to the United States); some are bilingual because of colonization (e.g., Aymara speakers in South America, where Spanish was imposed on them); some are bilingual because of education and extensive travel (e.g., those in the United States who learn French and have the opportunity to travel to France); some are bilingual for economic or professional reasons (e.g., Korean businessmen who learn English to do business with American companies); and some are bilingual because they grew up in households that spoke two languages. When the second language does not replace the native language, this is called **additive bilingualism** (Berry et al., 1992; Lambert, 1977). When the second language replaces the native language, this is called **subtractive bilingualism** (Berry et al., 1992; Lambert, 1977). Subtractive bilingualism is also called **language attrition** (Snow, 1993). Language attrition occurs when a language is not used often, even when the first language is very well ingrained.

> *When I was younger, I remember a cousin coming here from Japan when he was around 17. His English was so thick with a Japanese accent that it was hard to understand him at times. I saw him years later. He still spoke English with a Japanese accent, although it was much easier to understand him. However, to my surprise, he told me that he forgot how to speak Japanese. I wondered how this could be, given that he spoke Japanese until he was 17 and he still spoke English with a Japanese accent.*
>
> Jeremy, 40+-year-old Japanese-American Man

When two languages are used in the household so that people become bilingual from birth, this is called "**native bilingualism**" (Snow, 1993). Moreover, there are both cognitive and social consequences of bilingualism (Lambert, 1967, 1977, 1980).

Cognitive Consequences of Bilingualism

Early studies indicated that bilingual children performed less well than did their monolingual counterparts (Lambert, 1977; Matsumoto, 2000). However, Lambert and his colleagues criticized those early studies for not controlling for social class or educational opportunities (Lambert, 1977; Lambert & Anisfeld, 1969; Peal & Lambert, 1962). When studies were controlled for these factors, Lambert and Anisfeld (1969) and Peal and Lambert (1962) found that bilingual children actually performed better on various measures of intelligence. Price-Williams and Ramirez (1977) suggest that this performance might be the result of increased levels of cognitive flexibility among bilingual individuals.

additive bilingualism–the acquisition of a second language that does not replace the native language.

subtractive bilingualism–the acquisition of a second language that replaces the native language.

language attrition–equivalent to subtractive bilingualism.

native bilingualism–the ability to speak two languages from birth, acquired because both languages are spoken in the household.

There is evidence that acquiring a second language changes the brain location of certain concepts or at least causes a change in category clustering of concepts. Grabois (1999) studied native Spanish speakers (NSS), expert speakers of Spanish (ESS), Spanish learners (L2), foreign-language Spanish learners (FL), and native English speakers (NE). NSS participants were monolingual Spanish speakers who spoke Spanish from birth. ESS participants were native English speakers who lived in Spain for at least three years and achieved a level of expertise in the Spanish language. L2 participants were native speakers of English who were advanced learners of Spanish and who were studying abroad in Spain for 1 year. FL participants were enrolled in advanced Spanish-language courses and had been learning Spanish for about 2 years. NE participants did not have any expertise in Spanish. Grabois examined how these participants responded to sets of words that related to emotional terms (love, happiness, fear, and death). The closer participants were to NSS participants, the more similar their clusters of responses were to those of the NSS group. In other words, ESS participant clusters looked much more like the NSS clusters than did the FL participant clusters. From a cognitive perspective, this would suggest that the actual mental structure changes according to one's proficiency in the second language.

Alvarado and Jameson (2002) replicated the Grabois (1999) findings using a color-naming task. They presented monolingual English speakers, monolingual Vietnamese speakers, and bilingual Vietnamese and English speakers certain colors and asked them to name or describe those colors. They used colors such as brick, clay, pale blue, and intense green as the stimuli and examined the degree to which individuals used single-word descriptors of the colors (e.g., "brick") or modifiers (e.g., "pale blue"). They found that bilingual speakers were more similar to monolingual English speakers in their use of language than to monolingual Vietnamese speakers when describing these colors. However, they were still distinguishable from both monolingual speaking groups. It must be noted that these bilingual speakers were fairly proficient in English, since they were college students and thus had enough English proficiency to perform at the college level.

Interestingly, although popular wisdom has it that children acquire second languages faster than do adults, systematic investigation proves otherwise (Snow, 1993). This is true for both formal and informal acquisition of the language (Snow, 1983, 1987; Snow & Hoefnagel-Höhle, 1978). However, older learners may be more "fossilized" in their native languages, so accents from their first language will persist into their second languages (Krashen, Long, & Scarcella, 1982). Thus, an older learner's mastery of the second language may be inferior to that of a younger learner.

Social Consequences of Bilingualism

Speaking multiple languages has an effect upon one's identity (Berry et al., 1992). In fact, ability to speak the language reflective of one's racial/ethnic group is a dimension or a component of some racial identity models (Bernal et al., 1993; Isajiw, 1990; Mendoza, 1989; Phinney, 1992; Sodowsky, Lai, & Plake, 1991; Suinn et al., 1987; Zea et al., 2003). Many of you who speak a particular language

PICTURE 4.6   Maintaining one's native language can be a source of connection with others who also speak that language. *Photograph by Belen Gonzalez*

may feel an instant connection with someone else who speaks that language, or you may have observed people who seem to have such a connection with one another when they are speaking their native language.

Tsai, Ying, and Lee (2001) found that, in their Chinese-American sample, those who knew a great deal about Chinese culture and were proficient in Chinese language had higher self-esteem than did those who did not have such knowledge and abilities. Tsai and associates suggest that this increased self-esteem may be used to counteract racism and discrimination. However, the researchers note that their sample was taken from the San Francisco Bay Area, and because of the large numbers of Asian/Pacific Americans in that area, these results may apply only to people from that region. Certainly, you can imagine that if you have a friendship network in which it is the norm to speak the language of your country of heritage, someone who does not speak that language could feel excluded from the group at times, which may in turn have some negative effect upon his or her self-esteem.

In the short run, giving up one's language of origin may make it easier to fit into one's social environment when that environment does not support that language. Many of you remember your childhood, when anyone who deviated from the predominant group was teased and ridiculed. One of our students wrote about how she tried to eliminate any evidence of her difference from her peers:

> *The issue of acculturation is extremely interesting to me, especially since I am not an American citizen. I was born and raised in Munich, Germany, and didn't set foot on American ground until I was eleven years old. As we discussed in class on Wednesday, my quick assimilation into the new Californian life supports the fact that children adapt very quickly to their new environment. In my case this was primarily driven by the fact that I just wanted to fit in!*

In Germany I had stood out my entire life for being Eurasian (my father is Japanese, my mother German), and the taunting and constant questions were still too fresh in my mind. I was relieved to see that being Asian was of very little consequence in my Arcadia elementary class, since the majority of the other children stemmed from an Asian background. Hence, I was determined to fit in and appear "American" in every way. I asked my mother to pack me sandwiches instead of the Tupperware dishes filled with German or Japanese leftovers. I refused to wear some of the clothes I had brought over, simply because they didn't quite look like everyone else's. I learned to speak English (accent-free) over the next year, achieved primarily by watching countless episodes of "Full House" and "I Love Lucy." The end product resulted in my mother scolding me for "becoming completely Americanized" and trying to hide the parts of me that were the most special.

JUDY, 20+-YEAR-OLD WHITE/JAPANESE WOMAN

In other reaction papers, Judy indicated that she wished she knew more about her background, particularly her Japanese background. Her mother imparted much of her German knowledge, but her father was not very communicative about his Japanese background. Thus, while she was in Germany, even though her classmates knew she was Eurasian and identified her as Japanese, her lack of knowledge about her Japanese heritage left her with a sense of loss. Had she known more about her Japanese heritage and had she known some Japanese words, her teasing classmates might very well have expressed interest in her instead of taunting her. When she came to America, she tried to eliminate all aspects of her German heritage so that she would fit in with other Asian and Eurasian children in her school. We never asked her if she retained her German language, but it would be interesting to know the degree to which she still feels German.

SUMMARY

Grice (1975) identified some conversational conventions that make face-to-face communication a cooperative endeavor. These conventions go beyond the content of the communication and go into extraverbal issues such as turn taking, politeness, and relationships between the two conversational partners. This chapter dealt with many of these extraverbal issues. Sue and Sue (2003) identified some of these areas as proxemics, kinesics, paralanguage, and high- and low-context communication factors. We discussed some aspects of proxemics, kinesics, and paralanguage, but much of this chapter dealt with high- versus low-context communication.

Communication is more than just language. Words constitute much of the basis of our communication with one another, but they do not make up the entirety of what is being communicated. Societies that depend more on words than on the context within which the words are transmitted are called low-context (LC) communication societies. Alternatively, societies that depend more on the context to convey a message are called high-context (HC) communication societies. In general, Western societies tend to be LC and Asian societies tend to be HC. Connected with the LC–HC distinction is the distinction between direct and indirect communication. HC societies in particular make use of indirect communication. Part of this connection is that indirect communication in conjunction with contextual messages allows people to avoid conflict. In Asian cultures, this form of communication also allows people to save face.

There are many specific cultural differences in communication. HC communication is associated with Asian cultures. African Americans vary in their communication styles, primarily in ways that examine the authenticity of their conversational partners, particularly when their partners are White. Thus, they are attuned to issues such as stereotyping, honesty, and power. Latinos/as tend to be from "contact" cultures. Thus, they touch their conversational partners more and are more emotionally expressive. The use of metaphors, proverbs, and sayings (*dichos*) is also common in Latino–particularly Mexican-American–communication. American Indians appreciate silences more and are also governed by a time orientation of eras as opposed to chronology. Moreover, side-by-side conversations and less eye contact are more common among American Indians.

Elderly individuals may use language in ways that vary from young and middle-aged adult language. Most of the research in this area has been on grandparent-grandchild communication and reveals that the Erik Erikson notions of transmitting knowledge and wisdom govern this kind of communication. Grandparents are particularly interested in telling the story of the family, and grandchildren are particularly interested in these kinds of stories.

Gender differences are particularly interesting. Women more than men tend to use qualifiers and other forms of communication that indicate a tentativeness. One interpretation of that tendency is that women are less confident in their communication. However, another interpretation is that women are more inviting and polite in their communications, so they soften their words to allow their conversational partners to agree or disagree with them. It is important to note that women's conversations occur within the context of general societal sexism.

Some studies in the past indicated that bilingualism reduces one's ability to function in society. However, more modern studies have found that a second language actually seems to add to cognitive flexibility and ability. Snow (1993) pointed out that bilingualism can be achieved in a number of ways, such as learning a second language beyond one's native language, having a second language imposed on one, and learning two languages from birth because two languages are spoken at home. Lambert (1977) indicated that there are at least two consequences of bilingualism: cognitive and social. Besides cognitive flexibility, one cognitive consequence of bilingualism seems to be that clusters of concepts are influenced such that these clusters are a combination of the native language and the acquired language. Social consequences seem to be connections with others who also speak the language, contributions to one's identity, and ethnic pride.

Food for Thought

We all have a sense of the conventions of everyday speech. Did you ever watch the television series *Seinfeld*? Many episodes had as their central premise a violation of a conversational rule. Do you remember the episode of the close talker? How about the soft talker who got Jerry to wear a poofy shirt because he could not hear what she was saying and he inadvertently agreed to wear the poofy shirt on a national interview program? We cannot really verbalize what conversational rules are, but we can certainly recognize when they are violated. On situation comedy shows, those violations are funny; in our everyday lives, they make us feel uncomfortable. Think about times when you may have violated conversational conventions—for instance, talking louder to a person who does not understand English. After reading this chapter, you may be more conscious of how you interact with others in conversation.

Critical Thinking Questions

Have you ever been in a conversation with someone who violated one of the cooperative principles (e.g., that person kept talking and did not let you join in the conversation or stood uncomfortably close to you)? If so, how did that make you feel?

Can you recall ever being in a conversation with two (or more) people who seemed to have some inside information to which you were not privy? Did their conversation seem to leave you out of their discussion? If so, how did you signal to them that you did not know what they were saying?

Do you consider yourself a high-context or a low-context communicator? How have your conversations gone with those who tend to be the opposite of you in using context?

Do you tend to have a direct or an indirect communication style? How does it feel when you are in a conversation with someone who uses the opposite style of communication?

When you are in a conversation with someone from a different racial or ethnic group, are you aware of different styles of communication?

When interacting with elderly individuals, do you notice that they tend to like to transmit information about the past? When interacting with your grandparents, do they pass down family stories, particularly about your parents?

Do you notice any differences between the ways men and women talk?

Have you studied different languages? How fluent are you in those other languages?

Seek out people who have learned English as a second language. To what extent did they feel that English replaced their native language or to what extent did they feel that they were able to retain their native language?

CHAPTER 5

Immigrants, Refugees, and the Acculturation Process

IMMIGRANTS AND REFUGEES
  Immigrants
  Refugees
COMMON EXPERIENCES OF IMMIGRANTS AND REFUGEES
  Language Barriers
  Support Networks
  Family Hierarchies
  New Family Roles
  Employment
  Education
ACCULTURATION
  "Old" and "New" Immigrants
  Models of Acculturation
      Acculturation of Immigrants
      Acculturation of Ethnic Minority Populations

The Migration Process
Ecological Context and Fit
SUMMARY

I just recently got a job as an assistant social worker. This job entails visiting the elderly from different backgrounds (SES, culture, etc.) who are suffering physical ailments, some of which are debilitating. I am to assess their psychosocial support and their coping with their illness and provide resources upon request. I am also to provide "suggestive counseling" whenever patients (the term they use) are emotionally affected by their physical ailments. Most of these patients are depressed, some are alone, and this job is a test of keeping my boundaries. I visit these patients, at the very most, twice.

One of my patients was a Vietnamese man, who lived alone in a one-bedroom apartment, within a senior citizens' complex. This man meekly welcomed me into his very well-kept home. When I spoke to this man on the phone, prior to my arrival, he told me that he spoke very little English. Amazingly, when I began to assess him and started asking him questions, I found that he spoke English very well! I told him this and he shyly laughed. He mentioned afterwards that he has been here since 1986 and that he was a refugee from the Vietnam War and had escaped from jail, went from Malaysia to the Philippines, and finally into the United States. Anyhow, he was amazed at how many resources he could be given as a senior citizen with Medi-Cal. Apparently, he has been paying someone $50 each time he had to visit his doctor! This is a service he can get for about $.75 per ride from the county!

The most surprising aspect of my visit with this old man was a comment he made after I complimented his English. He said that he has not spoken English like he was speaking it with me. He said that he was surprised himself at how well he spoke the language. He suggested that it might be because I was not asking him to repeat words and I wasn't acting as if he was deaf and speaking in volumes that could have ruptured his eardrums. He described that for the most part, whenever he attempted to speak to people, they would always talk to him loudly and overly accentuate his words as if he was, in his words "stupid." White people did this for the most part, according to him, and this made him feel "less than a person." Therefore, he really stopped talking to people altogether. He said that "no one" would want to speak to an old, stupid man like him anyway. I held back the tears as I listened to him and couldn't even imagine not speaking to anyone due to fears of feeling "stupid." I couldn't imagine being all alone as this man was, and keeping everything he had to say to himself. After he said all this, he looked at me, smiled, and said, "Thank you for being my solace. Since 1987, you are the first person to talk to me." This was a man who thought that he did not speak English well. I told him that I was glad that he felt better and that I would be coming back to confirm if he indeed received all the services that we had set up that day. We stood up and before I knew it, this man took my hand and had it about two inches from his face, then gently put it down. After seeing the quizzical look on my face he told me that if I called him back, he probably would not remember my name, or my voice. He said that when people called on the phone, he gets scared about his English and blanks out sometimes. He told me that when I call next time, to say that I was the one whose hand he smelled. He said that this, he would remember. He said, "I may not remember your name, but I will always remember your scent. For an old man like me, anything you remember is always good." As I walked away, he put his arms together, as if in prayer and bowed. I smiled and did the same.

JAYMIE, 30+-YEAR-OLD BIRACIAL (FILIPINA/BLACK) WOMAN

The process of acculturation can indeed be difficult, and many stories attest to this fact. Here is another one.

My family lived in the Philippines until I was about twelve years old. Coming to America brought about mixed emotions because of stories we heard about the American people. First of all, we always saw Americans who looked like Ken and Barbie dolls, so we assumed that this is how they all looked. This somewhat prepared us for how different we would look beside them. Secondly, America was supposed to be a great country of opportunity and success. Everything that happened in between was never considered.

My sister was eight years of age and my brother five when we settled in America. The main reason we came was due to my father's job in a prestigious firm that was based in Michigan. We chose to live in California due to the numerous relatives we had residing in the state. My family immediately went through changes within the year that we had arrived. Due to these changes, and the incomplete and unrealistic stories we were told, my brother, my sister, and I became more different than we were alike.

I wanted to be American. I stayed in front of the television for hours at a time, attempting to rid myself of the Filipino accent. I was determined to stay out of the sun, so I could be more "white," and adopt the Californian accent. Most of my friends were White during high school, and my father was very proud.

My sister "hung out" with Filipinos and Asians. She insisted on being Filipino only, denying any other cultural parts that were a part of our own family, much less others. For the most part, she refused to eat like Americans, act like Americans, or be among Americans. She dated only Filipinos and Asians and never really looked at any other ethnic groups as dating partners.

My brother became a loner. He didn't associate with any ethnic/cultural group in particular. As a matter of fact, he prided himself in being different. He would go out of his way to be different from "the norm" of what a Filipino AND an American should be. Although he never got in trouble, he always made sure that he was noticed for being apart from everyone.

Now as adults, it is somewhat surprising that I am the one who took it upon myself to learn about my culture and my "different selves." I retained the language and cultural beliefs. My sister married an Asian man and my brother remains an "enigma" and continues to go "against the waves."

Although as a family, we went through many hardships and struggles, we were thankful that we had other family members to rely on when things became difficult. We were prepared to come to America, if not to survive, to live a dream. Those dreams changed as soon as we settled, but were revived as we grew to realize that holding on to our family was just as important as "fitting into" a society that struggles to accept us.

SYLVIA, 20+-YEAR-OLD FILIPINA-AMERICAN WOMAN

These two stories are similar in that they relate the hardship and struggles of people in a host country that differs greatly from their original country. However, we must also appreciate the differences in these people's experiences of adaptation and **acculturation**.

acculturation—experiences and changes that groups and individuals undergo when they come in contact with a different culture.

Although we specifically discuss immigrants and refugees in this chapter, acculturation does not occur only in individuals from other countries. We will see that other people who reside in the host culture also experience acculturation and stress. However, the discussion of immigrants and refugees helps us to make meaningful comparisons involving the acculturation process and facilitates further examination of multicultural topics.

We are all aware of how difficult it is to grow up and face developmental, societal, and economic changes in our own multicultural society. Can we, then, begin to imagine how hard it is for people who grew up in a different country with different norms? Can we imagine the acculturation process that occurs in a new host country? We must consider language, norms, education, family systems and more, as well as the confusing and sometimes heartbreaking experiences immigrants and refugees must endure. Some might argue that people can stay where they are and avoid this process, but as human beings, can we honestly deny to others the American ideal of "following your dreams" and wanting the best for yourself and your family regardless of the trials and tribulations?

IMMIGRANTS AND REFUGEES

According to Hong and Ham (2001), the term *migration* includes two phenomena: (1) the flight of refugees from their own countries because of the threat of persecution, imprisonment, or death, and (2) the voluntary departure of individuals from their own countries to some other country. The story of the Vietnamese man, a refugee, at the beginning of the chapter is an example of the first phenomenon, and the story of the Filipina woman and her siblings, immigrants, is an example of the second. According to Cheal (2001), *refugees* and *immigrants* have very different experiences when they arrive in their new host country. Their stories of acculturation and stress may differ because of the differences in how they came to decide to migrate to a new country.

Immigrants

Immigrants usually have some time to consider their migration. Their decision may be based on their desire to "do better" for their families. These individuals are usually employed in their own country and want to apply their knowledge, expecting that the host country will be able to provide them a higher salary and more success than their country of origin can. Immigrants usually have a job waiting for them or at least have some assistance in finding a job (Cheal, 2001).

Social support networks are available to immigrants, both in the host country and in their country of origin, so that contacts are maintained with family members from their own country even after they leave. In that sense, immigrants usually have constant social and economic support so that they do not feel "alone" in a new host country. With their migration usually planned, immigrants tend to seek out other support systems within their own cultural group, which serve as additional safe havens and extended families.

Immigrants have opportunities to plan their exit from their host country, make arrangements for orderly transportation to their chosen place of residence, pack their belongings, and say goodbye to family and friends. They are usually able to ship items to their arrival place, knowing that family members will be there to receive them. Family and friends are present to welcome immigrants to their new home and to help them learn to function within their new society (Cheal, 2001; Hong & Ham, 2001).

Central in importance to most immigrants is the opportunity to return to their home country periodically for visits. They usually do not feel restrained and can choose to return home if the host country is not what they thought it would be. Many immigrants return to their home countries in their old age, choosing to live out the rest of their days in the place where they were raised.

Refugees

Throughout most of this chapter we will discuss immigrants and the acculturation process, but it is important to understand that refugees are quite different from immigrants in a number of ways. **Refugees** leave their homes because of perceived or actual violence (Cheal, 2001; Hong & Ham, 2001; Prendes-Lintel, 2001). The Vietnamese man described at the beginning of this chapter left his home because of the Vietnam War. He and his wife and children attempted to leave together but were separated as they ran for their lives. He does not know whether his wife and children are dead or alive. As did most refugees, he left with no belongings except the tattered clothes on his back.

immigrants—people who move to another country voluntarily. The decision to move can take weeks, months, or even years, which allows these people to prepare for the move and to begin the acculturation process before the move.

refugees—people who are forced to move from their homelands because of war or political oppression. The decision to move is almost immediate, taking days, hours, or even minutes, which allows these people neither to prepare for the move nor to begin the acculturation process because they do not usually know in which country they will finally settle.

In contrast to most immigrants, this refugee did not want to leave his home. His sudden departure did not allow him to say goodbye to friends and family, and he could not stay behind. Quite often family members who leave together do not stay together. Some die during flight, and their bodies are left behind without a proper burial. Since refugees' flights are unplanned, they experience resistance, and sometimes violence, during their migration from individuals who are not welcoming and who are ignorant about refugees' cultures.

Vietnamese refugees are prime examples of this kind of refugee. Moreover, they represented the enemy to those in the United States who remember the Vietnam War, so some people were afraid of the Vietnamese refugees who came to America. Vietnamese refugees also endured overcrowded camps (Cheal, 2001) and an unfamiliar social system. They became vulnerable to anything that the host culture put them through, suffering an emotional as well as a physical sense of a roller coaster ride. Because of their lack of experience with the host culture, many refugees relied on rumors within the refugee community to obtain relevant information with the host culture. Reality quite often clashed with rumors, resulting in a distrust of others that kept the refugees from seeking medical help even when their lives were at stake. Even after they were able to settle into the new host country, most of these refugees, especially the older ones, had few skills with which to find and maintain employment. With no family to depend on for communication and support networks, they usually settled for jobs that were paid "under the table" and had terrible working conditions.

Quite often, students are unaware of the hardships their parents endured when coming to the United States. However, courses such as this stimulate their curiosity, and they either ask their parents about their migration history or the stories their parents told them bring their experiences into sharper focus. This student came to the realization of her father's hardships after class discussion:

> I always thought that my dad was an immigrant because, well, he "immigrated" from Vietnam. Although he had told me stories about how hard it was to come to America, I just associated it with the will for freedom and the will to create a better life for themselves and for their family. I can honestly say that I did not know the difference between a refugee and immigrant. I knew that they were leaving their country, but I did not know the purpose or meaning of it. My dad told me that he and 3 of his siblings, two younger brothers and a younger sister, had to leave Vietnam because of the war that was occurring. They were still fairly young, around their mid-teens and early twenties. He actually told me two stories but I'm not sure how they link together. They had to pay a lot of money to people that would smuggle them over in boats. When the boat was in the middle of nowhere, the smugglers robbed the passengers of whatever valuables they had, but my dad had hidden his money into the seam of his shorts. The details are quite fuzzy but my dad and his siblings made it safely to America.

My dad and his siblings somehow ended up in St. Paul, Minnesota, and we were sponsored by a middle-aged white American couple. They attended church, went fishing, and other activities that their sponsors introduced them to. They worked minimum wage factory jobs to get by each day. My aunt was a young teenager and was able and encouraged to go to school by her 3 brothers who worked to support each other. They shared a one-bedroom apartment, where my Aunt got the only room and my dad and his brothers slept in sleeping bags in the living room floor. They did not have the luxuries of eating out, wearing nice clothes, or a comfortable living environment. My dad told me that they shopped at thrift stores for clothes because they could not afford to buy new clothes. The extra money that they did have, they allowed my aunt to buy new clothes or supplies for school. They felt that it was better for one of them to be able to get an education, than for all 4 of them to be working in low-paying dead-end jobs.

CARLEY, 20+-YEAR-OLD VIETNAMESE-AMERICAN WOMAN

Berry (1988, 1991) discussed the notion of a "refugee career" (Table 5.1) and identified six stages of this career: (1) predeparture, (2) flight, (3) first asylum, (4) claimant, (5) settlement, and (6) adaptation. *Predeparture* refers to the conditions that force refugees from their homelands, such as wars, revolutions, and atrocities. *Flight* refers to the period of transit away from the home country. This is a period of maximum uncertainty, during which the refugees do not know where they are going. They know only that they need to flee from their homes and communities. Whereas immigrants plan their departures over the course of months or even years and know where they are going, refugees often make their decision to leave in a matter of days or even hours. Carley's story about her father nicely demonstrates Berry's model.

First asylum refers to the first place the refugees settle where they feel safe. Conditions in these places of asylum vary widely, however, from safe and relatively good to woefully underfunded and unhealthy. For example, after the Cuban revolution in the late 1950s, most Cuban refugees fled to the United States,

TABLE 5.1   **Berry's Six Stages of Refugee Careers**

Stage	Brief Description
Predeparture	Conditions that force refugees to flee their homelands
Flight	The period of transit away from the homeland
First Asylum	First place where refugees settle
Claimant	The first country of potential resettlement
Settlement	The country of settlement
Adaptation	Adjustment to the new country of settlement

particularly to the Miami area (Kitano, 1999). This was not only the first asylum area but also their settlement area. These refugees were generally well-off and were able to shelter their money in the United States before they fled Cuba. On the other hand, at the time of this writing, hundreds of thousands of refugees are crowded into makeshift refugee camps in the Darfur region of Sudan on the border of Chad. These camps are a first asylum and were designed only for tens of thousands of people, so there is an extreme shortage of food, water, and medicine. Some experts predict that half a million people or more will die because of these conditions (The Tragedy of Sudan, 2004).

Claimant refers to a country that grants asylum. At this point, there is still a possibility that the refugees can be deported or repatriated. Quite often, refugees are permitted to stay in this initial country for only a limited time. If they exceed the time limit, they are subject to deportation. *Settlement* refers to a country's formal acceptance of refugees who want to settle there. Finally, *adaptation* refers to the adjustments that refugees make to their new host country. This process is referred to as *acculturation* later in this chapter.

Because refugees generally flee extremely difficult circumstances, they often experience posttraumatic stress disorder (Prendes-Lintel, 2001). Frequently, refugees experience deaths in their families, threats of violence or death, separation from important family members, and other forms of trauma. Moreover, trying to adjust to a new country that may have a markedly different culture delays any recovery from the trauma they experience. Evidence of that trauma often includes somatic symptoms, such as headaches, stomach problems, extreme nervousness, and sleep disorders (American Psychiatric Association, 2000).

When discussing issues regarding refugees, many students gain more respect and appreciation for those who had to flee their circumstances and go to a world quite different from the one they knew. This student felt "humbled" by realizing his parents' ordeals:

> My parents and I are a refugee family. My parents were escaping persecution from the Communist Cambodian government during Pol Pot's evil regime where a genocide of Cambodians was taking place. Fortunately, we took refuge in a camp in Thailand. There at the refugee camp is where I, the oldest child, was born. . . .Less than a year later, my family and I ended up in Louisville, Kentucky, where my brother was eventually conceived. My parents told me that a church sponsored a cohort of refugees. Fortunately, my family was one of them. I couldn't imagine the difficulties and racism that my parents had in the acculturation process. A year later, we moved to California, where I suppose the acculturation process was a little easier due to a more diverse environment; but I cannot say for sure since I was too young to recall.
>
> The film [on refugees we saw in class] gave me a glimpse into my parents' life and I have never been so humbled. I have always considered myself to be "first generation" American because of the fact that I immigrated when I was less than a year old. American culture had more of an impact in my life than my culture of origin. Therefore,

PICTURE 5.1 Internal political conflicts can cause people to flee their home countries and seek asylum in other countries. *Photograph by Tom Zasadzinski*

my acculturation process has been facile. But after viewing the film and reflecting about my parents, I sympathetically realized why my parents never acculturated.

CHANNOCK, 20+-YEAR-OLD CAMBODIAN-AMERICAN MAN

Refugees often hope to return to their countries of origin. However, a lack of financial and social resources, and the perceived threat in their own countries, make return an unattainable dream for most of them. For the most part, they are left in the host country with other people of their ethnic group, as a type of extended family. They usually live in neighborhoods that are ethnically homogeneous, so that they are able to fulfill their needs without having to go too far "outside" their respective communities. This arrangement represents a double-edged sword. On the one hand, living within their communities allows them to settle in their new land with relative ease. On the other hand, it can set back the acculturation process in the long run (McGoldrick, 1982).

COMMON EXPERIENCES OF IMMIGRANTS AND REFUGEES

We have seen that there are many differences between immigrants and refugees, even when we consider only the reasons behind their migration. Just as important, however, are the potential similarities in the experiences of these groups once the individuals begin their lives in their new country.

People in the host country often do not distinguish between immigrants and refugees and use a convenient label to support a discriminatory stance. In other words, if it is convenient to label the targeted group as immigrants, then immigrants and refugees are lumped together under that label to support a person's stance that we should curb immigration. If it is convenient to label the targeted group as refugees, then immigrants and refugees are lumped together under that label to support a person's stance that tax dollars should not go toward supporting those fleeing from their countries of origin—freedom should be their payment.

Now let us take a closer look at some of the common experiences that immigrants and refugees face in their host country. Foremost among these experiences are problems with language barriers, support networks, changing family hierarchies, new family roles, employment, and education.

Language Barriers

I remember that my father was in this rage one day because someone had made a big deal about his accent at work. He came home and told us that from that moment on he did not want us to watch TV in Spanish. It was an "all" English-speaking world out there, and I felt like I had to change my ways and learn the language thoroughly. Years passed and I started losing a little bit of the Spanish language.
Speaking in English feels a lot more comfortable for me now. I would go visit my family in Mexico, and I was right back in the struggle. They would make fun of me because I had become too "Americanized" according to them. I felt like I was caught in between two worlds.

PATRICIA, 20+-YEAR-OLD MEXICAN-AMERICAN WOMAN

I don't know what my culture really is. I have mostly Asian friends, but they all speak as I do, English. I speak Mandarin to my mom but never to anyone else. I communicate to my younger brother in English, and he talks to our mom in Mandarin also. I only became aware of myself after I was set up on a blind date with someone who speaks Chinese. I talked to her in Mandarin, but I was very uncomfortable because the only person I talk to in Chinese is my mom. The date was a disaster because she never talked at all, and I was very frustrated at the fact that the person who fixed me up was not aware that I am pretty Americanized. Well, the fact that I was born in Taiwan doesn't mean much, but the fact that I was raised here in Los Angeles and didn't hang out with foreigners means much more. After that I never called that girl again and she never called me either. I realized only recently, after encountering a non-English-speaking person, that the very least someone has to be is English-speaking.

TERRY, 20+-YEAR-OLD TAIWANESE-AMERICAN MAN

People who come from other countries encounter language barriers that are sometimes hard to overcome. Differences in how individuals deal with the communication problems are apparent within the older and the younger generations.

As if the words are not hard enough to learn, the directness of the American culture clashes with the indirectness of certain other cultures to make an awkward and guarded relationship between people. Whereas the younger generation adapts more readily to the direct ways of this society, the older people find the directness rude and insensitive, which increases their dependence on the younger generation for communication.

Many individuals who migrate from one country to another have little or no exposure to the host country's language. This is especially true of people from third-world countries who migrate to more developed countries, such as the United States. How can we expect a person to succeed when that person does not know how to speak effectively with other people on a daily basis? The older generations that migrate have a harder time with the language barrier. They mostly rely on their children or the younger generation to communicate with others outside their community, a dependence that affects both the older people and the younger ones. The older people may feel alienated, insecure, distrustful, and useless, whereas the youth may feel overly responsible for their parents. Some of the youth, as exemplified by the Latina and the Asian male quoted earlier, begin to lose a sense of the importance of their native tongue. Fluency in the English language becomes the mark of a better person within these groups, and whether someone is a refugee or an immigrant, the less pronounced the accent, the more privilege that person achieves.

Whenever individuals feel unsuccessful within the mainstream society because of language barriers, they move into the part of the country, town, or city where most of "their own" live. This trend is apparent when we see that specific ethnic groups occupy certain towns or cities. These areas become safe havens for most immigrants or refugees and others who are experiencing **acculturative stress** (feelings of tension and anxiety caused by the inability to adapt in the new country). Those who retreat to these ethnic communities risk further isolation and discrimination from majority groups, but they are willing to take that risk in order to feel a part of a community that understands their needs and shares their language.

acculturative stress—feelings of tension and anxiety caused by the inability to adapt in the new country.

Whereas immigrants, who are usually prepared to migrate, may have some knowledge of the host country's language, refugees, who had no plans to migrate, are thrown into confusion and burdened with humiliation. This situation is due not only to their inability to speak the new language but also to their lack of social support networks willing to translate so that they can function and live properly.

Support Networks

Sonia has lived in East Los Angeles for 26 years, and people continue to wonder why she does not speak any English. She was born in Mexico and migrated to the United States when she was thirty years of age. She thought that she would be able to get a better job here. At thirty-five years of age, she was diagnosed with diabetes and her health deteriorated subsequently. According to her, Mexico could not offer ample medical benefits, so she felt "stuck" in the United States. All of her family members live in Mexico, and some travel back and forth from time to time for emotional support, but for the most part, Sonia is alone.

When I visited her, I found her living in a low-income apartment complex. She lived in a one-bedroom apartment, with all the shades drawn. She must have had all of her belongings accumulated from 26 years ago, because her home was cluttered and room was limited. She admitted to feeling depressed and alone. Given the 26 years that she had lived in the same place, she was unaware of any of the available community resources. Although she wanted to be able to talk to others who spoke Spanish, she didn't know where to look. Her health had gotten worse in the years, and she believed that she probably would be stronger if she had others to talk with.

We found an adult recreation and day program for Sonia, but we were not sure how often she will be able to go due to her ailing health. I wonder how much better she would be today, had we found her earlier?

JAYMIE, 30+-YEAR-OLD BIRACIAL (FILIPINA/BLACK) WOMAN

Whether an individual is an immigrant or a refugee, support networks become one of the most important factors within a societal context to assist the acculturation process. Although employment, language, roles, and education may be important, lack of support networks can be the greatest source of stress.

As we have noted, immigrants usually have more ready support networks than refugees do. Although that is the case, we must further consider the country from which the immigrant comes and the generation traveling to the new host country. Many Asian immigrants are typically cut off from their families in their country of origin, both socially and emotionally (Hong & Ham, 2001). Although their trip to America or some other host country may be planned, they usually do not have the financial resources to stay in contact with family overseas on a consistent basis. Many immigrate as single individuals, lacking the extensive support system that they had in their country of origin. Other social interactions or friendships take a longer time to establish (Hong & Ham, 2001).

According to Hong and Ham (2001), the lack of a support network leads to social isolation and stress for many immigrants, particularly when they encounter difficult situations. We may assume that the farther one's country of origin is from the host country, the harder it is to maintain contact with family members left behind. Whenever problems of any kind arise, the isolation and stress caused by the lack of support systems may lead to anxiety, depression, and marital conflict.

Although community resources are available, immigrants and refugees fear being turned away or humiliated because of their difficulty with English and their different ways of behaving, and they rarely reach out for help. Since there are limited community resources that target individuals who speak English as a second language, most immigrants and refugees remain isolated. Like Sonia in the preceding story, they may spend the rest of their days alone and unaware of available help. This lack of desire to reach out may not stem from total ignorance of available resources but, rather, may be due to previous experiences of alienation from the majority population.

Furthermore, Hovey (2000) states that among immigrants and refugees, *perceived* quality of social support may be a more accurate predictor of psychological distress than is the quantity of social support. Therefore, larger social networks may not offer more support than some other resource that the person believes can offer better support. Immigrants, who usually have a more positive view of their move, will have a more positive perception of support than will refugees, who did not want to migrate in the first place. These perceptions are an extra factor that we should take into consideration within the context of supportive networks.

Family Hierarchies

While migrating individuals struggle with language and maintaining social contact, changes are also taking place within their family structure. Decision-making power and the family hierarchy begin to shift.

> *Pablo and his family immigrated to the United States when he was only five years old. They were originally from Mexico and they wanted to succeed in the land of opportunity. Pablo was the youngest in the family and acculturated the fastest, but the family struggled seemingly more as they found out that the land of opportunity had rules one had to follow for success. Pablo's parents did not speak English and had difficulty finding jobs. Pablo witnessed his older brothers and sisters grow in different ways as the country "ate them alive." Pablo also saw how the family struggled because his father expected the same respect as head of household although his mother became the primary breadwinner in the home. This created an obvious rift in the home as his older brothers lost respect for their father who could not hold a job. In order to attempt maintenance of peace in the home, Pablo's mother still cooked, cleaned, and cared for the children while she worked full time outside of the home. Eventually, Pablo's two older brothers joined a gang, one older sister married early and moved out of the home, and Pablo moved out of the home to attend college.*
>
> *I go by Paul now. I don't like to talk about my family in first person because I don't feel like we are the same people we were before we moved here. I'm in college trying to get a doctorate degree. Everything has changed. I have no contact with my father and my mother died from a broken heart.*
>
> PAUL, 26-YEAR-OLD MEXICAN-AMERICAN MAN

In the United States, primarily individualistic and egalitarian principles prevail. That may cause problems in the realm of family hierarchies and organization after immigrants and refugees enter the country. Although the United States is known as a country driven by individualism, patriarchy still exists in many ways within the family if not also within the society as a whole. Some migrating individuals, however, come from countries that consider the mother the head of the family. People from Western culture tend to share the U.S. view of hierarchy and individualism, but some revere the mother most within the family. Meanwhile, individuals from the Eastern societies tend to be collectivistic, but some are still very patriarchal in beliefs. In light of all these differences, how can we begin to understand changes that take place in an individual's life after he or she moves or flees to the host country?

For example, although Mexican families stress affiliation and cooperation (Falicov, 1996), those values are supported with clear hierarchies. Parents and children try to achieve smooth relationships that avoid conflict. Respect for parents is a must, but in Mexican families, the mother commands much authority. For these groups, the status of the children is low, and the status of the parents is high. Although a patriarchal view persists, more complex dynamics exist, with a wide range from patriarchal to egalitarian and with many combinations in between (Falicov, 1996; Hong & Ham, 2001).

Whereas Americans attempt to maintain romantic ties even after having children, most immigrant couples begin to lose romantic ties and focus more on the parental dyads. The process of acculturation disrupts this hierarchy for most families as the children begin to command "equal time" and independence from parental decisions. The parents' views of "how things were in the old country" begin to conflict with the children's views of how things should be now that they are residing in a country that values individualism and egalitarianism. Women, who traditionally are lower in the hierarchy than their husbands and partners are, begin to demand equality, particularly after they gain employment. (Dual incomes

PICTURE 5.2 Latino families generally have more structured family hierarchies than do their Western counterparts. *Photograph by Sylvana Rodriguez*

are often necessary for the family to survive.) Daughters demand the same treatment as sons after learning about feminism and equal rights.

Most families migrating to the United States include grandparents who are regarded as the "root of the oak," commanding as much respect as the parents, if not more. Yet the elderly who migrated or fled to a new host country must also endure the changes in hierarchy. Outside responsibilities, the necessity that all members of the family be employed, and less respect for the "old ways" combine to lessen the importance of the elderly within U.S. culture (Lewin, 1941). Within the U.S. culture, the elderly are encouraged to remain independent regardless of ailment, whereas in other countries, the elders are viewed as part of the nuclear family.

Within the hierarchy are roles in the family subsystems that usually change. Many family members resist those changes, if only to maintain some stability, and find that other members rebel and eventually leave the system.

New Family Roles

Ed and Nancy (adopted American names) migrated from Japan in search of a better life for their son, whom Nancy was carrying at the time. After Nancy had the baby, Ed found it difficult to make ends meet with his salary as a factory worker. Initially, when Nancy suggested that she find work, Ed was enraged. He announced that he was the man and he should work while she took care of the baby. Besides, he thought that it would be ridiculous for other family members to help raise the child, even though they had aunts who were willing to help care for Mitchell, their newborn son. Finally, Ed relented and "allowed" Nancy to work. Nancy began to work 40-hour weeks while Ed's hours at work were cut in half. Nancy had to work overtime to help support the family. After work, she would pick Mitchell up from her aunt's house, bathe him, and then make dinner. At times, she would be so exhausted that she would doze off while they ate dinner. Eventually, she began to fight with Ed because even though he would come home from work earlier in the day, he would not pick up Mitchell and would wait for Nancy to come home to make dinner while he napped. Nancy and Ed fought for the most part around issues of Ed's refusal to take on any role that would equate him with a woman. He screamed about his father who worked for the family and his mother who did everything at home. He blamed Nancy's American friends for "poisoning her mind," making her believe that she should "talk back" to her husband. Nancy screamed about the fact that she did not "just" stay home, and that they were no longer living in Japan. She insisted that things must change before it was too late. Mitchell was 10 when Nancy divorced Ed. Ed eventually returned to Japan and remarried. Nancy is a single mother who vows to raise Mitchell with values of respect for his partner as an equal.

JAYMIE, 30+-YEAR-OLD BIRACIAL (FILIPINA/BLACK) WOMAN

Along with changes in the family hierarchy come changes in roles. Men who are used to being the breadwinners are exposed to a society that allows for "stay-at-home dads." Though fathers who decide to stay home are still somewhat under-appreciated in this society, in other countries this role *cannot* exist. Furthermore, men must give up their role as sole breadwinner in the household when their wives must enter the workforce to meet the family's needs. Women's role of housewife and mother changes to that of "supermom," who cleans the house, cares for the children, and works 40-hour weeks. Sometimes, the father must accept additional roles in child care and housekeeping, sharing those responsibilities with his partner.

Grandparents who migrate in their later years become strangers in the home. Their children and grandchildren are busy with their own lives, so the grandparents begin to associate with other seniors who share their values and circumstances and with whom they feel comfortable. Although they sometimes assume the role of "babysitter" for the younger children while parents work, they are not revered as they once were in their country of origin. Children of immigrant families have more household responsibilities than they did in premigration days because both parents are now working (Hong & Ham, 2001). They also become translators for their parents publicly, especially if the parents struggle with the language of the host country.

If the family has boundaries that are too rigid to adapt to the demands of their new situation, dysfunction can occur and relationships break down (Hong & Ham, 2001). Role changes between partners and the children may cause marital conflict. Children as family translators have too much power, and from a family-therapy perspective (Hoffman, 1981; Nichols & Schwartz, 1998), there is a violation of generational boundaries. What this means is that adults *should* be at a higher level in the family hierarchy than children, but because the children have more power around language issues, they enter into the adults' level of power.

For most families, the demands of changing roles present difficulties that eventually modify the family system. If families cannot adjust to these changing roles, they may face dissolution. For most of us, it is easy to say that change is necessary to maintain cooperation and avoid conflict, but for families who migrate with deeply rooted beliefs, such change is not an easy process. In a sense, it is impressive that so many families *are* able to adapt to these changes.

Employment

My wife and I thought how wonderful it will be to move from a third-world country to the United States. I had a degree as a Chemical Engineer and my wife was willing to stay home and care for our three young children. Most of our family lived here in the U.S. and have told many stories of how much easier it was to get jobs. One thing I didn't consider was how my degree was "no good" because I earned it from elsewhere other than the U.S. They said I need re-certification, which was a nicer way of saying that I needed to go back to school and learn "their way." Well, I couldn't do that because we had no money, and we had three children. My wife was unemployed and the rest of our family had to work to maintain their own household. I work at an ARCO gas station now and we've gotten robbed twice. I want to feel hopeful, but it has gotten harder and harder. I guess I just have to be thankful that I have a job. I want to go back "home," but we feel like it will be harder since most of our family is here.

ANDY, 30+-YEAR-OLD, IMMIGRANT-ASIAN MAN

According to Hong and Ham (2001), immigrants often cite greater freedom, a more stable political environment, and better opportunity for their children as reasons for immigration. Once they are settled in the United States, however, prolonged low-income employment or underemployment can eventually take its toll. Lacking English-language skills and enjoying only limited social support, most immigrants and refugees are forced to find employment in ethnic communities that are also limited in growth and income. Immigrants who have sufficient financial resources attempt to establish local businesses but must do so in high-crime neighborhoods. Some groups, such as Korean Americans (Hong & Ham, 2001), have financial assets tied up in their small businesses, which prevents them from moving into more favorable businesses or neighborhoods. Other groups settle into factory jobs and other low-paying, intensive manual labor that requires many hours.

Not only do these individuals face limited employment opportunities, but once they do find employment, their premigration experiences, limited English, and physical characteristics also become reasons for employers to discriminate against them. Promotions are nearly impossible, even for those who have held prestigious positions in their countries of origin. Degrees held by immigrants before their move are not as marketable in the United States, and they are forced to accept jobs with much lower status. Decline in status lowers self-esteem and increases disillusionment, and these factors can eventually cause family distress. For some individuals who have some social or familial support, further education to obtain equivalent credentials is possible. For others, the necessity of making ends meet makes such opportunities impossible. Most migrating people recognize that they need to attend English classes to move forward with employment, but they can't always do so.

Individuals who are unable to master the English language are easily taken advantage of and discriminated against by employers and other employees. These individuals may be forced to accept conditions that do not meet minimal legal standards, but their lack of education and their need to feed their families force them to tolerate such treatment and working conditions. Some immigrants who are able to establish businesses are leery of taking their small businesses outside the ethnic communities because they know that thriving within a bigger cosmopolitan setting is nearly impossible. Although some do dream that their established businesses within smaller, ethnic communities are only a stepping-stone to a well-accepted and profitable venture, such dreams rarely become a reality. To clinicians and other laypeople, these people present a picture of resilience, determination, content, and noble self-sacrifice (Hong & Ham, 2001). Yet underneath such external appearances can lie severe stress, doubt, and frustration (Hong, 1989; Hong & Ham, 2001).

Education

Some immigrants in the United States have had some secondary and more advanced education in their countries of origin. However, other immigrants and most refugees have limited educations, which can be a major problem when they attempt to find employment that pays well. Some adult immigrants who are able to go back to school, raise a family, and work at the same time can face problems of overstress, family discord, and marital conflict. Therefore, older immigrants and refugees often place the hope for higher education in their children.

Unfortunately for immigrant children, education can also cause stress within the individual and the family system. Immigrant children who attended school in their countries of origin have a difficult time adjusting to the U.S. school system. For most immigrant children, the values within the school system in the United States differ greatly from the values in their own countries. In many places, such as Mexico and Asian countries, respect for educators is demanded just as much as respect for parents. Talking back and holding an opinion that conflicts with a teacher's opinion are not tolerated in some countries.

Parents begin to have conflicts with children who rebel against the old ways. Change that is adaptive within the classroom is often brought into the home, which reinforces parents' thinking about the U.S. educational culture. Some parents become so worried about how their children will turn out after finishing their education that they choose to take the children out of school and place them in the job market. Laws mandating that minors attend school are ignored, and tension increases among the school system, the parents, and the children. Parents who hold traditional values are often viewed as rigid, by their children or those in the host culture. This perception can lead these children or authorities in the host culture to discount the parents' beliefs, even though some of these beliefs may be legitimate.

Although we highlight the preceding issues as major considerations in attempting to comprehend the experiences of immigrants and refugees, they are only some of the many issues that relate to the process of acculturation. How individuals adapt to the differences between their country of origin and their host country may determine their success. In defining the success of immigrants and refugees, we should not look at the success of individuals who have lived in the United States all their lives.

Some migrating individuals equate success with fulfilling basic needs such as food and shelter. Although we can argue that some citizens of this country also face unemployment and obstacles in attempting to achieve the "American dream" while we keep our gates open to others, we cannot blame immigrants and refugees for attempting to live the dream as well. While some citizens say "go back home, where you belong," newcomers are replying that "this is home and the welcome mat is displayed everywhere." If some people have the greater advantages of family and social support, knowledge of the language, and educational and occupational opportunities, and still struggle within this culture, imagine how difficult it must be to pursue the "American dream" for those who are not as privileged and who lack basic skills.

Since an individual's level of acculturation can determine his or her success, we will take a more elaborate look at what is involved in the acculturation process. In the next section, we apply the process of acculturation to "natural citizens" as well as to immigrants and refugees.

ACCULTURATION

According to various researchers, acculturation refers to the experiences and changes that groups and individuals undergo when they come into contact with a different culture (Brislin, 2000; Hall & Barongan, 2002; Hovey, 2000; Yeh, 2003). Depending on the changes that people go through, their stress levels will differ. Furthermore, Hovey (2000) found that *acculturative stress,* which is the tension and anxiety that directly results from and has its source in the acculturative process, is unrelated to one's level of acculturation. This finding implies that a person who is less acculturated may not experience more stress than one who is more acculturated.

Note that acculturation is a *process* as opposed to an *outcome.* In other words, those who immigrate to the United States are acculturating or adjusting to their new host country as opposed to trying to achieve a certain level of acculturation as an end point. Moreover, the host country (in our case, the United States) is also undergoing a process of adjusting to immigrants. For example, as the number of Latino and Asian groups has increased on the West Coast, more and more Latin American (primarily Mexican) and Asian restaurants have opened, and some restaurants are even specializing in "Fusion Cuisine," which is a fusion of American, Latin American, and Asian flavors.

According to Hall and Barongan (2002), acculturation is usually assumed to apply to ethnic groups whose immigration to the United States is relatively recent, such as Latino Americans and Asian Americans. However, we should keep in mind that because there are major differences between the dominant cultural group and both African Americans and American Indians, members of these two groups also may go through an acculturation process. In these cases, we see how racism and discrimination can affect the acculturation process even for those who are "natural citizens" of this country. Although immigrants and others who have moved here have been an important part of U.S. history, the topic of acculturation has only recently been addressed.

America has become more diverse. That diversity may be welcome to some, but for others, it creates confusion, fear, distrust, and hatred. Even with increasing research into acculturation and the processes that immigrants and refugees go through, most people still need to be educated about the inevitable experiences of those who move from a familiar environment to a new one that contrasts dramatically with the old one.

"Old" and "New" Immigrants

Those who curse at the continuing flow of immigrants into this country usually know little about issues of migration and acculturation. That ignorance goes back to earlier periods of immigration, when fear and denigration of immigrants were prevalent, especially in the 19th century (O'Brien, 2003). According to O'Brien, the predominant concern then was whether the country could "adequately assim-ilate" the large number of people who were moving into the United States, espe-cially between 1880 and 1920.

In the 19th century, differentiation between "new" and "old" immigrants began as a primary rationale for restricting entrance into the nation, and many other fears magnified the "threat" posed by immigrants (O'Brien, 2003). Both the "new" and the "old" immigrants were unwelcome because Americans feared that their jobs were being threatened. Furthermore, the "new" immigrants were re-garded as physically, mentally, and morally inferior to the older immigrants (O'Brien, 2003). As reported by many studies, "new" immigrants were viewed as "retarded," less intelligent, and frequently as occupants of mental institutions. Immigrants were objectified and associated with waste, animals, and catastrophic events (O'Brien, 2003). Diseases and crime were known to spread from areas where immigrants lived, which contributed to the already exaggerated fears about immigrants. (As we discuss in chapter 6, this concern is an example of the ulti-mate attribution error: the diseases and crime were blamed on the immigrants rather than on the social conditions.)

Today, most of the concerns of Americans focus on the job market and how immigrants are willing to work for low pay, taking away many jobs from Ameri-cans. And many Americans today still protest against the "mixing of the races," which was also a concern in previous eras. But have things fundamentally gotten better? Most people would say yes, but some of the old fears remain.

The focus of most research on immigrants has been on the image of immigrants and the fears of residents of the host country. Not enough research has been done on the experiences of migrating individuals before, during, and after their move. This type of examination might help Americans understand why people from other countries continue to "act the way they do," even though they have moved to the United States. Understanding the acculturation process might also shed some light on stereotypes, prejudice, discrimination, and racism (see chapter 6).

Models of Acculturation

Traditionally, researchers in the field have identified the process of adjusting to a new culture as being assimilated into that culture. These researchers contended that immigrants or refugees maintained their original cultures for the most part, then their children begin to transition to acquiring the norms and values of the host culture while they lose their connection to their parents' culture, then the grandchildren of the immigrants or refugees almost lose all connection with their grandparents' culture. By the time of the third or fourth generation, there is al-most no hint of the original culture in favor of the norms and values of the host culture (Gordon, 1964; Warner & Srole, 1946; see Kitano, 1997). However, most researchers now feel that there are different ways of acculturating into the new culture. They have examined models of acculturation to foster understanding of the processes that individuals undergo before, during, and after their move to the United States. (Keep in mind that the classifications in this model [and others] are processes as opposed to end points.)

PICTURE 5.3   Immigrant parents are often conflicted as to how "traditional" versus how "Westernized" their children should be raised in the United States. *Photograph by Diana Seif*

TABLE 5.2   Berry's Model of Acculturation

Status	Brief Descriptions
Assimilationist	An individual who has given up his/her identity of origin in favor of identifying with the host culture's values and beliefs
Separationist	An individual who identifies with his/her identity of origin and rejects all the host culture's values and beliefs
Marginalist	An individual who does not identify with either his/her original culture or the host culture
Integrationist	An individual who combines (integrates) aspects of his/her own culture and the host culture

Acculturation of Immigrants

Brislin (2000) and Leong (2001) describe Berry's (1990, 1997) model of how members of a recipient culture respond to various aspects of the donor culture. (See Table 5.2.)

My parents were born in India and came to America about 25 years ago. Even though I was born and raised in California, I am still aware of my Indian culture as well as the American culture. My cousins on the other hand, are of the third generation. Their grandparents immigrated here and their parents were raised here. My cousins are of the "straight line" model. They know nothing of the Indian culture that their grandparents brought with them. They consider themselves to be American, nothing else. There's nothing wrong with this, but in my belief, there should be a healthy balance of both cultures. Teach the good from both. When my aunt and uncle go out to the Indian cultural events, my cousins are clueless on what they are experiencing and I always find myself explaining to them every detail.

SANJAY, 20+-YEAR-OLD INDIAN-AMERICAN MAN

Are Sanjay's cousins' actions "bad"? That may depend on whom we ask. According to Leong (2001) and Brislin (2000), Sanjay's cousins may be representative of the **assimilationist** in the American society. The cousins have adopted values of their host culture, and it is apparent that they have basically given up the beliefs and values of their native country. They have essentially become "Americanized," and possibly in their own minds, that has made their transition easier. They may believe that they will be more accepted if they are "like everyone else." Assimilationists can also be said to believe in "guilt by association," in that they believe that they will increase their level of privilege if they are closely associated with the majority culture. However, is that true?

assimilationist–an individual who blends in completely into the host society, taking on the values of that society and rejecting his or her original values.

Tina moved to the United States as a teenager due to economic difficulties her family had in their native country. She is the oldest of three children, and her parents depended on her as the responsible person for her siblings. They relied on her to care for her siblings while they worked, as a dual income was necessary for the family to survive. Tina attended a high school, where she was definitely a minority, and she found herself searching for others who "looked like her." She insisted on speaking her native language with her friends in and outside her school, and especially at home. She made sure that her brother and sister were able to speak their own language and became especially upset when she noticed that her sister associated more with White Americans. She religiously followed traditions from her own country while she refused to celebrate more American traditions. She really did not associate with more "Americanized" folks besides those she worked with, unless she absolutely had to do so. She fraternized only with individuals who moved in a particular circle. That circle encompassed an area composed of only people from her own country.

JAYMIE, 30+-YEAR-OLD BIRACIAL (FILIPINA/BLACK) WOMAN

Some of us may applaud Tina's strict commitment to pursue and follow her own beliefs and her refusal to assimilate into the majority culture. However, some of us may wonder how Tina can ever become successful in America if she refuses to follow any of its traditions, especially if she intends to stay. According to Leong (2001), Tina's case is representative of the **separationist.** Separationists refuse to observe any traditions of their host country. They strongly maintain beliefs and values of their country of origin and are unwilling to identify with any other culture, even though they are confronted with the values of the host country on a daily basis. Tina and others like her may have observed and experienced discrimination because of their ethnic and cultural backgrounds. Whereas others prefer to join the majority to avoid the wrath of society, Tina chose to stay separate from the majority as much as she could for the same reason. Although Tina belongs in a different group from others who assimilate, hate and fear exist within both groups because of the experiences that they have been through.

separationist—an individual who refuses to take on any values of the host society, hanging on to his or her original values completely.

Joe was born and raised here in the U.S. Though his parents brought him up in a very strict, traditional home, Joe never really "felt like he belonged in his own cultural/ethnic group." He also did not like White people very much, so he really did not associate with many of them. So, Joe grew up in a predominantly Asian neighborhood, but he never really agreed with many of the norms of his culture. When Joe was about 16, he joined a Chinese gang. One of the things his gang did on a daily basis was to rob stores around his neighborhood. Chinese Americans in his area feared Joe and his gang, for they were known to hurt people. Joe and his gang also participated in drive-by shootings in other areas, and especially gang wars or "color wars." Joe never finished high school, though at the age of 32, he was able to leave the gang. Even after Joe left the gang, he did not pursue his education. Joe is now 40 years old, and he chose to be a proponent of anti-gang campaigns. He never finished his education and he makes just enough money to get by.

Jaymie, 30+-year-old Biracial (Filipina/Black) Woman

Joe is representative of the **marginalist** (Brislin, 2000; Leong, 2001). Marginalists are alienated individuals who neither adopt values of the host culture nor hold on to the values of their own culture. These people, as shown by Joe's story, have to create their own group, with separate norms and a different value system, which some of us may not completely understand. This group paints the classic picture of rebellion. They turn their backs on society, just as they feel that society has turned its back on them. They choose a family that accepts them regardless of where they come from. Although marginalist groups are considered the outcasts of society, they still come together having something in common. Besides the common experience of not belonging, they may share common ethnic backgrounds, religion, beliefs, and so on.

marginalist—an individual who does not adopt either the host society's values or his or her original values.

The last group is the **integrationists.** These individuals are able to "make the best of both worlds." They are able to hold on to their own values, beliefs, and culture while learning about and adapting to their host culture. Integrationists are

integrationist—an individual who holds on to his or her original values while also learning and adopting the values of the host culture.

the individuals who are deemed most likely to succeed. They also seem to be the most well balanced and the happiest of the four main groups. Although they can function in the host society, they are still able to relate to their own people without difficulty. We could suppose that integrationists are more readily able to deal with people from other ethnic groups because they have adopted a flexibility of association.

It could be that these acculturation groups are not necessarily stable, meaning there may be some fluidity in a person's status. More specifically, at age 14, someone may be grouped with marginalists, who choose to give up their own cultural beliefs while refusing to adopt those of the host culture. The changes that this same person experiences can later allow him or her to go from being a marginalist to being an integrationist. It could also be that a person is associated with more than one group in his or her lifetime. This fluidity suggests that there are more variables to consider when looking at the processes that immigrants and refugees must go through to appropriately acculturate into their host culture.

Acculturation of Ethnic Minority Populations

LaFramboise proposed a model of acculturation from her American Indian perspective that was designed to describe the acculturation process of American ethnic minority populations (LaFramboise, Coleman, & Gerton, 1993). Similar to the Berry model, the LaFramboise model (Table 5.3) includes *assimilationists,* who are also defined as those who completely absorb the dominant culture. Although assimilationists believe that complete absorption into the dominant culture ensures acceptance, they may experience rejection from the members of their own cultural group. Assimilationists also lose their original cultural identity, which may later cause guilt and isolation.

acculturated—
competent in host culture, but maintains own cultural identity as more essential.

LaFramboise and associates define individuals who are competent in a second culture without completely accepting it as being **acculturated**. This group seems to mirror integrationists in that people are able to show competence within the dominant culture. The difference is that individuals who are classified as acculturated

TABLE 5.3   LaFramboise and Associates' Model of Acculturation

Status	Brief Description
Assimilationist	An individual who completely accepts the host culture's values and beliefs
Acculturated	Being competent in the host culture without giving up one's culture of origin or completely accepting the new culture
Fusion	The process of combining one's culture of origin with the host culture, creating a somewhat new culture
Alternation	The process of alternating between one's culture of origin and the host culture depending on what the context dictates
Multiculturalist	An individual who understands that his/her culture of origin is acceptable by the host culture as one of many cultures connected by the social structure

are always identified as members of the minority culture, and they are relegated to a lower status and not completely accepted, even given their capabilities. Chao, Chen, Roisman, and Hong (2007) might call these individuals "bicultural essentialists" who believe that there is an essential quality to their ethnicity. Such individuals may experience more difficulties in switching between cultures than they consciously realize.

Another group defined by LaFramboise and associates (1993) is characterized by **fusion.** This idea is similar to the melting pot theory, wherein individuals come together to form a new, homogenous culture from parts of the different cultures. Fusion differs from Berry's assimilation group because aspects of multiple cultures are integrated into a new culture. Cultures of origin are not distinct and identifiable (LaFramboise et al., 1993). Fusion can sometimes be used as an excuse to "not see color" or other differences among people, which some people may argue is the perpetuating principle behind continuing racist acts.

fusion–the process whereby one's culture is completely dissolved into other cultures, forming a new, homogenous culture.

A group that seems to have similarities with Berry's (1990, 1997) integrationist model is the **alternation** group (LaFramboise et al., 1993). This group regards two cultures as equal. An individual does not have to choose between the two cultures and can alter his or her behaviors to fit the context. LaFramboise and associates see this group as the optimal one, just as Berry (1990, 1997) describes the integrationist group as his most positive one. Though the alternation group is optimal and many people would wish to be able to adjust themselves according to context, this kind of life is not easy. It is not always possible to maintain positive relationships, even when an individual can adapt and adjust accordingly. However, there does seem to be some evidence that individuals can master this process (Devos, 2006).

alternation–competence in both the host culture and one's original culture such that one is able to apply the values and behaviors that are appropriate for the situation.

The **multicultural** group, according to LaFramboise (1993), involves cultures with distinct identities joined together within a social structure. Individuals from one culture cooperate with those of other cultures to serve common needs. This is different from the melting pot notion in that each subculture can maintain its identity while living among others without necessarily assimilating or completely adopting the others' cultures. This group may be more accurately described by Jesse Jackson's[1] pluralistic quilt idea, in which each culture can be seen apart from the others, yet are all joined within the "same blanket." This is the optimal and most extreme definition of the multicultural model. When there is interaction, however, there also tends to be mutual influence, and cultures of origin tend not to be distinctly maintained. Thus, the multicultural group is difficult to achieve in practice (LaFramboise et al., 1993).

multicultural perspective–the perspective that there are multiple groups within a society and all groups are mutually appreciated.

The Berry and LaFramboise models of acculturation help us to determine the ways that people adapt to this society. These models could apply not only to immigrants and refugees but also to members of minority cultures who are trying to adapt successfully. However, as stated before, the process of acculturation and the success of immigrants who are attempting to adjust to a new culture can be

---

1. In his 1988 presidential campaign, Jesse Jackson described "a quilt of many colors" sewn by his grandmother. He said that a single patch of color was not large enough to provide warmth, but that when it was combined with other patches of color, the result was a quilt that could keep someone warm and safe.

determined by their experiences before, during, and after their arrival in the host country.

The Migration Process

There are three phases of migration to consider when speaking of immigrants and refugees: *premigration, migration,* and *postmigration* (Hong & Ham, 2001). The **premigration** period refers to the time before individuals leave their country of origin. We must consider the established set of values, beliefs, and familial relations imposed on individuals by the norms of their culture. Disruption of set patterns and norms can affect each person differently, sometimes depending on the age at departure to another country. Immigrants' experiences during the premigration period determine how readily able they will be to tolerate outside experiences and, at times, an imposed set of norms. In the premigration period, we must also consider rituals that are looked upon as "abnormal" in the host country; after migration, individuals often do not feel that they have the freedom to practice rituals that have been an important part of their lives. These individuals usually must reestablish their rituals in certain ethnic communities where they are welcome.

The second phase, **migration,** refers to the experience of actually leaving the country of origin. This phase includes the feelings of the migrating individuals when they are close to departure, saying goodbye to family members and friends, and then traveling. While they are departing, they have the opportunity to really think about the decision they have made, finalized by their departure. Some may feel fear and apprehension, and others may avoid having expectations for fear of disappointment. The separation from what is "known," safe, and comfortable may bring about feelings of isolation, loss, trauma, and sometimes suicidal ideation (Hovey, 2000). Still, people who leave their countries of origin often do so in search of something better than what they have had, so that they are somewhat prepared for the unknown. Immigrants have usually been prepared by social networks of people who already reside in the host country, so the shock of relocation is lessened.

The **postmigration** phase refers to the continued stress experienced by immigrants, specifically related to new societal and cultural contexts. An individual may experience feelings of ambiguity and confusion because of the desire to hold on to his or her own cultural beliefs while living in a country that holds different and sometimes opposing cultural views. The postmigration period is when language, new roles and hierarchies, education, and employment begin to change. Individuals who are unable to change during the postmigration period may suffer financially, emotionally, and/or mentally.

If we refer back to our two chapter-opening stories of the Vietnamese man and the immigrant family from the Philippines, we can see how the phases of migration become an important aspect to consider in predicting the outcome of the people's lives in the stories. Generally, the differences in the outcomes of their stories are rooted in the way they left their native countries and the resources they had when settling into their host country. Unfortunately, when we talk about adaptation, acculturation, and cultural issues, there is no one concept that can

---

premigration period—the time period before migration, when the acculturation process can begin to take place.

migration period—the period when a group is migrating from the country of origin to the host country. This includes the period immediately before the migration, when the final feelings about moving are experienced and leave is taken from family and friends from the country of origin.

postmigration period—the period after settling into the host culture, when the stress of migration continues to be experienced and the adjustment to the new culture takes place.

explain how some people end up living here successfully, whereas others continue to struggle for the rest of their lives.

Some people ask, "If one person were to successfully adapt within the host culture but also hold on to the most important cultural beliefs from their country of origin, could they be promised success?" Given that a glass ceiling exists for many people who were born into this society, can we honestly say that immigrants have a chance regardless of whether they assimilate or adopt a multicultural perspective?

We continue to ponder such questions because there is a lack of research on familial relations and outcome of migration (Kaslow, 1996). In addition, we have only recently begun to really push for multicultural research, which involves the study of topics ranging from migration to racism. For now, we can focus on the information that we have learned from past researchers. How can we determine how certain individuals become "more successful" in their lives after migrating to a new country?

Ecological Context and Fit

As one approach, consider some researchers' suggestions of a necessary ecological fit for migrating individuals (Falicov, 1996; Hong & Ham, 2001). By **ecological fit** or **ecological context,** we mean the degree to which there is a match between the sociocultural environment in the migrant's culture of origin and the country to which they are immigrating. Several layers of ecological context must be considered, and we cannot stress enough how important an individual's context is as he or she moves from the smallest layer or system of ecological context to the largest. Modified from Bronfenbrenner's (1979) model, the layers are *microsystem, mesosystem, exosystem,* and *macrosystem* (Figure 5.1). These layers are relevant

ecological fit/ ecological context— similarity of the social and cultural environments between an immigrant's country of origin and new host country.

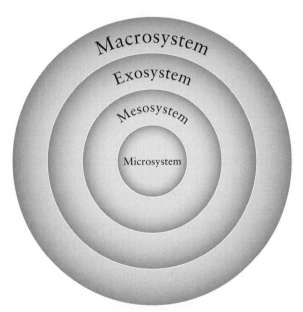

FIGURE 5.1 Bronfenbrenner's (1979) ecological model.

to acculturation because of possible stressors that exist within each layer and that may dictate an individual's degree of acculturation.

The **microsystem** includes relationships among family members. These relationships primarily involve the immediate family living in the same household. The **mesosystem** extends to relationships outside the family but is limited to the school, the workplace, extended families, and the community in which one lives. The **exosystem** involves the major societal institutions, such as the media, the government, and laws. Finally, the **macrosystem** encompasses the cultural norms and societal rules that determine the overall exchanges and interactions of the society in which we live. These four systems are interrelated, which means that things occurring at the smallest level of context can affect what occurs in the largest context (Hong & Ham, 2001).

When we observe the migration process, we can imagine how a person's ecological fit is disrupted. Immigrants and refugees are moved from a familiar environment where the rules of the government and their communities are well defined. During their flight or migration, their context changes, and all that they are familiar with becomes the unknown. We can see that as they go through the different stages of migration (premigration, migration, and postmigration), they will experience changes within the different layers or systems. Such changes are inevitable because of the different belief system and cultural norms that exist in their host country.

We can begin to see how the different systems are made up of a person's family, language, roles, and beliefs, but the geographical context also becomes an issue. In considering individuals outside the majority culture, intersecting layers of issues must be discussed within the same context. We cannot describe the reasons an individual has for leaving his or her country of origin without describing the changes that individual must endure. Additionally, the changes come from imposed rules within the host culture and affect rules learned from the country of origin. The changes, sometimes drastic, that take place during and after migration result in culture shock and acculturative stress. Most minority culture members must make a choice between holding on to their own culture and adopting the majority culture.

More specifically, certain migrating groups experience more culture shock and acculturative stress than do others. How can we explain that? Again, we go back to the question of which variables are to be taken into consideration when looking at a healthy acculturation process.

We can see that the reason behind the need to migrate to another country is where we should begin in consideration of the acculturation process. Although we noted earlier that the acculturation process is not limited to immigrants and refugees, most of our discussion related to the issues of migrating individuals. Individuals who undergo the process of acculturation and are natural citizens of this country do not experience the stressors of premigration and migration. They may share some postmigration experiences of immigrants and refugees, mainly involving stereotypes, prejudice, and discrimination.

Immigrants and refugees face the challenge of holding on to their own beliefs while they attempt to succeed in their host country. They must learn a different

microsystem—
a layer of context that includes relationships among family members living within one household.

mesosystem—
a layer of context that includes relationships in the immediate area outside the family, such as schools, work, the extended family, and the community in which one lives.

exosystem—a layer of context that includes major societal institutions, such as the media and the government.

macrosystem—
a layer of context that includes the cultural norms and societal rules that determine rules of conduct.

language and adapt to different roles to remain physically and mentally healthy. They have to deal with the changes that their children undergo and how those changes modify their family structure. They learn to accept their limitations and sharpen their skills so that they can maintain a certain lifestyle most befitting the "American dream."

SUMMARY

Quite often, people treat immigrants and refugees as being essentially the same. Both categories are people who come from foreign lands. However, there are some important psychological differences. Immigrants are those who decide to come to the United States for economic, political, and/or personal reasons. They plan to immigrate to the United States, and that planning process can take years. Thus, the acculturation process starts even before immigrants come to this country. They learn about U.S. culture and its norms, decide if those norms are consonant with their view of the world, and carefully decide where in the United States they will settle. Quite often, they have family and friends here who can assist in their immigration process or at least help them with the kinds of norms and services that can be of assistance.

In contrast, refugees have very little time to make their decisions to leave their homelands, often only a few hours. They do not want to leave their homelands but perhaps oppose those in power and have to flee political upheaval or the threat of death. They do not know where they will finally settle, since their overriding motivation to leave is to save their lives. After they leave their homelands, they typically are held in refugee camps that are overcrowded and unsanitary. Throughout the process of leaving (before, during, and after), refugees often experience a great deal of trauma, such as seeing family members and friends die or going through extreme hardships of transit. As a result of these circumstances, the acculturation process cannot begin before the refugees arrive in their host countries.

Once in their host countries, both immigrants and refugees must acculturate to their new surroundings; that is, they must adjust to the new country, with its unfamiliar customs and values. Among the challenges they face are language barriers, new family roles, employment opportunities, and educational opportunities. Quite often, children learn the new language much faster than do the parents and are able to interact with the social agencies of the new country. This gives the children more power than their parents have and leads to a disruption of the family hierarchy.

Researchers have developed models of acculturation that identify various resolutions of acculturation, such as maintaining two different cultural competencies, holding on to the traditional culture, blending the two cultures, or being confused about cultural issues. The degree to which immigrants and refugees successfully adjust to their host culture depends upon the degree to which they can successfully negotiate the blending of their traditional values with the new values of their host cultures.

Food for Thought

Most of you are in colleges and universities that have immigrants and refugees who have recently settled in the United States. If you know any immigrants or refugees, ask them if they might be willing to tell you why their families came to the United States. Were they immigrants or refugees? Note that some people came to the United States as small children and might not know all the circumstances that brought them here. If you engage in a conversation with an immigrant or a refugee, you might want to ask them if their parents feel a need to talk about their reasons for coming to the United States. More often than not, people want their stories heard, and you and your colleagues might be able to learn something from their parents.

Critical Thinking Questions

What is the history of your family in America? What hardships did your family experience when coming to America? What were the conditions of your family's ancestral homeland before they came to America?

If you are an American Indian, what hardships did your family encounter when it came in contact with European Americans/Whites? What were the conditions of your family's ancestral home before it came in contact with European Americans/Whites?

If your family immigrated to America, did it settle in an area known for immigrants from your family's country, or did it settle in an area that was widely integrated?

If your family immigrated to America, did your ancestors speak English, or did they have to learn English after arriving here? If they spoke a non-English language, what issues did your family encounter?

What roles within your family changed after your family arrived in America? How would you characterize yourself according to the acculturation models? Are you different from others in your family? If so, what are these differences?

CHAPTER 6

Stereotyping, Prejudice, Discrimination, and Racism

There's an old story about an elementary teacher. Her name was Mrs. Thompson. And as she stood in front of her fifth-grade class on the very first day of school, she told the children a lie. Like most teachers, she looked at her students and said that she loved them all the same.

But that was impossible, because there in the front row, slumped in his seat, was a little boy named Teddy Stoddard. Mrs. Thompson had watched Teddy the year before and noticed that he didn't play well with the other children, that his clothes were messy, and that he constantly needed a bath. And Teddy could be unpleasant. It got to the point where Mrs. Thompson would actually take delight in marking his papers with a broad red pen, making bold X's and then putting a big "F" at the top of his papers.

At the school where Mrs. Thompson taught, she was required to review each child's past records, and she put Teddy's off until last. However, when she reviewed his file, she was in for a surprise.

Teddy's first-grade teacher wrote, "Teddy is a bright child with a ready laugh. He does his work neatly and has good manners . . . he is a joy to be around."

His second-grade teacher wrote, "Teddy is an excellent student, well-liked by his classmates, but he is troubled because his mother has a terminal illness and life at home must be a struggle."

His third-grade teacher wrote, "His mother's death had been hard on him. He tries to do his best, but his father doesn't show much interest, and his home life will soon affect him if some steps aren't taken."

Teddy's fourth-grade teacher wrote, "Teddy is withdrawn and doesn't show much interest in school. He doesn't have many friends and he sometimes sleeps in class."

By now, Mrs. Thompson realized the problem, and she was ashamed of herself. She felt even worse when her students brought her Christmas presents, wrapped in beautiful ribbons and bright paper, except for Teddy's. His present was clumsily wrapped in the heavy brown paper that he got from a grocery bag.

Mrs. Thompson took pains to open it in the middle of the other presents. Some of the children started to laugh when she found a rhinestone bracelet with some of the stones missing, and a bottle that was one quarter full of perfume. But she stifled the children's laughter when she exclaimed how pretty the bracelet was, putting it on, and dabbing some of the perfume on her wrist.

Teddy Stoddard stayed after school that day just long enough to say, "Mrs. Thompson, today you smelled just like my mom used to." After the children left she cried for at least an hour. On that very day, she quit teaching reading and writing and arithmetic. Instead, she began to teach children.

Mrs. Thompson paid particular attention to Teddy. As she worked with him, his mind seemed to come alive. The more she encouraged him, the faster he responded.

By the end of the year, Teddy had become one of the smartest children in the class and, despite her lie that she would love all the children the same, Teddy became one of her "teacher's pets."

A year later, she found a note under her door from Teddy, telling her that she was still the best teacher he ever had in his whole life.

Six years went by before she got another note from Teddy. He then wrote that he had finished high school, third in his class, and she was still the best teacher he ever had in his whole life.

Four years after that, she got another letter, saying that while things had been tough at times, he'd stayed in school, had stuck with it, and would soon graduate from college with the highest of honors. He assured Mrs. Thompson that she was still the best and favorite teacher he ever had in his whole life.

Then four more years passed and yet another letter came. This time he explained that after he got his bachelor's degree, he decided to go a little further. The letter explained that she was still the best and favorite teacher he ever had. But now his name was a little longer—the letter was signed Theodore F. Stoddard, M.D.

The story doesn't end there. You see, there was yet another letter that spring. Teddy said he'd met this girl and was going to be married. He explained that his father had died a couple of years ago, and he was wondering if Mrs. Thompson might agree to sit in the place at the wedding that was usually reserved for the mother of the groom. Of course, Mrs. Thompson did.

And guess what? She wore that bracelet, the one with several rhinestones missing. And she made sure she was wearing the perfume that Teddy remembered his mother wearing on their last Christmas together.

They hugged each other, and Dr. Stoddard whispered in Mrs. Thompson's ear, "Thank you, Mrs. Thompson, for believing in me. Thank you so much for making me feel important and showing me that I could make a difference."

Mrs. Thompson, with tears in her eyes, whispered back. She said, "Teddy, you have it all wrong. You were the one who taught me that I could make a difference. I didn't know how to teach until I met you."

This story has been used repeatedly and in a wide variety of settings to inspire people—especially teachers—with the power of a single individual's influence on others' lives. Although the story is fictional, it illustrates what can happen when we help individuals in need and open them up to a world of possibilities. This version of the story traveled around the Internet a few years ago and has been published on Barbara and David Mikkelson's Web site (Mikkelson, 2005).

According to the Mikkelsons, the story was written by Elizabeth Ballard (now Elizabeth Ungar) for *Home Life* magazine in 1976. She combined two incidents—one she had heard of and one from her own life. In the first, a boy gave his Sunday school teacher a gift of perfume and a broken rhinestone bracelet. In the second, Ms. Ballard gave a box of handpicked pecans to her elementary school teacher. Her teacher stifled laughs from Ms. Ballard's classmates by saying that she was about to make some fruitcakes, and pecans were exactly what she needed to complete her baking. Thus, in a way, given how many lives Ms. Ballard has touched by writing this story, the essence of the Teddy Stoddard story is true.

As mentioned, this story is used primarily as a poignant way of inspiring teachers to inspire their own students. It appears in various forms on numerous Web sites (Cemy, no date; http://imateacher.itgo/three.htm; http://www.geocities .com/cubscoutpack501/WhyBeALeader.htm; http://www.hcc.hawaii.edu/intranet .committees/FacDevCom/guidebk/teachtip/m-files/m-3/lette.htm; http://www.k12 .wa.us/conferences/ospi2001/GomezPresentation/tsld001.htm; Vital Knowledge G.I.F.T.S., 2001). These Web sites actually number in the tens of thousands and contain different versions of the story. Why has the story become so popular? What is it about this story that resonates with people?

Besides demonstrating that "teachers can make a difference" (or, more broadly, that "people can make a difference") in other people's lives, this story also demonstrates how wrong we can be when we make judgments about others without really knowing their stories or personal histories. Let us explore this notion a bit further.

attribution theory—
a theory that
attempts to
determine the
cause of a behavior.
Two major
dimensions are
internal-external
and stable-unstable.

One of the more important theories in social psychology is **attribution theory** (Kelly, 1967, 1973), which describes how people explain the causes of human behavior. Attribution theory suggests that we use two primary dimensions to develop judgments (attributions) about others' behaviors: the internal–external dimension and the stable–unstable dimension. When combined, these two dimensions yield four possible explanations of another's behaviors: internal–stable, internal–unstable, external–stable, and external–unstable. For example, if you were to see Bobby hit Jimmy, you might say that Bobby is an aggressive child (an internal–stable attribution), that Bobby was in a bad mood (an internal–unstable attribution), that everyone hits Jimmy (an external–stable attribution, since this is external to Bobby), or that Jimmy just hit Bobby, so Bobby reciprocated (an external–unstable attribution) (Table 6.1).

TABLE 6.1 Attribution Theory: Four Kinds of Attributions for Bobby Hitting Jimmy

	Internal	External
Stable	Internal–Stable: Bobby is an aggressive child	External–Stable: Everyone hits Jimmy
Unstable	Internal–Unstable: Bobby was in a bad mood	External–Unstable: Jimmy just hit Bobby

According to Lee Ross (1977), we have a tendency to overuse dispositional (internal–stable) attributions and to underestimate external causes for behaviors. Thus, of the four attributions, we tend to believe that Bobby is an aggressive child before we believe any of the other three possible explanations of his behavior. This tendency is called the **fundamental attribution error** (Ross, 1977). Our assessment may or may not be an error, but if we ignore possible external reasons for certain behavior, then we may be committing this error. For example, Bobby may actually be an aggressive child, so our attribution of him as an aggressive child may be accurate. However, if he is *not* an aggressive child and we fail to take into account that Jimmy just hit him, we would be committing the fundamental attribution error if we were to assume that Bobby is aggressive. The tendency to commit the fundamental attribution error may be more of a Western error, because there are some indications that Eastern Asians do not have this tendency (Choi, Nisbett, & Norenzayan, 1999).

Let us consider the Teddy Stoddard story once again. How many of you automatically thought that Teddy Stoddard was a White child? That was our immediate reaction, too. Mrs. Thompson (whom we might also have assumed to have been White) turned this child's life around and made him a productive member of society. However, let us engage in a thought experiment: Suppose that Teddy Stoddard was an African-American child and Mrs. Thompson was White. What might have been the result? Mrs. Thompson might have responded in a different manner, still compassionate and caring, but different. She might have thought, Oh, what a shame that this child has had such a hardship! I should not be so hard on him. Maybe I will grade his papers with a bit more leniency.

We bring this up because in the story, Mrs. Thompson reacted to Teddy as an individual, and she gave him a kind of encouragement that resulted in his blossoming into a success story. In our thought experiment, Mrs. Thompson sees Teddy as a representative of all African-American children. Her caring for him might not have resulted in his flourishing but, rather, in his recognizing that not all White people are bad and that some will treat him with more kindness than others do. He might not necessarily have flourished intellectually but, rather, might have been less unforgiving toward Whites who treated him with less compassion. One of the challenges that ethnic minority individuals face is that the White majority culture tends to engage in another kind of attributional error: the **ultimate attribution error**. Thomas Pettigrew (1979) coined this term to mean that when attributions are directed toward individuals who represent a particular group, the internal and stable attributions are ascribed to the group members instead of just the individual. Again, in the case of Bobby hitting Jimmy, if Bobby were an African-American child, an ultimate attribution error would be to say that "African-American children are so aggressive" instead of limiting the aggression to Bobby. A student related the following story of the ultimate attribution error.

> Last week I was in the bank with a friend. As we waited in the long line, many people began to become impatient. The man two people in front of us in line was finally called to the window. It was soon very

fundamental attribution error–the tendency to overestimate dispositional (internal, stable) causes of behaviors and to underestimate external causes of behaviors.

ultimate attribution error–the tendency to ascribe the cause of a behavior to dispositional characteristics of the group rather than to an individual member.

clear that the bank would not cash his check. He calmly explained that the check was a payroll check, not a personal check, so there should not be any reason that they could not cash it. The bank teller told him that he could deposit the check, but his account would be on hold until the following Monday. He was obviously very upset by this and started yelling to speak to the manager. When the manager told him the same thing that the teller told him he became irate: he yelled, screamed, and hit the glass with his fists. Soon after the incident, the police came to make the man leave.

This story was multiculturally important to me because of the comments that were made by some of the other bank customers. The angry man was African American. People made terrible comments about him such as "That man is crazy" and "I wonder if he's on drugs." The worst comments that I heard were "Black people have short tempers" and "He's the type that give Black men a bad name." There were also other comments made attributing the man's behavior to his ethnicity. Nobody even stopped to think that maybe he was just having a bad day or a bad week and this incident was just the last straw. Maybe he needed that money to go grocery shopping for his family or to buy something important. I could not help but think that if he had been a White man their reactions would have been different. I believe that if the man had been White, people still would have made some of the comments that I heard, but I am certain that I would not have heard anybody attribute his behavior to his ethnicity. Nobody would have generalized his behavior by saying that all White people have short tempers.

AMY, 20+-YEAR-OLD WHITE WOMAN

CATEGORIZATIONS OF RACE AND ETHNICITY

I have a European-American friend who has for most of her life lived in a "white" community. I, on the other hand, have grown up with people of all ethnic backgrounds. When I met her, my first thought was that we would get along great. We had common interests and similar taste. The more we spent time together the more I realized she expressed herself as being superior. . . .

I recently bought a Louis Vuitton purse. For people who know about this couture brand, these bags are quite costly, ranging from $300 to $3500 dollars. When I received my bag I was ecstatic about my purchase and called everyone I knew to share the good news that I had one of the most popular couture bags in Southern California. When I called my friend "Brooke" (not her real name) she stood quiet for a second. When she finally spoke she said that it was impossible for me to buy such a costly bag. She said that whoever sold it to me had ripped

me off and sold me a knock off. I had explained that the bag I
purchased was at a price of over $600 and that it was definitely real.
What was mostly heartbreaking about this situation was that she
laughed at me, on the phone, and started chanting to her dorm friends,
or anyone who would listen, that her friend had just been made a fool
and had a fake bag. It was as if I had no common sense and most of all
didn't have the funds to have an item such as this.

A few weeks ago, I was talking with Brooke and she made an
indirect comment that Mexican people are mostly poor. It didn't occur
to me that I was included in this category of people until she stated that
I couldn't afford something that only wealthy people could afford. Or
should I say that only "white" people could afford. I have come to the
realization that there are many people like Brooke. These people look at
minority groups as not having the ability to live up to a higher standard
of living.

LAUREL, 20+-YEAR-OLD MEXICAN-AMERICAN WOMAN

Was Laurel's story one of stereotyping, prejudice, discrimination, or racism? Most social psychologists make a distinction among these forms of racial/ethnic categorization. Myers (2008) describes the differences as:

- **Stereotype**—a generalization about a group or its members on the basis of their categorization. A stereotype can be an accurate reflection of a group's norm; can be an overgeneralization, applying the norm to every member of the group or not allowing for variation about this norm; or can be simply inaccurate. Stereotypes are cognitive categorizations of people made on the basis of some demographic characteristic and do not necessarily convey positive or negative evaluations. For example, to say that Asians tend to be more collectivistic than Whites is an accurate stereotype. To insist that all Asians are collectivistic is an overgeneralization. However, to say that Asians are collectivistic is not to make a positive or a negative assessment of Asians on the basis of this categorization. Stereotypes are considered to be the *cognitive component* of categorization.

  stereotype–a generalization about a group or its members based upon their categorization.

- **Prejudice**—a judgment about a group or its members on the basis of their categorization. This judgment may be positive or negative, but it is typically thought to be negative. For example, someone may be prejudiced against Asians because they are collectivistic and tend to suppress individual freedoms or not express individualistic creativities. Prejudices are considered to be the *evaluative component* of categorization.

  prejudice–a negative judgment about a group or its members based upon their categorization.

- **Discrimination**—a negative behavior toward a group or its members on the basis of their categorization. For example, an Asian individual may not be selected for an assignment because it is assumed that this individual's collectivistic tendencies will not allow him or her to be creative enough. Discrimination is considered to be the *behavioral component* of categorization.

  discrimination–a negative behavior toward a group or its members based upon their categorization.

racism–
discriminatory
behavior that is
backed by
institutional power.

- **Racism**—discriminatory behavior that has institutional power behind it. This applies to those with institutional backing (those on the upside of power) who discriminate against individuals on the downside of power. For example, an individual may discriminate against an Asian individual and be backed by institutions of power. Most social psychologists feel that racism is a routine mistreatment of individuals on the downside of power, meaning that the mistreatment is part of institutional practices. Racism is considered to be the *institutional component* of categorization.

The description of racism also applies to other "isms," such as sexism, ageism, ableism, heterosexism, and anti-Semitism and other forms of religious discrimination. Institutional practices of the dominant society tend to suppress members of the nondominant parts of society. A former student wrote about her encounter with ageism:

In my community psychology class, every student had to do eight hours of community service. I did my community service at a convalescent home. It was interesting. While I was changing the decorations in the lunchroom, I noticed that there was an elderly woman who was crying and screaming. None of the other workers or nurses seemed to pay any attention to her. I also noticed that she was speaking in both English and Tagalog (the national language of the Philippines). This went on for about twenty minutes until finally one of the workers went to take the lady to her room. I asked that worker if the lady, Monica, could sit next to me while I was working. When Monica came over to sit next to me I asked her if she was Filipina, and I asked if she spoke Tagalog. She said yes and we started to have a conversation about the Philippines. She sat next to me for about an hour talking without screaming and crying. This was really amazing to me. Here was someone who just needs someone to talk to about something that she could relate to. It was amazing to see that just knowing a little bit about the Philippines and knowing only a few words would be an icebreaker between Monica and me. To me this just goes to show that understanding an individual's culture and background can do a lot. I hope that perhaps the elderly lady, Monica, for that hour felt really good having someone to talk to.

JESSICA, 20+-YEAR-OLD BIRACIAL (MEXICAN/WHITE) WOMAN

The practice of "isms" may not be intentional, and once it is exposed, members of the dominant group may be motivated to change the behavior to be more fair. However, until exposure takes place, the practice may have an element of suppression. For example, most universities heavily weigh teaching and research productivity for purposes of making tenure decisions. Members of the dominant group may feel that this emphasis is fair because it applies to all individuals equally. However, many ethnic minority individuals may have been hired to help advise ethnic minority students, make public presentations to community organizations, and engage in other activities related to their unique status within the university and the community at large. Such activities necessarily take away from their ability to publish as much as their White colleagues or to spend as much time on their articles—thus their work may not be acceptable to "prestigious" journals. Therefore, when compared with their White colleagues, they may not be evaluated favorably. However, if such inequities are pointed out and if the institution is motivated to be fair, community activities may be given some value in the tenure process, and articles published in some ethnically focused journals may be considered to be as scholarly as those in "prestigious" journals.

Did you notice that "stereotyping" and "prejudice" are internal activities? If I hold a stereotypic attitude toward you, or even a prejudicial one, but keep that attitude to myself, you are not hurt. It is not until my attitude is expressed either behaviorally (discrimination) or institutionally (racism) that you get hurt. It is difficult to get stereotypic or prejudicial attitudes out of our system, since many of them are products of years of "learning" or exposure. However, if we can become aware of such attitudes and work to counteract them, we will not hurt others. Once we act upon them, we have crossed the line to discrimination and/or racism.

Getting back to our discussions of the Rodney King and Donovan Jackson cases, do you feel they are evidence of stereotyping, prejudice, discrimination, or racism? As you have probably figured out, those incidents are examples of racism. As we know, many African Americans are routinely mistreated by those in power, such as police officers. It seems that unless these routine mistreatments are caught on videotape and the outrage of society is brought to bear upon the perpetrators, such incidents will continue unabated. It's both surprising and saddening that 11 years after the Rodney King incident, Donovan Jackson was beaten in the same area where the King incident occurred.

Stereotype Threat

Suddenly I was in the middle of this test with the question laid out before me and I started to panic. What if I couldn't write a good essay? What if I couldn't pass this most basic test? I think I spent most of the 75 minutes trying to talk away my anxiety rather than concentrating on the questions. I finished that test knowing that I didn't do my best on it. And then it hit me . . . could this be stereotype threat? Is this the fear that I would be confirming a stereotype that Asians "no speakie goodie ingerish"? Is this what I have been reading about in class? . . . Am I now feeling the insidious nature of racism? I am starting to wonder if taking this class is making me paranoid or more aware. Or maybe giving me a healthy dose of both. (Asian/Pacific Island female college student) (Mio & Barker-Hackett, 2003, p. 15)

This paragraph was part of a weekly reaction paper assignment written by a former student. She was one of the brightest students in her particular graduate program, but she was overcome with self-doubt when she had to take a writing test that her university required for graduation. All students had to pass this test before they could receive a degree. Just before the exam, she looked around her and saw a number of Asian students who spoke English as a second language (ESL). She was aware that most ESL students did not pass this test the first time they took it, and she was concerned that she would be lumped together with them and be stereotyped negatively.

Claude Steele (1997) has written extensively about what he has termed **stereo-type threat**—the threat that individuals belonging to a group that is negatively stereotyped will in fact confirm that stereotype when confronted with a difficult task that purports to measure differences in abilities. For example, Steele and Aronson (1995) reported on freshman African-American students who were extremely accomplished in English, as measured by their verbal scores on the Scholastic Aptitude Test (SAT), and were given the Graduate Record Examination (GRE) subject test in English. This test was four years beyond their education level, but they did not know that it was designed for students far more advanced than they were at that time. Still, these African-American students performed just as well as their White counterparts did when both groups were led to believe that the test was simply a very difficult test that was being administered because they had previously proven how accomplished they were. However, when the students were led to believe that the test would measure differences between Blacks and Whites, African-American student performance went down.

The same pattern was demonstrated for women taking mathematics tests. Freshman women who had received extremely high quantitative scores on their SATs were given the GRE subject test in mathematics. Again, these women performed as well as their male counterparts did when they were led to believe that the test was simply a very difficult one. However, when they were led to believe that it might measure gender differences in mathematics, the women's scores went down. This pattern also seems true with respect to gender differences in political knowledge (McGlone & Neal, 2003).

Steele (2001) states that stereotype threat occurs under specific circumstances. First, an individual has to excel in an area that is against the stereotype. In the areas examined in Steele's earlier studies, African Americans are not stereotypically considered to excel in English in comparison with their White counterparts, women are not considered to excel in math in comparison with their male counterparts, and women are not considered to be as interested in politics as men are. And, as exemplified in the preceding story, Asians—especially ESL Asians—are not considered to be fluent in written or oral English skills.

Second, the stereotype has to be negative. Verbal and mathematical skills are highly valued, and deficits in those areas are considered to be negative; politics are important in that they relate to how the country is run. For example, Derald Wing Sue, one of the most respected names in multicultural psychology, jokes about his inability to dance, saying that Asians are not really expected to dance well. Thus, although that is a negative stereotype about Asians, deficits in dancing are not threatening, because dancing is not a highly valued skill in mainstream America. However, if one does not speak English well in this country, one is considered to be less intelligent.

Third, the area in which the individual excels has to be important to him or her. The African-American and female research participants in Steele's earlier

stereotype threat– a fear that one will confirm the negative stereotype of a group to which one belongs in an area in which the individual excels.

studies excelled in English and mathematics, respectively, in high school, and they valued those skills. They were at the top of their high school classes and received much recognition for their accomplishments. The Asian student taking the writing test was in a graduate program learning to become a therapist, and obviously, verbal fluency skills are important to a budding therapist.

Finally, the test of the individual's skills must be challenging. Quite clearly, tests four years beyond one's current training would be challenging. In the Asian student example, the writing test was not difficult and merely involved developing a written argument about a topic; but because failing the test would mean not receiving a degree from the university; it was a "high stakes" test.[1]

Steele (2001) reasoned that the internal dialogue of victims of stereotype threat goes something like this: "Oh, no! I thought I was bright in this area, but now I am not performing well. I wonder if the stereotypes are true. Could it be that I have hit the limits of my abilities? Is my failure in this area only confirming the negative stereotypes that people have about me and people like me?" Contrast this internal dialogue with that of someone who is not threatened by such a negative stereotype: "Gosh, this test is hard!" The internal dialogue for these individuals is not as complex as the internal dialogue for those who are threatened by negative stereotypes. The internal dialogue for such threatened individuals adds a greater amount of stress, which interferes with their abilities to perform.

Steele (2001) suggests that none of us is immune from negative stereotypes. He cited a study conducted at a major university on White and Black athletes. As we know, the negative stereotype for White athletes is that they are not as naturally athletic as their Black counterparts, and the negative stereotype for Black athletes is that they do not think as well as their White counterparts. The researchers of this study told half of the group of athletes that a certain miniature golf course measured one's true athletic abilities, and they told the other half that the course measured one's ability to engage in complex planning. As would be predicted by the stereotype threat theory, the White athletes performed worse than their Black counterparts when told that the course measured true athletic abilities, and the Black athletes performed worse than their White counterparts when told that the course measured complex planning abilities.

How would you respond? Have you ever been in a situation in which you were performing some kind of activity that might support a negative stereotype about a group to which you belonged? Did your fear of confirming the stereotype interfere with your performance? If so, then you have firsthand experience of stereotype threat. According to Steele and his colleagues (Murphy, Steele, & Gross, 2007; Steele, 1997, 2001; Steele & Aronson, 1995), the signal of the threat can be very subtle. For example, Murphy et al. (2007) signaled the threat subtly by simply showing women taking math, science, or engineering (MSE) courses videotapes of such courses either having a balance of men and women taking the

---

1. Students are allowed to take this written test multiple times in order to pass it and receive a degree. However, failure on this test even once is a blow to the self-esteem of a student who is bright, so even the brightest students feel pressure when taking this test.

courses or of men far outnumbering the women. Remember, this happens only if you have high ability in a particular area, performing well is part of your identity, and the task you are doing is difficult (or there is pressure on you to perform exceptionally well on the task).

The Development of Negative Stereotypes

A biracial student wrote in one of her weekly reaction papers the following story about being stereotyped as a hoodlum:

> *After working out at [name of fitness center] in Sherman Oaks I noticed two security guards. They were both White males. One was on his walkie-talkie, and I just knew he was on the radio about us. I turned to my friend and said, "Oh gosh, here we go, I bet they have something to say . . ." I turned the corner and the other security guard put his radio away, and walked up toward me. With his eyes toward my basketball, he asked, "Is that the property of [name of fitness center]?" I said, "No, there is no basketball court, or basketballs at that facility. I'm sure [name of fitness center] didn't call you and complain about it."*
>
> *So, he followed me as I continued to walk toward the parking lot. I was bouncing the ball in the outdoor area. He said, "Don't bounce your ball on our floors." I was pretty upset, and I replied, "Am I disturbing the stores that are all closed, and the people that are not shopping or eating? Is it wrong to bounce my ball on your floors of dirty concrete and old pieces of gum? My ball is cleaner than your floor. I am disturbing no one." He stood quiet. Suddenly, there was a Black security guard. When I looked back the other security guard was walking away, now at a far distance.*
>
> *I couldn't figure out what had happened. I felt picked on, and belittled. I felt like I was some hoodlum who hadn't accomplished anything in life, and was destructive, as this is how I was treated. I realized that it just doesn't always matter who I am. People such as those guards will only see my outsides. I did notice their confusion from the way I spoke. My speaking probably wasn't what they expected from a Black person in sweats and a bandana. But, my way of speaking wouldn't outweigh my color, probably."*

TERRI, 20+-YEAR-OLD BIRACIAL (AFRICAN-AMERICAN/FILIPINA) WOMAN

How are negative stereotypes developed? Why do people hold such views? There are at least two ways in which such stereotypes are developed. One is somewhat benign and the other is somewhat malicious.

Hamilton and his colleagues have discussed how negative stereotypes can develop out of normal cognitive processes (Hamilton, 1981; Hamilton, Dugan, & Trolier, 1985; Hamilton & Gifford, 1976; Hamilton & Rose, 1980; Hamilton & Sherman, 1989, 1994, 1996; Hamilton & Trolier, 1986). Essentially, this perspective suggests that ethnic minorities (and other numerical and identifiable minorities) are labeled with negative stereotypes because of an overestimation of negative behaviors that occur with their minority status. Hamilton says that when two minority events co-occur, there is a natural cognitive process that takes notice of that co-occurrence. Because special note is taken, the overestimation occurs. Hamilton states that negative events are not as frequent as positive events in our lives. If an ethnic minority individual—who is in the statistical minority and by definition is less frequently encountered by the majority population—engages in a negative behavior, the observer sees two minority events happening together and registers that co-occurrence. Hamilton calls this overestimation **illusory correlation,** because the observer sees a correlation between the two events that really is not present. Thus, if Whites and Latinos have engaged in the same percentage of shoplifting in the past, store managers and workers may feel that Latinos engage in a higher amount of shoplifting (illusory correlation) because the co-occurrence of the minority group (Latinos) and the minority behavior (shoplifting) in the past had a greater impact upon perception.

illusory correlation–an overestimation of the co-occurrence of two minority events.

As evidence for this stance, Hamilton and his colleagues conducted a number of studies that demonstrated the relative ease with which illusory correlation can occur. They conducted these studies even without using ethnic minorities as experimental stimuli. Research participants received descriptors of two groups of people (Group A and Group B). Participants received 16 descriptions of positive behaviors and attributes of Group A and 8 negative descriptors. They also received 8 descriptions of positive behaviors and attributes of Group B and 4 negative descriptors. Thus, the participants received half as many descriptions of Group B as they did of Group A, and there were half as many negative descriptions as there were positive descriptions. In other words, both Group B and negative behaviors/attributes were minority events. Later, when the participants were asked to recall all the positive and negative events for both Groups A and B, they recalled about twice as many positive descriptors as negative descriptors for Group A (an accurate recollection), but they recalled about equal amounts of positive and negative descriptors for Group B (an overestimation of negative descriptors).

One way of understanding Hamilton's series of studies is to view illusory correlation as a form of Tversky and Kahneman's well-known **availability heuristic** (Tversky & Kahneman, 1973). A heuristic is a mental shortcut or rule of thumb used for making calculations or assessments of sometimes complex circumstances. Availability is a specific kind of heuristic in which the perception of frequency, importance, or probability of an event is based upon the ease with which this event comes to mind. In their original study, Tversky and Kahneman asked their research participants if there were more words that began with the letter *k* or words with the letter *k* in the third position. Many more participants said that there were more words that began with the letter *k* even though there are three times more words with *k* in the third position. Tversky and Kahneman suggested that since our minds are organized in something of a lexicon (dictionary-like) manner, it is easier to "look up" words that begin with the letter *k* than it is to look up words that have *k* in the third position. This relative ease in coming to mind was therefore translated into an assessment that there were more words that

availability heuristic–a mental shortcut whereby the importance, frequency, or credence of something is exaggerated because it comes to mind easily.

began with the letter k. If the co-occurrence (illusory correlation) of two minority events is noticed or registered more, it will come to mind more easily than the co-occurrence of two majority events or a majority and a minority event, so the co-occurring minority events will be judged to be more numerous or probable.

As the Tversky and Kahneman study on the letter k demonstrates, sometimes the availability heuristic can lead us to wildly disparate conclusions. Could it be that stores and shops are overlooking a number of shoplifters because they are overly focused upon ethnic minority customers? Quite possibly. The U.S. Government Accounting Office (2000) has found that this has been the case with screening airline passengers for possible drug trafficking. "Black and Hispanic men and women were about four to nine times more likely than White men and women to be x-rayed after being patted down or frisked" (2000, p. 13). Despite this disparity, ethnic minority women were actually *less* likely to be found with illegal drugs. "Hispanic women, for example, were four times as likely to be x-rayed as White women were, but they were about two thirds as likely to have contraband found during an x-ray" (p. 15). This GAO study concluded that the U.S. Customs Service would be more efficient if it did not engage in such biased racial profiling.

Many people recognize this racial profiling as "driving while Black" or "driving while Brown." A student of ours related this story:

> *The first week I arrived in this country, I was stopped by the police. He said I matched the description of someone spotted with a gun. He searched me and found nothing. I then inquired what the description was. The man they were looking for was Hispanic. The only matching aspect of our descriptions was that we were both wearing blue jeans.*

GODFREY, 20+-YEAR-OLD ZIMBABWEAN IMMIGRANT MAN

Of course, since Godfrey was driving, the police would not have seen his blue jeans, so they were obviously targeting him because of the color of his skin. Again, racial profiling is *inefficient* because the police have to spend some amount of time with an obviously innocent person while the real person who committed the crime is allowed more time to escape.

An extreme version of racial profiling was told to us by a former graduate student:

> *There was a commotion down the street from my apartment. There was a party, and someone shot off a gun. It took the police over an hour to get there. I was standing outside just to see what was going on.*
> *The police came up to me and questioned me about if I saw anything, and they eventually asked me if I had a gun. I said no, but I continued to watch what they were doing. They stopped every single ethnic minority person who walked by, despite the fact that the gun shot was at a party where there were almost exclusively White students and the alleged gunman was White.*

RAMÓN, 20+-YEAR-OLD MEXICAN-AMERICAN MAN

A former student who was conducting a literature search in preparation for a class project was astonished by the amount of racial profiling that has been documented:

This project has really opened my eyes and made me sick. I can't believe that racial profiling is as prevalent as it actually is. I just don't want to believe that people automatically think someone is guilty or suspicious just because their skin color is slightly different. I guess it's one of those things that has developed in America and appears to be beyond control. They have made it illegal but it still exists; what can we do to change it?

SCOTT, 20+-YEAR-OLD WHITE MAN

The less benign and more malicious reason negative stereotypes are developed is the need of those in power to justify the suppression of those out of power (Aronson, 1990; Mio, 2003). This stance is based upon **cognitive dissonance theory** (Festinger, 1957). According to Festinger, attitudes follow behavior. Cognitive dissonance theory suggests that when two cognitions are in conflict (dissonance), we are motivated to reduce that dissonance as we would be motivated to reduce hunger or thirst. Thus, if we were to observe ourselves behaving badly toward another person or a group of people, we might engage in the following internal dialogue: "I am a good person, but I behaved badly toward that other person. That person must have deserved such bad treatment." This reduces the dissonance and leaves us feeling justified in engaging in such negative behavior. As Aronson (1990) stated in his presidential address to the Western Psychological Association Convention, psychoanalytic theory suggested that if we felt hostility toward another individual, we should get the hostility out of our systems, and thus the process of catharsis would reduce our hostility toward that individual. However, cognitive dissonance theory predicted exactly the opposite (and more correct) result: "[I]f we hurt someone, it does not produce a release of hostile energy—on the contrary, it causes us to try to justify our actions by derogating our victim; this impels us to feel more hostility toward him, which opens the door for still further aggressions."

cognitive dissonance theory–a theory that suggests that when two cognitions are in conflict, a person will be motivated to change one of them to reduce the unsettled feelings caused by the discrepancy.

RACISM

Many people are familiar with the horrific case of Emmett Till (Williams, 1987). Till was a 14-year-old African-American boy from Chicago visiting his cousins in Mississippi. He was murdered, and his body was desecrated by Roy Bryant and J. W. Milam for simply saying "Bye, Baby" to Bryant's wife when leaving a general store. This was a famous case of racism made even more despicable by the fact that a defense lawyer addressed the all-White jury by concluding, "I'm sure that every last Anglo-Saxon one of you has the courage to free these men in the face of that [outside] pressure" (Williams, 1987, p. 52), and it took the jury one hour to find Bryant and Milam not guilty. They later acknowledged committing the murder because they were offended that Till would not beg for mercy for having flirted with Bryant's wife.

JEREMY, 40+-YEAR-OLD JAPANESE-AMERICAN MAN

The historic Black–White relationship has set the context within which racism has been discussed in the United States. The first African slaves in the United States arrived in 1619, when 20 slaves were sold to settlers in Virginia (Kitano, 1999). By 1860, shortly before the Civil War, nearly one-third of the population in slave-owning states and the District of Columbia were slaves (4 million out of 12.1 total people; Black, 1996). Although only 25% of the population actually owned slaves, the overwhelming majority of individuals in slave-owning states supported the practice for economic reasons. Moreover, "slavery also provided even the poorest of Whites with a sense of superiority over the African population, a superiority based on skin color" (Black, 1996, p. 58). For centuries, Whites tried to justify slavery, then segregation, then general mistreatment of African Americans in the United States. Consequently, institutional practices developed over the years disadvantaging African Americans and other ethnic minorities.

PICTURE 6.1   Overt forms of racism are more rare nowadays. *Photograph by Chris Dellosa*

Another example of overt racism in the United States comes from World War II. As most people know, Americans of Japanese ancestry in seven U.S. states (California, Idaho, Utah, Arizona, Wyoming, Colorado, and Arkansas) were "interned" (a euphemism for "imprisoned") during the war (Nagata, 1993, 1998). Following the attack on Pearl Harbor, the U.S. Government felt that these people were a threat to national security and removed them to concentration camps in the interior of the country. These Japanese Americans and resident aliens were transported with very little warning, and "evacuation sales" were forced upon many of them. The following is a story from such a sale.

> *We had two restaurants, and they were being taken away from us. In only a few days, I had to sell everything I could or else lose all that we had. I had to do this alone, because my husband was taken away the day the evacuation order was given because he was considered a community leader. All of these Americans came to our community to get the best deal they could. They didn't care that our lives were being taken away from us. I remember trying to sell one of our refrigerators for $10. A White woman said, "That refrigerator isn't worth $10. I wouldn't give you more than $5 for it." She was so uncaring; they were so uncaring. Our lives were bring ruined, and all they cared about was taking away our possessions for as little money as they could.*

MAKIKO, 80+-YEAR-OLD JAPANESE-AMERICAN WOMAN RECALLING HER EVACUATION SALE IN 1942 (TRANSLATED FROM JAPANESE)

Overt racism is often thought to be a relic of our past and not relevant to modern discussions of racism. In general, it is true that overt forms of racism are not as common as they used to be and that the public does not condone them. Modern forms of racism are much more subtle and much more difficult to detect. We need to be aware of them so that we can eliminate their influence on our everyday lives.

> *Our department was in the process of interviewing candidates for a tenure-track faculty position. As was our custom, each candidate interviewed with two faculty members at a time. On this particular day, I was paired up with one of our newest and youngest faculty members, a European-American male. The candidate was also a European-American male, but he was older, probably in his mid- to late-forties. We met in my office for the interview and, as the senior member of the team, I took the lead in asking the questions. I soon noticed that, although I asked most of the questions, the candidate directed all of his answers to my colleague. The candidate would not look at me, would not have eye contact with me, and even turned in his chair so he was facing my colleague. At the end of the interview, I stood up to shake the candidate's hand and say goodbye, but he turned his back and walked out the door and down the hallway without acknowledging me.*

I looked stunned, and so did my colleague, who turned and looked at me, a little red in the face, and just shrugged his shoulders. In the faculty meeting when we discussed the candidates, I shared this story and my colleague spoke up and confirmed that he experienced the interaction the same way I did. Interestingly, some other faculty members seemed to have been making excuses for his behavior, and one of the faculty members was even supportive of hiring him. However, fortunately, he had alienated many of the other female faculty members, too, and our department decided against making an offer to him.

LINDA, 30+-YEAR-OLD AFRICAN-AMERICAN WOMAN

This story illustrates a subtly (or not so subtly!) racist interaction that had costs for both the recipient and the offender. For the recipient, it was yet another slight in a long list of such insults. We all desire to have positive interactions, and each negative one stings us a little bit. For the offender, the obvious cost was that he was not offered a position in the department. A less apparent cost was that if this individual was completely unaware of how racist he came across in the interview, then he is destined to continue to offend others and be prevented from furthering his professional career. Our students have related many instances of modern forms of racism they have encountered:

As a Mexican-American female, I am always conscious of my racial identity, even though I have assimilated into the dominant culture. In American society, racial labels are very important. Everybody has to fit into a category. These categories allow people to generalize certain characteristics to a group. These stereotypes are often inaccurate. Recently, I was shopping at the Riverside Galleria, when an older white lady approached to ask me a question. Mistakenly, she confused me for a worker. It was an honest mistake until she questioned my ability to speak English. I was very offended by her preconceived notion. She presumed that because I am Latina, I must not speak English correctly. She did not realize how offensive her comment was and did not bother to apologize. On the other hand, I contemplate why this is a frequent encounter. As a minority, I am always pointed out that I am not part of the dominant society. I have done what society has asked me to do and assimilated. In the process, I lost my ancestral past. . . .

Recently I went to [name of store] with my mother to purchase her a perfume. A White female was working in the counter and refused to help me by pretending to be busy with paperwork. I stood at the counter for three minutes and no service. I finally left the counter and asked someone else to help me. The other salesperson was just as rude as the original clerk. Their behavior made me very uncomfortable and angry. At first, I just wanted to leave and not buy anything. I thought, Why should I spend my money here? But I did not leave. I was not going to let their discrimination break my spirit. My mother, on the other hand, was saddened by the experience. She refused the perfume I bought her because it was tainted by hate.

JUANITA, 20+-YEAR-OLD MEXICAN-AMERICAN WOMAN

When I first got the job I am currently at I had many problems with people talking about me and trying to keep me down. I am a very proud and intelligent person. I always held my head high no matter where I am and I believe they were very intimidated by that. Especially because I talked like I had some sense. Sometimes some of my co-workers would ask me if I was mixed because I don't talk "black," whatever that is supposed to mean. Even other African Americans tell me I talk white and that really upsets me because when they tell me that they are only bringing themselves down. When an African American tells me I talk like I am "white" just because I speak intelligently, it makes them look like they're unintelligent. Can't an African American speak intelligently without being told they are acting "white"?

ARIEL, 20+-YEAR-OLD AFRICAN-AMERICAN WOMAN

In the past, racism was overt and vicious; in the modern world, racism is disguised and subtle. To stop it, we must be able to identify modern forms of racism and make others aware of the ways in which they perpetuate it. Main forms of modern racism are *overt/covert racism* and *aversive racism*.

Overt versus Covert Racism

Ridley (1989, 1995) discussed the distinction between *overt* and *covert racism*. **Overt racism** is "old style" racism, in which those in the majority openly engaged in hostile and aggressive acts against ethnic minorities without fear of reprisal. Such acts included slavery, lynchings, and legal segregation (Jones, 1997). Jones's important book took a Black–White perspective, so those examples of overt racism are consistent with that theme. Hostility toward Blacks, the devastation of the American-Indian population and the later boarding-school phenomenon that took American-Indian children as young as 5 years old hundreds or thousands of miles away from their parents and tribes and "educated" them in Western ways (McDonald & Chaney, 2003; Tafoya & Del Vecchio, 1996), the internment of Americans of Japanese descent during World War II (Nagata, 1990a, 1990b, 1993, 1998), and social oppression of Latinos by the Immigration and Naturalization Service (Garcia-Preto, 1996) are just a few examples of how overt racism has affected the broad spectrum of ethnic minorities in the United States. While overt racism may be thought to be a thing of the past, many of our students have reported being the victim of overt racism or seeing it first hand:

I have personally been detained for reasons of DWB [driving while Black]. So often in fact that it was one of the first things I discussed

overt racism—
discriminatory behavior in which those in the majority engage in open, hostile acts of aggression against racial minorities consciously and unapologetically.

with my son when teaching him how to drive. "Always wear your seatbelt, signal long before you intend to turn, and when approached by the police, keep your hands on the steering wheel until instructed to move, and then do so slowly."

I have been given many excuses for being stopped including "you appeared to be weaving back there," and "we've had a rash of robberies in the area and are stopping everyone." But now and then a police officer will just come outright and state "this doesn't look like a car that you would own." Most of the time I simply sit quietly because if you speak up, you're asking for a ticket, or worse.

MIKE, 40+-YEAR-OLD AFRICAN-AMERICAN MAN

My best friend Theresa has been dating an African-American man for the past year. You would think that it wasn't a big deal, except she is white and her mother will not accept the relationship. . . . Obviously, this is very difficult for my friend. She cries almost once every week and often questions her relationship with her boyfriend. It is not his fault, however, there are times when she feels guilty, responsible for her mom's tears and disappointment. I personally have spent hours talking to her, reassuring her that her mom is wrong, that she is ignorant. At times I wonder if she will ever accept the relationship, what it would take for her to understand that she is racist?

Theresa's mother does not believe that she is a racist, nor that she is ignorant. When I come over to the house she yells at me, asking me what kind of friend I am to support this. Then she usually follows with questions about what kind of men I date and when I plan to start dating "blacks." It gives me the sickest feeling, I look at her with such shame. This is a woman that I once looked at as a second mother, never knowing her racist views. Now I am embarrassed to know her.

BARBARA, 20+-YEAR-OLD WHITE WOMAN

covert, intentional racism— discriminatory behavior that is intentional but is covered up so that one can deny that one is racist.

Ridley (1995) identified *covert racism* as a modern form of racism that seems subtle and even deniable. According to Ridley, covert racism can be either *intentional* or *unintentional*. **Covert, intentional racism** occurs when individuals are aware that they are acting in racist manners but try to disguise their true intent with a plausible story. For example, during a particular period of time, a public school system was having extremely severe financial difficulties [the particular school system, the time period, and the mayor are not being identified to protect the guilty]. When an outside consultant examined the financial books, the consultant found that the city had built 25 percent more schools than were ever needed. A friend of ours who grew up in the area knew exactly why this was, and he related this story to us:

Everyone knew that Mayor X was racist. Whenever an area began having more Black students near a White neighborhood, Mayor X would just build a new school in the Black area to keep the Black children from going to White schools. When questioned about this, he would always say that he was building a new school out of some discretionary funds he had, and that he was not being racist at all. In fact, he was helping these Black children by giving them a more modern school with modern facilities that the White schools didn't have. When he died, it was discovered that there was no "slush fund" at all, and he just built these schools with money he didn't have. That is why the school system is in such financial straits right now.

SEAN, 30+-YEAR-OLD EUROPEAN-AMERICAN MAN

Many people believe that affirmative action is an issue that draws covert, intentional racists. Certainly, there are individuals who want to eliminate affirmative action for principled reasons, such as the ideal of equality for all and the belief that favoring one group over another necessarily discriminates against the group not being favored. However, other individuals oppose affirmative action as a covert, intentional way of impeding the progress of any ethnic minority group.

Ridley felt that **covert, unintentional racism** is much more insidious and pervasive. Such racism may be expressed by anyone—even those who would consider themselves "enlightened." However, generally it is the kind of racism that is expressed by those who are unaware of the racist traditions of this country and perpetuate such racism without thought. A story that one of this text's authors tells in regard to covert, unintentional racism involves a discussion he had with a high school friend (Mio & Awakuni, 2000, p. 22):

> We were wondering who would be quarterback for the high school the following year, after Vince Ferragamo graduated. (I was in Ferragamo's graduating class, but I was worried for my friend's class the next year.) He suggested the name of an African American at the school, and I asked, How could he be quarterback? My friend said that this guy had a great arm, was fast, and could make quick decisions, but I still wondered how he could be quarterback. I had heard that Blacks could not be quarterbacks. and I blindly accepted this view, not knowing why people were saying such things. . . . I did not know that Blacks could become quarterbacks, as there were no professional Black quarterbacks at that time and very few on major college football teams. Boy, was I naïve! (JSM)

Another example of covert, unintentional racism came right after the 2002 Winter Olympics. As many Americans of Asian descent know, Asians are quite often seen as forever alien. One of America's best female figure skaters has been Michelle Kwan. She was born in the United States. In fact, her parents were born in the United States, so her family has been part of the American tradition for decades. During the 1998 Winter Olympics when Tara Lipinski beat Michelle Kwan for the gold medal, a headline on the MSNBC Web site read:

covert, unintentional racism—discriminatory behavior that is unintentional but serves to perpetuate ongoing racist acts or traditions.

American beats out Michelle Kwan

Of course, the headline implied that Kwan was not American. In 2002, when Sarah Hughes beat out Kwan for the gold medal, the *Seattle Times* (February 22, 2002), a newspaper in a state with the only governor of Asian descent (Gary Locke) in the continental 48 states displayed this amazing headline:

Hughes Good as Gold
American beats out Kwan, Slutzkaya

Again, the headline implied that Kwan is not an American. After being flooded with angry letters, the editorial staff of the *Seattle Times* apologized and recognized its error. At first, the newspaper tried to explain away its error by offering the rationale behind the headline: it did not want to repeat Hughes's name in the subheadline, so it replaced "Hughes" with "American." However, the public saw that explanation as an excuse and demanded that the newspaper take full responsibility for its error. The paper then issued a second, more sincere apology.

This kind of racism is directed even at very young children. Mio and Awakuni (2000) discussed how an African-American colleague's two-and-a-half-year-old son was adapting to a daycare center. Her son tried to kiss another two-and-a-half-year-old, and they bumped into each other and fell to the floor. Immediately, the teacher got upset and asked our colleague if her son bites. Meanwhile, two young White girls were fighting and pulling each other's hair, but the teacher patiently tried to separate them, saying gently, "It's all right, she didn't mean to hurt you," and so on. Our colleague decided then and there not to expose her son to such a subtly racist environment.

A student of ours identified how parents transmit racism to their children:

On Saturday, my work hosted a Valentine's Day event for children, while the mothers and fathers were able to conduct their shopping. We set up a table with crafts for the children to make and milk and cookies for them to eat, which we monitored at all times. I was one of the employees who was at the crafts table with the children. At one point I noticed that there were two black kids at the table sitting right next to each other and a white kid sitting across from them. They were interacting in such a positive manner, talking and laughing with each other. They were between the ages of three and six and seemed to be completely unaware of the difference in their ethnic backgrounds. So, then a white mother comes in with her two children. One of them takes a seat next to the black child and the other next to the white child. She is instantly aware of this and immediately moves her child sitting next to the black child to sit next to a white child. The mother then continues on with her shopping, leaving her children at the crafts table. Meanwhile, one of her kids manages to end up bonding with a black kid and gets up to sit next to him. They start helping each other with their crafts and are becoming good buddies. When the mother comes back to get her children she looks at her son sitting next to the black boy and rolls her eyes. At this point she seems extremely annoyed and demands her kids to finish up and that it was time to go. Her son was just so happy with his new friend and didn't want to leave, which made the mother even more upset with him, however, she did not appear to be upset with her other child who was sitting next to a white kid. They eventually gathered their belongings and left, but I was so irritated by this whole situation. I was not very surprised, just very bothered by the fact that parents continue to teach their kids racism.

KATRINA, 20+-YEAR-OLD WHITE WOMAN

Ridley feels that covert, unintentional racism is perhaps the most damaging of all forms of racism, because it is practiced by well-intentioned individuals who do not see themselves as racist at all. They are not motivated to change their behaviors or perceptions, because they do not equate themselves with obvious, overt racists of the past or the present.

The Response to Hurricane Katrina: A Case of Covert, Unintentional Racism?

On August 29, 2005, the nation watched in horror as Hurricane Katrina slammed onto shore near the Louisiana/Mississippi border. Soon thereafter, the levees surrounding New Orleans, LA, breached, and most of the city was flooded. People were trapped at the New Orleans Convention Center and at the Superdome, and relief was slow. Days after the breach of the levees, Federal Emergency Management Agency director Michael Brown did not know that there were people trapped at the Convention Center without food or drinkable water, and on September 2, 2005, President George Bush uttered those now-infamous words, "Brownie, you're doing a heck of a job" (CNN.com, 2005).

Two years after Hurricane Katrina hit the mainland, there were still hundreds of thousands of individuals waiting to receive the promised federal money to rebuild their houses (MacAskill, 2007). How can we understand this slow response to the rebuilding of the region after so many promises for immediate attention? Is this overt racism as most of the victims are of African-American descent, or are people responsible for the rebuilding process affected by covert, unintentional racism?

Sommers, Apfelbaum, Dukes, Toosi, and Wang (2006) believe that the media coverage of Hurricane Katrina reflected covert, unintentional racism. Such coverage can only affect those in charge of the rebuilding in a similar manner. Sommers et al. pointed out the now-famous identification of a White individual taking food from an abandoned grocery store as "finding food" versus labeling a near-identical picture of an African-American individual doing the same thing as "looting." The media used the term "refugees" to describe the victims of the hurricane. This term implied that the victims had less than full citizenship, whereas more neutral terms such as "evacuees," "victims," or "survivors" were not used until the media received criticism for their use of the term "refugees." Finally, the "story angle" of the media also reflected bias. They tended to report rumors of violent crime as fact, with stories about someone firing guns at helicopters trying to rescue people at a hospital (found to be untrue) or 40 murder victims being found in a freezer at the Convention Center (four bodies were found, only one of which seemed to have been murdered).

Covert, unintentional racism was reflected in the following student's reaction paper, but also understanding of the underlying racism of ignoring the problems of the community and also her own feelings of outrage to the situation and closeness to the victims once she had hands-on experience with them:

> *Over the weekend I traveled to New Orleans to help build houses for Habitat for Humanity with a club on campus. I had never been to the south before and I figured I would be able to apply things I had learned from this class while I was there, since the Katrina victims were refugees in a way and such. I did not anticipate how much I would really learn on this short visit. There is still a lot of work that needs to be done in the city but it is slowly coming together with the help of people from across the United States. I had never experienced some of the experiences I had on this trip.*
>
> *For the first time in my life I felt the meaning of white privilege* [to be discussed later in this chapter] *and/or at least identified it. I had never seen so many African-American people in my life. I am not saying this is a bad thing but I thought California was a very diverse state and well I assumed it would be about the same as New Orleans. I now understood why the whole Hurricane Katrina issue became such a racial and political event, because there really were so many African Americans who suffered from the storm and they were the ones that needed and still need the most help. Before while I was watching the news I did not understand why they were making it such a racial issue but after witnessing and hearing first-hand accounts of what happened after the floods I understand why it troubled so many people as being a form of racism coming from the government.*

AIMEE, 20+-YEAR-OLD EUROPEAN-AMERICAN WOMAN

As Aimee's experience indicated, she was profoundly changed when she had contact with the victims of Hurricane Katrina. This process was identified in Hunt's studies (Hunt, Armenta, & Seifert, in press; Hunt, Seifert, & Armenta, 2006). These studies found that the communities accepting evacuees from New Orleans were initially influenced by stereotypes of the evacuees. However, once these communities had contact with the evacuees, their feelings of prejudice went down, particularly if the communities did not feel overwhelmed by a large number of evacuees.

How did you feel about the victims of Hurricane Katrina? Did you have preconceived notions about them? Did Aimee's story change your mind about these victims?

Aversive Racism

Gaertner and Dovidio (1986) discussed **aversive racism**, a form of racism practiced by individuals who believe that they are not racist at all and who would find it offensive or aversive if they were thought to be racist. When their unconsciously racist views surface, these individuals cite "logical" or "commonsense" reasons for their views and thereby deny that they are racist. This is related to Ridley's covert, unintentional racism.

Dovidio (2001) and Dovidio and Gaertner (2000) reported on their studies that found support for their aversive racism concept. For example, when making hiring decisions between Black and White candidates, those scoring high on the aversive racism scale designed by the authors hired White candidates over their Black counterparts. When given the opportunity to discuss their decisions, aversive racists focused on the strengths of the White candidates and the weaknesses of the Black candidates. Another group of aversive racists hired more White candidates than Black candidates, but though the qualifications were exactly opposite to those of the first set of candidates, the second group's reasoning also focused on the strengths of the White candidates and the weaknesses of the Black candidates. In other words, hiring decisions were based upon exactly the opposite qualifications, yet the two groups always favored the White candidates and had "logical" reasons to back up their decisions. Figures 6.1 and 6.2 show Mio's (2003) depictions of data from the Dovidio and Gaertner study. Henkel, Dovidio, and Gaertner (2006) interpreted the responses to Hurricane Katrina in terms of aversive racism.

Some aversive racists may excuse racist symbols as "meaningless" or "part of tradition" with no intent to create a hostile racist environment. This student talked about her African-American friend who encountered aversive racists explaining away confederate flags flying all around a small town:

My friend, who is African American, is so excited to finally be finished up and is ready to go out and work as a full-blown doctor. He was offered a couple of different jobs and was telling me about how vastly different two of them were. For instance, he was offered a job in southern Georgia. He was explaining to me how different he felt from everyone else in that town because he was the only black person around anywhere. He told me he felt like everyone was looking at him strangely, "as if they had never seen a black man before." He himself never saw another black or ethnic person in that town during the couple of days he was there. But, he did tell me he saw confederate flags hanging everywhere throughout the town on buildings, cars, in restaurants, and even inside the place where he was interviewing. He

aversive racism— covert, unintentional discriminatory behavior practiced by individuals who would deny being racist and who would be appalled to realize that they were engaging in racist acts.

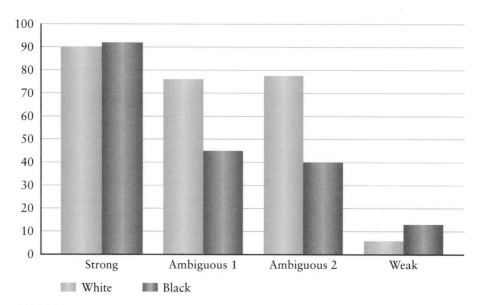

FIGURE 6.1 Representation of Dovidio's data on aversive racism—Probability of being hired. In Ambiguous 1, the White candidate was strong on Criterion A and weak on Criterion B, whereas the Black candidate was weak on Criterion A and strong on Criterion B. In Ambiguous 2, the White candidate was weak on Criterion A and strong on Criterion B, whereas the Black candidate was strong on Criterion A and weak on Criterion B. However, the White candidate had a higher probability of being hired in both ambiguous situations.

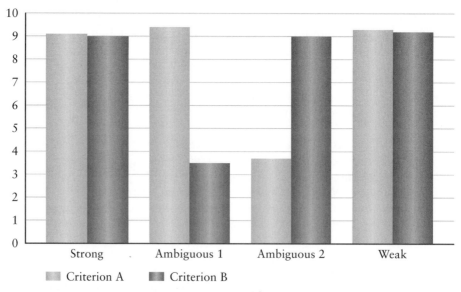

FIGURE 6.2 Ratings of importance of both of the criteria in Dovidio's study.

said this also made him feel really uncomfortable. Also, after his interview he told me that another doctor came up to him and told him not to worry about all the confederate flags hanging throughout their town. "It is just tradition around here," the doctor told my friend. "It doesn't mean anything though so don't worry about it," he said. This was another red flag for my friend not to take this job even though he was offered it. This made me realize, once again, that we still have a long way to go. It seems that racism will never be eradicated but it can certainly be decreased more, especially in areas were there isn't much diversity. It almost seems like the doctor who told my friend not to worry about the confederate flags was almost excusing the town's racist mentality by saying that it is just part of their tradition. This scares me. How can racism become a tradition? Sadly, it does for some.

GUADALUPE, 20+-YEAR-OLD MEXICAN-AMERICAN WOMAN

Although the following story is an example of aversive sexism rather than aversive racism, the principle is the same. The story is told by a colleague in a department with two different disciplines. One division had a gender balance, whereas the other division was all male. The names of the colleague and the department have been withheld to protect both from reprisal.

My department was conducting searches a few years ago. The other division had two positions for which it was searching. One of the positions was a "generalist" position, and the other position was a "specialty" one. The top two candidates for each position were a man and a woman. The generalist candidates differed in that the woman was finishing up her dissertation and the man had a postdoctoral position. The woman had one publication and several conference presentations, and her references said that she was a very promising candidate. The man, who had received his Ph.D. several years before, had a few publications and a contract for a book. The specialty candidates differed in that the man was finishing up his dissertation. Although he did not have any publications, he had several conference presentations, and his references said that he was a very promising candidate. The woman, who had received her Ph.D. several years before, had a few publications, had already published a book, and had received two fairly substantial grants. Amazingly, the chair of the search committee recommended that we offer the generalist position to the male candidate because he was a proven individual, and he also recommended that we offer the specialty position to the male candidate because he was a promising individual. Despite the fact that all of the women from my division of the department voiced their opposition to this ranking of candidates, the chair of the search committee stood his ground, feeling that he had made the right choices. It wasn't until a man from our division voiced his opposition to this ranking that the chair of the search committee agreed to reconsider the rankings. Sexism is alive and well in modern academia.

LONNIE, 30+-YEAR-OLD WHITE WOMAN

White Privilege

One of the most powerful treatises on the depth of unconscious White racism in this country was proposed by Peggy McIntosh (1988, 1995). The preceding story clearly illustrates **male privilege.** Not only was the search committee chair biased in favor of male candidates, he also ignored all the female voices that protested his decision, whereas he listened to the lone male who voiced his opinion. **White privilege** is similar to male privilege in that often many unearned advantages are given to White individuals without examination. If we are truly a fair society, such advantages should not occur. McIntosh presented many instances that might otherwise be left unexamined but that underscore the advantages of being White in this society. For example (McIntosh, 1995, pp. 79–81):

- I can avoid spending time with people whom I was trained to mistrust and who have learned to mistrust my kind or me.
- I can turn on the television or open to the front page of the paper and see people of my race widely and positively represented.
- I can talk with my mouth full and not have people put this down to my color.
- I am never asked to speak for all the people of my racial group.
- If my day, week, or year is going badly, I need not ask of each negative episode or situation whether it has racial overtones.

A biethnic female student wrote in one of our courses on multiculturalism about her reaction to reading McIntosh's treatise on White privilege:

When we discussed Peggy McIntosh's subtleties of racism, I especially liked "I am never asked to speak for all the people of my racial group." I notice that a lot of people do ask me to give the "Asian female" perspective, like I know what the Asian female perspective is. I am a fourth-generation Japanese and Chinese female, who does not for the most part know the language, customs, superstitions, culture tales, [or] traditions of both the Japanese and the Chinese cultures. I may know a few here and there, but by no means enough to "speak for all the people of my racial group."

When McIntosh said "I can turn on the television or open the front page of the paper and see people of my race," it also made me think of how much the Asian population is still not shown on television. My mother's cousin was an actor. As for major roles in television spots, he really did not have any. He had guest appearances on shows like

---

male privilege—the unearned advantages associated with being male, such as knowing that one's opinions will be respected. Women often feel that their opinions are not respected or are attributed to emotion, not sound reasoning.

White privilege—the unearned advantages associated with being White in America, such as knowing that Whiteness will be emphasized in the media. Ethnic minorities are not always portrayed in the media, and when they are, they are often portrayed stereotypically rather than as multifaceted individuals.

*Charlie's Angels, Silver Spoons, and many others, but never a real
leading role. In most of those shows he played the butler, the cook, the
Japanese tourist, and roles that were very stereotypical of Japanese men.
He did act in plays and was involved in other things, which supported
him, but he was not really seen regularly. I think times are changing.
More Asian actors and actresses are shown on television and movies,
but not at a rate that is proportional to the population.*

DEBBIE, 20+-YEAR-OLD BIETHNIC (JAPANESE/CHINESE-AMERICAN) WOMAN

Kliman (2005) discussed how she used her White and class privileges to demand medical attention for her husband who may have died had he not received
such attention:

> Frantic, I used class and other kinds of social privilege. I demanded
> immediate intervention. Did he survive at the expense of patients whose
> loved ones didn't share my entitlement, or of the overworked medical
> staff I pressed into action? . . . Race protected David, who is 6'4" and
> visibly strong. Toxic with infection, he was angry, confused, and probably
> frightening to others. I was aggressive on his behalf. What if we had been
> black or Latino, unprotected by our whiteness? Would antibiotics,
> sedation, or a call to security have come first? (p. 42)

In retrospect, Kliman expresses her guilt and acknowledges her privileged status;
an African-American or Latino-American wife may have had to retrospectively
discuss how racism took her husband.

Nowadays, McIntosh's article is standard reading for all graduate courses in
multicultural psychology courses, and it is almost always included in undergraduate
multicultural courses. Since one of the authors of this text is of Asian ancestry
(JSM), a particularly favorite observation is "I can turn on the television or open
to the front page of the paper and see people of my race widely and positively
represented." We particularly like to point out that unless one is viewing a mar-
tial arts movie, one almost *never* sees an Asian male on a television program or
in a movie. Asian females are typically presented as the girlfriends of White male
protagonists, but Asian males are almost never seen with White females and,
interestingly, are not even seen with Asian females. It is telling when we see students racking their brains trying to remember the last time they saw an Asian
man together with a White or an Asian woman on television. This seemed to
have resonated with a Chinese-American student, who wrote in one of her
reaction papers:

*"Oh, look, an Asian Guy!" My husband and I have gotten used to
using this phrase with each other as we watch television and look
through magazines. Why just this weekend I must have seen four or
five Asian men as extras on our favorite television shows. I don't know
why I was so excited to see them, because they were on the screen for
less than a blink of an eye. Only one of the four or five men that I saw*

PICTURE 6.2 Asians and Latinos have traditionally not been in positions of power. *Photograph by Tom Zasadzinski*

even had a line, the others only walked across the scene or were incidentally shot while the camera was panning onto one of the other major non-Asian actors. As we discussed in class, the incidence of seeing Asians on television is so rare that seeing three or four in a row is enough to make you wonder, "What's going on?"

MOLLY, 20+-YEAR-OLD CHINESE-AMERICAN WOMAN

Like Asian males, dark-skinned African-American women have a shortage of role models on television:

This weekend I paid close attention to commercials and movies to see how many Black faces I saw. One thing that I noticed was that I did not see very many "dark" Black women. Because I am an African-American woman with dark skin, I was looking to find women whom I could relate to physically.

Many of the Black actresses that are well known happen to be "light-skinned"; for example, Halle Berry and Queen Latifah. I wish there were more dark-skinned Black women on television to represent role models for other children to look up to. Lighter skin has always been preferred to darker skin. This is not always the case, but it is the majority from what I have observed. Growing up I did not think I was pretty because I was dark-skinned and I went to a predominately White school, and all of the other Black students were "light-skinned." I used to wish that I was light-skinned and had what is referred to as "good hair." I have slowly grown out of this way of thinking that dark-skinned people are not as pretty as light-skinned people. However, I still have issues sometimes when it comes to my confidence level.

SHARMAIN, 20+-YEAR-OLD AFRICAN-AMERICAN WOMAN

This issue of skin color is repeated by a number of students across a number of different ethnicities:

Ximena [who is Black/Panamanian] told us a story about her niece who wanted to take only her white dolls to the park. Her niece is only two years old, and she has already noticed the difference in skin color. She did not want to take her black dolls to the park because there are always other girls in the park, but she is the only black girl. . . . [This reminded me of] a recent event that happened to one of my friends (Christiana), who lives in Rancho Cucamonga. Last week her eight-year-old daughter was pretending to be sick for about three days, because she did not want to go to school. The school she is attending is mostly White. Christiana got very concerned by the third day, and started confronting her daughter. Alexandria, her daughter, told her that one of her classmates was telling everybody in the class not to play with her because she is Black. She is actually Hispanic, but she has very dark skin.

ISOLDA, 20+-YEAR-OLD COLOMBIAN-AMERICAN WOMAN

Before my sister got married and moved, I can recollect numerous episodes of her fretting about her skin color. My father is brown-toned and my mother is fair. Because of that, my two sisters are brown-toned and my brother and I are fair. In our Indian culture, being a girl and being brown-toned are two things that can severely work against you. No one saw how incredibly gorgeous my sister was because they focused on her skin color rather than her physical and inner beauty. My sister spent endless nights trying to fix this "flaw." I heard incessant comments from her about how jealous she is of my skin color and how much she wishes that she was more like Mom. She even got this cream that is commonly sold in India called "Fair and Lovely." She tried it; it obviously didn't work on making her either fair or "lovely." . . .

Once, an old and traditional relative of mine said to me that I have a very bright and beautiful future ahead of me. She also said that I must be more pure hearted than my sisters. I was first shocked at how she could even mention something of this sort aloud. I would feel ashamed for even having such thoughts enter my head, let alone be verbalized aloud! Then she went on to tell my mother, in front of my sister, that my sister is ugly only because of her dark skin and that she's going to have a horrible future. My sister will remember that forever and she continues to behave in ways that reveal how insecure she is about her skin color, even though her husband loves it.

I hate how these things work and I wish I had the power to change it. The place where I intend to begin first is within my own family.

INDIRA, 20+-YEAR-OLD INDIAN-AMERICAN WOMAN

Articles such as McIntosh's help us to understand how White people can assist in eliminating racism. Her insights help other Whites to see how society is set up to give an advantage to one class of individuals over other classes of individuals. Thus, the basis of our form of government—that all people are created equal—is not true unless we help make it true and form "a more perfect union." One step in helping to form a more perfect union is to produce more people like McIntosh—individuals who have power merely by their status but who are willing to give up some of their power to help those on the downside of power gain more equality, what writers in the field call a development of **allies** (Kivel, 1996; Mio & Roades, 2003; Roades & Mio, 2000; Rose, 1996; Tatum, 1997). Allies are those individuals on the upside of any form of unearned power and privilege, such as White privilege, male privilege, heterosexual privilege, and ability privilege, who are willing to work for social justice in giving those on the downside of power and privilege equal status. As Tatum (1997) has written, many of her White students feel powerless when they study racism, but when she talks about allies and how allies can help eliminate racism, her White students all of a sudden feel empowered because this mindset helps them understand how they can confront this otherwise daunting issue.

A former student felt energized by the discovery of White privilege and he was excited to apply it to his life:

allies—individuals who are on the upside of power who cross a demographic boundary to advocate for those on the downside of power.

There are many reasons why I truly enjoy this class. The biggest reason is the fact that things are brought to my attention that were right in front of my face for as long as I can remember, but I never saw them until now. I am talking about white privilege. The fact that I am white might be the sole reason that I have never realized it until now.

The part that I enjoyed was the fact that white males are privileged enough to move away from all minorities and be entirely surrounded by other white people. A white male could move up to northern Idaho and never see a minority unless he wanted to. I never thought about this until it was brought up in class.

MARK, 20+-YEAR-OLD EUROPEAN-AMERICAN MAN

Yet another student resonated to our class discussion of male privilege as related to White privilege:

The topic of male privilege in our society is quite interesting because it's something that probably goes unnoticed. Males are born into a society that is dominated by men, which makes it somewhat implicit. Males become a part of the dominant culture, and gain access to all of the advantages of being male. These individuals unintentionally become oppressors, as their unearned privilege places females at a disadvantage. This is something hard to recognize because it is the norm, and it isn't really an explicit form of oppression.

MITCHELL, 20+-YEAR-OLD EUROPEAN-AMERICAN MAN

Here is an example of a very effective intervention by one of our students serving as an ally:

I really hate how many people in society are homophobic, especially men and especially Latino men. For instance my boyfriend, who is Mexican American [and] very smart is about to graduate next month with his master's [degree] . . . but when it comes to homosexuality he is very ignorant and homophobic, [and] so are his friends. I know in the Latino culture, homosexuality is viewed as shameful or deviant, but I wish the younger and more educated generations would be able to get past this. For example I dragged my boyfriend to go see "Brokeback Mountain" with me when it was in the theaters. Well when his friends found out he went to go see that "gay" or "homo" movie they gave him a hard time. It really offended me that they would be so close-minded and ignorant, that I confronted their sexist and "machismo" opinions. Still today they nickname my boyfriend "Brokeback," [and] still to today I debate with them on gay and lesbian rights issues and on their ignorant statements.

I have several close gay and lesbian friends, and I am very liberal minded when it comes to gay and lesbian rights. I believe in gays and lesbians deserving to be legally married and have equality in the adoption process. So when I hear people use derogatory terms regarding gays or voicing homophobic beliefs I get really upset and usually confront them about it.

DELINDA, 20+-YEAR-OLD BIRACIAL (MEXICAN-AMERICAN/WHITE) WOMAN

However, being an ally can come with a cost. One of our students discussed how difficult it would be to be an ally. On the other hand, this is the only way that society can change:

Becoming an ally would take a lot of courage. I think it would be very scary to stand up against injustice toward a minority group. For example, a White person speaking out against the [anti-]immigration issue that is going on today. Those in power are White and are going to ultimately make the decision of what is going to happen. A White citizen would not want to suffer the consequences of losing their job because they were marching, getting beaten up for being a "beaner lover" (I heard this term on the street the other day. It was said to a White girl who had a Mexican boyfriend.), or being seen as a traitor to their own culture. . . .

We have seen in the past that the oppressed groups who have overcome their unjust situations have been those who have been allied by more powerful groups. If Martin Luther King had not appealed to White people with his message of equality and peace then perhaps many White people and White leaders would not have joined his cause. Since they did, they helped change history.

CORINA, 20+-YEAR-OLD MEXICAN-AMERICAN WOMAN

SUMMARY

Bias comes in many shapes and sizes. Some forms of bias are subtle and some are quite striking; some are unintentional and some are intentional. One of social psychology's basic theories—attribution theory—explains how bias can be revealed in our categorization of events. Ways of categorization can lead to stereotyping, prejudice, discrimination, and racism. Stereotyping and prejudice occur within ourselves and do not hurt others, whereas discrimination and racism are actions against others and consequently cause damage. This damage can be as minor as a mild irritation or a strained relationship, or as serious as blatant unfairness or even death.

Ultimately, however, racism hurts all of us. The targets of racism are, of course, hurt by the racist comments or actions. The perpetrators are also hurt, because they live in fear of those whom they categorize negatively, and when someone's racist attitudes become public, that person may even lose a prestigious position. Racism can be overt and intentional, and thus easily identified, but it can also be covert and unintentional, and difficult to identify.

Many modern forms of racism are difficult to detect. Moreover, most individuals who hold racist views are unaware that their views are racist and would even vigorously deny that they are racist. These modern forms of racism are often unintentional, but they cannot be eliminated unless people are willing to examine their own contribution to a racist atmosphere. Peggy McIntosh (1995) identified the various advantages of her "White privilege." These privileges are unearned and unconscious unless brought to light. For example, she can know that White people will be characterized positively in almost any newspaper or television show, whereas most ethnic minorities may never see characters of their ethnicity portrayed as part of American life. By identifying these privileges, she makes herself aware of the advantages that come with her skin color and the special burden such privileges place upon her to make her work harder for social justice.

Food for Thought

You can extend Peggy McIntosh's concept of White privilege to privileges of all kinds. Men are privileged in our society over women, heterosexuals are privileged over gay and lesbian individuals, and able-bodied individuals are advantaged over individuals with disabilities. As a man (JSM), I think nothing of staying in my office late at night, then walking to my car to go home. However, my female colleagues need to be concerned about this. They can avail themselves of the escort service our campus police department provides at night, but it is inconvenient for my female colleagues to do this. This is just one example of male privilege. We encourage you to think of other kinds of privileges from which you have benefited. In so doing, you will begin to think like an ally in working toward social justice.

Critical Thinking Questions

Have you ever attributed something to someone's personality but later found out it was the context that determined that person's actions? Have you ever felt that someone else unfairly attributed something you did to your personality or character when it was actually the situation that determined your action? Did you ever get the chance to talk with the other person in either of these situations so that you could develop better understanding?

If you have ever seen a television news report that a Person of Color has engaged in some criminal action, have you immediately attributed that action to others in that person's racio-ethnic group?

What institutional practices can you identify that unfairly disadvantage People of Color? What institutional practices can you identify that unfairly disadvantage women? What institutional practices can you identify that unfairly disadvantage

continued

people of nondominant sexual orientations? What institutional practices can you identify that unfairly disadvantage people of nondominant religions? What institutional practices can you identify that unfairly disadvantage people who have physical disabilities? What institutional practices can you identify that unfairly disadvantage anyone of any nondominant group?

What negative stereotypes can be attributed to a group to which you belong? Have you ever experienced stereotype threat based on these negative stereotypes?

What kinds of covert forms of racism can you identify around you?

What kinds of dominant group privilege can you identify that benefit you?

What kinds of things related to your dominant group privilege can you do to intervene on someone else's behalf?

CHAPTER 7

Cultural Identity Development

A MODEL OF PERSONAL IDENTITY
RACIAL IDENTITY DEVELOPMENT
    African-American Identity Development
    White Identity Development
    Multiracial Identity Development
    Gay/Lesbian Identity Development
    Racial and Cultural Identity Development Model
A CRITIQUE OF THE STAGE MODELS
MULTIPLE LAYERING OF IDENTITIES
SUMMARY

Who am I?

All human beings, at some point in their lives, face that question. Erik Erikson (1950/1963) stated that one of the major developmental tasks for human beings is the establishment of an identity. Our search for an identity takes place across many domains—physical appearance, personal interests, career plans, religious beliefs, gender roles, and so on.

Although every individual struggles with identity questions, individuals from cultural minority groups face a unique challenge. They must also resolve conflicts related to their minority status, whether that is based on race, gender, sexual orientation, physical ability, or some other trait that makes them "different" from the American mainstream. Society reacts to those differences, often in negative ways, and the individual must come to terms with the prejudice, discrimination, and oppression based on his or her membership in that group. Women experience sexism, People of Color experience racism, gays and lesbians experience heterosexism. Individuals from minority backgrounds struggle to make meaning of the fact that some aspect of their being is not accepted by society.

In her aptly titled book *Why Are All the Black Kids Sitting Together in the Cafeteria?* Beverly Daniel Tatum (1997) explains what happens to African-American adolescents as they experience society's negative reactions to their blackness. When they are young, color is often not an issue for African-American children who grow up in predominantly White or mixed neighborhoods. They may make friends and interact easily with children from other racial backgrounds. African-American children often have not had negative experiences associated with their race because the White world does not yet see them as a threat.

However, as they get older, things start to change. The African-American adolescent girl who goes shopping at the mall with her European-American friends sees the salespeople follow her around to make sure she does not shoplift, but they do not do this to her friends. She may also notice that the salespeople rush to help her friends but ignore her. The African-American adolescent boy might notice that European-American women clutch their purses more tightly when he walks by, or look nervous when he enters the elevator, or cross to the other side of the street to avoid him. African-American young people might also notice that their friends' parents do not mind if their children have Black friends but draw the line when it comes to dating. Tatum says,

> Why do Black youths, in particular, think about themselves in terms of race? Because that is how the rest of the world thinks of them. Our self-perceptions are shaped by the messages that we receive from those around us, and when young Black men and women enter adolescence, the racial content of those messages intensifies. (pp. 53-54)

When African-American youth try to discuss their thoughts and feelings about racially motivated incidents with their European-American friends, they get little support. Their friends may respond, "Oh, I'm sure they didn't mean it like that!" or "Just forget about it. It's not a big deal." But when they relate the experience to their African-American friends, they might say, "The same thing happened to me!" or "I know just how you feel." From their European-American friends they get denial and minimization; with their African-American friends, they find similarity, understanding, and support. Therefore, they gradually drift away from their European-American peers and toward their African-American peers. Tatum says,

> When feelings, rational or irrational, are invalidated, most people disengage. They not only choose to discontinue the conversation but are more likely to turn to someone who will understand their perspective. . . . Not only are Black adolescents encountering racism and reflecting on their identity, but their White peers, even when they are not the perpetrators (and sometimes they are), are unprepared to respond in supportive ways. The Black students turn to each other for the much needed support they are not likely to find anywhere else. (pp. 59-60)

African Americans, as well as young people from other cultural minority groups, must cope with society's reactions to their "other-ness." This is an important part of their identity development process.

A MODEL OF PERSONAL IDENTITY

Sue (2001) proposed a **Tripartite Model of Personal Identity.** An old Asian saying goes something like this: "All individuals, in many respects, are (a) like no other individuals, (b) like some individuals, and (c) like all other individuals." "While this statement might seem confusing and contradictory, Asians believe this saying to have great wisdom and to be entirely true with respect to human development and identity" (Sue & Sue, 2003, p. 11). The Tripartite Model is illustrated as three concentric circles (see Figure 7.1), which describe the individual, group, and universal levels of personal identity.

On the *individual level* "all individuals are, in some respects, like no other individuals." Each person is unique in genetic makeup, personality characteristics, and personal experiences. Our individual uniqueness sets us apart from all other human beings and is an important part of our identity.

The second part of the adage says, "All individuals are, in some respects, like some other individuals." This is the *group level* of personal identity, which focuses on similarities and differences among individuals. As mentioned earlier, society divides us up into groups based on various demographic characteristics (e.g., gender, race, socioeconomic status, religious preference). Therefore, a part of our identity is based on our membership in these various groups.

The third part of the saying reflects the *universal level* of personal identity: "All individuals are, in some respects, like all other individuals." There are characteristics we all share as members of the human race, such as biological and physical similarities, common life experiences (e.g., birth, death, love, fear), and common practices or behaviors (e.g., language).

In this chapter we focus on the second level of personal identity development, the group level. Membership in groups shapes the way we see ourselves, others in our group, and others outside our group. As we mentioned earlier, membership in

Tripartite Model of Personal Identity— the understanding that our self-perceptions are made up of unique, individual aspects, aspects of groups to which we belong, and universal aspects of human beings.

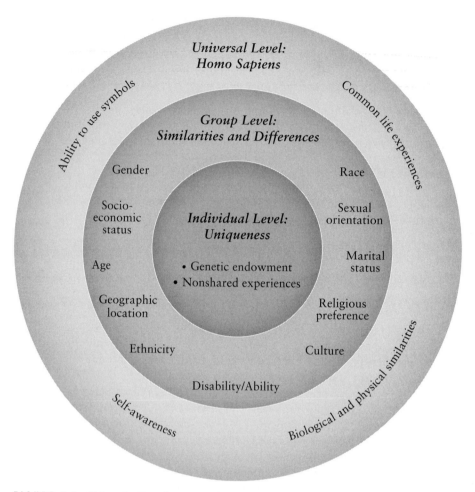

FIGURE 7.1 Tripartite Development of Personal Identity. *From D. W. Sue (2001)*

some groups is valued over membership in others—men over women, Christian over Muslim, able-bodied over disabled, White over Black. Society's reactions to our group membership influences group identity formation. A large body of literature exists on the cultural identity process, and there is no way to cover all of it, but this chapter will introduce you to it. The large majority of this literature focuses on racial identity development, so that is where we begin.

RACIAL IDENTITY DEVELOPMENT

My memory may be a bit tainted, but I think my daughter was about 5 years old, shortly after entering kindergarten, when she began to talk about race and features. I guess before that, she was exposed to very few children. She was always with my family, wherein the subjects of race, identity, discrimination, and such topics were never discussed.

When she was 5, I believe that I was still struggling with my own identity, so I really never talked about her multiracial identity. She came home and asked me why her friend's hair looked different from hers. She said that she touched it and everything, and it felt different too. I asked her "what her friend" was and she told me her friend's name. "No," I said, and I proceeded to ask about where she was from, and the color of her skin, but my daughter just concentrated on the texture of her hair, while she answered that she was from the same school and that her color was dark brown. This is going to sound amazing, but although I never had conversations with my daughter, prior to that day, about race, I thought she knew Black people from White people, Asian people from Hispanics, Whites from Asians, and so on and so forth. I believe that my assumptions were based on my own worldview and knowledge base, and I may have been projecting some feelings onto my daughter. The contradiction was that even though in my mind, I assumed that she knew the differences among different ethnic groups, I was not surprised that she couldn't tell between the racial features! How then did I think that she would know the differences between ethnic groups if she had no basis for that knowledge? I think because I assumed that a person's identity would be determined by how they looked alone, and that's how I went about defining my own ethnicity then, I assumed that my daughter and everyone else would think the same way. It was also because many people assumed that they knew exactly "what I was," based on how I looked, and for the most part, they were wrong! I was annoyed at my daughter for not knowing what I meant when I asked "what her friend was." I hated having to explain more about the one thing that I avoided all of my life. To define myself, my family, and my daughter was to justify many things that I didn't feel I should have to explain. Nowadays, I talk freely to her about ethnicity, discrimination, and such issues, because now that she is older, she too has experienced being "the other." Seeing who her friends are and how she has evolved now that I have educated myself, in turn increasing my ability to educate her, makes me feel confident that although she will continue to face obstacles along the way, she is better equipped to do so, as I am now.

DEANA, 20+-YEAR-OLD FILIPINA/AFRICAN-AMERICAN WOMAN

Deana describes a number of phases she went through in her own identity development. At first she saw her mixed racial background as negative; she denied it and avoided dealing with it. However, her daughter's questions about racial differences forced Deana to come out of denial. Through educating her daughter and herself, Deana got to the place where she gained more confidence in dealing with issues of racial identity. Although not everyone has the same experience as Deana, all individuals from racial minority backgrounds face similar questions about their identity and go through similar phases in addressing those questions.

African-American Identity Development

Research on cultural identity began with African Americans and can be traced back to a landmark experiment conducted by the husband-and-wife team of Kenneth and Mamie Clark, two African-American psychologists, in 1939. In their study the Clarks presented African-American children with Black and White dolls and asked them a series of questions, such as which doll was the prettiest, smartest, dirtiest. They found that African-American children consistently attributed more positive traits to the White dolls and negative ones to the Black dolls. The Clarks concluded that these results demonstrated the low self-esteem and negative self-image of Black children and attributed this to the racism, oppression, and discrimination experienced by Black children in White America. The Clark study had widespread influence in the field of psychology and beyond, and was used as evidence in the 1954 *Brown v. Board of Education* decision by the Supreme Court that segregated schools were unconstitutional (Clark, Chein, & Cook, 2004; Pickren, 2004).

Joseph White (1970) wrote an article in *Ebony* magazine on Black identity development. He intentionally published in that source to make his ideas more accessible to the general African-American community and not necessarily to researchers in psychology. A major influence on the study of cultural identity development professionally was an article published by William Cross in 1971 titled "The Negro-to-Black conversion experience." Cross outlined stages that African Americans go through in moving from self-hatred to self-acceptance. He called this process "nigrescence," or the process of becoming Black. The model contains four (originally five) stages. They are *pre-encounter, encounter, immersion-emersion,* and *internalization.*

At the **pre-encounter** stage, individuals are programmed to think of the world as non-Black or anti-Black. They think and act in ways that devalue their Blackness and idealize Whiteness. In other words, they have internalized society's attitudes about White superiority.

In the **encounter** stage, individuals experience some significant or startling event that forces them to reevaluate their previous ideas about race. Cross mentions the assassination of Dr. Martin Luther King, Jr., as an event that forced many in our country to reevaluate their attitudes about race.

In the third stage, **immersion/emersion,** a reversal occurs wherein people idealize Blackness, totally immerse themselves in Black culture, and reject anything that is not Black.

Cross's final stage is **internalization,** wherein people feel positive and secure about their Black identity but also exhibit increased comfort with and acceptance of other cultures. Although Cross made some revisions to the original theory on the basis of subsequent research (1991, 1995), the basic structure of the model remains the same.

Mike, whom we felt was in Cross's internalization stage, was able to be self-critical in observing his own inconsistencies:

> *I was raised in such a way as not to be prejudiced against anyone but have other black friends who are prejudiced against Mexicans or Asians or even non-American blacks. I also have to admit that I have*

PICTURE 7.1   Racial identity development models suggest that African Americans should develop a sense of pride about being of African descent. *Photograph by Erica Preston*

picked up some political prejudices myself. For example, I could never bring myself to purchase a German-made car because of the atrocities committed in World War II. I have owned Japanese cars almost exclusively even though I also know of similar atrocities committed by the Japanese against the Chinese. To me this just points out the irrationality of prejudice.

MIKE, 40+-YEAR-OLD AFRICAN-AMERICAN MAN

Deana was in the pre-encounter stage when she avoided dealing with her multiracial background. Her daughter's questions about racial differences moved her into the encounter stage. In the end she appears to achieve some positive resolution about her racial identity and reach the internalization stage. In the following story, see if you can identify the different stages of racial identity development.

It was 1963. I was only 3 years old. My family and I were sitting in the living room of our small house in East Los Angeles watching the news on television. Suddenly, the images of the civil rights protests in Birmingham, Alabama, flashed across the screen. I was stunned to see Bull Connor order the fire hoses and dogs unleashed on the African-American children. My mother rushed to turn the channel, but . . . it was too late. The images were already burned in my mind. I asked her, "Why are they doing that to those children?" As my mother stood at the ironing board pressing clothes, she somberly said, "Just because they're Negroes, honey. Just because they're Negroes." I immediately responded in a chipper voice, "I'm glad I'm not a Negro!" The reaction from my family members was swift and forceful. They all immediately said together in a loud chorus, "Yes, we are!" I burst into tears as the realization flooded into my little 3-year-old mind. If those children were being treated that way just because they were Negroes, and if I was a Negro, that meant the same thing could happen to me. That was the beginning of my long journey of fear, guilt, and shame regarding my racial identity.

Moving forward a few years, my family moved to the suburbs, bought a house in a predominantly White neighborhood, and enrolled me in a predominantly White school. I was usually the only Black child in my class and one of only a handful in the whole school. I felt different from the very first day, and spent almost every day in the first grade sitting on the White teacher's lap crying. I didn't understand why, when the White girls flung their hair, it gently fell back into place. If I tried to fling my hair, it stayed standing straight up. And they laughed. I went home and told my mother that I wanted straight hair. She took me to the Black beauty shop on the other side of town and had a relaxer put in. My hair promptly fell out, leaving me bald. I ended up wearing a wig until my hair grew back. Imagine my humiliation, going to grade school, wearing a wig.

My sense of alienation, shame, fear, and guilt about my race lasted for years. It wasn't until I entered high school that I began to have some positive identification with my Blackness because there were finally more Black kids that I could relate to and hang out with. But, the pain of those years still lies deep in my soul. When my sister and I recounted that and other various hair traumas with my mother, tears welled up in her eyes as she said, "We just did what we thought was best."

MARIE, 40+-YEAR-OLD AFRICAN-AMERICAN WOMAN

Did you recognize any of Cross's stages as you read Marie's story? Her first encounter experience occurred at 3 years old. She became very aware of her race but continued to carry feelings of guilt and shame about it for many years. In high school she finally had some African-American peers to "hang out with," and that helped her to develop more positive feelings about her racial identity. Perhaps that marked her entrance into the immersion-emersion phase.

Since Cross first published his stages of nigrescence in 1971, racial identity development has become one of the most widely researched topics in multi-cultural psychology (Parham, 2001). Parham and Helms (1981) constructed the Racial Identity Attitude Scale (RIAS) to measure Cross's stages (see Box 7.1). The RIAS has been used to explore the relationship between racial identity and a wide variety of other variables, such as self-esteem (Parham & Helms, 1985a), demographic factors (Parham & Williams, 1993), affective states (Parham & Helms, 1985b), and the counseling process (Helms, 1985). There has also been a proliferation of other cultural identity models. There are at least 11 other models for African Americans alone (Cross, Parham, & Helms, 1991; Helms, 1990).

There are also models for Asian Americans (e.g., Kitano, 1982), Latinos (e.g., Ruiz, 1990), and European Americans (e.g., Helms, 1984, 1990, 1995b), as

Box 7.1   The Racial Identity Attitude Scale (RIAS) (Helms, 1990)

A number of measures have been developed to capture cultural identity. One of the most widely used, the Racial Identity Attitude Scale (RIAS), was developed by Parham and Helms (1981) to measure Cross's stages of Black racial identity development. Here are some sample items from the RIAS. Although the scale was originally designed for African Americans, we have left the race blank so that you can fill it in with your own race.

Pre-encounter

I believe that large numbers of _____ are untrustworthy.

I believe that White people look and express themselves better than _____ do.

I feel very uncomfortable around _____ people.

Encounter

I feel unable to involve myself in White experience, and am increasing my involvement in _____ experiences.

I find myself reading a lot of _____ literature and thinking about being _____.

I feel guilty and/or anxious about some of the things I believe about _____ people.

Immersion/Emersion

I have changed my style of life to fit my beliefs about _____ people.

I believe that everything _____ is good, and consequently, I limit myself to _____ activities.

I speak my mind regardless of the consequences (e.g., being kicked out of school, being imprisoned, being exposed to danger).

Internalization

People, regardless of their race, have strengths and limitations.

I feel good about being _____ but do not limit myself to _____ activities.

I am determined to find my _____ identity.

well as for other identities such as gender (Kohlberg, 1966) and sexual orientation (e.g., Cass, 1979). It is beyond the scope of this chapter to describe all of these, so we will discuss two other models related to race (White racial identity and multiracial identity), one non-race-based identity model (homosexual identity), and one final model that attempts to summarize them all.

White Identity Development

I just recently started dating Tim, and I'm a little bit worried about where this relationship is going. Tim was raised in a predominantly White neighborhood. He attended all-White schools and he only recently moved to California. I think I'm the first Pacific Islander woman that he has exclusively dated. When we started to see each other more frequently and it became obvious that it was becoming more serious, the topic of race and culture came about (brought up by me). Tim was FASCINATED! He listened for hours to the stories that I told about my own and my family's experiences with racism, and there were moments when he would become emotional about them. He would often apologize that I had to go through such damaging experiences. Here's the part where I become unsure about our relationship. When I began to be more specific about these stories, I reiterated the fact that most of those who were discriminating and racist were Whites. Tim immediately became defensive when I said that lack of exposure to cultural issues makes one insensitive to such issues. He would immediately talk about the fact that his family never raised him to be a racist and that he doesn't see me as any different from anyone else. "That's a problem," I said, "because, I AM DIFFERENT. I want you to see me differently and respect those differences. I don't want to be like everyone else, and by clumping me with everyone else, I am denied my culture and those who are a part of my heritage." Tim became quiet although I could tell that he was confused and somewhat angry. Tim comes from a very liberal family, and he prided himself in being a liberal person. I think Tim is confusing liberalism with full acceptance of others, regardless of color, gender, beliefs, etc. I'm not sure how things are going to go, but I know that Tim is struggling with my confrontations regarding his lack of knowledge about Persons of Color.

TESA, 20+-YEAR-OLD FILIPINA-AMERICAN WOMAN

Most often, cultural identity development is discussed as a minority phenomenon, in which members of minority groups struggle with the negative attitudes of and treatment by the dominant culture. What about those in the dominant group? Do they struggle with such questions as well?

Tesa's story says that the answer is yes. By being in a relationship with a Filipina woman, Tesa's European-American boyfriend, Tim, was forced to confront his own attitudes about race. A number of multicultural psychologists have addressed the issue of White racial identity (Carter, 1995; Corvin & Wiggins, 1989; D'Andrea, 2003; Helms, 1984, 1990, 1995b; Ponterotto, 1988). They believe that members of the dominant group must confront racism and oppression from the other side—as perpetrators rather than recipients. A number of models of White racial identity development have been proposed (see Rowe, Bennett, & Atkinson, 1994), but arguably the most cited and most researched is the one developed by Janet Helms (1984, 1990, 1995b).

Helms assumes that racist attitudes are a central part of being European American and that development of a healthy White identity requires abandonment of racist ideas and the definition of oneself as nonracist. She delineates six stages (originally five) that European Americans go through in this process. She now uses the term "statuses" instead of "stages" to reflect the fact that individuals may exhibit attitudes and behaviors of more than one stage at the same time and that identity development is a dynamic process rather than a static condition that a person "achieves" or a category to which the person is assigned (Helms, 1995b).

In Helms's first status, **contact,** White people are unaware of and uninformed about racism, discrimination, prejudice, and privilege. They have minimal experience with people from other backgrounds and may profess to be "color-blind," making such statements as "I don't see color," "People are people," and "We're all the same under our skin." Individuals in this stage hold two opposing beliefs—one, that everything White is superior and everything minority inferior; and two, that racial and cultural differences do not matter. Tim was raised in an all-White environment and had little exposure to minorities before he began to date Tesa. He professed to be liberal, seeing all people as equal, and even told Tesa he did not see her as "different."

contact—the status in which White people are uninformed about the realities of racism and privilege.

A rather incredible illustration of this first status of contact came from popular television host Bill O'Reilly. He and the Reverend Al Sharpton went to dinner in Harlem, and O'Reilly expressed surprise that there was no difference between this Black-owned restaurant and a White-owned restaurant (Bauder, 2007).

Increased exposure to people from different backgrounds moves individuals into the second status, **disintegration.** Increased experience with People of Color leads to information that is incongruent with a person's previously held notions; the contradiction causes dissonance. For example, working with an African-American colleague on a project and seeing what a good job he or she does contradicts the belief that Black people are unintelligent and incompetent. Seeing that same colleague passed over for promotions challenges the belief that everyone has an equal chance of success, regardless of color. Tesa's stories about the racism and discrimination suffered by her family forced Tim to confront his previously held beliefs. The struggle to make sense of those contradictions may result in feelings of guilt, depression, anxiety and helplessness. To reduce that conflict, Whites may avoid members of minority groups, try to convince others that minorities are not inferior, or convince themselves that racism does not exist or at least is not their fault.

disintegration—the status in which White people are in enough contact with ethnic minorities that their naïveté about racism is shattered.

Upon exposure to the injustices that American Indians have endured throughout history, this student expressed her disappointment and guilt:

It is disappointing that once again Americans have used another minority group and trampled all over them. It is making me ill to continue to read through the chapters only to find out how cruel we were to people who didn't look or act American enough for the government and some citizens. I am horrified that I may be associated with these low-life people just because I am not a minority. I try to contribute as a voting citizen in favor of the American Indians and other minority groups to bring justice.

In last week's lecture, I learned for the first time that American Indian children were taken from their homes and put into boarding schools. The treatment and suffering those poor children went through was more than I could take for one lecture. It is just disappointing that again someone with power took advantage of those with less power . . . just because they can.

JANENE, 20+-YEAR-OLD EUROPEAN-AMERICAN WOMAN

reintegration—the status in which White people retreat to their comfort zone within their White communities.

Most likely, according to Helms, Whites resolve the conflict by retreating to the comfort and acceptance of their own racial group and, either passively or actively, supporting White superiority. This is the defining characteristic of the third status, **reintegration.**

The fourth status in Helms's model of White Racial Identity Development is **pseudoindependence.** This marks the first phase in the development of a nonracist White identity. Whites begin to acknowledge some existence of racism but see the solution in changing Blacks, not Whites. They may reach out to Blacks, wanting to help, but do so by imposing White standards. They struggle to find a new White identity but lack positive examples for how to accomplish this.

pseudoinde-pendence—the status in which White people begin to acknowledge the realities of racism but believe that it is Blacks who should change, not Whites.

In **immersion/emersion** a more positive White identity begins to form. Whites take time to explore their own culture, learning what it means to be White in a diverse society. They no longer focus on changing Blacks but on changing Whites and understand that a central part of White identity is letting go of one's own racist attitudes and actively fighting the racist attitudes of others.

immersion/ emersion—the status in which White people begin to form a more positive White identity and to focus on changing Whites, not Blacks.

The final status, **autonomy,** represents the accomplishment of a positive White racial identity. Whites feel good about their group but also find contact with individuals from other groups mutually enriching. They expand their sensitivity beyond racism to include other forms of oppression, acknowledge their privilege, and act as allies who actively seek to combat discrimination.

autonomy—the status in which White people are comfortable with their White identity, understand that racism is connected with other forms of oppression, and work to address all forms of oppression.

I am a bigot. I think I need to call myself that just as a now sober, once alcoholic person continues to call him/herself an alcoholic. I think that will always be a part of me, no matter what happens in my life now. I never thought of myself as a bigot until I met Wanda. Wanda is a beautiful, educated, and headstrong African-American woman, and I fell head over heels in love with her. We worked in the same place and I initially admired her only from afar. I mean, I thought at the time that I could never date this woman because in my mind I knew I couldn't be seen with her. At the time, these were thoughts that were in my head, probably subconscious. One day, I bumped into her and that was the end of me. We had so much to talk about that we were late coming back from the break room, and I HAD to ask her to have coffee after work. We began dating, and Wanda was never shy about issues regarding racism and discrimination. She would try to get me to have discussions with her, but I told her that I completely agreed with her thoughts and that there was nothing more disgusting than racist people. She would laugh, and I would quiver with disgust at myself for the lie that I told. After about 6 months of dating, Wanda asked me to meet her parents and I happily agreed. I thought her parents lived in the same neighborhood that she did, but was I wrong! A White man going into South Central (Los Angeles) with a Black woman at 8 p.m. for dinner was not fun for me. I was scared, and I think most of the Black men who killed me with their looks knew that, too. I don't know what I expected when I entered the home. Although humble, it was clean and the smell of food was all over. Her parents were really nice people, unlike the rest of them, were my thoughts. A couple of months later, Wanda began to ask questions about my family and friends. She began to wonder why she had not met any of my friends or family members, and I didn't know what to say. One day, Wanda finally lashed out, called me a racist, and walked out. I knew that I was, but I didn't want to lose her. I tried to talk to her and tell her some of the things that I was doing in order to educate myself, but she told me that she would know if I was telling the truth. She quit the job, and stopped taking my calls. Very recently, I saw Wanda at a coffee shop that we used to frequent, and she was pleasant. I asked to talk to her, and I proceeded to tell her about all of the feelings that I had while we dated. I talked about my ignorance, denial, and racist beliefs. I said that I was confused about my attraction to her because I've never looked at a woman of color twice, but I admitted that being called a racist was the best thing that has ever happened to me. Wanda reached out and touched my hand, gave me a hug, and walked away from my life, and I haven't seen her since. I know that I have so much more to learn, but now I know that I can and will.

STEVE, 30+-YEAR-OLD EUROPEAN-AMERICAN MAN

In Steve's story we see several aspects of Helms's model, such as his acknowledgment that he is racist and will probably always have some racist ideas, his conflicted feelings about being attracted to and dating a Black woman, and his attempts to be honest, to grow, and to educate himself. Which status do you think best describes Steve's racial identity?

If I were to distill my feelings about my ethnicity, I would say that being White, straight, and middle-class puts me on an incredible footing to speak out against defamation and bigotry, because I am speaking out against my own self-interest. An interest in politics has also made me an advocate of equality for all human beings, because I have read accounts of history and see every day on the news what and who "my people" have exploited and continue to exploit to get where they are. If I were to label myself I would say I am American, Oklahoman, and human. I sometimes feel guilty for calling myself an American because too many people have died to put me where I am today. I have come to be proud of that label though, because to me it embodies those who have willingly and unwillingly sacrificed so much.

BILL, 20+-YEAR-OLD EUROPEAN-AMERICAN MAN

All the racial identity development models discussed thus far apply to individuals from one racial background. What about people from multiracial backgrounds? What challenges do they face in their identity development process?

Multiracial Identity Development

In 1967 the Supreme Court declared antimiscegenation laws (laws that forbade individuals from different races to marry) unconstitutional. At the time, 16 states still had antimiscegenation laws on the books. Since that time, the number of interracial marriages and multiracial births has been on the rise (Spickard, 1989). According to U.S. Census data, the number of interracial marriages increased from 149,000 in 1960 to 1,461,000 in 1990. Between 1990 and 1998 there was a 41 percent increase (U.S. Census Bureau, 1999). The 2000 census was the first to allow individuals to mark more than one race. Of those counted in the last census, about 2 percent (6.8 million) identified themselves as multiracial. The growth in the multiracial population is also seen in the number of multiracial children. Four percent of children under 18 were identified as multiracial, compared with 2 percent of adults (U.S. Census Bureau, 2001). With these changing demographics have come changes in attitudes. Surveys over the last 20 years suggest that Americans show increased approval of interracial marriages (Root, 1996, 2001).

As the number of multiracial people in the United States has risen, increased attention has been paid to their unique identity development process. Individuals from multiracial backgrounds face a more complex identity process than do those from monoracial backgrounds (Kerwin & Ponterroto, 1995). These individuals must reconcile the heritage of parents from two racial backgrounds and must decide where they fit in a society that likes to pigeonhole people into single categories (Keerdoja, 1984). In addition, they may face discrimination from both groups because they are not seen as full members of either one (Johnson, 1992; Sue & Sue, 2003). Multiracial individuals may feel pressured to identify with one group over the other. Often society's reactions are based on the person's appearance—that is, what racial group he or she looks like. Many parents now encourage their children to identify with both racial/ethnic groups (Smolow, 1993). We also see more multiracial individuals who, instead of identifying with one or both of their racial groups, identify with a third multiracial group that is unique and distinct from the others.

> *As a multiracial individual sometimes it feels like I have no culture at all. I am Caucasian, Hispanic, and Native American. My family has lived in the United States for as long as any of us can remember. Any ethnic culture that we had seems to have gradually disappeared over time as my family members assimilated themselves into American society leaving behind their old identities and embracing a new American culture. . . .*
>
> *I am very grateful for what my parents have given and sacrificed for my well being. They've done a lot and worked hard to get where they are now and have never left me with a want or a need. Though if I could request one thing out of them it would be to teach me more about what it means to be a Hispanic, European, and Native American.*

MONA, 20+-YEAR-OLD MULTIRACIAL
(LATINA/AMERICAN INDIAN/WHITE) WOMAN

PICTURES 7.2   Biracial and multiracial individuals have increased in numbers in recent years. *Photographs by Corrine Sheldrake*

We see many of the conflicts related to multiracial identity described in Mona's story: confusion about her ethnic status, the need to express gratitude to her parents to cover up her guilt about being angry at them for not teaching her about her multiple ethnicities, and ultimately a wish that she knew more about her heritage. This new confusion has affected both individual and researcher (Jeo, 2004).

personal identity—the stage or status in which a child bases his/her identity on personal factors, such as self-esteem, instead of on race or ethnicity.

choice of group categorization—the stage or status in which a child is forced to choose which race or ethnicity he/she should use as the basis of his/her identity.

enmeshment/denial—the stage or status in which a child feels guilty about choosing one race or ethnicity over the other, because this is an implicit rejection of the parent whose race or ethnicity was not chosen.

appreciation—the stage or status in which a child/adolescent begins to broaden his/her perspective to include the race or ethnicity not initially selected for his/her identity.

integration—the stage or status in which a child/adolescent/adult sees the benefits of embracing both races or ethnicities.

A number of models of multiracial identity development have been proposed (Jacobs, 1992; Kerwin & Ponterotto, 1995; Kich, 1992). The first of these models was Poston's (1990) five-stage model of biracial identity development. At the **personal identity** stage, the young child's sense of self is independent of his or her racial group. Identity is instead based primarily on personal factors, such as self-esteem, that develop within the context of the family. In the second stage, **choice of group categorization,** the young person feels pressured to choose one identity over the other. That pressure may come from family members, peers, physical appearance, or society (Hall, 1980, 1992). In the next stage, **enmeshment/denial,** feelings of guilt and self-hatred arise from choosing one group over another. A positive multiracial identity begins to emerge in the **appreciation** stage, when the person begins to broaden his or her perspective and begins to explore the previously rejected side of his or her racial heritage. Finally, in the fifth stage, **integration,** the person sees the benefits of embracing both identities.

Poston's model suggests that healthy resolution of the multiracial experience entails integration of and appreciation for both racial backgrounds. There is an implicit assumption in his model that all biracial individuals follow the same path. Root (1990, 1998, 2004) agrees that multiracial individuals need to come to terms with both sides of their heritage but describes four possible resolutions to this process. Root says that the multiracial person may choose to (a) accept the identity society assigns, (b) identify with both racial groups, (c) identify with a single racial group, (d) identify with a new "mixed-race" group, or (e) identify with the race considered as the one with the lower-status culture in this country/higher-status culture in this country (hypodescension/hyperdescension).[1] According to Root, each of these can represent a healthy adjustment to one's multiracial background, although accepting the identity that society assigns is passive and may not be as secure as the four other, more active resolutions of one's identity.

However, just because someone has resolved his/her biracial identity does not mean he/she has escaped the sting of racism. This student discussed the racial tension still felt in his parents' families of origin:

I am the product of an interracial couple—my mom's ethnic background is German American while my dad's ethnic background is African American, specifically Kenyan. I am also currently in a relationship that is very serious and interracial to an extent. My fiancée

---

1. Root (2004) has added a fifth resolution: symbolic identity. There is typically a "hypodescencion" of identity wherein one identifies with the lower-status culture in this country. For example, if someone is an offspring of one Black and one White parent, the person's identity is generally considered to be Black. In symbolic identity, there is a hyperdescencion of identity. In other words, the person identifies as being White and consciously knows that this is a nonstandard identity. Being half Black is only symbolic to the person; the person knows he or she is half Black, but it does not have much relevance in his or her life. This is akin to the situation of someone with Irish ancestral roots who may become more aware of his or her Irish heritage on St. Patrick's Day but for whom being of Irish descent does not have much bearing on his or her day-to-day life.

is predominantly white. What is amazing to me is the ignorance that we thought was out of our society regarding race, and how it can still [affect] our relationships today. When my parents got married, my grandfather, my mom's dad, refused to come to the wedding, much less give her away. My uncle had to give my mom away and it broke her heart that her father could not accept the fact that she was happy. It took my mom and grandfather a long time to mend the pain that was caused by that argument. My grandfather finally saw that my dad was a good man regardless of the color of his skin, and that he had no intention of leaving my mom, and my mom was finally able to forgive him for what he did to her. Also my grandfather's mom and dad never spoke to my mom again.

JACK, 20+-YEAR-OLD BIRACIAL (AFRICAN-AMERICAN/WHITE) MAN

As we have mentioned, racial identity has dominated the field of cultural identity development. However, there are several models that address other minority identities. Here we present a model of homosexual identity development as an example.

Gay/Lesbian Identity Development

I was 7 and I think I knew I was gay. I always felt more comfortable "hanging out" with my girl cousins, playing with dolls, and watching stars on TV (all men, of course). I swooned with them over these hunks on TV, and they didn't seem to mind. I remember my dad always threatening me about how he would knock my hips back in place if I didn't learn to walk like a boy. I couldn't help it that I loved my girl cousins and the way they played pretend. I would beg for them to put makeup on me and they always did because I always had the longest eyelashes. Though, when we got a little older, my cousins began to get weird. They started to say that I was weird because I didn't like to play with the boys. People started telling my father right in front of my face that he better beat it out of me before "it" got worse. Because of all of my family members, my school friends, and even my parents' friends calling me weird, I really started to look at my behaviors and think, "Am I weird?" Especially when I started 6th grade and I always admired this boy who had black hair and green eyes. I always told myself that it was because he was "cool" and that I wanted to be cool too. While I admired this boy from afar all the other boys bugged all of the girls. Even though deep inside I knew that I was gay from a very young age, it was not confirmed until I was in 8th grade. I was in the boy's bathroom at school and some guy kissed me . . . for a long time! He was a loner kid. I think we made out until we heard other boys coming. I was excited! He moved away after a semester, which was probably good because I've had to maintain an image because of the years that have passed that my dad threatened me constantly. I had transformed into this stud whom all the girls wanted. Besides, I really didn't want to be different from all the boys. I even got myself a pretty girlfriend. I guess back then, looking straight and being gay was okay for me. It helped me fit in for a little while. Never mind the fact that I really had to watch out and not stare at boys too long. Never mind the fact that I was truly hiding under a stone. I had to do what I had to do to fit in.

RUDY, 20+-YEAR-OLD GAY EUROPEAN-AMERICAN MAN

coming out–the process by which a gay, lesbian, or bisexual individual openly expresses his/her sexual orientation.

Rudy's story describes the phases he went through in his coming-out process. **Coming out,** or the process by which gay, lesbian, and bisexual individuals come to terms with their sexuality and share that orientation with others, is a unique aspect of their identity development. Homosexual individuals face heterosexism in that everyone is assumed to be heterosexual. Coming out is also not a one-time event. It happens over time and in different contexts. Whenever the homosexual person meets someone new, he or she must decide whether or not to divulge his or her sexual orientation (Israel, 2004).

identity confusion–the stage or status in which a gay, lesbian, or bisexual individual begins to question his/her sexual identity.

identity comparison–the stage or status in which a gay, lesbian, or bisexual individual recognizes his/her feelings about same-sex individuals.

Cass (1979) proposed a series of six stages that help to explain some of the thoughts and feelings Rudy had about his sexual orientation. According to Cass, the first stage that young people go through when questioning their sexual identity is **identity confusion.** This is when the first awareness of being "different" from same-sex peers occurs. During childhood or adolescence, the young person begins to recognize feelings, thoughts, and behaviors that are homosexual in nature, such as preferring activities or having interests typical of the opposite gender. Rudy noticed that he liked hanging out with his female cousins, playing with dolls, and admiring male television stars. At first that was acceptable, but soon others made fun of him because of it. Feelings and thoughts of attraction toward same-sex peers may not be apparent at this stage, but the feelings of being "the other" or "different" are enough to cause the child or adolescent to withdraw from family members and peers.

The next stage is **identity comparison.** In this stage the differences are more pronounced, and the homosexual child recognizes how he or she is different. Thoughts and feelings about same-sex peers become more conscious. A girl who finds herself attracted to another girl sees that other girls talk about boys. This creates incongruence because the girl knows she's a girl and has most likely been socialized as "a girl." All of a sudden, things change and she has feelings that are not part of the rule book for being "a girl." She now questions why she is so different. When Rudy heard the comments and questions by his family members and friends about his behavior, he began to question himself and asked, "Am I weird?" In the 6th grade he consciously noticed himself admiring another boy in his class.

identity tolerance–the stage or status in which a gay, lesbian, or bisexual individual fully recognizes his/her homosexual feelings but attempts to hide them from others and from himself/herself, by trying to believe, for example, that it is just a "phase" he/she is going through.

The third stage of homosexual identity development in Cass's (1979) model is **identity tolerance.** In this stage the individual learns to walk a tightrope. The homosexual is now fully conscious that he or she has sexual feelings toward others of the same sex but keeps them to himself or herself. Others most likely remain unaware that the individual has this orientation. This is what we typically describe as "being in the closet." The person may work very hard to keep his or her orientation a secret, but that results in feelings of guilt, pain, anger, and self-hatred. The individual is in constant turmoil because he or she must constantly internally justify his or her actions. The individual also holds out hope that this may "just be a phase." Rudy confirmed his homosexual feelings when he made out with another boy in the locker room in the 8th grade. However, he then became the "stud" that his father wanted him to be and that all the girls desired. He even got a girlfriend and worked hard to fit in with the other boys, all the while being careful not to stare at other boys too long.

Stage four is **identity acceptance.** Here the person moves one step closer to coming out. In acceptance the individual can no longer deny his or her homosexuality. Nonetheless, the individual continues to live in a secret world where his or her homosexual relations occur "underground" in very limited, specific environments (e.g., gay clubs) and infrequently for fear of being discovered. The person continues to internalize society's negative views of homosexuality as evil, sinful, and unacceptable. This may lead to feelings of hopelessness and even suicide. The suicide rate is high for individuals who come to accept their homosexuality as a fact but lack the social support needed to assume pride in their orientation—rates for gay, lesbian, and bisexual youth range from 20 percent to 50 percent (Tremblay, 1995).

> **identity acceptance**—the stage or status in which a gay, lesbian, or bisexual individual fully accepts his/her sexual orientation and is about to "come out" to others.

The next stage in Cass's model is **identity pride.** In this stage the person formally "comes out of the closet." The homosexual now feels pride in his or her orientation and finds causes (e.g., rallies, clubs, walk-a-thons) to explore, express, and celebrate his or her newly found voice. Yet, there is not a complete association of personal identity with his or her homosexuality. For example, a man may come out to his parents and begin to join marches and rallies for homosexual pride, yet may still not be "out" at work or with some of his friends, and may expend a great deal of energy maintaining these multiple identities.

> **identity pride**—the stage or status in which a gay, lesbian, or bisexual individual openly expresses his/her sexual orientation and takes pride in that identity.

In the final stage, **identity synthesis,** one is able to integrate his or her homosexuality with his or her other identities (e.g., woman, African American, student). The individual is comfortable with his or her orientation and no longer feels the need to justify his or her being. Self-acceptance provides him or her with the coping mechanisms needed to endure and fight the ignorance and discrimination he or she will face in embracing his or her diverse self. This positive self-acceptance is most possible when the individual has a strong social support system to help him or her withstand societal pressures. However, that support may be difficult to obtain from family members and friends who are unwilling to accept the person's sexual orientation. It may take some time and effort to build a new support system, and this may include relocation to an environment that is more supportive (e.g., moving to a city with a large, visible homosexual population).

> **identity synthesis**—the state or status in which a gay, lesbian, or bisexual individual is able to integrate all aspects of his/her identities, such as ethnic minority status and gender.

Rudy does not describe his movement through the last two stages, but the following story describes some struggles faced by a young woman in her coming-out process.

I wanted to be straight for a long time, but I've known that I was a lesbian for an even longer time. Anyway, when I came out to my parents, I guess I was hopeful. My dad said that he would pray for my salvation, and my mom didn't say a word. After eight years, you'd think that one of them knew that I was not straight (I brought home my first girlfriend when I was 12). I knew I was queer before that, but I was too afraid to make any moves toward any girls. Then I turned 18, and I met the most beautiful girl in the world. I wanted to let everyone know that she was my girl. Her parents were really cool and she had been "out" for a long time. I thought it was time to come out of the closet after many years of feeling like crap and being and staying invisible. Anyway, I told my parents that I was queer, but they really reacted more violently after they found out about Michelle. I guess it was okay to say I was queer, but it wasn't okay to have proof that I am. Nowadays, Michelle and I live together. She and I go out to West Hollywood on weekends and once in a while we go to "Pride" parades, but I'm not really sure what to call us, or myself for that matter. I know that I love her, that I'm queer, but there still feels like something's missing. I remember having to write a paper in college recently, asking the question, Who are you? I wasn't sure how to answer it because being a lesbian is the most predominant identity that "rules" my life right now, but I know that I'm more.

LETICIA, 20+-YEAR-OLD LATINA LESBIAN

What stages of identity development do you see in Leticia's story? What stage is she currently in?

Racial and Cultural Identity Development Model

Racial and Cultural Identity Development Model (R/CID)—a general model that covers all forms of cultural identity and addresses how one relates to oneself, to others of the same culture, to others of different cultures, and to the dominant cultural group.

conformity—the stage in which an individual sees the dominant culture as better and superior to all groups, and sees his or her own cultural group as "less than" or inferior.

At this point you might be thinking, "I'm confused. There are too many of these identity models and they all sound alike!" It is true. There are many cultural identity development models, and we have covered only a few. They sound similar because of the influence of the original model proposed by Cross and because all people in minority groups have the shared experience of oppression. A group of multicultural psychologists proposed a comprehensive model of cultural identity development that pulls together the common features of all the models for different groups. The first was done by Atkinson, Morton, & Sue (1979, 1989, 1998), who called it the *Minority Identity Development Model (MID)*. The model was later revised by Sue and Sue (1990, 1999, 2003), who called it the **Racial and Cultural Identity Development Model (R/CID)**. Each stage in the R/CID addresses how the individual feels about himself or herself, others of the same group, others of another minority group, and members of the majority or dominant group (Sue & Sue, 2003). The model is summarized in Table 7.1.

The first stage of the R/CID is **conformity**. Here individuals show a strong preference for the values, beliefs, and features of the dominant culture over their own. They have incorporated society's view that the dominant culture is superior. The individual has strong negative attitudes toward the self, his or her own group, and other minority groups. Members of the dominant groups are respected, admired, and emulated.

TABLE 7.1 The Racial/Cultural Identity Development Model

Stages of Minority Development Model	Attitude toward Self	Attitude toward Others of the Same Minority	Attitude toward Others of a Different Minority	Attitude toward Dominant Group
Stage 1—Conformity	Self-depreciating or neutral due to low race salience	Group-depreciating or neutral due to low race salience	Discriminatory or neutral	Group-appreciating
Stage 2—Dissonance and appreciating	Conflict between self-depreciating and group-appreciating	Conflict between group-depreciating views of minority hierarchy and feelings of shared experience	Conflict between dominant-held and group-depreciating	Conflict between group-appreciating
Stage 3—Resistance and immersion	Self-appreciating	Group-appreciating experiences and feelings of culturocentrism	Conflict between feelings of empathy for other minority	Group-depreciating
Stage 4—Introspection	Concern with basis of self-appreciation	Concern with nature of unequivocal appreciation	Concern with ethnocentric basis for judging others	Concern with the basis of group-depreciation
Stage 5—Integrative Awareness	Self-appreciating	Group-appreciating	Group-appreciating	Selective appreciation

Source: Atkinson, D. R., Morten, G., & Sue, D. W. (1998). *Counseling American minorities: A cross-cultural perspective* (5th ed.). Dubuque, IA: Brown.

dissonance—the stage in which there is a sudden or gradual "occurrence" that challenges a person's belief that the dominant group is superior and minority groups, including his or her own, is inferior.

Next is the **dissonance** stage. At some point, the individual encounters information that contradicts his or her cultural values and beliefs. For example, a closeted gay male who thinks all homosexuals are "fairies" may meet a gay man who is very masculine. An Asian-American person who thinks racism does not exist any more may experience a racist incident. Although movement into the dissonance stage may occur very suddenly with a traumatic event (as discussed in Cross's model), the developers of the R/CID model believe it occurs slowly through a gradual breakdown of denial as one questions his or her attitudes from the conformity stage. In dissonance the person is in conflict between positive and negative views of the self, members of his or her own group, members of other minority groups, and members of the majority. This student discussed her own transition from the conformity stage to the dissonance stage:

> I always thought that being and acting Filipino would not allow me to have American friends because my culture is so different than Americans. I thought that I wouldn't fit in unless I acted like them. Sadly, I have sacrificed on many occasions that opportunity to teach my friends that other cultures are great if only they would give it a chance instead of making jokes about how weird other people are. I let them put me down when I would wear certain clothes or do my hair a certain way because it made me look more Asian. I have to say that I have learned that many of my so-called friends really aren't my friends. They don't want me to be who I am, they want me to be who they are, and I can't any longer. I'm not too sad to cut some of these people out of my life because I have had to deal with trying hard to be like them for so long that I just made myself exhausted. This class has taught me the beauty in understanding who I am, and where I came from. I also was able to look at other cultures' perspectives, and I have gained a lot of respect for them as well. I am choosing to become an ally for my fellow culture, as well as other minority cultures.

CELESTE, 20+-YEAR-OLD FILIPINA-AMERICAN WOMAN

resistance and immersion—the stage in which the person becomes more immersed within his or her own cultural group, rejecting the dominant culture with extreme feelings of anger, guilt, and shame for his or her initial preference of the dominant culture and rejection of his or her own.

The third stage of the R/CID model is **resistance and immersion.** In this stage the person does an about-face and completely espouses minority views and rejects the dominant culture. The person feels guilt and shame about previously being a "sellout" and contributing to the oppression of his or her own group. There is anger, distrust, and dislike for the dominant group. The person is motivated to discover more about his or her own culture and builds a stronger sense of connection to his or her own group. Relationships with other minority groups tend to be transitory and superficial.

introspection—the stage in which a person becomes less angry at, and distrustful of, the dominant group, less immersed in his or her own group, more appreciating of other cultural groups, and more apt to educate him or herself about his or her own identity, though the process still creates some inner conflict.

In the **introspection** stage the individual begins to let go of some of the intense feelings of anger toward the dominant culture and redirect that energy into greater understanding of himself or herself and his or her own group. The person moves away from total immersion in his or her own group toward greater autonomy, but there is some conflict about this. There is also more of an attempt to

PICTURES 7.3   From the early racial identity development models arose more general racial/cultural identity development models, encouraging cultural pride across many groups. *Photographs by Alejandro Santander*

understand the attitudes and experiences of other groups, including a struggle to sort out the positive and negative aspects of the dominant group.

The final stage of the R/CID is **integrative awareness.** Here the person achieves an inner sense of security and appreciates both the positive and the negative aspects of both his or her own culture and the dominant culture. The person has a positive sense of group pride but is also able to question group

integrative awareness—the stage in which a person finds greater balance, appreciates his or her own group as well as other cultural groups, and becomes aware of him or herself as an individual and a cultural being, recognizing differences in different cultural groups, both positive and negative.

values. The person sees himself or herself as a unique individual, a member of a cultural group, and a member of the larger society. The person now reaches out to members of other minority groups to gain a greater understanding of their attitudes and experiences and expresses support for all oppressed people. The person also distinguishes between people in the dominant group in deciding whom to trust and in determining who also actively seeks to eliminate oppression.

The R/CID attempts to pull together the common characteristics of all the stage models. Do you think it is useful to have one comprehensive model of cultural identity development, or do you think each group has unique characteristics and experiences that need to be taken into account? Try going back to previous stories in the chapter (e.g., Deana, Marie, Rudy, Leticia) and applying the stages of the R/CID.

A CRITIQUE OF THE STAGE MODELS

Although cultural identity models have made a huge contribution to the field of multicultural psychology and to our understanding of human behavior and our diverse society, they are not without limitations. Most models of cultural identity development suggest a linear progression through each of the stages. In other words, it is assumed that all individuals begin at the first stage and gradually work their way through all the stages in the order described. However, that is not necessarily the case. Parham (1989) suggests that people may cycle back and forth through the stages across the life span. For example, in Cross's model, someone who has reached the final stage of internalization might have an experience that throws him or her back into the encounter or immersion-emersion stage. We mentioned previously that Helms (1995b) changed the term "stages" in her model to "statuses" to reflect the idea that these identities are not static categories but represent a dynamic developmental process.

Another observation is that not all minority individuals begin their developmental process in a stage where they idealize Whiteness and denigrate their own racial minority background. For example, in Cross's model, not all African Americans begin at the pre-encounter stage. Children who grow up in predominantly Black environments or in homes where they are taught to have a sense of pride in their racial identity may begin at a later stage. However, negative racial experiences during adolescence (such as those described in Tatum's book) can cause them to have attitudes and behaviors more characteristic of the pre-encounter, encounter, and/or immersion-emersion stages of the Cross model.

Another criticism of the cultural identity models is that they assume one definition of mental health, judging the final stage of the model as the "healthiest." In the final stage of most of the models, the individual achieves pride in his or her own group but also reaches out to other groups and incorporates positive aspects of the dominant group into his or her identity. However, for some individuals, immersion in their own group may be an adaptive response for their particular situation. The R/CID model assumes that a healthy identity includes some degree of autonomy, but in some instances, sublimation of one's individual needs for the sake of the group may be a healthy choice. We need to be careful in assuming that one identity outcome is the healthiest for all members of a particular group and under all circumstances (Barker-Hackett, 2003). Some critics of the stage models question the relevance of such models for different generations (Krate, Leventhal, & Silverstein, 1974). Others criticize the models for overemphasizing reactions to racism and oppression (Akbar, 1989; Nobles, 1989) and lacking empirical evidence to support some of the stages (Behrens, 1997; Cross, 1995; Helms, 1989).

MULTIPLE LAYERING OF IDENTITIES

Remember Leticia, the Latina lesbian in the preceding story? When faced with the question, Who are you? she wasn't sure how to answer. She felt her lesbian identity dominated at the time, but she also felt that she was more than that. Leticia is Latina, but she does not specifically mention her ethnic identity in her story. We may wonder where she is in her ethnic identity development and how that is related to her sexual orientation identity. The emotional turmoil of the homosexual identity process is painful enough, but People of Color who are homosexual face even more oppressive consequences. They face a unique challenge—integrating two identities, one pertaining to their ethnicity and the other to their sexual orientation—in a society that does not fully accept either one. Lesbian Women of Color face "triple jeopardy," since they must cope with oppression occasioned by their race, their gender, and their sexual orientation (Akerlund & Cheung, 2000; Greene & Boyd-Franklin, 1996).

We may also wonder about the reaction of Leticia's family members to her sexual orientation. Was it due to their culture? their religion? We all have multiple identities. We are not just a woman or a man, gay or straight, Catholic or Protestant; we are all these things. Membership in each of these groups shapes our experiences and our worldview. It has a powerful influence over how society views us, how we view ourselves, and how we view others (Atkinson et al., 1998; Sue & Sue, 2003).

All of us belong to more than one group (e.g., Leticia is a female, a lesbian, a Latina), but one of those identities may be more important to us than the others (e.g., sexual orientation over race). Characteristics of the person and characteristics of the situation interact to determine which identity is most salient at a particular time (Sellers et al., 1998). For example, if Leticia is at a club with all lesbian women but is the only Latina in the room, her race may become more salient than her sexual orientation.

The work of Sellers and colleagues (1998) helps to explain this shifting in the salience of identities. They examine the significance of race in the overall self-concept and define **racial salience** as "the extent to which one's race is a relevant part of one's self-concept at a particular moment or in a particular situation" (p. 24). In other words, the significance of one's race varies across individuals and across situations. For example, being the only African American in a class may make race salient for one person but not have an impact on another African-American student in the same situation, because of that

racial salience—at a particular time or in a particular situation, the extent to which one's race is relevant in self-concept.

student's own attitudes and beliefs about his or her racial identity. The following story illustrates the multiple layering of identities and how the salience of these identities can shift.

> One summer while I was in graduate school I traveled through Europe with three girlfriends, all of whom were African Americans. It was our first time in Europe, and we were constantly amazed at the reactions we got from people. At first we couldn't understand these strange and different feelings we were experiencing. Then it dawned on us, people were reacting to us based on our culture (as Americans) and our gender (as females). At home we were used to walking in places and being ignored or having people react negatively to us simply based on our color. We were used to being on guard, ready for people to do or say something negative, hurtful, or offensive. But in Europe that wasn't happening. Or, if it did happen, it was based on something else, such as us being American or being women, not because we were Black. In fact, being Black was a positive. Our Blackness was considered beautiful. And we weren't used to that.
>
> This realization really hit us during an incident that happened when we were in Greece. We were out on the island of Santorini. The island was full of young people from all over the world, and all the hotels were full. The only place we could find to stay was a room in a private home. Well, I'm being nice by calling it a room. It was really the unfinished upper level of a house. The floor was cement, there were no windows, no doors, and only patio lounge chairs to sleep on. During the day we thought we might be able to do it, but after dark, and after some strange men moved into the "room" next to ours, we decided we had to find another place to stay, and—thank God—we managed to find a beautiful (and complete!) room at a nearby hotel. We were so relieved and excited that we ran back to that house, packed up our things, and promptly left without telling anyone.
>
> The next day we wanted to do some laundry, so we took our bags of dirty clothes to the only laundromat in the little seaside town where we were staying. As we approached the storefront we saw a man talking with a group of young people and overheard him say, "Well, some American girls were supposed to stay there last night, but I don't know what happened to them." I did not think their conversation had anything to do with me, but one of my girlfriends leaned over and whispered, "He's talking about us." "What?" I asked, still totally oblivious. "He's talking about us," she said a little more emphatically. "What? Really? Oh!" The light dawned. The owner of the laundromat was also the owner of the "house" we vacated the night before, and we were the "American girls" he was talking about. But, American? Me? I'd never ever identified as being American. Black, yes. But, American? No. (The term African American was not in popular usage yet). So

many negative things went along with being American. Americans were
racist. Americans were the oppressors. I'm not American. But, that is
how that Greek man saw us. Americans first. Girls second. Black was
somewhere farther down the list. At home we would have just been
"the Black girls." I was stunned. It threw me for a loop. [LAB]

In LAB's story we see that a major factor in the ordering of her identities, with race as the primary one, was the negative reactions she received from others as a Black woman in the United States. Keeping race as the top priority served as a coping strategy against racist assaults, large and small. However, in Europe, the circumstances changed, and others in her environment no longer reacted primarily to her race but, rather, to her culture and gender. This forced reordering of identities was a shock for LAB.

What groups do you identify with the most? Which group identity is most salient for you? Why? Does the salience of your identities ever change? If so, how? Why?

SUMMARY

The study of identity development is one of the most popular in the field of multicultural psychology. Cultural minorities face unique identity challenges because of the racism, discrimination, and oppression from a society that does not value their differences. Psychologists attempt to understand how personal, social, political, and cultural factors interact to shape one's identity. These models began with racial and ethnic groups but quickly expanded to other groups, such as gay, lesbian, and bisexual groups, multiracial groups, and women. Many models of cultural identity development exist, reflecting the unique situations of the various groups.

The models share some common characteristics. Most assume that cultural minorities begin in a stage where they devalue their own culture and idealize the dominant culture. However, life experiences challenge that perspective and force them to reevaluate their beliefs. This moves them into a stage where they immerse themselves in their own culture and devalue the dominant culture. Resolution is achieved when the individual has a positive view of his or her own group but also identifies with and incorporates positive aspects of other groups.

Identities are not unidimensional. All of us have multiple identities, such as woman, student, daughter, and member of an ethnic minority group. At times one of those dimensions becomes more important, and at other times another dimension becomes more important. Sometimes these dimensions can conflict. For example, if you are a woman who is a member of an ethnic minority group and the discussion turns to physical abuse, as a woman you might feel it important to speak out to put an end to this abuse, but as a member of an ethnic minority group, you might feel that your discussion of this topic may unfairly lead others to conclude that all male members of your group engage in abuse. The more secure you are in all your identities, the less these conflicts will interfere with your ability to speak your mind with confidence.

Food for Thought

The cultural identity development models have made a huge contribution to our understanding of human behavior and our society as a whole, but perhaps the most important contribution is an increased understanding of ourselves. If you have not explored your own cultural identities, we strongly suggest that you begin such an exploration. Some people tell us, "I'm a Heinz 57—I am a mix of so many different cultures that I don't know what I am other than an American." We tell them to go home and consult with their parents and/or grandparents. They will discover that they do have some identifiable ethnicities that can be a source of interest and understanding. These students soon come back to us and say, "I was wondering where this particular characteristic came from, and then my grandmother told me that when she was growing up, she learned to behave in this manner. I guess I just picked it up from my mother, who had picked it up from my grandmother. I then looked up the country where my grandmother's parents came from, and everything began to make sense." By completing this kind of examination, you might discover how enriching it can be.

Critical Thinking Questions

How are you like everyone else? How are you like a group of identifiable people? How are you unique?

How are you like others in your racio-ethnic group? What similarities do you see among people of other racio-ethnic groups?

When interacting with people of different racial and ethnic groups, have you noticed that some seem to be more connected with their groups than others are? Have you noticed that some seem to reject interactions with you, whereas others seem quite open to interacting with you?

If you are multiracial, with what group or groups do you feel most comfortable? What group or groups seem to be most accepting of you? If you know people who are multiracial, with what group or groups do they feel most comfortable?

If you are lesbian, gay, or bisexual (LGB), how comfortable are you with your sexuality? If you know people who are LGB, how comfortable are they with their respective sexualities?

What other identities do you have? Do they ever come into conflict with your racio-ethnic identity? If so, how have you resolved those conflicts?

CHAPTER 8

Culture and Health

HEALTH AND HEALTH BEHAVIORS
HEALTH DISPARITIES DEFINED
CAUSES OF HEALTH DISPARITIES
    Racism
    Poverty
    Structural Barriers
    Access to the Health Care System
    Differential Treatment
MISTRUST OF THE HEALTH CARE SYSTEM

WHY SHOULD WE CARE?
BRINGING ABOUT CHANGE
SICKLE CELL ANEMIA–A CASE STUDY
SUMMARY

*I don't want to be treated any better than anyone else, yet it happens on
a daily basis. I remember about a year ago I had an experience with this.
I had to go to the emergency room at the . . . hospital because I got a
concussion. Me, and my other white friend, walked in and were served
immediately, very fast service. I was checked in with a room in just a few
minutes. The problem with this was that I could not help but notice that
the waiting room was packed full, with people standing even. The
majority were not white. The thought of this still haunts me. It was so
sad to see the babies crying and families just waiting. Then there I was
getting the royal treatment. It was not right. All I could say to the nurse
was Busy night? and she replied, Yes, very. I think about that night all
the time, and whether or not I should have said something. I should
have insisted that they be served first. It is such a sad thing, and I feel
like I am on the bad side.*

BRIDGET, 20+-YEAR-OLD EUROPEAN-AMERICAN WOMAN

*An incident took place that is a prime example for discrimination
between ethnic groups. A young 23-year-old black woman came into
the hospital because she had a Caesarian about three days prior. She
complained of abdominal pain and she was not immediately treated by
the facility. They had her waiting in the emergency room for seven
hours. At the same time an older white woman was complaining of
abdominal pain as well, I think it was kidney stones or a urinary tract
infection. But anyways they both came in at the same time and had the
same chief complaint, but the white female was called in before the
black female even though she had a baby three days prior. The white
woman was promptly treated and given antibiotics and discharged.
When the black female was called in and treated she [had to be]
admitted to the hospital and immediately scheduled for surgery because
the doctor who performed her C-section left part of the placenta in her
stomach that was causing infection. This incident happened on my shift
and it is only one of many amazing stories that display racial
discrimination within the healthcare system.*

ADRIAN, 20+-YEAR-OLD EUROPEAN-AMERICAN WOMAN

This chapter addresses health psychology as it relates to health disparities and
health care disparities in ethnic minority groups. *Ethnic minority groups* refers to
people who are disadvantaged and lacking privilege because of their race/ethnicity,
socioeconomic status, disability, age, gender, orientation, geographic location, special health care needs, long-term-care needs, or need for end-of-life care. *Health
disparities* refers to different rates of health or illness that ethnic minorities have in

comparison with their White counterparts, whereas *health care disparities* refers to the differential access to or treatment by the health care system in this country. Although we may not be able to address the specific health and health care requirements of each group, we will elaborate on the needs as a whole so that we begin to explore ways to make improvements in meeting those needs.

As some of us are already aware, ethnic minorities do not receive optimal care for illnesses, whether or not those ailments can be traced primarily to nonmajority groups. Ethnic minority health has never received the attention that it should have, so many people continue to ask "the chicken or the egg" question: do ethnic minorities receive suboptimal care because they do not seek medical attention and insist on self-care or "ignoring" their illnesses, or do they choose to "deal" with their illnesses on their own because they have continually received suboptimal care? In examining ethnic minority health, it becomes clear that questions about health go hand in hand with questions about health care. We cannot discuss health without discussing health care, especially as it relates to health disparities in ethnic minority groups.

First, we address definitions of health, health behaviors, and health psychology. Next, we take a look at general health problems that are more common to different minority groups than to Whites. These health issues will help us develop a more elaborate view of health disparities, the definitions involved, possible causes, and their link to health care disparities. Finally, we discuss goals and limitations regarding health and health care disparities.

HEALTH AND HEALTH BEHAVIORS

Taylor (2003) cited WHO's definition of **health** as a complete state of physical, mental, and social well-being—not merely the absence of disease or infirmity (World Health Organization, 1948). Therefore, a person is not necessarily healthy just because there is an absence of symptoms. We can argue that different ethnic minority groups suffer from illnesses that do not afflict the majority population as much, and the ways in which such illnesses are treated may be defined by looking at people's health behaviors. Those health behaviors are influenced by people's beliefs about their health and its treatment.

health—a complete state of physical, mental, and social well-being—not merely the absence of disease or infirmity.

PICTURE 8.1   Maintaining one's health partially depends upon one's access to treatment. *Photograph by Erica Preston*

More simply stated, thoughts about health and the treatment of health issues influence how people behave or seek treatment to maintain or improve their health. For example, if you feel that your health problems are due to a chemical imbalance of some sort, you will tend to seek out a healer who will prescribe a medication. On the other hand, if you feel that your health problems are due to a dietary imbalance, you will seek out a healer who will map out a diet program for you. Furthermore, ethnic minorities' thoughts about health may also be influenced by those from whom they seek treatment, such as indigenous healers who have markedly different worldviews about the nature of disorders from those of more Western-oriented healers.

health behaviors—behaviors undertaken by people to enhance or maintain their well-being.

Health behaviors are behaviors undertaken by people to enhance or maintain their health. Health behaviors differ according to demographic factors. Younger, more affluent, better-educated people under low levels of stress and with high levels of social support typically practice better health habits than do people under higher levels of stress with fewer resources, such as individuals in lower socioeconomic classes (Taylor, 2003). Some individuals who are not familiar with the behaviors and beliefs of ethnic minority groups continue to question the need to improve health care disparities when they observe those individuals behaving in ways that may not fit the Western conception of a healthy lifestyle. Again, we need to pay attention to people's belief systems and the ways in which they influence their behaviors.

health psychology—the study of psychological influences on how people stay healthy, why they become ill, and how they respond when they do get ill.

Health psychology is devoted to understanding psychological influences on how people stay healthy, why they become ill, and how they respond when they do become ill. For example, a health psychology researcher may be interested in why people continue to smoke even though they know that smoking increases their risk of cancer and heart disease (Taylor, 2003). On the positive side, a health psychology researcher may be interested in the factors behind why some people engage in very strict regimens of good diet and exercise.

Health Belief Model—a set of assumptions that suggests that one's health behavior is affected by one's perception of a personal health threat as well as by how a particular health practice would be effective in reducing the personal health threat.

According to the **Health Belief Model** (Taylor, 2003), an individual's health behavior is affected by that individual's perception of a personal health threat, as well as how a particular health practice would be effective in reducing the personal health threat.

> *For the first couple of years that my family and I arrived to the U.S., we did not have health insurance, and indeed, we would not go to a doctor unless it was something very critical. Actually, we would not even go to a doctor when something serious arose, we would actually go straight to the hospital, which meant waiting in line in the emergency room. Furthermore, we would even sometimes hesitate to go to the hospital because none of my family members were able to speak English. . . . Many of the times we would revert to home remedies and would not visit a hospital until it was imperative.*
>
> JAIME, 20+-YEAR-OLD MEXICAN-AMERICAN MAN

HEALTH DISPARITIES DEFINED

Many researchers have identified health disparities (e.g., Buki, Borrayo, Feigal, & Carrillo, 2004; Clegg, Li, Hankey, Chu, & Edwards, 2002; Gilliland, Hunt, & Key, 1998; Li, Malone, & Daling, 2003; Schiffner & Buki, 2006). Our goal is to

PICTURE 8.2   People's health behaviors depend upon their health beliefs. *Photograph by Megan Prior*

look at the cyclical pattern that ultimately results in widened disparities in health care between minority groups and the majority and in continued discrimination of minority groups. According to the U.S. Department of Health and Human Services (2003), there is inequality in the quality of care given. If a White person suffered from a cardiovascular disease and a Person of Color suffered from the same illness, would they be given equal treatment? The U.S. Department of Health and Human Services (2003) defines **disparity** as the condition or fact of being unequal, as in age, rank, or degree. Synonyms for disparity include *inequality, unlikeness, disproportion*, and *difference*.

> **disparity—the condition or fact of being unequal.**

According to the National Cancer Institute, the first attempt at an official definition for "health disparities" was developed in September 1999, in response to a White House initiative. The National Institutes of Health (NIH), under the direction of then-director Dr. Harold Varmus, convened an NIH-wide working group, charged with developing a strategic plan for reducing health disparities. That group developed the first NIH definition of "health disparities:"

> Health disparities are differences in the incidence, prevalence, mortality, and burden of diseases and other adverse health conditions that exist among specific population groups in the United States.

Before we discuss more specific causes of health disparities, let us consider some of the more common health issues faced by minority groups. Some of these health issues can be seen by comparing health problems of minority groups with health problems of the majority population, and others can be seen by comparing health problems of different ethnic minority groups with one another.

TABLE 8.1   **Major Health Disparities**

- Minorities are more likely to be diagnosed with late-stage breast cancer and colorectal cancer than are Whites.
- Patients of lower socioeconomic position are less likely to receive recommended diabetic services and more likely to be hospitalized for diabetes and its complications.
- When hospitalized for acute myocardial infarction, Hispanics are less likely to receive optimal care.
- Many racial and ethnic minorities and persons of lower socioeconomic position are more likely to die from HIV. Minorities also account for a disproportionate share of new AIDS cases.
- The use of physical restraints in nursing homes is higher among Hispanics and Asian/Pacific Islanders than among non-Hispanic Whites.
- Blacks and poorer patients have higher rates of avoidable admissions. African Americans have the highest rate of cardiovascular disease in the world (USDHHS, 2001).
- Diabetes has reached epidemic proportions among Native Americans, African Americans, and Hispanics.
- African Americans, Asian Americans, and Hispanics have a disproportionate burden for cancer deaths compared with the White population.
- Elderly African-American men have significantly higher levels of race-related stress than do elderly African-American women. Higher incidences of stress-related diseases (e.g., hypertension, coronary heart disease, and cancer) occur mostly among African-American men because of their chronic exposure to racism and discrimination.

Source: *National Healthcare Disparities Report, Executive Summary,* U.S. Department of Health and Human Services (2003), Edwards (2003), and Utsey, Payne, Jackson, and Jones (2002).

TABLE 8.2   **Gender Differences in Health Disparities**

- African-American women have a shorter life expectancy than do White women by 5 years.
- African-American women have 50% higher all-cause mortality rates, as well as death rates from major causes such as heart disease, cerebrovascular diseases, and diabetes that are often 2 to 3 times higher than those for White women.
- Though breast cancer incidence is similar for African-American and Caucasian women, Black women have higher breast cancer mortality.
- Among younger and reproductive-age women, maternal mortality and homicide rates are 4 times higher for African Americans than for Caucasians.
- HIV-related death is 12 times higher for Black women than for Caucasian woman.
- Today, the women's health agenda includes conditions that occur throughout the entire life cycle and all types of diseases, as well as more general problems such as depression, lack of health care, and domestic violence.
- Among Native Americans and African Americans younger than 45 years, death rates were 47% and 42% higher, respectively, than would be expected on the basis of death rates for Whites.
- HIV/AIDS has higher burden for African-American and Hispanic women as a mainstream women's issue, and osteoporosis affects proportionately more White than minority women.

Source: Kumanyika, Morssink, and Nestle (2001).

TABLE 8.3 Disparities in Substance Abuse

- The socioeconomic disparities among racial/ethnic subgroups in the United States, combined with the associations between low socioeconomic status and substance abuse, would indicate that an increasing number of members of racial/ethnic minorities may be at risk of substance abuse.
- Persons of Chinese, Japanese, and Filipino ancestry or origin accounted for about 60% of the Asian/Pacific Islander (API) population. API prevalence of substance abuse, alcohol dependence, and need for illicit-substance-abuse treatment is low compared with that of the total U.S. population, although it is high enough to warrant attention. Males have a higher prevalence than females do, but the gender gap is larger among the APIs than among the total U.S. population.
- Among the Hispanic subgroups, there is much variation in the prevalence of substance abuse, alcohol dependence, and need for illicit-drug-abuse treatment. Mexicans and Puerto Ricans have a high prevalence of illicit drug use (marijuana, cocaine), heavy alcohol use, alcohol dependence, and need for drug abuse treatment. Caribbeans, Central Americans, and Cubans have low prevalence, and South Americans and other Hispanics have prevalence that is close to that of the total U.S. population. As far as cigarette use is concerned, Puerto Ricans have a relatively high prevalence, Caribbeans and Central Americans have relatively low prevalence, and Mexicans, Cubans, South Americans, and other Hispanics have an intermediate prevalence, all of which are relative to the total U.S. population.
- Native Americans, who are identified as those having origins in and maintaining cultural identification with any of the original peoples of North America, including American Indian tribes and Alaskan Natives, have very high prevalence of past-year substance use (including cigarettes, alcohol, and illicit drugs), alcohol dependence, and need for illicit-drug-abuse treatment. This is relative to the total U.S. population.
- Individuals in low-income-family households have a higher prevalence of substance abuse, and Hispanics and non-Hispanic Blacks have a higher percentage of families with low-income households.
- Regardless of racial/ethnic subgroup, adolescents who dropped out of school or who reside in households with fewer than two biological parents have relatively high prevalence of past-year use of cigarettes, alcohol, and illicit drugs.

Source: *National Household Survey on Drug Abuse,* Substance Abuse & Mental Health Services Administration (SAMHSA), 2003.

Disparities are most easily identified when there is a clear reference point for what is appropriate and reasonable to expect. Table 8.1 displays some prominent health disparities between ethnic minority populations and their White counterparts.

Although health disparities in general exist between ethnic minority populations and Whites in the United States, there are more specific health disparities between ethnic minority women and their White counterparts. Table 8.2 displays some of those differences.

Although some may argue that substance and alcohol abuse and/or dependence should be considered with mental health problems, it is a medical fact that such abuse and dependence eventually produce physical illnesses. Many illnesses caused by years of substance abuse are often irreversible and sometimes fatal. That is why health professionals focus on substance abuse along a continuum of physical health as well as on its interactions with mental disorders/difficulties. Table 8.3 lists some of the disparities in substance abuse among ethnic minority populations.

While we can look at different illnesses and health practices of ethnic minority groups in comparison to the majority population, we should take a look at other, more specific causes to continuing health disparities. Inequalities in health care that affect some racial, ethnic, socioeconomic, and geographical subpopulations in the United States ultimately affect every American (U.S. Department of Health and Human Services, 2003). The Department of Health and Human Services report further states that persistent disparities in health care are inconsistent with *American* values. This statement provides additional "food for thought," because it would be interesting to see how different individuals would define "American."

CAUSES OF HEALTH DISPARITIES

Let us use the premise cited by Taylor (2003) involving the Health Belief Model to begin exploring the causes of disparities in health and health care. An individual's perception of a health threat is influenced by at least three factors: (1) general health values, (2) specific beliefs about vulnerability to a particular disorder, and (3) beliefs about the consequences of the disorder. A person's perception of a health threat cannot completely influence him or her to change health behaviors more positively.

We should also consider whether a person believes that a health measure could reduce the threat, which involves the individual's perception of the effectiveness of the treatment as well as the cost of the treatment. For example, we see that an individual must place a large degree of trust in the diagnosing health professional to believe that a health threat exists. The individual must also believe that treatment costs are valid and worthwhile.

It may be hard to imagine anyone distrusting a medical professional who is supposedly trained to diagnose correctly and treat effectively, but we need to take a look at the issue of trust from a different point of view. Through the eyes of a minority group member, health professionals do not look as reliable as they do through the eyes of a majority group member. Though we focus on the health professional as the one who is distrusted, is the health professional really the fundamental cause of health/health care disparities?

I used to work as an independent contractor assistant social worker. Our company was contracted by home health care agencies that provided home care for predominantly senior citizens. During one of my many visits in Los Angeles, I was to provide service for an African-American male, age 70. When I arrived at the home, I saw this man on the couch, lethargic and sickly thin. I approached and realized that he was blind. The man was a diabetic who had glaucoma and became legally blind. Shortly after I arrived, a neighbor came in and said that this man used to have his daughter helping him, but she recently died from cancer. I asked my questions in order to ascertain which services he needed. The man had not eaten in a day, and this was dangerous, especially for a diabetic. He had Medicaid and Medicare and earned monthly SSI, but was unable to acquire the needed help. Amazingly, this man was still receiving home care, which meant that a nurse visited him on a daily basis to administer the insulin injections. I immediately called the home care agency to question the staff about this particular patient. They said that the reason I was sent was to figure out what kind of help the man needed. All this time they were seeing this man, no one took the initiative to help him. Amazingly, the staff knew that he needed a caretaker and some food, but they waited awhile to contact someone to help him. We ended up having to institutionalize the man because he didn't have enough money to pay a round-the-clock caregiver and he was unable to care for himself at all. His home was not conducive for living in, since he was blind. The man died two months after being moved into a convalescent home.

Here's a similar story: I visited another man, Caucasian, age 68. This man was also a diabetic, with almost the same amount earned, but this man was on Medicare and another supplemental type of insurance. The one thing that was different was the type of care that this man received from the same home health care agency. This man was released from the hospital, and because he had more than himself to speak about his needs (he had family members), the home health care agency became more an advocate for him. He had equipment in the home to help him be more comfortable. I remember that a nurse was present during my visit with this man. She said that she wanted to make sure that I had all of the information that I needed in order to help "her" patient. After this visit, I asked the nurse about the African-American man from the previous story, and this was when I found out that he died in the convalescent home. I was infuriated, and I asked her why it took their agency so long to help that man who didn't have any family members left, while they were "on top of things" with this patient who seemed to have many family members supporting him. She had no explanation for me. I told myself that this was how things were, and I began to plan my future because I know that my story might parallel that of the African-American male more so than the Caucasian male patient.

RAFAEL, 30+-YEAR-OLD MEXICAN-AMERICAN MAN

Should we assume that these two stories differ because of the difference in family support? If the African-American man had had more family members advocating for him, would his story have had a different ending? We can make different assumptions about these stories, but we should take a look at the underlying causes of the disparities in treatment and care between the two men. As in many cases, whether they involve health, finances, or education, and so on, we will find that there is more than one aspect to consider in any attempt to obliterate the negative forces that make our society the unequal and disparate place that it is still today. We need to look at racism, poverty, and structural barriers to getting health care, as well as ease of access to the health care system. Finally, we should also look at differential treatments in healthcare as a continuing cause for disparities.

Racism

About one-third of the U.S. population is expected to be Asian/Pacific Islander, African American, or of Hispanic origin by the year 2010 (U.S. Census Bureau, 2004). By the year 2050, almost 50 percent of the U.S. population will be non-White (Edwards & Erwin-Johnson, 2003). Clearly, the ethnic minority population is increasing at higher rates than the White population is. If the ethnic minority population is increasing, then we can assume that there will be an increase in numbers among our elderly and our children. These two subgroups constitute increasing numbers of those in poverty (Edwards, 2003; Utsey et al., 2002).

These demographic trends indicate that the number of Americans who are vulnerable to the effects of disparities in health care delivery will rise over the next half century (U.S. Department of Health and Human Services, 2003). Should we focus primarily on health and health care disparities? Or is there a bigger underlying factor that needs to be addressed to decrease disparity among minority groups in relation to the majority group?

Many readers may recognize that, once again, racism—and in this case institutionalized racism—seems to be the culprit. Because racism, operating through varied interpersonal and institutional pathways, is a fundamental cause of racial/ethnic health disparities, the elimination of those disparities cannot be achieved without first undoing racism (James, 2003). Some may reject that idea, thinking "Are they using '*that*' again"? The answer is, absolutely. Until we as a society realize that the hand of racism has its fingers in many pockets of societal endeavors, which we all would like to consider democratic and ideal, we will see "*that*" over and over again in many areas.

As far as racism and its involvement in health and health care disparities go, there are aspects that we would like to highlight because they seem to be repeated in many research studies regarding disparities. This is not to say that other factors under the umbrella of racism should not be considered, but for purposes of this chapter, we focus primarily on factors that are most prominent within health issues. We hope that readers will be able to see how the chapters in this book relate to one another and how they all should come together as proof of what our society needs to do to improve the way we fulfill our democratic, "American" ideals.

It is important to note that there can be huge differences within ethnic groups, but our focus is minority groups in relation to their White counterparts. If we fail to mention certain minority groups more specifically, it is because we intend to deliver a message that is needed to help *all* minority groups improve the standards that they have learned to live with thus far. In addition, when examining racial and ethnic differences within populations, we have found that many data sets often do not include information about patient socioeconomic status, language, population subgroup, understanding of health information, cultural competency, and special health care needs (U.S. Department of Health and Human Services, 2003). Limitations in the data pertaining to individuals in certain ethnic groups make it difficult to be more specific with respect to those groups.

The vast majority of empirical research on prejudice and discrimination has been conducted among African Americans, and few studies have systematically addressed how prejudice and discrimination affect other racial/ethnic groups, such as American Indians, Asian Americans, and Latinos (Cain & Kington, 2003). Since racial/ethnic bias has affected the social position of each racial/ethnic group in the United States, bias may have unique associations with health for each group. Bias against People of Color exists in many sectors of our society (Cain & Kington, 2003), and there is a suggestion of existing mental and physical consequences for people who routinely live with discrimination. Cain and Kington (2003) also report that the ways in which racial/ethnic bias can affect health range from economic deprivation and limits on access to quality medical care to the physiological responses to the experience of chronic discrimination and to inequitable exposure to occupational and environmental hazards.

Racism is a fundamental, underlying cause of health and health care disparities (Edwards & Erwin-Johnson, 2003; Utsey et al., 2002), but we should begin to take a look at the ways in which we can organize proof of the injustice to minority groups.

Poverty

Poverty contributes to disparities in health care. James (2003) identified a contradiction that exists in our society: racism is incompatible with democratic ideals, but both are deeply characteristic of U.S. society. Racism and democratic ideals coexist partly because of the moral economy of the U.S. society, which refers to the norms that govern, or should govern, economic activity in a given society and that set either tight or loose constraints on the ability of dominant groups to treat subordinated others as undeserving of the protections and privileges they accord themselves. Inequalities in wealth and health result from such constraints but are publicly rationalized as logical.

James (2003) further adds that this explanation has been uncontested and dominantly used as the reason for the nation's persistent racial/ethnic health disparities, and it has taken root in the American psyche without a shred of empirical evidence to support it. James argues that the entire argument rests on an edifice of negative moral sentiments and stereotypes about some racial/ethnic minorities. On one hand, the negative sentiments and stereotypes increase minorities' vulnerability to economic exploitation in the marketplace, and, on the other hand, they portray minorities—subtly or overtly—as undeserving of the protections and privileges of citizenship that are readily available to others.

How do ethnic minority groups, especially those who have limited resources, begin to find out about health care access? Gaining initial entry into the health care system includes such measures as looking up health professionals who are in the local area, after the minority group member actually acquires a way to pay for

PICTURE 8.3   Poverty is related to poor health. *Photograph by Janice Morrissey*

the needed medical treatment (determining whether health professionals take cash for people who are unable to acquire insurance). Many if not most people gain initial entry by calling around, using the Internet, and following up on referrals from other individuals.

That may seem easy enough, but if we consider the limitations of minority group members, the commonly used ways to gain entry into the health care system may prove more troublesome. Some minority groups do not have telephone access in their place of residence. Most do not have access to the Internet. Those who live in certain neighborhoods have no reliable referrals because they live with other individuals facing similar challenges regarding the health care system. Entry to the health care system may prove more difficult than it seems to be for Whites. Poverty hinders minorities from utilizing resources, but when we consider this along with structural barriers, it becomes clearer how disparities continue.

Structural Barriers

Kim had been in the United States for about 5 months. She had to wait for her paternal uncle to petition her from Korea and for the papers to be approved, before she agreed to migrate. Kim was very scared to move to the U.S., but she knew she had to for her kids back home. Her husband died recently and she had no one else besides her grandmother back in Korea. During her 5th month in the U.S., Kim began to get headaches daily. She lived in a tiny apartment with her uncle, aunt, and their five children. This neighborhood was primarily low-income, immigrant Koreans. Although Kim was a "legal citizen," she refused to go to the doctor for help. In her mind, she really didn't know how to begin the process. She was told that she needed a "card" to get medical help and she really didn't know how to do that. Her uncle would help, but he was the only one who worked and the family was poor. Kim needed help but was too embarrassed to ask. She really didn't know where to begin and where to look first.

JAYMIE, 30+-YEAR-OLD BIRACIAL (FILIPINA/BLACK) WOMAN

For ethnic minority group members who are limited not only by the color of their skin but also by language barriers or their immigrant/undocumented status, entry into the health care system becomes a maze with no beginning and no end. An individual's cultural beliefs may be a contributing factor to his or her resistance to seeking help in the United States, but certainly the lack of cultural competence among health professionals does not inspire minority group members to be trusting of such help. Many racial and ethnic groups, as well as poor and less educated patients, are more likely to report poor communication with their physicians and to report more problems with some aspects of patient–provider relationships (U.S. Department of Health and Human Services, 2003). For example, Asians, Hispanics, and people of lower socioeconomic status (SES) have greater difficulty accessing health care information, including information on prescription drugs.

Furthermore, the Department of Health and Human Services executive reports state that geography can play an important role in health care disparities. Remote rural populations, for example, are clearly at risk for having worse access and receiving poorer quality care. Gaining entry into the health care system seems to require more competence from the patient, who may be linguistically, economically, and educationally challenged, than from the health professionals who are in charge of healing and advertising assistance. For most minority group members, it is easier to stay within their own community and "deal" with their ailments according to how it was done "from where they came" than to fight their way through mazes while they deal with their pain.

As readers can surmise, there are many challenges for People of Color, the young, the elderly, the impoverished, and those with special needs—the "unseen people" in our society—just in considering entry into the health care system. It is clear that certain injustices, whether within the health care system or any other aspects of our society, are interconnected, which suggests that resolving these underlying issues could eventually put an end to discriminatory practices.

Once ethnic minority group members gain entry into the health care system, they may not be able to see their health professional right away. Ethnic minority group members must consider such issues as transportation to the doctor's office, making appointments, and referrals to specialists (U.S. Department of Health and

Human Services, 2003). Most ethnic minority group members need to be hospitalized before they are made aware of resources that are available to them.

Some groups are unable to get care because of limitations that go beyond those that most health care providers are prepared to address. According to Ashton and associates (2003), African Americans and Latinos have lower incomes, less education, lower rates of private health insurance coverage, a higher probability of being underinsured, and greater dependence on public health care programs than do Whites—all of which impede their ability to seek and obtain timely services.

Most health care providers are limited when communicating with ethnic minority patients. This limitation is due either to the health care professional's lack of cultural competence in dealing with individuals from different minority groups or, simply, to language barriers.

Another factor to consider regarding access to health care involves patients' perceptions, which focus on patient–provider communication and relationships, cultural competency, health literacy, and health information (U.S. Department of Health and Human Services, 2003). According to the National Healthcare Disparities Executive Reports, although African-American and Hispanic patients are more likely to report that their provider usually asks about medications prescribed by other doctors, people of lower SES, Asians, and Hispanics report greater difficulty understanding health care information from their doctor's office. In addition, people of lower SES and Hispanics are more likely to report one or more communication difficulties with their physicians.

Patients' perceptions seem to be most important in considering access to health care because we can assume that most individuals have to be comfortable with the professionals providing health care if they are to continue seeking care. Because of the trouble they had gaining entry to begin with, most minority group members enter the health care system already suspicious of the care or the lack of care that they might receive. After they experience discrimination from the health care professionals to whom they are supposed to entrust their lives, why would they continue to seek care?

Access to the Health Care System

It seems as if in most of our research, we can organize the disparities under two headings: access to care and quality of care. According to the National Healthcare Disparities Executive Reports (2003), access to health care is a prerequisite to obtaining quality care, and both are independent and additive.

Therefore, we can start by looking at how access to health care can affect an individual's quality of care and how both are influenced by discrimination and racist ignorance. We should be able to see how one is influenced by the other, and how the cycle continues up to now. The National Healthcare Disparities Executive Reports (2003) organized access to services into four main categories: entry into the health care system; structural barriers; patients' perceptions; and utilization of care. We will discuss these topics in the sections that follow.

We have found that access to health care directly affects the quality of care that patients receive, especially people from minority groups. According to the U.S. Department of Health and Human Services report (2003), because an individual must have access to health care before quality care is acquired, we must consider multiple factors that lead to differences in health care. Such factors include different underlying rates of illness owing to genetic predisposition, local environmental conditions, and lifestyle choices. The report further states that the differences in care-seeking behavior of patients vary because of differing cultural beliefs, linguistic barriers, degree of trust in health care providers, or variations in the predisposition to seek timely care. If there is so much to consider when examining access to health care and care-seeking behaviors, what type of care should we expect for minority groups?

When we take a look at the factors that affect access to health care services, we see many overlapping issues that must be dealt with before minority group members are able to receive quality care. For example, poverty and lack of resources leave many minority group members uninsured. That limits their ability to gain entry into the system. If for some reason they are able to gain entry, they must make appointments and find a way to get to the health care professional. Making the appointment, finding a way to the health care professional, communicating with health care professionals, and ensuring understanding of what they need to do to continue or maintain care can all be hindered by language barrier problems (only one of the many barriers). Language problems (which, along with skin color, tend to signal minority group membership) influence patients' perceptions of how they are treated by the health care professional. Those perceptions help them eventually

PICTURE 8.4 Health disparities are related to one's access to the health care system. *Photograph by Darren Tatham*

decide whether or not to return, live with the illness, or continue to search for a "better doctor" or "better help." This cycle continues, and meanwhile the sick get sicker and the quality of care continues to decline.

> *Ever since I [can] remember I've always served as an interpreter for my mom and my grandma. It all started when I was in junior high, whenever there was a Parent–Teacher Conference I had to translate for her because some teachers did not speak Spanish. It was a difficult situation because sometimes I just couldn't find the exact word to get the right meaning across. My mom would also get frustrated but I felt that she didn't understand how troublesome it was for me. I remember she would always say that she didn't know why it was so hard to translate; if I knew both languages then there shouldn't be any problem. I would try to explain to her that I was able to understand but I just couldn't find the appropriate translation.*
>
> *Later I learned that translating for teachers was nothing compared to translating for doctors. When I would take my grandma to a doctor's appointment or whenever she was hospitalized I had to try my best at interpreting. Sometimes it was entertaining because my grandma would just start talking without being asked anything and then the doctor would ask me what she had said. Like I mentioned earlier, it was difficult to find a good word in English to translate her conversation. There are some words that just don't have an equivalent in another language. Not only was it troublesome to paraphrase my grandma's conversation but it was worse to translate all the scientific words that doctors use. I would always ask myself, How in the world am I going to explain this to her?*

BEATRICE, 20+-YEAR-OLD MEXICAN-AMERICAN WOMAN

As we note how the quality of care declines, a look at differential treatments between ethnic minority groups and the majority population reinforces how the sick get sicker.

According to the U.S. Department of Health and Human Services (2007):

- About 30 percent of Hispanic and 20 percent of Black Americans lack a usual source of health care compared with less than 16 percent of Whites.
- Hispanic children are nearly three times as likely as non-Hispanic White children to have no usual source of health care.
- African Americans and Hispanic Americans are far more likely to rely on hospitals or clinics for their usual source of care than are White Americans (16 and 13 percent, respectively, versus 8 percent).

Differential Treatment

My father studied in our country and achieved a Master's Degree in Business Administration. Unfortunately, when we migrated to the U.S. his Master's degree did not matter and certainly did not compete with younger students who also had a Master's degree. My father, who was a very strong man back home, became ill with diabetes and high blood pressure 5 years after we moved to the U.S. My mom says that it was from all of the stress that he had to go through. My father, who held a high position back home, had to humble himself to be a door-to-door salesman. One time, I went with my dad to the doctor because he had to get some checkups done (he never said what for), but I thought it was pretty serious because he never took me to checkups before. It ended up being an extra checkup due to his diabetes and the inconsistent blood sugar levels that he was experiencing. I didn't hear any information that the doctor gave because he merely gave my dad a prescription and began to leave the room. My father called out because he had some questions, but the doctor kind of waved him off and said to try the medication first and set another appointment in two weeks. My dad didn't say a word and neither did I. We left the room and were passing by the nurses' station when we spotted the same doctor talking to a White man about this patient's exercise regimen and how it would be beneficial and so on and so forth. I thought to myself, He couldn't answer my dad's question, but he can talk to that man about exercise? My dad looked at me as he saw what I saw and smiled meekly.

PRISCILLA, 20+-YEAR-OLD FILIPINA-AMERICAN WOMAN

As this story demonstrates, although certain illnesses are more common among Persons of Color, those illnesses are more likely to be treated inappropriately because treatment professionals are influenced by lack of knowledge, prejudice, and discrimination. For example, White physicians have been known to misdiagnose symptoms of heart attack in Black patients at a much higher rate than in White patients with identical symptoms (Schulman et al., 1999).

Perceptions and experiences of racial/ethnic bias leading to unfair treatment can result in personal negative emotional and stress responses for ethnic minority groups (Cains & Kington, 2003). These responses in turn have been shown to be related to hypertension, cardiovascular disease, mental health, and other negative states of health (Cains & Kington, 2003; Clark et al., 1999; Myers, Lewis, & Parker-Dominguez, 2003; Utsey, 1997; Utsey, Bolden, & Brown, 2001; Utsey & Payne, 2000). For example, racism can lead to chronic stress, which has been demonstrated to be associated with a suppression of immune responses. This leaves individuals vulnerable to invasive organisms such as bacteria and viruses, leading to an increased vulnerability to disease (Clark et al., 1999; Cohen & Herbert, 1996). Table 8.4 lists some other such differences.

The use of physical restraints in nursing homes is higher among Hispanics and Asian/Pacific Islanders than among non-Hispanic Whites. Poorly managed care or misdiagnoses result in expensive and avoidable complications, which can lead to significant morbidity, disability, and lost productivity at the individual level (U.S. Department of Health and Human Services, 2003). At the societal level, increased costs result from missed opportunities to intervene and reduce the burden of illness.

TABLE 8.4   Differential Treatments Received by African Americans

- African Americans have suffered substandard health care, which has led to higher death rates for African Americans in the categories of HIV/AIDS, cancer, and heart disease.
- Minorities are more likely to receive less desirable surgical procedures, such as amputations, at a rate up to 3.6 times greater than their White Medicare peers.
- Minorities, especially African Americans, are sicker and die more often from treatable, preventable illness than any other ethnic group in the United States.
- Of the 15 leading causes of death, African Americans have the highest incidence rates in 13 of them, according to Rodney Hood, M.D., past president of the National Medical Association.

Source: Edwards and Erwin-Johnson (2003).

African Americans and Hispanics are as much as three times more likely than are Whites to feel that minorities receive a lower level of care (Roach, 2003). Furthermore, whereas one in five Whites acknowledges that minorities receive lower levels of quality medical care than White Americans do, two-thirds of African Americans feel that way, as do 41 percent of Hispanics (Late, 2003). In the following story, Abigail recognized the differential treatment that ethnic minorities and Whites received in her local hospital.

> *I remember before I got my insurance through my husband's work that I had to take my son to get his immunizations for school and I had to go to a clinic in Pomona. I had to apply for Medi-Cal so I could get the immunizations free of cost, and when I went in there, most of the patients if not all of them were Mexican or Latino. What was really surprising to me was that although this was a doctor's office I couldn't help noticing how dirty it was. I just felt so out of place and then on top of it, I felt bad for feeling like that, because I am no better than anyone else, no matter what background they are from, but I had never in my life had to go to a doctor's office that wasn't clean, nor did I ever have to apply for Medi-Cal. Once more, the doctor's office I go to now is much cleaner and bigger. I also noticed that most of the patients were Caucasian, or if they were Hispanic or African American, they were upper-class. All my life I have had insurance and good healthcare, so it was a real eye-opener for me. I can now sympathize with those who don't have it or the access to it due to circumstances beyond their control.*

ABIGAIL, 30+-YEAR-OLD EUROPEAN-AMERICAN WOMAN

According to the U.S. Department of Health and Human Services (2007):

- **Heart disease**—African Americans are 13 percent less likely to undergo coronary angioplasty and one-third less likely to undergo bypass surgery than are Whites.

- **Asthma**—Among preschool children hospitalized for asthma, only 7 percent of Black and 2 percent of Hispanic children, compared with 21 percent of White children, are prescribed routine medications to prevent future asthma-related hospitalizations.
- **Breast cancer**—The length of time between an abnormal screening mammogram and the followup diagnostic test to determine whether a woman has breast cancer is more than twice as long in Asian-American, Black, and Hispanic women as in White women.
- **Human immunodeficiency virus (HIV) infection**—African Americans with HIV infection are less likely to be on antiretroviral therapy, less likely to receive prophylaxis for *Pneumocystis* pneumonia, and less likely to be receiving protease inhibitors than other persons with HIV. An HIV infection data coordinating center, now under development, will allow researchers to compare contemporary data on HIV care to examine whether disparities in care among groups are being addressed and to identify any new patterns in treatment that arise.
- **Nursing home care**—Asian-American, Hispanic, and African-American residents of nursing homes are all far less likely than White residents to have sensory and communication aids, such as glasses and hearing aids. A new study of nursing home care is developing measures of disparities in this care setting and their relationship to quality of care.

Most of us would oversimplify the problem by stating that if people would simply learn English and get a job, most of these issues would disappear. Why then do English-speaking minority group members, such as White women, children, and ethnic minorities who are U.S. born or "without an accent," and those who struggle for employment, continue to report discriminatory practices by health professionals? According to Roach (2003), there are several reasons for the unequal treatment of minority group members, including cultural and language barriers and discrimination on the part of health professionals. The report also revealed that large numbers of Americans support penalizing providers and insurers with a history of delivering unequal care based on a person's race or ethnicity. In 2002 the landmark Institute of Medicine report found that although there are complex reasons for racial and ethnic health care inequities, evidence suggests that bias, prejudice, and stereotyping on the part of doctors and other health care providers contribute to the problem (see Roach, 2003). According to Edwards and Erwin-Johnson (2003), not understanding a patient's culture contributes to health disparities that lead to increased risks for disease and death, and the connections between health disparities, cultural competence, and quality care are undeniable.

We can change gears and still see how quality of care is mismanaged and unequal. In U.S. society, one predominant minority group is women. According to Kumanyika, Morssink, and Nestle (2001), U.S. ethnic minority health issues involve racial/ethnic disparities that affect both women and men, even though women's health advocacy in the United States does not consistently address problems specific to ethnic minority women. An important milestone in the women's health movement was the *Roe v. Wade* decision of 1973, with the ensuing legislative struggles over reproductive rights and concerns that led to increased advocacy for control of more general health matters and to greater attention to women's issues in mainstream medical research (Kumanyika, Morssink, & Nestle, 2001). Although there has been much improvement in the area of women's health, women still receive less information about their health from their doctors than do their male counterparts. In the study on differences in diagnosis and treatment of symptoms of heart attack between Whites and Blacks, mentioned earlier in this chapter, those differences were found to be even more prevalent between men and women (Schulman et al., 1999). Women were even less likely to be correctly diagnosed with heart attack symptoms than were Blacks in the study, and White men received the highest percentage of correct diagnoses.

MISTRUST OF THE HEALTH CARE SYSTEM

I can't believe it! This is our own government! How could they do something like this? I always knew that there was some racism in our country, but I can't believe that our own government could be so cruel in its participation in this study. Before I read about this, I wanted to deny that racism was that big of a deal. This stuff happened in the days of slavery, but not today. But when I read that our own government approved of a study to simply watch people die when they knew there was a cure totally blew me away!

DARCY, 20+-YEAR-OLD WHITE WOMAN

That response was from a student who read about the infamous Tuskegee Experiment (Sue & Sue, 2003; Williams, 1974b). In this "study," the U.S. Public Health Service recruited more than 600 African-American men from rural Alabama. Approximately 400 of them had a latent stage of syphilis, and 200 were studied as controls for those infected with syphilis. From 1932 until 1972, the infected men were not treated for their disease but, rather, were simply observed. Ultimately, 7 of the men died directly from syphilis, and 154 died of heart failure most likely connected to their untreated condition. The revelation of this study, which was exposed only because of the Freedom of Information Act (passed because of suspicions about how the country became involved in the Vietnam War), is widely considered to be the impetus behind the federal government's implementation of ethical research standards for human subjects (U.S. Department of Health, Education, and Welfare, 1979).

Kumanyika and associates (2001) mention the ethnic minority health movement evolving as an offshoot of the civil rights struggle, with the current advocacy anchored in a 1985 federal task force report documenting "excess deaths" among ethnic minority groups compared with the White population. These authors further reported that disparities in some areas were seen to have persisted or worsened even in the presence of societal changes intended to improve the health care condition of minority groups, which according to some minority observers is a deliberate effort to encourage the gradual disappearance of an unwanted group. There seemingly is such a deep distrust of the majority group that we cannot ignore the social explanations that stem from experiences of discrimination by the minority groups that could lead them to this type of conclusion.

How could an entire group manifest behaviors that have such underlying distrust of this society? Kumanyika and colleagues (2001) specifically address ethnic minority women's health as being fraught with vestiges of the historical relations between the White American majority and People of Color. These historical relations include the stigmatization of people with dark skin, legal and de facto segregation and discrimination, and a host of painful historical associations with slavery, the Tuskegee study, involuntary sterilization, and internment in wartime relocation camps. Such historical facts describe the worst type of quality of care, if we can even refer to such events with the word "care." We can also assume that such experiences shaped the lives not only of ethnic minority women but of all persons in ethnic minority groups.

WHY SHOULD WE CARE?

If you receive relatively good health care or if you have reasonably good access to the health care system, you might be tempted to ask, Why should I care about other people not receiving adequate health care? First of all, since you are reading this book on multicultural psychology, you probably already care somewhat about this issue. Second, on a broad level, persistent disparities in health care are inconsistent with American values. This country was founded on the belief that everyone is equal and that justice should apply to all. If there are systematic disparities in health care that are due to correctable factors, we should be motivated to address those problems (U.S. Department of Health and Human Services, 2003).

On a more pragmatic level, continued health disparities will ultimately strain our health care system. To the extent that such persistent disparities will ultimately cause a rise in the cost of health care in our society, we will all pay for such disparities. For that reason, we must address these problems before they strain our economy beyond our capacity to pay for them.

BRINGING ABOUT CHANGE

Some readers may be interested in finding out how we can measure quality of care so that we can ascertain that improvement has occurred. Although that task may be impossible because of data limitations and some bias of measures, reports from the U.S. Department of Health and Human Services (2004) cite five varying aspects of quality of care from the report on health disparities: effectiveness, safety, timeliness, patient centeredness, and equity. Considering everything that we have discussed in this chapter, it is clear that most ethnic minority group members are still lacking in those areas of quality of care. If all groups do not have equal access to health care in the first place, then we can assume that quality of care will not be equal among all individuals.

Another difficulty in measuring quality of care is that there are indications that the federal government is still trying to cover up health care disparities (Edwards, 2003). A report released by the Special Investigations Division of the minority staff of the Government Reform Committee found that the Health and Human Services reports altered the information to minimize "the scope and extent of racial and ethnic health disparities in the United States." For example, Edwards (2003) noted that Health and Human Services reports tend to emphasize less serious health disparities, such as "Hispanics and American Indians or Alaska Natives are less likely to have their cholesterol checked" as opposed to more serious disparities, such as racial and ethnic minorities being more likely to be diagnosed with late-stage cancer, to die of HIV, to be subjected to physical restraints in nursing homes, and to receive suboptimal cardiac care for heart attacks. Another example of such downplaying is the report that American Indians/Alaska Natives have lower death rates from all cancers without mention of the fact that overall life expectancies for American Indians and Alaska Natives are significantly shorter than for other Americans or that their infant mortality rates are substantially higher. Since the reporting procedures of our reporting agencies are open to question, we may not be able to see the true extent of disparities in the quality of care that all people receive within our society.

A Latino patient we visited reported (translated from his native Spanish language):

> I remembered things like having to use the bathroom, pressing the button for a nurse and waiting so long that I had to "go on myself." When the nurse did show up, she became infuriated at the mess that I made, and I remember being pulled and pushed to the bathroom so hard that I threw up. This infuriated her even more and she screamed at me. Although I couldn't understand it because it was all in English, I remembered the word "stupid" once or twice. I don't want any trouble from her and I am not trying to get anyone fired. I just needed to get this off my chest, because I continue to have nightmares about it. It will be better now because I was able to "let it out."

JULIO, 60+-YEAR-OLD LATINO-AMERICAN MAN

After that incident was reported, a social worker was assigned to Julio's case and confirmed that this nurse had been abusive to many patients. The nurse was disciplined, and Julio was able to receive services he needed. Can we call Julio's story one with a happy ending? The answer depends on how we want to look at things. As a health care society, we seem to be more reactive than preventive, especially with ethnic minority group members such as Julio.

How would we like to see things change? What goals should we set to improve our health care system? Are there easy answers? Since it seems that institutionalized racism is the underlying theme within health/health care disparities, much work has to be done to document improvement in the narrowing of health/health care disparities. At this point, we need to focus on specific issues that we

PICTURE 8.5   Increasing the number of ethnic minorities in the health care profession can help to overcome the distrust that many People of Color have toward the system.

can directly observe, measure, and report to improve health disparities. Although there seems to be much to improve regarding health disparities in our society, we must say that all is not lost.

Because it has been shown that official reports of disparity seem to highlight the less severe examples of disparities in minority health, one goal should be the systematic collection and analysis of health care data—to help policymakers discern areas of greatest need, monitor trends over time, and identify successful programs for addressing those needs (U.S. Department of Health and Human Services, 2003). We need much more data, as well as plans for addressing disparities. Recognition of these needs is increasing.

Late (2003) suggested that important steps in solving problems in health disparities include helping ethnic minorities take part in their own treatment decisions and increasing the number of minorities in the health care field. Training existing health care delivery professionals to be culturally competent is also essential for meaningful health education. Other important steps are increasing awareness of available health services, making services consistent with cultural norms, understanding rights and protections, ensuring accurate diagnoses and proper treatment of illness and other medical conditions, and engaging in informed consent process (Edwards & Erwin-Johnson, 2003). Most ethnic minority group members do not feel wanted as soon as they gain access to the health care system. Adherence to these recommendations by health care professionals will make ethnic minority group members feel more welcome, and compliance with treatment regimens will increase, thus decreasing existing health care disparities.

Healthy people 2010 (www.healthypeople.gov) propose "a systematic approach to health improvement," which suggests a need to recognize goals and objectives for change as part of a larger, systematic approach to health improvement.

SICKLE CELL ANEMIA—A CASE STUDY

Sickle cell anemia is an inherited blood disorder primarily affecting people of African descent. Symptoms include swelling of hands and feet, pain that can last from a few hours to several weeks, fever, fatigue, shortness of breath, blindness, and slow growth rate. The symptoms are caused by defective hemoglobin molecules. Red blood cells become stiff, cluster, and form sickle shapes. These clusters cannot pass through small blood vessels and thus deprive organs of oxygen-carrying red blood cells. Those with this condition are vulnerable to infections. Infants and children can die from this disorder because they cannot fight off bacterial infections. Advances in treatment have increased life expectancy, but there is no cure for this disorder (U.S. Department of Energy, Biological, and Environmental Research, 2004).

Sickle cell anemia occurs in about 1 in every 500 African-American births in the United States. According to the U.S. Census Bureau (2004), there are about 39,000,000 African Americans in the United States, so sickle cell anemia affects about 78,000 African Americans. Although it does not seem to affect many other ethnic groups, about 1 in every 1,000 to 1,400 children born to Latino Americans is diagnosed with this disorder.

For comparison purposes, let us consider cystic fibrosis, another inherited disease. This disorder generates thick, sticky mucus that can obstruct airways to various organs, particularly the lungs, leaving the sufferer vulnerable to bacterial infections (National Institutes of Health, 2004a). Although death is not typically associated with this disease, those afflicted with it are subject to infections, coughing, and wheezing, and men (but not women) can become infertile.

Cystic fibrosis occurs in about 1 in every 3,000 Caucasian (White) births in the United States. The U.S. Census Bureau (2004) statistics show that there are about 237,900,000 Whites in the United States. Thus, about 79,300 White individuals are afflicted with this disease.

Sickle cell anemia and cystic fibrosis afflict about the same numbers of people in the United States. Sickle cell anemia seems to be more deadly, but according to the National Institutes of Health (2004b), about $95 million was spent on studies examining sickle cell anemia in 2003, whereas about $117 million was spent on studies examining cystic fibrosis in the United States. This indicates that about 23 percent more funding is available to study a disease that is less often lethal but afflicts primarily White individuals than is available to study a disease that is more often lethal and afflicts primarily Black individuals. Our purpose is not to attempt to pit one disease against another or to suggest that money be taken away from studying one disease and given to the other disease for study. However, statistics such as these lead one to understand why African Americans are distrustful of the commitment of the U.S. government for the betterment of the health of Blacks as compared to Whites.

SUMMARY

Health disparities exist among ethnic minority group members, between groups, and between minority group members and Whites. A look at ethnic minority groups as a whole, however, makes it easier to pay close attention to what might be involved in eliminating disparities in health and health care.

Health beliefs involve individuals' perceptions of their illness and how susceptible they are, based on their trust in the health professional who makes the diagnoses and the cost of such treatment. Health beliefs dictate the ways that minority groups maintain their health. Since health behaviors contribute to the continuation of healthy or unhealthy lifestyles, ethnic minority group members who typically seek less care and receive suboptimal care compared with Whites have a lower quality of life.

The health of minority group members depends on their ability to access care. Accessing health care in this society has proven to be more difficult for ethnic minority groups than for Whites. Gaining entry into the health care system, structural barriers (such as transportation and getting appointments with doctors), patients' perceptions of the care they may receive or have received, and utilization of care are all categories of difficulties to consider in accessing health care. These difficulties in accessing health care ultimately determine the quality of care that ethnic minority groups will receive.

Since access to care and quality of care seem to go hand in hand, as well as possibly being independent of each other, a common theme in both is institutional racism. Institutional racism dictates that health professionals remain incompetent in cultural issues (communicating with patients, understanding cultural norms when it comes to treatment, providing appropriate information and diagnoses, etc.). Racist beliefs also disempower ethnic minority groups by making them fully reliant on health professionals' decisions about their treatment. Ethnic minority groups remain uneducated about their health issues.

Research and data on health and ethnic minority groups are limited and some that exist are questionable. Only a limited number of ethnic minority group members work within the health care system. Racism is apparent in the ongoing struggle of ethnic minority groups in the health care system; hence, health disparities continue to exist.

Food for Thought

Our goal is to undo discriminatory practices within the health care system. Since we know that such a goal is vague and idealistic, at this time we think it best to target incremental policy changes. These changes involve additional research, training of health professionals as well as the ethnic minority groups to become more aware of cultural issues to improve communication and treatment of illnesses, creating a system to ensure that such changes are made, and enlisting more minority group members/leaders in the effort to bring about change. The apparent limitations are that to begin change, we would need revolutionary policy changes, and that would involve getting our political leaders to take a closer look at current policies and to vote for better health care for the entire society. Are you ready to work for those changes?

Critical Thinking Questions

Think back to when you were growing up. Did your family have health coverage? How did your family pay for visits to the doctor?

What kinds of healthy behaviors were around you (e.g., jogging, going to the gym.)? What kinds of unhealthy behaviors were around you (e.g., smoking, drinking alcohol)? Did friends of different ethnicities have different kinds of health behaviors around them?

How easy was it for you to see your family doctor? How easy was it for you to get to a local hospital? Did your family speak the same language as your doctor, or did you need an interpreter?

How much did you trust your family doctor? How much did you trust other elements of the health care system?

CHAPTER 9

Culture and Mental Health

CULTURE AND DIAGNOSIS

The *Diagnostic and Statistical Manual of Mental Disorders*:
  A Classification System

Culture and the Expression of Symptoms

Cultural Group Differences and Mental Health

  The Epidemiologic Catchment Area Project (ECA)

  National Comorbidity Survey (NCS)

  Minorities Not Well Represented in the Large Epidemiological Studies

  Problems with the Epidemiologic Studies

  Conclusions from Existing Data

Gender Differences

Culture-Bound Syndromes

Eating Disorders: An American Culture-Bound Syndrome?

CULTURE AND THE TREATMENT OF MENTAL DISORDERS

Denise—a 20-year-old, African-American, lesbian college junior—was majoring in sociology at a large, predominantly White university in the southwestern United States. Denise came to the university counseling center to address feelings of depression and loneliness related to chronic difficulties with interpersonal relationships, particularly with her peers and family members, surrounding her sexual orientation.

Denise was assigned to an African-American female counselor and appeared somewhat anxious during the intake session. She verbalized her ambivalence about discussing her problems in counseling because she had received numerous messages from her parents and other family members about the taboo of going to a mental-health counselor to address "personal things." Denise said she had "trust issues" and that she would feel more comfortable knowing something about the counselor. She asked the counselor about her credentials and whether or not she was a "liberal person." After her counselor responded honestly to these questions, Denise appeared to relax.

Denise discussed some of the adjustment difficulties she was having at the university, feeling as if she was "too different from any of these people here" and as though she didn't fit in. More specifically, Denise believed her interpersonal difficulties were related to her inability to deal effectively with the heterosexist attitudes of many students. She also shared that others' negative treatment of her in this regard affected her self-esteem. While her family always fostered a sense of pride about her racial identity, they were also "intolerant" of her sexual orientation. She stated they frequently told her that she was "going to burn in hell" because of her sexual orientation. She felt the African-American students on campus were also judgmental and "unaccepting" of her sexual identity.

During the first few sessions Denise explored her feelings of sadness and anger related to feeling unsupported and oppressed by people in her social and family circles because of her sexual orientation. She also explored issues related to her own internalized heterosexism, racism, and sexism. As her counselor helped her identify various cultural identities and validated her struggles to consolidate them, Denise claimed she was feeling increasingly comfortable with the idea of working to synthesize her multiple identities to formulate a more integrated sense of her being. She also stated that she was beginning to feel less depressed. Denise was also able to take some responsibility for her interpersonal interactions. She came to recognize that her difficulties with trust, while warranted on many occasions because of heterosexism, sometimes contributed to her feelings of isolation and sadness. Denise traced some of her "trust issues" to relationships with girls in junior high who betrayed her "secret" of being a lesbian. She discussed at great length her feelings of disappointment and anger related to not feeling "unconditionally loved" by her family and was beginning to accept the fact that her family members "may never be okay with my being gay." Denise and her counselor also spent time exploring their relationship with regard to cultural differences, issues of trust, and issues of power. She also spoke about her initial fear of being "rejected" by her counselor, an African-American woman. Denise spoke of feeling empowered by her experiences of feeling supported, validated, and challenged in counseling, and she expressed an interest in joining a lesbian support group on campus so she could obtain support and continue struggling with her issues. (Adapted from Sue, Ivey, & Pedersen, 1996, pp. 115–117)

As we will see, Denise's case illustrates a number of issues regarding culture and mental health. A major premise of multicultural psychology is that all behavior occurs in a cultural context. Therefore, mental health is influenced by culture. We can see the effect of culture on mental health in many ways, including the types of symptoms experienced, the manner in which those symptoms are expressed, and the meaning those symptoms have for the individual, his or her family, and his or her community. Culture influences how clients cope with their troubles, whether or not they seek help, and from whom. Culture also plays a role in the causation of mental disorders, their prevalence, and their treatment.

Culture influences not only the client but also the counselor or therapist and the institutions that provide mental health treatment. Mental health professionals bring their own culture, including their attitudes and beliefs, to the setting, which can influence their diagnosis and what strategies are used to help the client (U.S. Department of Health and Human Services, 2001).

In Denise's case, we see first a complex interaction among her symptoms of depression, loneliness, isolation, and interpersonal conflicts with her multiple identities as an African-American lesbian woman. Her presenting issues went beyond her internal thoughts and feelings and were affected by her interactions with and the attitudes of other college students, particularly African-American students, and her family regarding her sexual orientation. She was hesitant to go to therapy because of the negative stigma attached to it by her family but also because of her difficulties trusting others, even her African-American female therapist. Denise benefited from therapy for a number of reasons, including her therapist's ability to see beyond Denise's initial presenting problems and to effectively connect her issues to the larger cultural context. In this chapter we discuss these and many other aspects of culture's impact on mental health and the diagnosis and treatment of mental health problems.

CULTURE AND DIAGNOSIS

Diagnostic and Statistical Manual of Mental Disorders—the primary reference manual used in all mental health fields to classify mental disorders. Published by the American Psychiatric Association, this manual is currently in its fourth edition (1994), with a text revision made in 2000.

We cannot have a discussion about culture and the diagnosis of mental disorders without talking about the *Diagnostic and Statistical Manual of Mental Disorders* (*DSM*). The *DSM* is the primary manual used by health and mental health professionals in the United States to diagnose mental disorders. The *DSM* has gone through several revisions. The most current version is the *DSM-IV-TR*, or the fourth version with a text revision (American Psychiatric Association, 2000).

Although the *DSM* is used in other countries, there are other diagnostic manuals, including one developed by the World Health Organization (WHO), the *International Statistical Classification of Diseases and Related Health Problems*, currently in its tenth version (*ICD-10*). The developers of the *DSM-IV-TR* and the *ICD-10* worked closely together, so the two manuals are compatible. Individual countries also have their own diagnostic manuals. For example, in China they use the *Chinese Classification of Mental Disorders, Second Edition* (CCMD-2) (American Psychiatric Association, 2000).

The *Diagnostic and Statistical Manual of Mental Disorders: A Classification System*

Diagnostic categories in the *DSM* are based on empirical research and focus on behavioral descriptions of symptoms. Specific diagnoses represent clusters of symptoms that typically are seen together and that have some defining feature. A diagnosis is made on the basis of a set of behavioral criteria. If the person exhibits a minimum number of symptoms in the list, then a specific diagnosis is made. For example, Major Depressive Disorder has a list of nine symptoms, including depressed mood, loss of interest or pleasure in usual activities, weight loss, and insomnia. For a diagnosis to be made, the person must experience five or more of those symptoms for at least 2 weeks. By focusing on behavioral manifestations of symptoms, the *DSM* attempts to be neutral. This enables it to be a useful communication tool for people from an array of professional backgrounds (e.g., psychologists, medical doctors, social workers), with different theoretical orientations (e.g., behavioral, psychodynamic, family/systems), in a variety of settings (e.g., hospitals, clinics, private practice) (American Psychiatric Association, 2000).

The *DSM-IV* (American Psychiatric Association, 1994) was the first version of the *DSM* to systematically include cultural issues. Now, a section on cultural issues is included with each of the diagnostic categories. In addition, there is an Outline for Cultural Formulation, which is a guide that helps mental health professionals systematically review the client's cultural background, the role of culture in the expression of the client's symptoms, and the role that cultural differences may play in the relationship between the client and the therapist. The outline identifies five areas that the therapist should cover in making a cultural assessment of the client and his or her presenting problems: (a) the cultural identity of the individual; (b) cultural explanations of the individual's illness; (c) cultural factors related to psychosocial environment and levels of functioning, including culturally relevant social stressors and available social support; (d) cultural elements of the relationship between the individual and the clinician, including how cultural differences between the client and the therapist may affect the treatment; and (e) overall cultural assessment for diagnosis and care, where the therapist incorporates all these cultural factors to plan the most appropriate course of treatment (American Psychiatric Association, 2000).

The *DSM-IV* also includes a Glossary of Culture-Bound Syndromes, which are disorders that tend to occur only in certain cultures. (These *culture-bound syndromes* will be discussed in more detail later). Although the inclusion of cultural issues in the *DSM-IV* represents an important step forward in the field, some psychologists are critical, saying it does not go far enough (Lopez & Guarnaccia, 2000; Parham, 2002).

While the DSM strives to be an objective diagnostic tool, research studies repeatedly demonstrate clinician bias in applying diagnostic criteria. Clients reporting the same symptoms are given different diagnoses. Several studies have shown that African-Americans are more likely to be diagnosed with schizophrenia and less likely to be diagnosed with a mood disorder, while the opposite is true for non-African-Americans (e.g., Adembimpe, 1981; Neighbors, 1997; Trierweiler et al., 2005). In other words, there is a tendency for therapists to give the more serious, chronic, stigmatized diagnosis of schizophrenia to African-American clients and a less severe diagnosis, such as major depression, to European-American clients.

Culture and the Expression of Symptoms

An accurate diagnosis depends both on the client's ability to describe his or her symptoms and on the clinician's ability to observe and to accurately interpret those symptoms. Culture influences the way in which individuals express the symptoms of various disorders. People from different cultures may experience the same disorder but may experience and describe their symptoms in very different ways. The manifestation of symptoms can vary with age, gender, race, ethnicity, and culture.

Let us again use the example of depression. Certain cultures might experience and express more physical symptoms than mood symptoms. This is known as **somatization,** or the expression of psychological symptoms through physical ones. For example, individuals from Latino and Mediterranean cultures may complain of "nerves" or headaches, those from Middle Eastern cultures may complain of problems of the "heart," and Asians may talk about weakness, tiredness, or "imbalance." It is important for the clinician to be aware of such cultural differences in expression to avoid misdiagnosis. For example, some individuals may express a fear of being hexed or bewitched, or may report vivid feelings of being visited by someone who has died. These may be acceptable and understood experiences in some cultures but could be mistaken by a traditional Western therapist for symptoms of psychosis.

somatization—the expression of mental disorders through physical disorders.

In addition, the expression of depressive symptoms can change with age. The symptoms described in *DSM-IV-TR* criteria typically describe how depression is experienced by adolescents and adults. Children may have somatic complaints as well as irritability and social withdrawal, and their depression often coexists with other behavioral problems, such as disruptive behavior, hyperactivity, and inattention. In contrast, depressive symptoms in the elderly may include disorientation, memory loss, and distractibility. These must be distinguished from the symptoms of dementia (American Psychiatric Association, 2000).

Chanda relocated to the United States after surviving the horrors of Pol Pot's regime in Cambodia. While living in Cambodia she lost most of the members of her extended family who were either killed by the Khmer Rouge (the ruling party) or from starvation. Chanda was married four times. Her first husband was beaten to death by the Khmer Rouge. Her second husband died of an illness while they were awaiting resettlement in the refugee camp. Her third husband left with another woman, and she separated from her fourth husband. Chanda was pregnant 12 times. She lost six to miscarriages and two died from starvation. She has four surviving children—one who was the only one to survive the Pol Pot era, the second who was born in a refugee camp, and the last two that were born after she immigrated to the United States. She describes the living conditions on one of the farms she worked in Cambodia:

> When the floods came we had nothing to eat at all. Living there, you know? And from working and over-exhaustion, having nothing to eat. Some months, when there was no rice at all, they would make soup out of rice peel (husk) for us to eat. There were even people who ate their own children. There was a lady who ate her dead baby, too hungry! If you don't believe me, go see for yourself, and you'll see that this village is full of skeletons. . . . We would walk around looking for food, even one little plant; we left no leaves on it.

Chanda resettled in the United States in 1983. Since then she has suffered continuously from various forms of illness, physical pain, constant coughing, feeling that something was stuck in her throat, allergies, hearing voices, and seeing spirits. Chanda describes going to the hospital where they took X-rays, but the medical people were unable to determine the cause of her problem because nothing showed up in the photos. She says:

> I told them that I had fever and things. As soon as I came down with a fever, it was like "a hundred ghosts took over my body." I was sick on that day. Within one hour, it was like I was sick with 10 different illnesses. I would sit there and hear ringing. I told the doctors that this hurt and that hurt, because it really did hurt inside my body. My arm hurt, to this day it hurts where I extend my arm and the pain won't go away. If I don't take painkillers I would "sleep in tears" every night.

Chanda also experienced spirit visitations. She says these spirits keep telling her things, and she keeps seeing something from another world. Chanda's descriptions of her visitations from spirits caused her to be hospitalized for a week. (Adapted from Morelli, 2005, pp. 130-134)

Although Chanda may have some physical symptoms as a result of her many years of starvation, we can also see the tendency to somaticize, or to express psychological symptoms as physical ones. We also see some symptoms that the traditional Western doctors diagnosed as psychosis (visitations from spirits) but that may represent a culturally appropriate or acceptable experience.

Cultural Group Differences and Mental Health

In the field of public health, **prevalence** is defined as the current rate of existing cases of a disorder at a given point in time. An example would be the number of people currently diagnosed with schizophrenia. Another term used quite often when reporting rates of various disorders is **incidence,** which refers to the number of new cases of a disorder that occur during a given period of time, such as the number of people who will be diagnosed with schizophrenia this year. **Lifetime incidence** refers to the number of cases of a disorder that occur during one's lifetime. Therefore, if an individual was diagnosed with schizophrenia two years ago and continues to suffer from this disorder, that person would be included in the prevalence rate, would not be included in the incidence rate in the past year, but would be included in the lifetime incidence rate.

> **prevalence**—the current rate of a particular disorder at a given point in time.

> **incidence**—the number of new cases of a disorder diagnosed in a given period of time.

> **lifetime incidence**—the number of cases of a disorder that occur during one's lifetime.

There is a great deal of interest in comparing the incidence and prevalence rates of disorders in the different ethnic groups. The literature is mixed, with some studies showing lower rates of mental disorders in ethnic minority populations and some showing more, making it difficult to draw conclusions about ethnic group differences and mental disorders. However, the results of a few large epidemiologic studies reveal some trends.

The Epidemiologic Catchment Area Project (ECA)

The Epidemiologic Catchment Area Project (ECA) was the first and the largest mental health study ever conducted in the United States (Robins & Regier, 1991). Data were collected between 1980 and 1983 from almost 20,000 adults in five communities—Baltimore, Maryland; St. Louis, Missouri; Durham, North Carolina; Los Angeles, California; and New Haven, Connecticut. Participants represented people living in the community as well as those in mental hospitals, jails, residential drug and alcohol treatment centers, and nursing homes. Participants were interviewed using the Diagnostic Interview Schedule (DIS), a structured interview that contains questions based on *DSM* criteria.

Results of the ECA indicated that nearly 20 percent of the U.S. population were currently experiencing a mental disorder, or had within the last 6 months. The most common lifetime disorders were phobia (14.3 percent), alcohol abuse/dependence (13.8 percent), generalized anxiety disorder (8.5 percent), major depressive episode (6.3 percent), and dysthymia (3.2 percent) (Robins & Regier, 1991).

The ECA sample included mostly European Americans ($N = 12,944$), with large enough numbers of African Americans ($N = 4,638$) and Latinos/as ($N = 1,600$)

TABLE 9.1 Rates of Psychiatric Disorders for Blacks, Whites, and Hispanics— ECA Study (Percentages)

Disorder	Current			Lifetime		
	Black	White	Hispanic	Black	White	Hispanic
Affective	3.5	3.7	4.1	6.3	8.0	7.8
Alcohol abuse	6.6	6.7	9.1	13.8	13.6	16.7
Drug history	—	—	—	29.9	30.7	25.1
Drug abuse	2.7	2.7	1.9	5.4	6.4	4.3
Schizophrenia	1.6	0.9	0.4	2.1	1.4	0.8
Generalized anxiety	6.1	3.5	3.7	—	—	—
Phobic	16.2	9.1	8.1	23.4	9.7	12.2
Any disorder	26.0	19.0	20.0	38.0	32.0	33.0

Source: Robins and Regier (1991).

to allow meaningful comparisons of the rate of mental disorders in these three groups. However, rates for Latinos/as and Latino/a Americans should still be interpreted with caution because the large majority came from only one ECA site (Los Angeles). The number of participants from other groups, such as Asian/Pacific Americans ($N = 242$) was so small that few studies included them in their comparisons (Chang, 2002). One exception was a study by Zhang and Snowden (1999). Table 9.1 summarizes the ECA findings in regard to European Americans, African Americans, and Latinos/as.

If you look at the bottom line and the rates for any type of mental disorder, it appears that African Americans have both a greater current and a greater lifetime rate of mental disorders. However, if you look more closely you see that the only category in which African Americans truly have greater rates than European Americans and Latino/a Americans is for anxiety disorders (generalized anxiety disorder and phobias). These numbers are responsible for the overall higher rate for African Americans. African Americans reported higher lifetime rates of simple phobia, social phobia, and agoraphobia than European Americans. African Americans also tended to have higher rates of generalized anxiety disorder, but no consistent differences emerged for panic disorder. In terms of duration, African Americans experienced longer durations of panic disorder but shorter durations of phobic disorder (Brown, Eaton, & Sussman, 1990). Latinos/as had the lowest current rates of phobias, but lifetime rates were between those of African Americans and those of European Americans.

ECA data also revealed slightly higher rates of schizophrenia for African Americans, but those differences disappeared when adjusted for age, gender, marital status, and socioeconomic states (SES). Latinos'/as' rates for schizophrenia were lower than those for both African Americans and European Americans. Latinos/as also had the lowest rates for drug abuse and use, but current rates of alcohol abuse were lower for both African Americans and European Americans than for Latinos/as. For affective disorders, African Americans had the lowest rates, Latinos/as had the highest current rates, and European Americans had the highest lifetime rates.

Although there were some ethnic group differences in the specific disorders, the overall conclusion from the ECA is that there are very few ethnic group differences in the rate of psychiatric disorders.

As mentioned earlier, Zhang and Snowden (1999) analyzed ECA data from the community sample and included Asian/Pacific Americans in their ethnic group comparisons (see Table 9.2). They found that the overall rates of mental disorders for Asian Americans were generally lower than those for the total sample. When

TABLE 9.2   Lifetime Prevalence Rates of Mental Disorders for the United States

	United States		
Mental Disorder	ECA[a] (N = 19,640)	ECA Asians[b] (N = 242)	ECA-LA Asians[b] (N = 161)
Mood Disorders			
Major depressive episode	6.3	3.4	3.2
Dysthymia	3.2	3.0	3.3
Manic episode	0.8	0.0	0.0
Anxiety Disorders/Somatization			
Generalized anxiety disorder	8.5[+]	—	—
Panic disorder	1.6	—	—
Any phobia	14.3	6.6	5.6
Agoraphobia	5.6	—	—
Simple phobia	11.3	—	—
Social phobia	2.7	—	—
Obsessive-compulsive disorder	2.6	1.0	0.2
Somatization	0.1	—	—
Substance-Use Disorders			
Alcohol abuse/dependence	13.8	7.1	7.1
Drug abuse/dependence	6.2	2.3	2.1
Other Disorders			
Schizophrenia/schizophreniform	1.5	0.2	—
Antisocial personality	2.6	0.2	0.2

[+]Assessed in only 3 of 5 sites.

Source: [a]Robins & Regier (1991).
   [b]Zhang & Snowden (1999).

compared with European Americans, Asian/Pacific Americans exhibited approximately equal rates of disorder for only dysthymia, with significantly lower rates of all other forms of disorders that were measurable. There were no diagnostic categories in which Asian/Pacific Americans had higher rates than European Americans.

National Comorbidity Survey (NCS)

A second national epidemiologic study of mental disorder was the National Comorbidity Survey (NCS) (Kessler et al., 1994). This study tried to improve upon the methodology used in the ECA. It included a nationally representative sample of more than 8,000 people living in the community. This study utilized a modified version of the Composite International Diagnostic Interview (UM-CIDI), which is based on the DIS and also yields diagnoses based on *DSM* criteria.

The NCS results showed a higher overall prevalence rate for psychiatric disorders than the ECA showed, with nearly one half of the sample meeting the criteria for at least one *DSM* diagnosis. The most common lifetime diagnoses were alcohol use/abuse (23.5 percent), major depression (17.1 percent), social phobia (13.3 percent), drug use/dependence (11.9 percent), and simple phobia (11.3 percent).

The NCS sample included 4,498 European Americans, 666 African Americans, and 719 Latino/a Americans. The Latino/a sample was limited in that only English-speaking people were interviewed. The numbers for all other ethnic groups in the NCS were so small they were lumped together in the "other" category and were not included in ethnic group comparisons (Kessler et al., 1994).

See Table 9.3 for a comparison of NCS data from European-American, African-American, and Latino/a-American samples. In the table, the first column shows the percentage of people in the general population with a particular diagnosis. Columns two and three show ethnic group ratios comparing African Americans with European Americans and Latino/a Americans with European Americans. A ratio greater than 1.0 indicates which group had higher rates of that disorder. A ratio less than 1.0 means that group had lower rates of that disorder. Overall, Table 9.3 reveals higher rates of mental disorder for Latino/a Americans and lower rates for African Americans in all categories in the NCS study. The greatest differences are seen in the lower rates of substance abuse or dependence

TABLE 9.3 Overall Prevalence and Ethnic Ratios of Psychiatric Disorders—National Comorbidity Survey

Disorders	Prevalence in General Population (%)	Ethnic Ratios	
		Black/White	Hispanic/White
Any affective disorder	11.3	0.78	1.38
Any anxiety disorder	17.1	0.90	1.17
Any substance abuse or dependence	11.3	0.47	1.04
Any disorder	29.5	0.70	1.11

Source: Kessler et al. (1994).

for African Americans and the higher rates for affective disorders among Latino/a Americans.

Unlike the ECA, the NCS did not find any ethnic group differences in panic disorder, simple phobia, or agoraphobia. However, a closer look at the data suggests an interaction between gender, race, and diagnosis of a phobia. Using NCS data, Magee (1993) found that European-American men had higher rates of agoraphobia, simple phobia, and social phobia than did African-American men, and African-American women had higher rates of agoraphobia and simple phobia than did African-American men.

Another large national epidemiologic study was recently conducted, which sought in part to replicate the NCS and to include larger samples of participants from various ethnic groups—the Collaborative Psychiatric Epidemiology Studies (CPES; Heeringa et al., 2004). For example, one of the studies in this collaborative focuses specifically on Latinos/as and Asians—the National Latino and Asian American Study (NLAAS). While results have been published from this collaborative for specific groups (e.g., Abe-Kim et al., 2007), no references were found that yet compare rates between the ethnic groups. It will be interesting to see those when they come out.

Minorities Not Well Represented in the Large Epidemiological Studies

Until the more recent results are published, small sample sizes in both the ECA and the NCS studies allow few conclusions to be drawn regarding the rate of mental disorder among Asian/Pacific-American groups as compared to other groups. The study by Zhang and Snowden (1999) concluded that Asian/Pacific Americans have rates of mental disorder equal to or lower than those of European Americans. A study by Sue and associates (1995) sheds some light on one particular Asian ethnic group—Chinese. The Chinese-American Psychiatric Epidemiological Study (CAPES) was conducted in Los Angeles in 1993 and 1994 and included more than 1,700 U.S.-born and immigrant Chinese, with immigrants constituting the clear majority (90 percent). When rates in the ECA and NCS were compared with rates in the CAPES, the Chinese participants had lower lifetime prevalence rates of psychiatric disorders. More specifically, Chinese Americans had lower rates of generalized anxiety disorder, simple phobia, panic disorder, agoraphobia, and social phobia. Major depression was the only area in which their rates were higher than in the ECA study but lower than in the NCS data. As mentioned previously, results from the CPES should increase our knowledge of rates of mental disorders in Asian populations.

No large epidemiologic studies have been conducted that included sufficient numbers of American Indians or Alaskan Natives to be able to make meaningful comparisons between the ethnic groups. A few small studies were found that shed some light on the mental health status of American Indians. Beals and colleagues (1991) report that depression, suicide, and alcoholism are the most common mental health problems among American Indians. Alcoholism and alcohol-related problems seem to be a particular problem in some American-Indian communities (Johnson, 1994). Their suicide rates are also high, at two times the national average, with the highest rate of completed suicide for any ethnic group (Debruyn, Hymbaugh, & Valdez, 1988; Herring, 1999).

Costello and colleagues (Costello et al., 1997; Costello, Farmer, & Angold, 1999) compared the rates of mental disorder between a sample of Cherokee Indians and European Americans living in the Appalachians. They found no differences in the overall rate of mental disorders between the two groups but did find that certain problems, such as parental violence, substance abuse, and crime, were greater among Cherokee families than among European-American families. The American-Indian Vietnam Veterans Project (AIVVP) was a community-based epidemiological study in which the rates of PTSD and of alcohol abuse and/or dependence for American-Indian veterans in the study were significantly higher than for European-American, African-American, and Japanese-American veterans (National Center for Post-Traumatic Stress Disorder and the National Center for American Indian and Alaska Native Mental Health Research, 1996).

Problems with the Epidemiologic Studies

The question of ethnic group differences in the prevalence of mental disorders may be a natural one to ask, but it is a complicated one to answer (Chang, 2002). The epidemiologic studies just cited represent the largest, most rigorous studies to date. However, they are not without problems. Chang (2002) discusses a number of these concerns. One problem is the small sample sizes of some groups. Few comparisons were made for Asians, and no comparisons were found that included American Indians, or other growing groups in the United States, such as Arab Americans.

A second problem is within-group heterogeneity. Aggregate data that combine all members of an ethnic group ignore the large variation that exists within groups. For example, among immigrant groups, such as Asians and Latinos/as, there is considerable variation based on generation, acculturation, linguistic ability, and socioeconomic status. Many authors call for research that examines particular groups in more detail (Sue et al., 1995). Chang (2002) and others note, lumping all members of an ethnic group together ignores critical within-group differences. The differing rates of mental disorder among Latinos/as illustrate this point. A series of studies shows that Mexicans born in the United States exhibit higher rates of mental disorder than those born in Mexico. In the ECA, U.S.-born Mexicans had prevalence rates of mental disorder similar to those of European Americans but higher than rates of those born in Mexico. Those born in Mexico had rates lower than both European Americans and U.S.-born Mexicans. The same pattern was seen in the NCS, and more recently in the National Latino and Asian American Study (NLAAS; Alegria et al., 2007). A third study conducted with Mexican Americans living in Fresno County, California, found a similar pattern (Vega et al., 1998). About 25 percent of immigrants had some disorder, whereas 48 percent of those born in the United States did. The length of time in the United States was a factor: immigrants who had been in the United States at least 13 years had higher prevalence rates than did those in the United States less than 13 years. A similar pattern was observed among Asian/Pacific Americans, with those born outside the United States showing lower rates of mental disorder and lower usage of mental health services than those born in the United States. Although Asian/Pacific Americans born in the United States had lower overall rates of mental disorder than did European Americans, their rates were still higher than those of Asian immigrants and Asians living outside the United States (Abe-Kim et al., 2007; Chang, 2002; Takeuchi et al., 2007).

A third concern has to do with diagnostic accuracy. Diagnoses in the large studies mentioned were based on *DSM* criteria. The *DSM* is based on Western diagnostic concepts that may not fully recognize cultural variations in experience and expression of psychological symptoms, such as the tendency for somatization. In addition, questions may not be fully understood, respondents may not answer in a completely honest manner, and interviewers may not accurately interpret participants' responses.

Fourth, available diagnostic categories may not fully cover the range of symptoms or disorders experienced across cultural groups, such as culture-bound syndromes (see discussion later in this chapter). Williams and Harris-Reid (1999) also discuss the difficulties in generalizing the findings on ethnic group differences in mental health. They cite limitations related to different research methodologies, different criteria for identifying mental disorder and minority status, the heterogeneity of minority groups, and the lack of research available on some groups.

Conclusions from Existing Data

What conclusion can be drawn from the data on mental disorder and ethnic group membership? The *Surgeon General's Report on Mental Health: Culture, Race, and Ethnicity* (U.S. Department of Health and Human Services, 2001) concludes that the prevalence rates for mental disorders in the various ethnic groups are virtually equal. In other words, there are no significant differences in the overall rate of mental disorder in the different ethnic minority groups. Nonetheless, the report also notes that current research is limited and that much more research needs to be done. Williams and Harris-Reid (1999) conclude, "Despite decades of research, we lack a clear picture of the mental health status of the principal minority populations in the United States" (p. 304).

So far, our discussion about cultural group differences and mental health has focused on differences among ethnic groups in the United States. If we look at the prevalence of mental disorders across the globe, certain disorders appear with relative consistency. Schizophrenia occurs at a rate of about 1 percent, bipolar disorder 0.3–1.5 percent, and panic disorder 0.4–2.9 percent (World Health Organization, 1973; Weissman et al., 1994, 1996, 1997, 1998). The consistency in the occurrence of these disorders across different countries, combined with the results of family and genetic studies, suggests that there is a strong genetic component to these disorders and that cultural factors play less of a role (U.S. Department of Health and Human Services, 2001). Differential rates across cultures suggest that culture plays more of a role in other disorders, such as depression, for which the rates range from 2 percent to 19 percent across countries (Weissman et al., 1996). This result suggests that cultural factors, such as poverty and violence, may play a greater role than genetics does in the causation of major depression (National Institute of Mental Health, 1998).

We can also see the influence of culture on mental disorder in the development of Posttraumatic Stress Disorder (PTSD). PTSD is a disorder that develops following exposure to a traumatic event whereby the person witnessed or experienced actual or threatened death or serious injury to himself/herself or others.

PICTURE 9.1 More ethnic minority therapists are needed in psychology. *Photograph by Tom Zasadzinski*

Examples of traumatic experiences include rape, combat, and natural disaster. Symptoms include reexperiencing the event through things such as troubling or intrusive memories, dreams, or flashbacks; avoidance of situations that remind the person of the trauma; sleep disturbance; and hypervigilance (American Psychiatric Association, 2000).

Traumatic experiences are particularly common for immigrants from countries in turmoil. Higher rates of PTSD have been observed in these populations. Kinzie and associates (1990) found that 70 percent of a sample of Vietnamese, Laotian, and Cambodian refugees met the criteria for PTSD, and that 82 percent of them experienced the most common symptom of PTSD—depression. Blair (2000) studied a random sample of Cambodian adults and found that 85 percent had experienced horrible traumas before immigrating to the United States, including starvation, torture, and the death of family members. About 45 percent met the criteria for PTSD, and about 81 percent reported five or more symptoms.

The diagnosis for Chanda, whose case was described earlier in this chapter, was most likely PTSD. Some people may maintain that Chanda's reactions were *normal* or *expected* given her horrific history, but in the eyes of our diagnostic system she still would be classified as suffering from PTSD.

Gender Differences

We cannot leave a discussion of group differences in mental health without talking about gender differences. Data from the NCS show that there are no overall differences in the rates of mental disorder between men and women, but there are gender differences in the particular types of disorders experienced (Iwamasa & Bangi, 2003; Kessler et al., 1993, 1994). Women have higher rates of depression and anxiety, and men have higher rates of substance abuse and antisocial disorders.

The differentiation has been described as women having higher rates of "internalizing" disorders and men of "externalizing" disorders. What this means is that women tend to focus their feelings on the self, whereas men project their feelings outward and express them through overt behaviors. According to Rosenfeld (1999), this means that women more than men live with profound feelings of sadness, loss, low self-esteem, guilt, hopelessness, and self-blame. They suffer more anxiety, ranging from fears of specific objects or situations, to panic attacks, to free-floating anxiety and constant worry. In contrast, men consume more alcohol and drugs, and do so more frequently than women. Abuse of alcohol and drugs leads to more negative physical consequences for men, such as blackouts and hallucinations, and it interferes with their lives more often, causing more problems at work, at school, or in the family. Men are more likely to exhibit aggressive and violent behavior (Mio et al., 2003). They are also more prone to criminal behavior, deceitfulness, impulsivity, irresponsibility, and recklessness.

> Ms. S. had a history of being battered by her husband, leaving that relationship and eventually marrying another man. Her own children, who were born on the reservation, had several fathers. One son was killed. Ms. S. divorced her last husband because of his repeated infidelity and moved her family, which included her mentally retarded oldest daughter and disabled mother, to a city to support them better.
>
> Ms. S. had her son arrested after he threatened her with a knife and raped her. He justified his behavior by saying that he was too drunk to know what he was doing. When he pleaded with his mother to have the authorities release him, she agreed to drop the charges. Seven months later, he was accused of sexually abusing her two granddaughters, ages 5 and 7, which he had apparently been doing since before the rape. . . .
>
> Ms. S. was referred for therapy to help her regain custody of the children. The focus of the HSD [New Mexico Human Services Department] treatment plan was to help her overcome her depression and enable her to "regain self-control, particularly with regard to defending herself from her son." She also felt abused and disempowered by the state social service and legal systems. Her family life had been completely disrupted by her son's behavior, its discovery by a foreign agency (HSD), and the interventions imposed by a hostile and alien system. (LaFramboise, Berman, & Sohi, 1994, p. 57)

This case illustrates the point that women tend to internalize their disorders, whereas men externalize their disorders. Hence, Ms. S. was diagnosed with depression, and many of the men in her life engaged in violence, alcoholism, and infidelity.

These gender differences are consistent across cultures, leading some to believe there is a biological basis. However, studies that vary the social conditions, such as wives being employed outside the home, demonstrate that differences in the rates of disorder between men and women are the same or reversed. This evidence points more to social causes than biological causes for these differences (Rosenfeld, 1980, 1999).

Rosenfeld (1999) believes these differences are more accurately explained by life circumstances, such as women having less power (e.g., women earning less than their husbands), greater responsibility for taking care of the home and raising children, and stronger social ties. Decreased power and control and increased social responsibility and their different interpretations of those circumstances, combined with different coping strategies, lead women to have higher rates of depression and anxiety than men. For example, combining the roles of worker and parent means different things to men than to women. For a man to work outside the home is consistent with his role as the breadwinner for the family. However, for a woman, providing care, nurturance, and attention for her children is more central to her role as parent than earning an income. Thus, women have higher levels of distress in combining these roles than their husbands do (Simon, 1995).

There is also discussion about whether the different disorders exhibited by men and women are really in response to different circumstances or if they are instead different reactions to the same circumstances. Norms for the acceptable expression of emotions differ drastically between men and women. These norms are socialized into boys and girls from a very young age. How many men reading this book were told, "Stop crying. Boys don't cry," "Don't be a sissy," or "Suck it up and be a man!" Men are discouraged from expressing feelings, especially those that are defined as feminine or weak, such as worry, fear, and helplessness—all emotions associated with anxiety and depression. Feelings such as anger are more acceptable for men. One study showed that men who come into psychiatric emergency rooms with depressive symptoms were hospitalized at a much higher rate than women with the same symptoms, whereas women who came in exhibiting antisocial symptoms or substance abuse were more likely to be hospitalized than men reporting the same problems (Rosenfeld, 1984). Men may attempt to hide or avoid the forbidden feelings related to anxiety and depression. Drinking accomplishes that goal.

Thus, it seems that men and women have different disorders both because they encounter different social experiences and because they have different kinds of reactions to circumstances (Rosenfeld, 1999).

Culture-Bound Syndromes

culture-bound syndromes— disorders that tend to occur only in certain cultures.

Although mental disorders conforming to *DSM-IV-TR* criteria can be found across cultures, there are illnesses found only in particular areas. These are known as **culture-bound syndromes,** or "clusters of symptoms that are much more common in some cultures than others" (U.S. Department of Health and Human Services, 2001, p. 11; Trimble & Mertz, 1999). Although there may be some overlap, there typically is no *DSM-IV-TR* category that corresponds directly to a culture-bound syndrome.

The *DSM-IV-TR* lists some of the most researched culture-bound syndromes. One example is *ataque de nervios*. This condition is typically reported among Latinos/as, especially those from the Caribbean (Lopez-Baez, 1999; Oquendo,

Horwath, & Martinez, 1989). Symptoms include uncontrollable shouting, attacks of crying, trembling, heat in the chest rising to the head, fainting spells, and verbal or physical aggression. Generally, the victims report feeling out of control, and the experience often occurs in response to a stressful event, such as news of the death of a close loved one. The episodes are usually discrete, with the person quickly returning to his or her usual level of functioning.

Another example of a culture-bound syndrome is *brain fag*. This term comes from West Africa and refers to a condition experienced by high school or university students wherein they report difficulty concentrating, remembering, and thinking. Students report that their brains are "fatigued" or tired from too much thinking (Prince, 2000). Some of you may be saying, "That's not a culture-bound syndrome. I experience that every night when I try to study!"

Yet another example of a culture-bound syndrome is *taijin kyofusho*, a form of social phobia observed in Japan and Korea. The individual suffers from extreme anxiety that his or her body or its functions are offensive to others, such as through eye contact, body odor, or misshapen physical features. Although this syndrome may seem similar to Social Phobia or Body Dysmorphic Disorder, the key feature is extreme fear of offending others. This makes sense if you put the symptoms in the cultural context of concerns about harmonious social interactions that characterize traditional Japanese culture (American Psychiatric Association, 2000; Atkinson, 2004; see our discussion of individualism versus collectivism, chapter 3).

Although some culture-bound syndromes have similarities to *DSM-IV-TR* diagnoses, there are important differences. The culture-bound syndromes represent local, folk diagnostic categories. Diagnostic labels are developed within a cultural context. The diagnostic categories of the *DSM* reflect Western culture and Western medicine.

The existence of culture-bound syndromes that do not fit into any particular *DSM* category illustrates some of the difficulties that occur when one considers cultural manifestations of psychopathology. Western health and mental health workers may misunderstand, misdiagnose, and mistreat symptoms exhibited by members of cultural minority groups (Lin & Cheung, 1999). Research has not yet determined whether culture-bound syndromes are variants of *DSM-IV* diagnoses or separate and distinct disorders. Although there may be some overlap, it is still important to note the differences, for both the professionally sanctioned diagnoses of the *DSM* and the culture-bound syndromes may be manifestations of the specific ways that the cultural and social environment interacts with genes to produce a particular illness (U.S. Department of Health and Human Services, 2001).

Eating Disorders: An American Culture-Bound Syndrome?

Eating disorders present an interesting example of some of the issues regarding culture and mental disorder discussed earlier. The most common eating disorders include *anorexia nervosa* and *bulimia nervosa*. **Anorexia nervosa** is characterized by extreme weight loss, the intense fear of gaining weight, and distorted body image. The individual continues to see herself or himself as fat even though by

anorexia nervosa— an eating disorder marked by such a severe restriction of one's diet that the sufferer's weight falls far below what would be expected, given her/his height and age.

bulimia nervosa—
an eating disorder
marked by the
consumption of a
large amount of
food in one sitting—
called a binge—
followed by the
purging of that
food, most typically
through vomiting
but also through
extreme exercise or
the use of laxatives.

objective standards she or he is significantly underweight. **Bulimia nervosa** is characterized by binging and purging. The individual has episodes during which she or he consumes excessively large amounts of food; afterward, the person engages in extreme activities to avoid gaining weight, such as vomiting, excessive exercise, and the use of laxatives or diuretics (American Psychiatric Association, 2000). Besides just looking at full-blown eating disorders, many researchers also consider subclinical levels of disturbed eating and body image to be important. In other words, there are many people who have significant issues with weight, eating behaviors, and body image who may not meet the full criteria for an eating disorder.

It is a commonly held belief that eating disorders are most common in Western, White, female populations (Crago, Shisslak, & Estes, 1996; Dolan, 1991; Pate et al., 1992). Most research studies focus on this population (le Grange, Telch, & Tibbs, 1998; Thompson, 1994), but there are a large number of studies that examine the prevalence of these disorders in different cultural groups. Some of these studies suggest that eating disorders are less common among ethnic minorities living in Western societies, but the results are inconclusive (Wildes & Emery, 2001).

For example, some studies suggest that African-American women are less likely to develop anorexia and bulimia nervosa than their European-American counterparts (Gray, Ford, & Kelly, 1987; Hsu, 1987). Although African-American women are typically heavier than European-American women, fewer African-American women exhibit problematic eating behavior (Abrams, Allen, & Gray, 1993; Dolan, 1991; Rand & Kuldau, 1990), and they possess greater body satisfaction than do European-American women (Harris, 1994; McCarthy, 1990). In addition, African-American women have been found to have less of a discrepancy between their perceived and their ideal body size (Rucker & Cash, 1992). Some studies also show lower rates of dieting behaviors, body dissatisfaction, weight concerns, and eating disorders for Asian and Asian-American women (Akan & Grilo, 1995; Dolan, 1991; Lucero et al., 1992). However, Lerner and associates (1980) found that Japanese women had lower self-esteem, self-concept, and body-image scores than Americans, and Lee (1993) found that Chinese women were similar to their Western counterparts in their desire to be thin. Interestingly, that preoccupation with thinness did not lead to changing or restricting their eating behaviors. Lucero and colleagues (1992) found that Latina-American women weighed more but were less concerned with their weight than were European-American women (Lucero et al., 1992), but Fitzgibbon and associates (1998) found Latina-American women to have a greater severity of binge-eating symptoms and a lower body-image ideal than African-American and European-American women. Liddi-Brown, Barker-Hackett, and Grizzell (2002) conducted a study with a large, multicultural college student sample that included nine measures of disordered eating and body image. They found that Latinos/as had a stronger drive to be thin, and Asian/Pacific Americans and African Americans exhibited more uncontrolled overeating. Some measures of body image in their study showed that Asian/Pacific Americans and African Americans had more positive body image than did Latino/a Americans and European Americans.

As you can see, the results are mixed. Although most studies suggest lower rates of eating-related problems for ethnic minority women, a few found the rates to be higher. To settle the controversy, Wildes and Emery (2001) conducted a meta-analytic review that involved 35 studies, with a total of more than 17,000 participants, that looked at eating disturbance and body dissatisfaction in ethnic minority and White populations. They found that Whites reported greater eating disturbance and body dissatisfaction than did ethnic minorities across all measures used in their study. Although African Americans had lower levels of eating disturbance than did White women, the opposite was true for Asian/Pacific-American women. The differences were greatest for subclinical levels of eating disturbance, and virtually nonexistent for clinical levels, meaning that the rates of anorexia and bulimia nervosa were approximately the same for Whites and non-Whites. Thus, the authors clearly conclude that White women living in Western countries experience greater eating disturbance and body dissatisfaction than do non-White women (Wildes & Emery, 2001).

Thus, the most consistent finding in the literature is that symptoms related to eating disorders are more prevalent in White than in non-White populations. This finding has led some to describe eating disorders as culture-bound syndromes, because culture obviously plays a role in their development (Crago, Shisslak, & Estes, 1996; Keel & Klump, 2003; Pate et al., 1992). However, some finer distinctions may need to be made. Keel and Klump (2003) review the literature looking at incidence rates and historical evidence, as well as the genetic heritability of anorexia nervosa and bulimia nervosa, and conclude that bulimia nervosa seems to be a culture-bound syndrome but anorexia nervosa does not. They attribute this to the fact that there seems to be a greater genetic base for anorexia nervosa.

Why do you think eating disorders might be more common among Whites than among ethnic minorities? Most authors relate this to cultural differences in standards of beauty, with the Western ideal being a very thin body type. Some authors believe that eating disorders are on the rise in non-White, non-Western cultures because of increased exposure to Western standards of beauty through the media and the adoption of those standards through acculturation (Bowen, Tomayasu, & Cauce, 1991; Davis & Yager, 1992; Nasser, 1986). For example, Becker (1995) found that before 1995 Fijians had a strong admiration for robust body shapes and a tolerance for obesity. After broadcast television became widely available in Fiji in 1995, bringing American, British, and Australian programming to the island, attitudes shifted, and young Fijian women began developing a desire to be thin.

With regard to Latinas, Lopez, Blix, and Blix (1995) found that the ideal body image was similar for European-American females and Latinas born in the United States. However, Latinas born outside the United States who immigrated at age 17 or older tended to select a larger silhouette as their ideal body image, whereas Latinas who were 16 or younger at immigration tended to fit within the norm of U.S.-born European-American women. These findings support the notion that cultural norms in Western societies promote smaller body sizes and increased body dissatisfaction. Wildes and Emery (2001) tested the effects of acculturation in their meta-analysis, but their findings were inconclusive.

In our discussion so far, we have highlighted the impact of culture on mental health. Although there are some variations in the prevalence of various disorders

PICTURE 9.2   Whereas eating disorders have been primarily associated with American White women, Asians are increasingly suffering from eating disorders as they are being exposed to American standards. *Photograph by Katherine Song*

among groups, the current consensus seems to be that there are far more similarities than differences. Some of you may have been surprised by the lack of group differences in the rate of mental disorders. You may have assumed that the rates would be higher for groups such as African Americans because of factors like racism, discrimination, and poverty. Those factors are important. Remember that when group differences were observed, they were most often explained by the varying circumstances of the groups. For example, some of the differences disappeared when factors such as gender, age, and SES were controlled, meaning that racial group membership was not the most important factor, but the fact that race intersects with other things, such as poverty, was. This finding points to the need to consider the context in which these disorders occur, the largest being the cultural context. Williams and Harris-Reid (1999) "emphasize the need for identifying the ways in which the mental health problems of each group emerge from the larger social context in which the group is embedded" (p. 296) and the need to examine the ways in which social economic, political, and cultural factors affect the mental health of minority groups.

CULTURE AND THE TREATMENT OF MENTAL DISORDERS

Just as culture affects the expression and occurrence of various mental disorders, it also affects treatment of those disorders. Treatment typically refers to counseling and psychotherapy. We noted in chapter 1 that the history of multicultural psychology is rooted in efforts to address cultural differences in counseling and psychotherapy. Sue and Sue (2008) argue that to adequately assist individuals from diverse backgrounds with mental health issues, counseling and psychotherapy must be culturally sensitive. That means mental health professionals must consciously, actively, and effectively address cultural issues in the therapeutic setting. This section covers a number of multicultural treatment issues, including underutilization of services, barriers to treatment, and various attempts at providing culturally sensitive treatments.

Underutilization of Mental Health Services

In 1978 the Special Populations Task Force of the President's Commission on Mental Health concluded that ethnic minorities are underserved or inappropriately served by the mental health system in the United States (Special Populations Task Force, 1978). More than 20 years later, in 2001, the Surgeon General's report on culture, race, and ethnicity also concluded that significant disparities exist for ethnic minorities in mental health services (U.S. Department of Health and Human Services, 2001).

In general, only about 1 in 3 people who need mental health services actually uses them. Thus, underutilization is an issue for all segments of the population, but it is especially so for ethnic minorities (Robins & Regier, 1991). Many authors in the psychological literature have noted that ethnic minorities are less likely than European Americans to seek mental health treatment (e.g., Kessler et al., 1996; Sussman, Robins, & Earls, 1987; Vega et al., 1998; Zhang, Snowden, & Sue, 1998). African Americans and Asian/Pacific Americans are also more likely to delay seeking treatment until their symptoms are more severe (U.S. Department of Health and Human Services, 2001; Chen et al., 2003). Research on Asian Americans shows that about one third who requested an intake appointment from a mental health program failed to show up for this initial session (Akutsu, Tsuru, & Chen, 2004). If they showed up, dropout rates' after the intake session ranged from 10 to 22 percent (Zane, Hatanaka, Park, & Akutsu, 1994). Ethnic minorities are also more likely to seek help from other sources for psychological problems, such as their primary-care physician, clergy, traditional healers, family members, and friends (Buchwald, Beals, & Manson, 2000; Cooper-Patrick et al., 1999; Levin, 1986; Neighbors & Jackson, 1984; Peifer, Hu, & Vega, 2000).

The general conclusion in the literature is that members of ethnic minority groups underutilize mental health services (Sue & Sue, 1999). Cheung and Snowden (1990) review the literature on ethnic minority utilization of mental health services and conclude that African Americans use services more than expected, and Asian Americans and Pacific Islanders use services less. Latino/a Americans', American Indians', and Alaskan Natives' use of services varies according to type of service. These results indicate that there may be important differences in help-seeking behavior between various ethnic groups.

Although it is important to study variations in help-seeking patterns among ethnic groups, it is also important to remember that there may be significant within-group differences. Within-group differences have been observed among different Asian groups (Tracey, Leong, & Glidden, 1986), between Mexican

Americans and Mexican immigrants (Keefe, 1982), and in the African-American community (Neighbors, 1984, 1985, 1988; Neighbors & Jackson, 1984).

Research shows that if ethnic minorities do go to therapy, they do not stay as long as European Americans. Several studies revealed that ethnic minority clients are much more likely to terminate therapy after just one session than are their European-American counterparts (Sue, 1977; Sue, Allen, & Conaway, 1975; Sue et al., 1991; Sue, & McKinney, 1974; Sue et al., 1974).

Barriers to Treatment

It is generally accepted that ethnic minorities tend to underutilize mental health services. What are some of the barriers that prevent them from getting the services they need? Is it that they have negative attitudes toward seeking help? toward psychotherapy? Or, is it that they have negative experiences once they go to therapy?

It has been suggested that ethnic minorities' negative attitudes toward psychotherapy prevent them from seeking help in the first place. For example, some authors have suggested that African Americans are reluctant to utilize mental health services because of a history of negative experiences with racism. African Americans go into the therapeutic setting viewing the European-American therapist as an agent of an oppressive society who may use the information disclosed in therapy against them (Ridley, 1995; White & Parham, 1990). In the NCS study, participants were asked a series of questions that assessed their attitudes toward mental health services. For example, they were asked how likely they would be, if they had a serious emotional problem, to seek help, how comfortable they would be talking to a professional about their personal problems, and how embarrassed they would be if their friends knew they were getting professional help for an emotional problem.

Diala and associates (2000) compared the responses of European-American and African-American participants' to those questions. Surprisingly, they found that initially, before receiving any type of professional help, African Americans had more positive attitudes about mental health services than did European Americans. However, once they received help, their attitudes changed and became more negative. This change suggests that their encounter with professional mental health services was negative and that something about the experience turned African Americans off. This change, considered along with the findings mentioned previously that ethnic minorities tend not to come back after the first session, suggests that we need to examine what happens in the therapeutic setting with ethnic minorities.

Sue and Sue (2008) articulate what they see as the three major barriers to effective multicultural counseling and therapy: (a) culture-bound values, (b) class-bound values, and (c) language variables (see Table 9.4).

Culture-Bound Values as Barriers

culture-bound values—core beliefs of one culture that relate principally to that culture and may be inappropriate for another culture.

Psychotherapy is directly influenced by the culture within which it was developed. Psychotherapy was originally developed by Western Europeans (e.g., Freud); therefore, it reflects a Western perspective, and some of the central values of that perspective may be in direct conflict with the values of clients from other cultures.

TABLE 9.4 Sue and Sue's (2008) Barriers to Multicultural Counseling and Therapy

Culture-Bound Values

    Focus on the individual

    Verbal/emotional/behavioral expressiveness

    Insight required

    Self-disclosure (Openness and intimacy)

    Scientific empiricism

    Clear distinctions between mental and physical well-being

    Ambiguous and unstructured therapeutic process

    Different patterns of communication between client and counselor

Class-Bound Values

    White middle- to upper-class values

    Implicit inferiority of lower-class values

Language Variables

    Emphasis on verbal communication

    Monolingual English assumptions

    Lack of bilingual therapists

    Use of standard English

    Implicit inferiority of nonstandard English (e.g., Black English/Ebonics)

Sue and Sue (2008) describe some of the European-American values embedded in psychotherapy that may conflict with values of clients from other cultures. They refer to these as **culture-bound values.** Culture-bound values in counseling and psychotherapy include individualism, verbal/emotional/behavioral expressiveness, insight, openness and intimacy, analytic/linear/verbal (cause–effect) approach, clear distinctions between mental and physical well-being, ambiguity of process, and communication patterns from client to counselor.

In chapter 3 we discussed the differences between individualism and collectivism. Psychotherapy tends to be a very *individualistic* process. If we look at the most popular theories of human development—Piaget, Erickson—we see that they emphasize individuation—the development of an autonomous, independent self—as healthy development. If we look at the goals of some of the main orientations to psychotherapy, we also see this focus on the individual. For example, Carl Rogers emphasized self-actualization, or the development of one's full potential. Alfred Adler emphasized the concept of self-esteem; how one feels about himself or herself is seen as a critical component of mental health, and a person's self-esteem is greatly influenced by one's personal accomplishments. This concept just does not make sense in collectivistic cultures where people have an interdependent sense of the self. As discussed in chapter 3, this may also be related to the difference be-tween guilt and shame. Guilt is an individual emotion, whereas shame appears to be a group emotion, because one's behavior reflects upon his or her family or group. In some cultures, too much emphasis on the self is seen as unhealthy. For example, American culture says, "The squeaky wheel gets the oil." In contrast, Japanese culture says, "The nail that sticks out gets beaten down." In American culture, the loud, assertive person gets positive attention, but in Japanese culture, assertiveness is seen as being selfish and against group standards.

> *My friend is Persian and the counselor she's seeing is White. She told me that she was having trouble trying to explain to her counselor some of the cultural differences between Persian and American individuals. Persians are more collectivistic—they will sacrifice their time in order to please some family members. Also, Persians tend to be very traditional and their religion plays an important role in their everyday life.*
>
> *One of the things she told me was that her White counselor was unable to understand why she would place her brother's business before her studies and why she didn't find it easier to do her own thing in order to succeed herself. This may be easy for a White person to state, because Whites are extremely individualistic, and they fail to understand that family members in some cultures are placed before one's self.*
>
> LANA, 20+-YEAR-OLD ARMENIAN-AMERICAN WOMAN

The second culture-bound value described by Sue and Sue (2008) is *verbal/emotional/behavioral expressiveness*. Different cultures place varying emphasis on acceptable ways to express emotion. Western cultures tend to value open and outward expression of emotions, whereas other cultures, such as Asians, value emotional restraint (see our discussion of direct versus indirect expression in chapter 3). Members of ethnic minority groups, because of mistrust, may with-hold true feelings in situations where they feel threatened, such as an African-American client with a European-American therapist. In the Western tradition, where outward emotional expression is valued and expected, clients who do not express enough emotion are labeled as resistant, restricted, and repressed by their therapists.

The third culture-bound value described by Sue and Sue (2008) is *insight*. Many traditional forms of counseling and psychotherapy (e.g., psychoanalytic, humanistic) believe that the path to wellness lies in insight, or the client's under-standing of the underlying dynamics of his or her problems. Other cultures do not see the need for such in-depth self-exploration. In fact, in some Asian cultures it is believed that thinking too much about something can make the problem worse. Asian elders advise children not to think about the problem because then you are thinking about yourself too much, instead of the family. The following story illustrates a conflict over this value of insight.

My family went to therapy once because my teenage sister was getting into a lot of trouble, and my mother didn't know how to handle her anymore. We were assigned to a White male therapist. In the first session the therapist asked my mother a lot of questions about her own feelings and actions. I could see my mother was getting a bit irritated. She didn't understand why the therapist was focusing on her and not my sister. At the end of the session the therapist suggested that my mother keep a journal, record her thoughts and feelings for the week, and bring them back to the next session. We never went back.

BELEN, 20+-YEAR-OLD MEXICAN-AMERICAN WOMAN

In this story, we can see the factors that resulted in this family's terminating after the first session. One main factor was the clash in the culture-bound value of insight. This mother wanted practical advice on coping with her daughter's behavioral problems. Instead, the therapist assigned the mother to keep a journal. We can assume that the therapist had good intentions, believing that the problems lay with the interactions between the mother and the daughter, and that the mother needed to become more aware of these interpersonal dynamics. However, this was not culturally sensitive intervention, and the family never went back.

The fourth culture-bound value is *self-disclosure,* or intimacy and openness. In therapy the client is supposed to share the most intimate details of his or her life. In many cultures such personal disclosures are reserved for only the closest family and friends. Intimate relationships are developed over time, not once a week in a 50-minute session.

I will admit that there are times when I feel anxious, depressed, and angry. I think at some point in their lives everyone does. However, even though I've had such feelings, it has never crossed my mind, the idea of going to therapy. I guess it has a lot to do with the way I was raised. Growing up in Mexico, I only knew of one person—in my entire life over there—that was going to therapy. . . . Everyone around town would say that he was crazy because he was going to therapy. I was about ten at the time, and I felt fear towards him. I would always avoid getting close to his house because since he was "crazy" he would probably hurt me. My family and I then migrated to the United States, and about four years ago I met him at a family wedding. Turns out we are distant relatives. Furthermore, he is a great person. I did not see any crazy in him that I won't see in any other person. I asked about the time [in Mexico] when he attended therapy. From what he told me it was nothing very out of the ordinary. Things were just not going well for him at the time and his parents misinterpreted that. However, he did tell me that he did enjoy therapy and that it did help him.

JAIME, 20+-YEAR-OLD MEXICAN-AMERICAN MAN

The fifth culture-bound value is *scientific empiricism*. Psychology patterns itself after the physical sciences, which emphasize objective rational linear thinking. In Western approaches, the therapist is supposed to be neutral, rational, and logical, like a scientist. Mental health concerns are approached through linear problem solving and quantitative evaluation through the use of tools such as psychodiagnostic tests (e.g., intelligence tests, personality tests). Instead, many other cultures take a more circular, holistic, harmonious approach to the world. For example, instead of breaking nature down into its components to study it, control it, and exploit it for profit, as Western cultures do, American-Indian culture emphasizes harmonious living with the world. Instead of emphasizing rational, reductionistic problem solving, they believe in the value of intuition.

Sixth, Western philosophy also draws a *distinction between mental and physical functioning*. In other words, the mind and the body are seen as two separate entities, and there is a clear distinction between mental and physical health. That distinction is not made in other cultures. Thus, there is no difference in going for help with an emotional problem to your regular physician or your priest. Just as the doctor prescribes a specific, tangible solution to the problem (e.g., medication), the counselor or therapist may be expected to do the same.

A seventh culture-bound value, *ambiguity*, refers to the unstructured nature of the therapeutic setting. Some societies, such as Latino/a cultures, have very clear social structures and patterns of relationships (e.g., the father is the head of the family; the mother takes primary responsibility for rearing the children). People from different cultures may be unfamiliar with the relationship structure of Western therapy and may find it uncomfortable and confusing.

Finally, along similar lines, *patterns of communication* differ from one culture to another. In some cultures, such as Latino/a ones, children are reared to respect their elders and authority figures, and they do not speak until they are spoken to. The therapist may be viewed as an authority figure, and the culturally different client may come in and wait for the therapist to speak first and take the lead in running the session. However, in many traditional Western therapies, the client is expected to do most of the talking and take responsibility for directing the session while the therapist takes a less active role. Therapists may misunderstand and misinterpret the behavior of the culturally different client who comes in and does not say much.

Class-Bound Values as Barriers

class-bound
values—core
beliefs of one
socioeconomic class
that relate
principally to that
class and may be
inappropriate for
another level of
socioeconomic
status.

Effective multicultural therapy can also be hindered by **class-bound values**. According to Sue and Sue (2008), the values that underlie typical mental health practices are decidedly White middle class and often fail to recognize the economic implications for the delivery of mental health services. "Class-bound factors related to socioeconomic status may place those suffering from poverty at a disadvantage and obstruct their efforts to obtain help" (Sue & Sue, 2003, p. 55). For example, poor clients may not have transportation to get to sessions and may not have the money or the insurance coverage to pay for services. A therapist who wants the poor client to openly express intimate parts of his or her life, to introspect, and to gain insight into the underlying dynamics of his or her behavior may be in direct conflict with a client who is more concerned about finding a job, putting food on the table, or finding adequate care for his or her child. Clients who are in survival mode, just trying to make it from day to day, may expect more tangible advice and suggestions from the therapist. It is also often difficult for a therapist who comes from a middle- to upper-class background to relate to the circumstances and hardships affecting the client who lives in poverty.

> *We were in a faculty meeting discussing the final comprehensive exam for our graduate students. In part of the exam students must answer questions related to a clinical vignette. A number of faculty wrote possible vignettes, and we were trying to decide which one to use in the exam. I wrote a vignette about a 5-year-old boy who was referred for treatment for acting out at school. In the family background I mentioned that the mother lived in a small apartment where a lot of different people came in and out, many who abused drugs. One night, when the client was an infant, the mother could not get him to stop crying. One of the mother's friends, who was high on drugs, grabbed the small boy and tried to throw him off the balcony. When we got to that part of the vignette, a White male faculty member said, "We can't use that one. That would never happen in the real world." I immediately spoke up and said, "Well it does in my world. That was based on an actual case." The other faculty member turned a bit red, looked a little sheepish, but said nothing. We ended up using that vignette.*

Linda, 30+-year-old African-American Woman

The inferior and biased treatment of lower-SES clients is well documented in the literature (APA Task Force on SES, 2006). For example, in a study by Garfield, Weiss, and Pollock (1973) counselors were given identical descriptions of a 9-year-old boy who exhibited negative classroom behavior. The only thing that differed was his socioeconomic status (SES). Counselors who were told the boy belonged to the upper SES expressed more of a willingness to become involved with the boy than those who were told he was from the lower SES. Lorion (1973) found that psychiatrists more often referred clients like themselves (i.e., White, upper SES) to therapy. These findings illustrate some of the class-bound variables that affect the provision of mental health services for members of minority groups.

Language as a Barrier

The third barrier to effective multicultural therapy described by Sue and Sue (2008) is **language.** United States society is monolingual, at least in its values. The reality is that hundreds of languages are spoken within the United States, but the preferred language is English. Because psychotherapy is a "talking cure," the client and the therapist must be able to accurately and appropriately send and receive both verbal and nonverbal messages for therapy to be effective.

Individuals who do not speak English may be completely shut out from mental health services because of a lack of bilingual counselors and therapists. Those who speak English as a second language may be at a disadvantage because

language issues— differences in language (e.g., an English-speaking therapist and a Spanish-speaking client who may have some limited facility with English) or language usage (e.g., Ebonics or Black English).

they cannot express their thoughts, feelings, and experiences in as complex, deep, or rich a manner in English as they can in their native tongue. Those who speak nonstandard English, such as some African Americans who use Black English/ Ebonics, may use words, phrases, and expressions with which the European-American therapist is unfamiliar.

Experience with Racism

A major barrier to seeking treatment is mistrust, which is connected to the very real experiences of ethnic minority groups with racism, both currently and historically (U.S. Department of Health and Human Services, 2001; Duran, 2006; Ridley, 1995; Sue & Sue, 2003; Trimble & Gonzales, 2008). Clients may be reluctant to seek professional services because of the perceived racism of the mental health system and their actual racist encounters with various social agencies. For example, therapists may fall prey, whether consciously or unconsciously, to their own racist stereotypes, biases, and prejudices. Sue and Sue (2003) see these more subtle forms of unintentional racism as even more detrimental to the therapeutic process because they are unseen and more pervasive.

Well-meaning therapists unwittingly convey their negative attitudes to clients. They may be more resistant to seeing the harm that they do and to changing their ways because they see themselves as moral, just, fair-minded, and decent. Also, because of their lack of familiarity and discomfort with other cultures, therapists may unconsciously do things to push culturally different clients away, such as not putting much effort into building rapport, concluding that the client is resistant or not well suited to psychotherapy, or determining that the client's needs would be better served elsewhere. Sue and Sue (1999) gave a perfect illustration of these factors:

> I have worked with very few African-American clients during my internship at the clinic, but one particular incident left me with very negative feelings. A Black client named Malachi was given an appointment with me. Even though I'm White, I tried not to let his being Black get in the way of our sessions. I treated him like everyone else, a human being who needed help.
>
> At the onset, Malachi was obviously guarded, mistrustful, and frustrated when talking about his reasons for coming. While his intake form listed depression as the problem, he seemed more concerned about nonclinical matters. He spoke about his inability to find a job, about the need to obtain help with job hunting skills, and about advice in how best to write his résumé. He was quite demanding in asking for advice and information. It was almost as if Malachi wanted everything handed to him on a silver platter without putting any work into our sessions. Not only did he appear reluctant to take responsibility to change his own life, but I felt he needed to go elsewhere for help. After all, this was a mental health clinic and not an employment agency. Confronting him about his avoidance of responsibility would probably prove counterproductive, so I chose to focus on his feelings. Using a humanistic-existential approach, I reflected his feelings, paraphrased his thoughts, and summarized his

dilemmas. This did not seem to immediately help as I sensed an increase in the tension level, and he seemed antagonistic toward me.

After several attempts by Malachi to obtain direct advice from me, I stated, "You're getting frustrated at me because I'm not giving you the answers you want." It was clear that this angered Malachi. Getting up in a very menacing manner, he stood over me and angrily shouted, "Forget it, man! I don't have time to play your silly games." For one brief moment, I felt in danger of being physically assaulted before he stormed out of the office.

This incident occurred several years ago, and I must admit that I was left with a very unfavorable impression of Blacks. I see myself as basically a good person who truly wants to help others less fortunate than myself. I know it sounds racist, but Malachi's behavior only reinforces my belief that they have trouble controlling their anger, like to take the easy way out, and find it difficult to be open and trusting of others. If I am wrong in this belief, I hope this workshop (multicultural counseling and therapy) will help me better understand the Black personality. (pp. 27-28)

This case illustrates several of the potential barriers to effective multicultural therapy. In this example we see the clash between the therapist's bias toward the values of individualism, independence, and self-exploration. The therapist felt the client's focus on finding a job was a way to avoid doing "real" therapeutic work. From an individualistic perspective, the person is also responsible for his own actions, so if something goes wrong, it is his fault. This therapist clearly placed the responsibility for therapy going awry in the lap of the client. In addition, the client's frustrations with the therapist may have stemmed from the therapist's insistence on retaining an objective, distant stance (individualistic, rational, scientific), rather than making an effort to genuinely connect with him.

There was also a cultural difference in their modes of expression and the client's willingness to do self-disclosure and self-exploration, which the therapist misinterpreted as "guarded" and "mistrustful." The therapist's perceptions of his African-American male client were colored by his negative stereotypes of the aggressive, violent Black male and of African Americans as lazy and unmotivated. These were evident in the therapist's fear for his safety when the client became angry and his frustration with the client for looking to the therapist for help in finding a job.

Culturally Sensitive Therapeutic Approaches

With all these barriers to minority groups seeking and receiving appropriate mental health services, it might seem like an impossible task for members of those groups to get the help they need. A number of approaches have been developed to overcome these obstacles and provide services that are more appropriate for culturally diverse groups.

Essentially, three basic approaches are described in the literature: (a) Train personnel in mental health service agencies; (b) establish separate services for minority groups within existing agencies; and (c) create separate facilities for the specific purpose of providing services to culturally diverse groups (Sue, 1977;

Uba, 1982). Along the same lines, Rogler and associates (1987) suggested three levels of services. The first level involves providing services in the native language of the clients, coordinating with other organizations in the ethnic community, and creating an atmosphere in the organization that is open to the cultural values of the community it serves. The second level involves selecting mainstream treatments (i.e., traditional approaches to therapy) that fit with ethnic culture. The third layer involves creating interventions designed specifically for ethnic cultures.

In the following sections we will discuss some of the approaches that have been developed to provide effective mental health services to diverse populations. More specifically, we will cover the training of mental health professionals, cultural matching between clients and therapists, and culture-specific approaches.

The Training of Mental Health Professionals: Multicultural Competence

One way to overcome barriers to effective multicultural therapy is to increase the ability of mental health professionals to work with culturally diverse populations. Sue and Sue (1999) state:

> It is our contention that the reasons why minority-group individuals underutilize and prematurely terminate counseling/therapy lie in the biased nature of the services themselves. The services offered are frequently antagonistic or inappropriate to the life experiences of the culturally different client; they lack sensitivity and understanding; and they are oppressive and discriminating toward minority clients. One of the major reasons for therapeutic ineffectiveness lies in the training of mental health professionals. (p. 11)

In other words, the way to effective multicultural therapy is through training and education of mental health professionals. That leads us to the issue of multicultural competence. In chapter 1 we discussed the struggles associated with getting APA to officially adopt a set of multicultural competencies and thereby set the standard for the training of professional psychologists and counselors to conduct therapy with individuals from diverse backgrounds. We now examine more closely the issue of multicultural competence and what it means.

multicultural competence—the ability to work and be effective with individuals who are of a different culture from yours.

In general, **multicultural competence** refers to effectiveness in working with people who are different from you. More specifically, Pope-Davis, Reynolds, Dings, and Ottavi (1994) defined multicultural competence as

> an appreciation of and sensitivity to the history, current needs, strengths, and resources of communities and individuals who historically have been underserved and underrepresented by psychologists. . . . Specifically, these competencies entail the following: an awareness of one's own biases and cultural assumptions, content knowledge about cultures different from one's own culture, an accurate self-assessment of one's multicultural skills and comfort level, an appropriate application of cultural knowledge to the counseling process, and an awareness of the cultural assumptions underlying the counseling process. (p. 466)

Multicultural competence utilizes a broad definition of culture (see chapter 1) whereby any kind of difference between the therapist/counselor and client is considered a cultural encounter. That means a male therapist working with a female client, a straight therapist working with a gay client, a European-American therapist working with an African-American client, a Protestant therapist working with a Catholic client, and so on. Since every individual, including therapists and clients, brings his or her own unique set of cultural identities to the therapy office, all therapy could be considered multicultural therapy (Pedersen, 1988).

The multicultural competencies were developed by a number of psychologists, most prominently Derald Wing Sue and Patricia Arredondo (Arredondo et al., 1996; Sue et al., 1982; Sue, Arredondo, & McDavis, 1992; Sue et al., 1998) (see chapter 1). There are three main areas of multicultural competence: (a) the counselor's awareness of his or her own cultural assumptions, values, and biases; (b) an understanding of the client's worldview; and (c) the development of culturally appropriate intervention strategies and techniques.

One of the primary aspects of multicultural competence is self-awareness. In other words, counselors and therapists cannot be effective in working with individuals from different backgrounds unless they first understand themselves. That includes an understanding of their own cultural heritage, the impact it has on their attitudes and behaviors, and an understanding of the attitudes they have toward other groups, such as biases, prejudices and stereotypes.

Second, effective counselors and therapists need to be able to see the world through their clients' eyes. They need to have basic information about the various groups they encounter, such as history of the group, current issues facing the group, and typical values held and practices followed by the group. That knowledge should not be used to formulate stereotypes or to make hasty judgments about members of particular groups but should be used to formulate hypotheses that can be explored with the client. For example, if you are a therapist with a Latina client, you might assume that she is Catholic and ascribes to traditional gender roles. Those things may exemplify Latino/a culture in general but may not hold true for an individual Latina client in your office. These are issues that need to be explored with her to see if they apply.

Third, therapists and counselors must develop a repertoire of culturally appropriate strategies, such as the ability to assess level of acculturation and ethnic identity, comfort discussing difficult topics such as racism and sexism, and collaboration with other institutional, community, and indigenous sources of help.

See Table 9.5 for a more detailed description of the multicultural competencies. This table elaborates the attitudes and beliefs, knowledge, and skills that are needed in each of the three main areas of multicultural competence.

The case of Denise at the beginning of the chapter illustrates a number of the dimensions of multicultural competence. First, it might be assumed that Denise and her counselor would have an automatic rapport because they were both African-American women. However, there were important differences between them, the most salient being sexual orientation. This illustrates the point that all counseling is multicultural counseling, because we each have multiple identities. Denise and her counselor openly discussed these differences. In the

TABLE 9.5   Multicultural Counseling Competencies

I. Counselor Awareness of Own Cultural Values and Biases
  A. With respect to *attitudes and beliefs,* culturally competent counselors:
  - believe that cultural self-awareness and sensitivity to one's own cultural heritage is essential.
  - are aware of how their own cultural background and experiences have influenced attitudes, values, and biases about psychological processes.
  - are able to recognize the limits of their multicultural competencies and expertise.
  - recognize their sources of discomfort with differences that exist between themselves and clients in terms of race, ethnicity, and culture.
  B. With respect to *knowledge,* culturally competent counselors:
  - have specific knowledge about their own racial and cultural heritage and how it personally and professionally affects their definitions of and biases about normality/abnormality and the process of counseling.
  - possess knowledge and understanding about how oppression, racism, discrimination, and stereotyping affect them personally and in their work. This allows individuals to acknowledge their own racist attitudes, beliefs, and feelings.
  - possess knowledge about their social impact on others.
  C. With respect to *skills,* culturally competent counselors:
  - seek out educational, consultative, and training experiences to improve their understanding and effectiveness in working with culturally different populations.
  - are constantly seeking to understand themselves as racial and cultural beings and are actively seeking a nonracist identity.
II. Understanding the Client's Worldview
  A. With respect to *attitudes and beliefs,* culturally competent counselors:
  - are aware of their negative and positive emotional reactions toward other racial and ethnic groups that may prove detrimental to the counseling relationship. They are willing to contrast their own beliefs and attitudes with those of their culturally different clients in a nonjudgmental fashion.
  - are aware of stereotypes and preconceived notions that they may hold toward other racial and ethnic minority groups.
  B. With respect to *knowledge,* culturally competent counselors:
  - possess specific knowledge and information about the particular client group with whom they are working.
  - understand how race, culture, ethnicity, and so forth may affect personality formation, vocational choices, manifestation of psychological disorders, help-seeking behavior, and the appropriateness or inappropriateness of counseling approaches.
  - understand and have knowledge about sociopolitical influences that impinge on the lives of racial and ethnic minorities.
  C. With respect to *skills,* culturally competent counselors:
  - familiarize themselves with relevant research and the latest findings regarding mental health and mental disorders that affect various ethnic and racial groups.
  - become actively involved with minority individuals outside the counseling setting so that their perspective of minorities is more than an academic or helping exercise.

III. Developing Culturally Appropriate Intervention Strategies and Techniques
   A. With respect to *attitudes and beliefs,* culturally competent counselors:
   - respect clients' religious and spiritual beliefs and values, including attributions and taboos, because these affect worldview, psychosocial functioning, and expressions of distress.
   - respect indigenous helping practices and respect help-giving among communities of color.
   - value bilingualism and do not view another language as an impediment to counseling.
   B. With respect to *knowledge,* culturally competent counselors:
   - have a clear and explicit knowledge and understanding of the generic characteristics of counseling and therapy and how they may clash with the cultural values of various cultural groups.
   - are aware of institutional barriers that prevent minorities from using mental health services.
   - have knowledge of the potential bias in assessment instruments and use procedures and interpret findings in a way that recognizes the cultural and linguistic characteristics of clients.
   - have knowledge of family structures, hierarchies, values, and beliefs from various cultural perspectives. They are knowledgeable about the community where a particular cultural group may reside and the resources in the community.
   - are aware of relevant discriminatory practices at the social and the community level that may affect the psychological welfare of the population being served.
   C. With respect to *skills,* culturally competent counselors:
   - are able to engage in a variety of verbal and nonverbal helping responses. They are able to send and receive both verbal and nonverbal messages accurately and appropriately. They are not tied to only one method or approach to helping but recognize that helping styles and approaches may be culture bound.
   - are able to exercise institutional intervention skills on behalf of their clients. They can help clients determine whether a problem stems from racism or bias in others so that clients do not inappropriately personalize problems.
   - are not averse to seeking consultation with traditional healers or religious and spiritual leaders and practitioners in the treatment of culturally different clients when appropriate.
   - take responsibility for interacting in the language requested by the client and, if not feasible, make appropriate referrals.
   - have training and expertise in the use of traditional assessment and testing instruments.
   - attend to and work to eliminate biases, prejudices, and discriminatory contexts in conducting evaluations and providing interventions, and develop sensitivity to issues of oppression, sexism, heterosexism, elitism, and racism.
   - take responsibility for educating their clients to the processes of psychological intervention, such as goals, expectations, legal rights, and the counselor's orientation.

Source: Adapted from Arredondo et al. (1996) and Sue et al. (1998).

very beginning, Denise asked the counselor to share personal information about herself and her political attitudes. In some orientations it is taboo for the counselor to share personal information about herself, but the fact that Denise's therapist did so helped Denise to feel more comfortable and overcome some of her "trust issues" and some of the stigma she felt about seeing a mental health professional. Denise's counselor demonstrated a level of comfort and skill in discussing difficult and potentially uncomfortable and conflictual issues, such as heterosexism. To do so effectively, Denise's counselor had to be aware of her personal attitudes on those topics. The counselor was also able to work effectively with Denise because of basic knowledge she had about lesbian lifestyle and the reactions of various communities to this, as well as skill at connecting Denise with other institutional supports (i.e., the lesbian support group.) Thus, Denise's counselor was successful in helping her cope with her presenting problems by demonstrating the three areas of multicultural competence—attitudes and beliefs, knowledge, and skills.

Cultural Matching

When I was 15 years old I was removed from my mom's home and placed in foster care. As part of entering the system I was required to go to therapy once a week. The first therapist they sent me to was a White man in [name of affluent, predominantly White neighborhood]. I immediately felt very uncomfortable. I was supposed to open up and talk about my past and what I had been through and all that, but I did not feel comfortable doing that with him. It felt very stiff and too structured. I remember him taking out these cards and laying them out on the table and asking me what the expressions meant and all that. I don't remember why he did that. I also remember him asking me about fees and how was he going to get paid. I told him I was a ward of the court and didn't know anything about that. That made me feel as if he was not there for me; he was just doing his job. After about five sessions I asked my foster mother, "Can you find me someone Black?" She talked to someone and after that I started seeing an African-American male therapist in the same city. I immediately felt comfortable. It was much less structured. It felt like talking to someone I already knew. I could understand what he said and relate to the language he used. I continued to see him every week for the required amount of time, which was probably about three months.

JAMES, 40+-YEAR-OLD AFRICAN-AMERICAN MAN

James's story brings up a question that naturally arises when thinking about culturally sensitive approaches to therapy: Will therapy be more effective if the client and therapist are of the same background? Like James, would you feel more comfortable talking with a therapist of the same race? The same gender? The same socioeconomic status?

Karlsson (2005) reviewed the literature on ethnic matching between clients and therapists. He divided the studies into three main types—analog studies, archival studies, and process–outcome studies. Analog studies are typically conducted with college students, who are presented with a simulated therapy session and simply asked whether or not they would prefer an ethnically similar therapist (e.g., Lopez, Lopez, & Fong, 1991), or to rank order which therapist characteristics are most important to them, including ethnicity (e.g., Atkinson, Furlong, & Poston, 1986). Archival studies review clinic and hospital records to look at number of attended sessions and dropout rates. The third type of research, rather than looking at data from simulated therapy sessions as analog studies do, or examining the statistics of therapy as archival studies do, examines what happens in actual therapy sessions. These are known as process and outcome studies.

The answer to the question of the effectiveness of ethnic matching between therapist and client is different depending on which kind of study is done. Karlsson (2005) says that the best conclusion for analog studies is that sometimes there is a preference for ethnic matching, but that other therapist characteristics may be judged as more important. For example, one study found ethnic matching to be ranked higher for Native-American students than European-American students, but both groups ranked similarity in attitudes and behaviors as more important than ethnic match (Bennett & BigFoot-Sipes, 1991). Attendance and dropout rates in archival studies do seem to indicate that ethnic matching is important. A large archival study was conducted by Sue and his colleagues (1991), which included a sample of more than 13,000 African-American, Asian-American, Mexican-American, and European-American clients, using data from the Los Angeles County outpatient mental health system. They found that a match between client and therapist in language and ethnicity predicted a decrease in dropout and an increase in the number of sessions. For clients with English as a second language, matching was also a predictor of treatment outcome. In contrast, studies of actual therapy process and outcome suggest that ethnic matching between client and therapist is not important. Jones (1978, 1982) conducted experiments in which he manipulated ethnic match between European-American and African-American clients and therapists. Using the therapists' assessment of treatment outcome, he found that the outcome of the therapy did not differ based on the ethnic match between clients and therapist.

After reviewing and critiquing the literature from all three types of studies on ethnic matching, Karlsson (2005) concludes that "the empirical support for ethnic matching is, at best, inconclusive and lacks a foundation of rigorous research designs" (p. 124). He calls for more and better designed studies, particularly process and outcome studies. Until then, he says "it is still unclear how mental health professionals should optimally serve ethnic minorities in a most advantageous fashion" (p. 124). In other words, research to date does not give a clear answer as to whether or not clients do better when they see a therapist from a similar ethnic background.

Is the effectiveness of cultural matching really unclear? James's story at the beginning of this section might suggest differently. In fact, James's experience is not uncommon. Sue and Zane (1987) concluded that therapy crucially related to how credible a therapist is. Ethnic minority clients may see an ethnically matched therapist as being credible simply because of the matching of their culture. Sue and Zane would call this "ascribed credibility." While this is only a superficial form of credibility, the therapist can earn a deeper level of trust and credibility over time, called "earned credibility." If a therapist is not matched for ethnicity, a client may reject the therapist and not return to therapy or drop out at a higher rate. Certainly, this was the finding of the Sue et al. (1991) large-scale study discussed earlier. However, *if* the client were to remain in therapy with the mismatched therapist, a good therapist can earn credibility. In the Jones studies cited above, the data collected were *therapists'* assessments of the treatment outcome. Therapists may be motivated to believe that they did a good job with any client, so this may be why matched and mismatched therapists were not different from one another when they assessed their own therapy sessions. This conclusion would have been strengthened if a measure of client assessment were also taken. We would echo Karlsson's call for more empirical studies involving process and outcome studies, but we would also call for assessments from both the therapist and the client.

Culture-Specific Therapies

Another approach to providing culturally sensitive therapy is to tailor interventions to the needs and characteristics of specific groups. The idea is that to be effective, psychotherapy must address specific issues that members of particular groups face. Throughout this chapter and this book, we have emphasized that there are cultural, social, political, historical, and economic factors affecting members of culturally diverse groups that make their situations, their perspective, and their behavior unique. For members of various groups to benefit from mental health services, those factors need to be acknowledged and openly addressed in the therapeutic process.

Although much work has been done in developing strategies for conducting counseling and therapy from a multicultural perspective, some psychologists feel this work is too broad and leads to overgeneralizations. They are now calling for more cultural specificity in theoretical constructs, research strategies, and treatment modalities (Boyd-Franklin, 1989; Nobles, 1986; Parham, 2002; Yang, 1997). In speaking about the needs of African-American clients, Parham (2002) states, "Although efforts at multicultural counseling have vastly improved over what historically existed in the profession, they are, nonetheless, limited in their utility because they lack the cultural specificity necessary to more effectively intervene with the African-American population" (p. 9). Parham (2002) disagrees with the notion that a generic set of multicultural skills can be learned by all counselors and therapists that will make them effective with individuals from all different backgrounds.

There is a large and growing literature that describes strategies for tailoring mental health services to various culturally diverse populations. Database searches reveal hundreds of articles focused on therapeutic approaches for different cultural groups. There are journals that focus on particular groups (e.g., *Hispanic Journal of Behavioral Sciences, Journal of Black Psychology*). Most books on multicultural counseling carry separate chapters that highlight the issues faced by particular groups and make suggestions for working with them (Atkinson, 2004; Pedersen, Draguns, Lonner, & Trimble, 2008; Sue & Sue, 2008). In addition, books are available that are dedicated to treatment issues for just about every group, including gays and lesbians (Perez, DeBord, & Bieschke, 2000), women (Barret & Logan, 2002; Enns, 1997; Sechzer et al., 1996), Asian/Pacific Americans (Hall & Okazaki, 2002; Lee, 1997), Latinos/as (Falicov, 1998; Zea & Garcia, 1997), American Indians/Alaskan Natives (Witko, 2005), and African Americans (Jones, 1998; Parham, 2002).

Since so much information on therapeutic approaches for particular cultural groups is available elsewhere, in the next section we focus on treatment issues and strategies for just one group—sexual minorities. For a very complete example of a culture-specific form of treatment, see Parham's (2002) discussion of African-centered therapy for African Americans.

Treatment Issues and Strategies for Sexual Minorities

In 2000, the APA published *Guidelines for Psychotherapy with Lesbian, Gay, and Bisexual Clients*. The document includes 15 guidelines. For example, the guidelines encourage therapists to recognize that homosexuality is not a mental disorder, recognize how their own attitudes about sexual minorities influence their practice, understand the impact of social stigma on the mental health of sexual minorities and how they present in therapy, gain knowledge about and respect for homosexual relationships, understand the unique challenges faced by homosexual parents and the complex family structure for some sexual minorities, and understand the effect of an individual's sexual orientation on his or her family relationships. A number of authors have suggested specific strategies for implementing these guidelines (Perez, DeBord, & Bieschke, 2000; Pope, 2008). The following story illustrates some of the issues unique to clients from sexual minority groups.

It is very interesting how some people feel the need to try and impose their thoughts and "visions" on to others. They seem to have a need for those around them to "stay within the lines" of their perspective.

Letting my "family" (those I have adopted as my own) know about my relationship with my partner was a very difficult decision for me. In telling those close to me I was concerned that it would change how they felt about me, that they would quite possibly see me in a different way, even to the point of no longer being part of my life.

I had heard many stories from other women who chose to tell their family and friends about their same-gender relationships and lost some of those close to them in that process. In my case I am very blessed. Everyone who means much to me was very accepting of my life partner and my lifestyle with the exception of one of my friends.

This individual (in my own view) has a need to have everything in its place and in the way that she sees fit. She has very specific beliefs about what's right and appropriate, especially when it comes to relationships. I had told all of my other friends about my relationship with my partner except this one. After a while it became difficult to avoid the subject in her company. I had to tell her. I did not want to because I didn't want to have to deal with whatever came out of her mouth. She can, at times, say things that are very hurtful.

Anyway, I told her about my relationship. She immediately responded with, "That's not my vision for you." She saw me married to a man with a few children. She also stated that this was just a "fad" I was going through. Never did she ask if I were happy or how I came to this decision. In future conversations she never asked about my partner. When I mentioned her she pretty much ignored what I said, but she would go on and on about her relationship with her husband. She totally and completely discounted the relationship—and in essence me—as insignificant.

For quite some time prior to telling her I had not shared very much of myself with her. I no longer trusted my inner self with her based on hurtful things she'd said to me in the past. My telling her about this very important relationship in my life, and her response further indicated to me she is not open to receive anything that is not sanctioned and approved of by her. Since then I've withdrawn from her even further.

KATHY, 40+-YEAR-OLD AFRICAN-AMERICAN BISEXUAL WOMAN

Kathy's story illustrates some of the unique issues faced by sexual minorities (i.e., gays, lesbians, bisexual, and transgender individuals). Some of these include coming out, heterosexism, homophobia, reactions of family members and friends, and religious views on homosexuality. Kathy struggled with coming out to her friend.

Coming out is not something that heterosexual people and those from other minority groups, such as women, and those from physically visible racial backgrounds (e.g., African Americans, Asian/Pacific Americans), typically have to worry about. In our society, it is automatically assumed that you are heterosexual. When you walk into a room, most people form judgments about your racial group membership based on your appearance, although people from racially mixed backgrounds whose appearance is ambiguous often get the question, What are you?

Coming out has serious risks. Being openly gay or lesbian opens the person up to potential discrimination and harassment, and can even be life-threatening. (Think about what happened to Matthew Sheppard, the University of Wyoming student who was beaten to death in 1998 because he was gay.) Individuals who come out to their families also risk rejection by family members. Kathy talked about the "family" of friends that she adopted. Sexual minorities face heterosexist attitudes or the belief that being heterosexual is normal and best (Barret & Logan, 2002). Heterosexism was evident in the "lines" drawn by Kathy's friend in her "vision" that Kathy have a husband and children. There is a growing literature on working with sexual minority clients, and APA published guidelines for therapists working with these groups (American Psychological Association, 2000b). In short, culturally sensitive therapy with sexual minority clients requires that the therapist pay attention to these issues.

Measuring multicultural competence has been a subject of much research (Coleman, 1996; Constantine & Ladany, 2001; Pope-Davis & Coleman, 1997). Although such general competencies have gained support, others suggest that specific theories and techniques for specific populations be measured for the effectiveness of such approaches. This would be a natural next step and is a challenge for researchers in the next few decades.

SUMMARY

There are many issues related to culture and mental health, including the prevalence of disorders in different groups, how symptoms are expressed, and how disorders are diagnosed. The American mental health system uses the *Diagnostic and Statistical Manual of Mental Disorders (DSM)*, currently in its fourth edition with a revised discussion of disorders (*DSM-IV-TR*). Although there are many similarities in disorders across the world, there are also some culture-bound syndromes. These disorders seem to be specific expressions of disorders that are connected to cultural values and traditions. For example, although many people may not conceptualize them as such, eating disorders may be a culture-bound syndrome here in the United States.

Treatment issues include barriers to effective multicultural treatment and efforts at overcoming those barriers, such as training mental health professionals to be multiculturally competent, providing monolingual clients with therapists able to communicate with them, cultural matching between client and therapist, and culture-specific therapies. One mismatch between many ethnic minority populations and mainstream modes of treatment is that modes of treatment are based upon values of the majority culture, which may not resonate with the diverse populations that are being treated.

In conclusion, we cannot emphasize enough that, like every other aspect of human behavior, culture influences mental health. If psychotherapy is be effective in helping people from culturally diverse backgrounds, culture must be an integral part of any approach.

Food for Thought

Most of us have encountered mental health difficulties in our lives. Have you ever been so anxious before taking a test that you could not sleep the night before or concentrate on your studies for the test? Have you ever broken up with a boyfriend or a girlfriend and become very sad about this, making it difficult for you to enjoy things you usually enjoy? These are common forms of mental health difficulties, called anxiety and depression. When people encounter issues such as these, they usually can get through a brief period of discomfort, then begin feeling back to "normal." However, when these problems persist, professional intervention might be needed. Some people can find appropriate mental health professionals to help them get through these periods without much difficulty. Just think how it might be if you could not find a therapist with whom you feel comfortable enough to be able to discuss your problems. Many people from backgrounds different from therapists have just these problems.

Critical Thinking Questions

Have you or anyone in your family ever needed the services of mental health professionals? If so, what was your/their experience like? Would you/they ever go again? How comfortable did you/they feel with your/their therapist? Was the therapist of the same racio-ethnic group as you or your family member, or was he or she from a different group?

If you have seen a mental health professional in therapy, was your therapist of the same gender as you, or was he or she of a different gender? Did you discuss issues related to gender? If so, what were they? If not, why not? If you have never seen a mental health professional, ask these questions of someone who has seen such a professional and who is open to discussing matters such as these.

If you have needed to see a mental health professional, how easy or difficult was it to find such a professional? How easy or difficult was it to find a professional who spoke your preferred language? How easy or difficult was it to find transportation to this professional?

CHAPTER 10

Where Do We Go From Here? Building Multicultural Competence

Today I got a job at Disneyland. I'm so excited. I think I'm glad to be part of a working society now. Well, during the interview process I was asked a few questions. During one of my responses I was able to talk about my major, GEMS (Gender, Ethnic, and Multicultural Studies), and relate the importance of multiculturalism. I told the interviewer that I was well versed in dealing with different groups of people. I said that I realize that Disney deals with all types of people from all over the world. I said that being culturally aware and being sensitive to different customs and people are useful assets to working in a diverse atmosphere such as Disneyland.

To my surprise the gentleman truly liked my answer. He said that that was right. So I learned the value of being diverse and culturally sensitive. It made me feel good that the education that I am receiving is going to be of some value and use in the real world. I think that Disney is one of those companies that rely on people from different cultures and backgrounds as the bread and butter of their success.

JEANNIE, 20+-YEAR-OLD AFRICAN-AMERICAN WOMAN

In her story, Jeannie learned the value of multicultural competence. It illustrates the value of multicultural competence for everyone, not just counselors and therapists. In this chapter we would like to help you on your way to becoming multiculturally competent.

Our main goal for this book is to increase your knowledge and understanding of multicultural issues and to bring those issues to life by sharing the personal stories of real people. By now you probably have a good understanding of the theories, concepts, and methods of multicultural psychology, and you are probably more aware of how those issues affect you and those with whom you live, study, and work every day. We hope that you are now motivated to continue learning and growing as a person living in a diverse world. We hope that this is just one step in your development of multicultural competence.

What is multicultural competence? As we discussed in chapter 9, **multicultural competence** means effectiveness working with people who are different from you. It is the ability to have positive, productive, and enriching experiences with people from different backgrounds.

The concept of multicultural competence originally related to the training of professional psychotherapists and counselors to work effectively with clients from diverse backgrounds. However, multicultural competence is not just for people in the helping professions. Each of us can benefit from increasing our level of multicultural competence. In chapter 1 we described the growing diversification of American society. Such diversity affects almost every aspect of life and increases the chances that you will interact with people who are different from you in many ways.

Right now, if you are studying in a library or some other public place, chances are if you look around you will see someone of a different background—a different race, gender, age, sexual orientation, religion, or physical ability. As you sit in your classes each day, most likely you are in rooms with people of different backgrounds. Or, at work, there probably are co-workers, customers, clients, and supervisors from different backgrounds. What about in the building or neighborhood where you live? The stores you shop in every day? The point is that we live in a multicultural society and an increasingly diverse world.

Have you heard the term "global village"? It refers to the fact that the world is getting smaller and smaller every day because of increased mobility and technology that allow us to travel and communicate with people all over the world in an instant. We live and work in a world full of many kinds of people, and it is important to learn to interact with them effectively. For example, if you go to school with people from different backgrounds, it would benefit you to be able to study and do projects with them more effectively. When you are job hunting, it looks good to potential employers if you have skills in working with diverse groups of people. Multicultural competence is a vital skill for everyone today.

multicultural competence—the ability to work and be effective with individuals who are of a different culture from yours.

HOW TO INCREASE YOUR MULTICULTURAL COMPETENCE: THE MULTICULTURAL COMPETENCIES

Chapter 9 discussed the specific areas of multicultural competence for professional psychologists. The three general areas of professional multicultural competence are (1) counselor awareness of own cultural values and biases, (2) an understanding of the client's worldview, and (3) development of culturally appropriate intervention strategies and techniques. Each of these areas is further broken down into attitudes and beliefs, knowledge, and skills.

Although these competencies were developed for professional counselors and therapists, they can be applied to your everyday life. In other words, each person can use these guidelines to improve relationships and interact effectively with people of different backgrounds. If we apply these principles to everyday interactions, they could read as follows: (1) **awareness of your own cultural attitudes,** (2) **understanding other worldviews,** and (3) **development of culturally appropriate interpersonal skills.** Let us explore each of these areas further and see how they can be used to develop personal multicultural competence.

AWARENESS OF YOUR OWN CULTURAL ATTITUDES

Multicultural competence begins with awareness of your own attitudes and beliefs. An old African proverb says "Know thyself." This is an important starting point in the development of multicultural competence. Most multicultural psychologists would agree that knowing your own beliefs, values, perceptions, feelings, reactions, and so on is critical in effective interactions with others. One way to increase self-awareness is to know how you react in multicultural situations. In other words, how do you think, feel, and behave in situations with people who are different from you?

> *I went out with a friend from school to celebrate the birthday of a friend of hers. After a nice dinner at [restaurant's name], we decided to exercise our amazing vocal talents at a karaoke bar. We arrived at a long strip-mall where the bar was located. I walked up to the door with my friend to meet the group from dinner, and we entered the building to see a small entry room connected to a long hallway. The room was painted a pale green and had off-white linoleum. The dim fluorescent lighting added to the dull setting of my surroundings. One girl from our group spoke to the Asian man at the front counter in Chinese, resulting in him leading us down the hallway to one of the doors spanning the hallway's walls. Inside we found a small room with bench seating around a table with a small karaoke machine. A book with songs was passed around as we crammed in around the table to pick something to sing. I looked at the pages and all the words were in Chinese. I felt extremely uncomfortable as I realized not only was my friend Chinese but the rest of the group was as well and I was in a Chinese karaoke bar. Music started showing a video on the screen with Chinese characters at the bottom. It looked like Chinese Backstreet boys and my new friends sang along. I was extremely conscious of my Caucasian background that did not fit into the situation. I wanted to run out of there but I had no ride. I felt my face flush thinking I didn't belong. I tried but I must not have hidden my reaction well because my friend rescued me after a couple songs. My friend rescued me by asking me in a whisper if I was ready to go. I tried to hold back the enthusiasm behind my answer of "yes." She graciously took the responsibility for us leaving the fun, explaining that she had to go, giving me the opportunity to say my good-byes and a final exclamation of "happy birthday" to her friend. I felt relief flow through my body as we left the bar and drove away in the safety of her car.*

DAVID, 20+-YEAR-OLD WHITE MAN

---

awareness of your own cultural attitudes—the part of multicultural competence that involves an individual's being aware that his/her own attitudes may be heavily influenced by his/her own culture and may be different from those of a person with whom he/she is interacting.

understanding other worldviews—the part of multicultural competence that involves an individual's knowing that other cultures may have ways of seeing and interpreting the world that are markedly different from his/hers.

development of culturally appropriate interpersonal skills—the part of multicultural competence that involves an individual's knowing how to apply his/her knowledge about someone else's worldview to behaviors that appropriately take into account that knowledge, effecting positive change.

Have you ever been in a situation like David's? What did you think? How did you feel? Did you, like David, try to make a quick escape? Chances are that you have been in a situation where you felt very different and that, like David, you felt very uncomfortable. Such experiences are very common and can help us understand the dynamics of multicultural interactions.

Dr. Shelly Harrell, a professor of psychology at Pepperdine University in California, describes the personal dynamics of difference to explain how people react in multicultural situations (1995; See also Barker-Hackett & Mio, 2000.). We can all think of times when we felt different. Perhaps as a child you were the last person picked for a dodgeball team, or were teased about being fat, or were the only person of your ethnicity in a class. Maybe you have been to a party where you felt out of place because you did not know anyone there. Maybe you were the target of taunts and prejudiced remarks for being gay. Often experiences with being different are tied to a range of negative emotions, such as fear, humiliation, rejection, alienation, sadness, and anger. Our natural tendency is to avoid such painful and uncomfortable experiences and to minimize or hide the differences.

> *I come from a predominately White, conservative town. The people who live there are not as open-minded as they could be. Growing up in that type of environment, then attending a school such as [name of school that is highly multiculturally composed] was indeed a culture shock. When I received my roommate's number whom I was supposed to live with, I was scared to call because I could not pronounce her name. I thought that it was going to be difficult to live with someone whose name I couldn't even say. When I finally called her she seemed nice, but it was hard to understand her. I had never been around an individual who had this type of accent. When it finally came to the week of moving into the dorms, I was scared. As I was moving in, I saw many types of individuals—Caucasian, African American, Asian, Peruvian. After I had lived there awhile I was used to meeting new individuals and was no longer as close-minded. Now I wish that people from my hometown could feel as I do about meeting different types of individuals and learning about their culture.*
>
> NINA, 20+-YEAR-OLD WHITE WOMAN

Nina's experiences going from a predominantly White hometown to a culturally diverse college campus illustrate some of the dynamics of difference. In particular, Nina described the fear she felt at the prospect of living and interacting with her new roommate, who was obviously from a different culture. This type of fear and discomfort is normal in situations that are unfamiliar and where we feel different. But what do we do with that fear and discomfort?

The Five D's of Difference

Harrell (1995) uses the "Five D's of Difference" to explain people's reactions in situations in which they feel different. They are *Distancing, Denial, Defensiveness, Devaluing,* and *Discovery* (Table 10.1).

TABLE 10.1 Harrell's (1995) Five D's of Difference

"D" Term	Definition
Distancing	Avoiding situations where one feels different
Denial	Pretending that differences do not exist
Defensiveness	Defending or protecting oneself from pain and fear
Devaluing	Evaluating a difference from oneself as unimportant or deficient
Discovery	Embracing differences and seeking opportunities to gain familiarity

distancing—
avoiding situations
in which one feels
different. Distancing
can occur
physically,
emotionally, or
intellectually.

Distancing

The first "D of Difference" is **distancing,** or avoiding situations in which we feel different. If we do not get too close to the difference, the possibility of negative experiences is minimized. Distancing can occur physically, emotionally, or intellectually. We may avoid going into situations in which we know we will be different. Many people do this by always hanging out with people of similar backgrounds. Or, once we are in a situation in which we feel different, we may get out of there as soon as we can. David was anxious to get out of the karaoke bar and felt relief once his friend had "rescued" him. He put *physical* distance between himself and that uncomfortable situation.

Harrell (1995) suggests that pity is a form of *emotional* distancing. The person feeling the pity may feel superior to those in the other group, and the recipient of the pity may feel ashamed or deviant. This emotional distancing prevents meaningful, sincere, honest interaction between the individuals as equals. (See the story analysis in chapter 6 that asks what would have happened had Teddy Stoddard been Black.) People can also distance themselves *intellectually* and take a more scientific or objective stance to the situation.

A student volunteered to do research with me, but she admittedly had little experience with multicultural issues, my main area of research. I suggested that she take part in the Cross-Cultural Retreat sponsored by our campus every year to help her learn more and to develop her own level of multicultural competence. When she returned I asked her how it went. She proceeded to give me a very objective, intellectual discussion about how she observed other people and their interactions during the weekend. When she finished, I suggested to her that perhaps it was easier to take the role of observer than to actively get involved and participate where she had to experience and evaluate her own personal issues. She admitted that this was true and that she has always avoided dealing with her own ethnic background because she is very uncomfortable with the topic. She also admitted being very uncomfortable with people from other backgrounds, especially gays and lesbians, and that she'd felt "surrounded by them" at the retreat.

LINDA, 30+-YEAR-OLD AFRICAN-AMERICAN WOMAN

The student in Linda's story chose to intellectually distance herself by becoming the objective, scientific observer. That was her way of dealing with the discomfort of being around those whom she perceived as different from herself and with the discomfort of having to face issues regarding her own ethnic identity.

Denial

When we encounter people and situations that are different or unfamiliar, our tendency may also be to **deny** the difference. This involves pretending not to see the difference, minimizing its importance, or ignoring it altogether. Common denial statements include "People make too much out of differences. Aren't we all human beings? Don't we all have the same red blood running through our veins?" People have said to me (LAB), "Oh, I don't see your color! You're just like everyone else to me!" I am sure the people who said that were well intentioned and thought they were paying me a compliment, but it was actually an insult. Why? Because they denied, minimized, and ignored an important part of my identity. The implication was that if they noticed I was African American, it would be negative; in reality, to me it is positive. Harrell (1995) says that when statements are made to her such as "I don't really see you as a Black person," her internal response is "Then you do not really see me." Would it be credible if a man said to a woman, "I don't see you as a woman, I only see you as a person?" Although it is true that many common experiences bind us together as human beings, there are also things that make us different and unique. Denying those differences may make others feel invisible, ignored, discounted, and unimportant, and that limits the ability to have meaningful, enriching interactions with one another.

denial—pretending that there is no difference between oneself and another, minimizing its importance, or ignoring the difference altogether.

Defensiveness

The third "D of Difference" is **defensiveness**. Being defensive means trying to defend or protect oneself. Being different is often associated with pain and fear. We try to protect ourselves from that fear and pain. Unfamiliar situations are often perceived as threatening; therefore, people react by trying to protect themselves from the perceived threat. People who get defensive maintain that they are not bothered by the difference.

A classic example of a defensive statement is "I'm not a racist!" Instead, the negative feelings associated with the difference are externalized and attributed to those other "bad, racist people." Another classic defensive statement is "I have lots of friends who are [fill in the group]." This again is evidence that the person is trying to prove that he or she is not bothered by the difference. This attitude may even be seen among people who are very involved in working with oppressed groups. Their involvement may be their defense against the discomfort they feel with the difference.

defensiveness—trying to protect oneself from acknowledging the difference between oneself and another to avoid the discomfort created by that difference.

It is often hard for people to admit that they are bothered by difference. To admit that they do have some racist or heterosexist ideas would be a threat to their self-image as an unbiased, fair, caring individual, especially in American society, where a high value is placed on equality. These people would be classified as aversive racists (see discussion in chapter 6); that is, they consciously feel that racism is aversive, yet they unconsciously hold racist views. To confront their discomfort with the difference would reveal a conflict of values. Those individuals who get involved in diverse communities may feel hurt, rejected, disappointed and confused when confronted with this contradiction. This dynamic was seen among European Americans involved in the Civil Rights Movement during the 1960s.

> *In the summer of 1964 large numbers of college students, Black and White, went to Mississippi to work with SNCC (the Student Non-violent Coordinating Committee). This became known as "Freedom Summer." While Blacks and Whites previously worked side by side in the Civil Rights Movement with few problems, many of the Blacks felt threatened because of the influx of larger numbers of Whites during that summer. "Now Black organizers were expected to welcome a bunch of cocky White kids, with advantages that African Americans could scarcely dream of, and watch them be hailed as the movement's saviors. For more than a few, it was an unbearable thought" (p. 294). As a result, some of the Black workers were cold and aloof with the White volunteers. Others took pleasure in intimidating the young, White volunteers, challenging them on everything from race to politics to sexual attitudes. On the other hand, a number of the White volunteers, oblivious to the wounded feelings of their Black co-workers, indeed had a "missionary attitude" that they were there to save the Blacks of Mississippi. Some, feeling they were more articulate and educated, aggressively told the Blacks how they thought things should be done.*
>
> *Sally Belfrage, a White female volunteer, wrote about her experiences in Freedom Summer. "She and other volunteers were mesmerized by the charismatic SNCC veterans, wanted to be like them, and were deeply hurt when they realized that they would never be fully accepted by their heroes. 'And this raised the question: Why, then, am I here? If they're not grateful for my help, if we are supposed to be struggling for brotherhood and can't even find it among ourselves, why am I here?' This was each one's private battle, rarely discussed. To do so would have meant admissions, giving words to certain uncomfortable doubts'" (p. 298). A White psychologist at Oxford who worked with the volunteers said the Whites were naïve, believing they understood the SNCC workers because they "feel for the Mississippi Negro." But, he added, "They can't feel like the Mississippi Negro. They know it and it makes them unhappy. . . . They don't like to find out they're insensitive about anything" (pp. 298–299).*
>
> ADAPTED FROM OLSON, *FREEDOM'S DAUGHTERS* (2001)

The experiences of the students during Freedom Summer illustrate some of the dynamics of distancing. Both the Black and the White volunteers engaged in distancing behaviors and attitudes. For example, some of the Black workers, feeling threatened by the larger numbers of Whites coming into the movement, distanced themselves emotionally and intellectually by becoming cold and aloof or by being outright hostile and challenging. The Whites reacted with hurt and shock, feeling that they had come to Mississippi to help and that their good intentions were not appreciated. The relationships between Black and White civil rights workers during Freedom Summer also illustrate the fourth "D of Difference"—devaluing.

Devaluing

Often when we encounter something that is different or unfamiliar, we evaluate it. Unfortunately, we often have the tendency to see things that are different or unfamiliar as strange, weird, or even scary. This reflects the tendency to **devalue,** which is the fourth "D of Difference." Thomas Parham, co-author of the book *The Psychology of Blacks* (Parham, White, & Ajamu, 1999), calls this the "Difference Equals Deficiency Bias." In other words, we tend to see things that are different as deficient, or less than.

devaluing— assessing the difference between oneself and another as deficient or less important.

Think about your initial reaction when someone wants you to try a new food. You may turn your nose up at it before you have even tried it! The automatic assumption is I'm not going to like that!

What about when you meet someone, such as a new roommate or co-worker? On one level you may be excited about meeting the new person, but on another level you immediately begin to form a social hierarchy. Is this person taller than I am? more attractive? smarter? wealthier? You want to see how you measure up in comparison with him or her. Our natural tendency as human beings is to preserve and increase our self-esteem, so we naturally want to place ourselves higher on the scale than the other person. In other words, we find ways to devalue things about the other person to help ourselves feel more comfortable.

Another way to look at it is that to devalue is to maintain a feeling of superiority. We feel better about ourselves when we see others who are different as deviant, primitive, immoral, lazy, stupid, and so on. When we devalue people who are different, it is easier to justify our negative feelings. The fear and threat may then become anger and rage. We can justify our negative feelings about "those people" because of their bad or immoral behavior. Examples of devaluing statements are "AIDS is God's punishment on gay people for their immoral behavior" and "If Black people would just work harder, they could find jobs, do better in school, and get ahead in this world."

During Freedom Summer, the White workers devalued the Blacks living in Mississippi by taking on the "missionary attitude" and seeing them as lesser beings in need of saving. They also devalued them with their feelings that they were more articulate and educated than the Black workers and therefore had the right to tell them how to do things. They failed to recognize that the Black volunteers had been running their own movement successfully for several years before the White volunteers arrived that summer. Following is an example of devaluing.

I have to start this off by listing my "non-racist" credentials. I'm very pro-equal rights for all people of all races, genders, and orientations. I speak out against racism and other discrimination, and am committed to lowering the levels of stereotype and prejudice in my own life. However, I have noticed an uncomfortable trend in my thoughts that I wish to be rid of. Whenever I hear someone "talking black"—that is, using urban-style slang, possessing a southern-like accent, using "ebonics," etc.—I sort of . . . well, have a prejudiced reaction. I tend to associate the speaker as lower economic class, probably less intelligent, and generally in the "different sort of person than me" category, unlike African Americans who do not have extremely pronounced accents. I do not negatively react in any way if I just see an African American or hear someone who is black speaking in a more "normal" Southern California accent, but if they have a pronounced accent I've noticed I almost always jump to (quite frequently) erroneous conclusions. Case in point, one of the professors in the Sociology Department at my school is an altogether engaging and wonderful black woman, but when I first heard her speaking I assumed she was simply an older undergrad and not a Ph.D. This was embarrassing to me, since I feel quite uncomfortable when I catch myself indulging in a prejudiced reaction, clearly when there is no reason I should do so.

I also admit to having uncomfortable reactions to people wearing things I know are or have been very gang-related clothing, but my hometown (La Habra, CA) is not exactly Beverly Hills. There were several small-time gangs in my area, mostly populated by Latino kids, so I tend to react poorly to the standard "gang" attire or anything that reminds me of it. This has extended minorly to black people as well, though I am actually less familiar with general black gang clothing indicators since my neighborhood was nearly all Latino, white, and Asian, so I kind of give them a little bit more benefit of the doubt. Still, I do tend to find urban fashions ugly, and I doubt I would object nearly so strongly if some little prejudicial whisper in the back of my mind didn't keep suggesting "gangster" when I notice those sorts of clothes.

I often actively try to correct my negative thoughts and am working on getting rid of them. Chief among the ways I am trying is simply by exposure. As I mentioned before, there were very few African-Americans around when I grew up, and it may just be a familiarity thing. I'm trying to increase the number of African-American friends I have (previously, the only black friends I had used pretty normal Californian speech patterns). I figure if I make some good friends who have accents but are also obviously intelligent people, I might be able to both get used to it and prove my bad assumptions wrong. For the record, whatever reaction I have doesn't do a whole lot to my overall interaction with people; it is merely a first impression kind of thing, but those do matter in the long run. I somehow doubt I am the only person who does this—it may merely be that others are too embarrassed to talk about it. I just wanted to, well, perhaps confess a bit.

BOB, 20+-YEAR-OLD EUROPEAN-AMERICAN MAN

*At the third biannual Multicultural Conference and Summit,
Dr. XX shared a story. She was in a meeting in which a European-
American female graduate student addressed each faculty member in
the room as 'Dr. So-and-So,' but when she got to Dr. XX the student
referred to her by her nickname. Dr. XX immediately corrected the
young woman, stating that she deserved the same respect as the other
faculty and expected to be addressed in the same manner. The young
woman later came privately to Dr. XX's office and apologized, but
Dr. XX refused to accept her apology. She told the young woman that
her statement was made in a public forum; therefore she expected an
apology in a public forum. On the same conference panel, Dr. YY,
an African-American gay man, related a similar story, stating that his
colleagues are often introduced as 'Dr. So-and-So,' but he is introduced
by his first name. Dr. YY felt that these seemingly simple, unconscious
acts show that his Ph.D. is not valued as much as that of his European-
American colleagues. I looked around the room and saw many heads in
the audience nodding in agreement, including myself. We had all had
similar experiences.*

LINDA, 30+-YEAR-OLD AFRICAN-AMERICAN WOMAN

As you see from these stories, devaluing can be very subtle. Sometimes we devalue things that are different and do not realize it. For example, sometimes people describe something or someone from a different culture as "exotic." Often they mean that as a compliment, but to the intended recipient it can be an insult. Whereas some might see it as positive, the word "exotic" also implies "different" or "strange," and hence not understandable. At the very least, it means something unlike me.

*I went to a party with a girlfriend being thrown by another girlfriend,
"T.," up in the hills above Hollywood. T. was dating an Italian guy at
the time. There were people of all different races there, but my girlfriend
and I were two of just a handful of Blacks. T. introduced us to some
White guys saying enthusiastically, "They're doctors!" as if that was
supposed to really impress us. I engaged in conversation with one of
them and at one point he said, "I like your hair. It's pretty. It's not all
Chzghzch! like other Black girls." He made a crunching sound,
punctuated with a crooked, twisting hand movement to describe what he
thought about natural Black hair. I was insulted and quickly put an end
to the conversation. I've never forgotten that, but it was typical of
incidents encountered at mixed clubs and parties we frequented during
that time. As White guys ingested more alcohol their inhibitions lowered.
Although they might be very nice people, they always ended up saying
something culturally insensitive that made me angry.*

JANICE, 30+-YEAR-OLD AFRICAN-AMERICAN WOMAN

Thus far, the "D's of Difference" sound very negative, but they are natural human tendencies. It is natural to feel uncomfortable in an unfamiliar situation, and we naturally respond by trying to decrease that discomfort. As we said in chapter 6 regarding stereotypes, it is not bad that we have them, but it is bad when we let them negatively affect our relationships with others. The same is true of the "D's of Difference." We need to be aware of the feelings, acknowledge them, and then take action to prevent them from negatively affecting our interactions.

Discovery

The last "D of Difference" is a positive experience, **discovery**. Encounters with people from different backgrounds are opportunities for discovery. Discovery means embracing and seeking greater familiarity with difference (Harrell, 1995). It involves working through the discomfort and anxiety, rather than avoiding it. It means experiencing differences as challenges and opportunities for learning and growth.

An attitude of discovery means being willing to stretch and get outside our comfort zones. It means taking risks and feeling uncomfortable sometimes. It means keeping an open mind and being open to new experiences, new places, new things, and new people. By doing so, we enrich our own lives and the lives of others. The negative feelings associated with difference are natural. We all experience them. Their purpose is to protect us. We will not be able to eliminate those negative feelings, but with them comes the opportunity for personal growth and improved intergroup relations.

> **discovery—** appreciating the difference between oneself and another, seeing how enriching that difference may be, and seeking out opportunities to gain familiarity.

I had the opportunity to go to a community in Mexico to fellowship with the people there. The first year I did not go, because ultimately the language barrier made me feel uncomfortable. I kept focusing on the fact that I would be in a community of people for an entire week and I could not say anything but Hola *and* Adiós. *I was scared of social situations. I did not want to have to face the "awkwardness" of not understanding someone in conversation. In the five D's of difference, I was distancing myself from a situation that was unfamiliar to me. However, the next three years in a row, I decided to go and I experienced discovery there. I realized just how quickly one could pick up a language when they are immersed in it for a period of time. I was able to make lasting friendships, and to think I never would have had the blessing of experiencing such friendships and such all because I was afraid of something that was unfamiliar to me.*

I have realized and encouraged others to realize, that staying in one's comfort zone is, well, comforting, but it's not nearly as rewarding as stepping out of it to find so much more about other people, and even oneself.

KATIE, 20+-YEAR-OLD EUROPEAN-AMERICAN WOMAN

Katie's experience illustrates the benefits of *discovery*. She came from a predominantly White background. She felt uncomfortable when she encountered

PICTURE 10.1 Experiencing other cultures can be an enriching experience.
Photograph by Tom Zasadzinski

individuals of a different culture for the first time. However, instead of doing one of the other "D's of Difference," such as devaluing or distancing, she took on an attitude of discovery. She opened her mind, took a risk, got out of her comfort zone, and took advantage of the opportunity to learn and experience something new.

Discovery can also be fun if you can fight through your initial desire to distance yourself from the situation. Rayanne discovered this in a tasty way:

Since it was around Christmas and I was meeting new people I decided to get dressed up. Around the holidays my family always gets dressed up when they get together—nothing too fancy, maybe a nice sweater or blouse. Besides that, I wanted to look cute, after all I was

PICTURE 10.2 Stepping outside one's comfort zone can lead to discovery about oneself. *Photograph by Juliam Hsu*

meeting my boyfriend's family for the first time. Unfortunately I looked too nice—in fact I stood out from everyone else. Since his family was making tamales, which are very messy, his family was dressed in old jeans and sweatshirts. On top of being the new girl they looked at me funny for wearing a skirt to make tamales.

After a couple of minutes I was no longer uncomfortable by my appearance. It was a long night of making tamales but I enjoyed the time I spent with them. When we left they invited me back to eat the tamales with them on Christmas Eve. So, the next night I went back and enjoyed the food we worked so hard to make the night before.

It was very interesting to observe his family's traditions. Every year his family does the same thing around Christmas . . . I've discovered that other Hispanic families do the same thing around Christmas. They go to a relative's house to make tamales the day before Christmas Eve and then come back on Christmas Eve to eat them and open presents up at midnight. At first I compared my family to his and made remarks like "that's not what my family does," but now I embrace our differences.

RAYANNE, 20+-YEAR-OLD EUROPEAN-AMERICAN WOMAN

Remember Nina's story at the beginning of this section? She was afraid to meet her new roommate whose name she could not pronounce, but instead of avoiding the situation and asking for a new roommate, she had the courage to go ahead and live with her. She also had the courage to get to know other people in the dorms from different cultures. In the end she realized how valuable it was to develop relationships with people different from her.

Universoul Circus took me by surprise. People were standing all the way out to the parking lot, waiting to buy tickets. Thankfully, mine were already bought. The enormous big top was situated in Hollywood Park off of Prairie Avenue. I have never seen a big top other than on television and I was extremely excited to go. Moreover, the fact that most of the intense performances would be executed by African Americans thrilled me even more. If it wasn't for my friend's family, I would never have heard of a circus team called Universoul. Founded in 1994, the circus has expanded and has since traveled to 32 cities, including a tour in South Africa in 2001. Cedric Walker, the founder and CEO of Universoul Circus has been quoted to say that his dream was to have "hip-hop under the big top." The vision of this circus is to find African-American performers who have talents other than sports, singing, and dancing. However, the circus also searches for performers who are not of African descent to perform talents that come from their own culture as well. So in a sense, the circus has become a multicultural event that shows off each culture's unique talents that other cultures may have not been aware of. The big top had enough room to fit around 2,000 people and there were no empty seats. As soon as the lights went up, hip-hop music ruptured through the speakers and the performances began. From African-American ice skaters dancing to hip-hop music, to an African-American woman lion tamer, the talents seemed to only get better. During breaks between acts the announcer would have activities that would involve the crowd, such as naming famous 80's African-American TV show song themes. There was an activity where the announcer brought up five men and women who were 25 and older and five men and women who were 18 and younger and they had a dance off to different kinds of music. The interaction with the crowd was wonderful, especially since every activity had a theme that pertained to the African-American community.

What I loved the most about the circus was that I don't believe the performers were originally from America. My friend had mentioned to me that they found most of the performers in Africa and Asia. Sharing my culture with people from an entirely different culture (who recently adapted to my own culture) was very significant for me. The very fact that Universoul Circus wasn't primarily made up of African Americans but Africans and Asians made me understand that the name "Universoul" wasn't used to target only our community. Ideally, they are looking for a whole genre of crowds that doesn't necessarily just include African Americans. I appreciated this because although the circus was initially made to identify with my culture, it now tries to involve people from other cultures. It was quite a sight to see men and women of various ages interacting with each other, when usually in our culture, older men and women seem to focus more on parenting rather than socializing with younger children. But with the charming ambiance and playful atmosphere, Universoul Circus knew no boundaries when it came to interacting with the young and old. Everyone connected with each other because of each person's similar background. For example, during one of the activities, the announcer played different songs and the audience had to yell out what it was. What surprised me was how many people, young and old, knew the songs. It didn't matter when the song was made; I saw little African-American kids singing, "We are Family," right along with their parents. There was a cultural connection that was shared that night because of Universoul. It targeted an audience that had similar experiences in life because of the culture they shared and gave them something they could all have fun with.

Universoul Circus was a great experience for me because it put me in a position where I was surrounded by people who were like me. I am rarely around people who share my same culture and it was surprisingly a relief to be able to easily connect with people who had similar tastes and likes. The circus is something all cultures generally enjoy in America, but Universoul Circus gave me an amazing feeling because I felt like this was something that I could personally connect with. The jokes, the music, the all-around atmosphere had me feeling very comfortable because I understood what they were trying to achieve. They wanted the audience to feel like this was dedicated to them; the whole purpose of this circus was a commitment to our community and culture as a way of saying, "This belongs to you." Universoul impacted our society because it shows the positivism of our culture rather than the expected stereotypes and stigmas.

ALICIA, 20+-YEAR-OLD AFRICAN-AMERICAN WOMAN

The Three S's of Similarity

Alicia's story shows how comforting it can be to be around others who are similar to us. We like what is similar, or familiar. Why? One of the authors (LAB) gives three reasons, which she calls the "Three S's of Similarity." (See Table 10.2.) We like things that are familiar because they are *simple,* make us feel *safe,* and help us feel *sane.*

Simple

simple—things that are similar to us or our values are easy or comfortable.

It is **simple,** or easy, to stick with what is familiar. It is more challenging to get out of our comfort zones and explore new people and new places. When we encounter something that is different, we feel uncomfortable and have to work harder to function in the situation. When we stay in situations with which we are familiar, we do not have to consciously process as much information. Things are accomplished automatically without much effort or thought.

TABLE 10.2 The Three S's of Similarity

"S" Term	Definition
Simple	It is easy to stick with the familiar
Safe	It feels comfortable to stick with the familiar
Sane	Being around others who are similar to us makes us feel normal or at least not unusual

Safe

Sticking to what is familiar is also **safe.** As we have said, things that are different are often perceived as a threat. If we do not encounter them, we continue to feel safe. We do not have to risk suffering the potential negative consequences. This recently happened to Bill Cosby when he made negative comments about uneducated African Americans to a predominantly African-American audience. He did not realize his comments would cause such a fervor, probably because he was speaking to his own group, which felt familiar and safe.

Sane

We also like things that are similar because they help us feel **sane,** or at least normal or not unusual. We mentioned earlier that we have a natural tendency to preserve and build up our self-esteem. Being around people who are similar to us is validating. It affirms that we are okay if other people act, think, and feel the same way we do. When we encounter people who act, think, and feel differently, we question ourselves. Think about groups of teenagers in junior high and high school who hang out together. They dress alike, talk alike, do their hair alike, listen to the same music, and so on. We do the same thing. If you think of times when you have been in a new or unfamiliar situation, such as going to a new school, chances are the friends you made were people similar to you.

safe–things that are similar to us or our values are not a threat because we know how to deal with them and do not have to encounter unsettled feelings of going beyond the familiar to the unknown.

sane–things that are similar to us or our values help us feel normal because if we are like everyone else, we are not out of step; we are validated or affirmed.

> *I had a teacher asking me, "Why do all of the Black kids hang out together?" I responded, "Have you noticed that all of the White kids hang out with one another, too?" Immediately, her face turned red and she tried to explain that she didn't think anything was wrong with the Black kids hanging out together, she was just curious why they felt the need to do so.*
>
> DOLLY, 30+-YEAR-OLD AFRICAN-AMERICAN WOMAN

A similar issue came up in an article in one of our alumni magazines. LAB felt the need to respond to the article and write about how Black students were not trying to separate themselves but how we needed those times alone together to refuel to face the many small, sometimes large, racist insults and challenges we faced each day on a predominantly White campus (Barker-Hackett, 1999). White students often fail to realize that when ethnic minorities hang out with one another, it is not an insult, but perhaps it should be a message.

Beverly Daniel Tatum, in her aptly titled book *Why Are All the Black Kids Sitting Together in the Cafeteria?* (Tatum, 1997), says she has been asked that question hundreds of times. She discusses the coming together with others of the same background as an important step in adolescent racial identity development that reflects their response to racial messages received from the environment. As young people reach junior high and high school, race becomes more salient and they experience more racist encounters. Black youth growing up in racially mixed neighborhoods may notice that they are no longer invited to the birthday parties of their White friends. Black girls may notice that when their White friends start to date, they do not. When they try to discuss these things with their White friends, they may find their friends just do not "get it." As a result, "the Black students turn to each other for the much needed support they are not likely to find anywhere else" (p. 60). Tatum (1997) says, "We need to understand that in racially mixed settings, racial grouping is a developmental process in response to an environmental stressor, racism. Joining with one's peers for support in the face of stress is a positive coping strategy" (p. 62).

Black students are not the only ones who tend to stick together. Walk into a cafeteria on any high school or college campus and chances are you will find Latinos sitting with Latinos, Asians with Asians, and Whites with Whites, although few people comment when all the Whites sit together. On our campus the students know the areas where the Asians, Indians, Arabs, gay and lesbian students, and others tend to hang out.

Examining Your Biases, Prejudices, and Stereotypes

The "D's of Difference" and the "S's of Similarity" are useful in increasing awareness of your own attitudes and beliefs regarding muliticultural issues. They help you understand your desire to stick with situations and groups that are familiar and how you react when you encounter people, things, or situations that are different or unfamiliar. You can also increase your multicultural competence by becoming more aware of your attitudes and beliefs about other cultures.

Increased awareness includes examining your own biases, prejudices, and stereotypes. In chapter 6 we mentioned that biases, prejudices, and stereotypes by themselves are not necessarily bad. We naturally develop them as human beings. Stereotypes help us summarize and organize all the millions of bits of information our senses and brains are bombarded with every day. Biases and prejudices are a natural outcome of growing up in a society built on them.

The Museum of Tolerance in Los Angeles has an exhibit with two doors. One is marked "Racist," the other "Non-Racist." You must pass through one of these doors to continue to the next section of the museum. The only problem is that the door marked "Non-Racist" is locked, which forces everyone to go through the door marked "Racist." The point is obvious: We all harbor racist thoughts and ideas. These things become bad when we allow them to negatively affect our relationships with others. Even if we are not aware we have them, they still have an effect on us. The goal is to be aware of our racist thoughts and ideas so we can better control them and prevent them from negatively affecting our interactions.

Learning about Your Own Culture

Self-awareness also involves learning about your own culture and its effect on your personal attitudes and beliefs. As we discussed in chapter 7, your personal perceptions and feelings about your own culture are an important part of your ethnic identity. These feelings may be positive, negative, or mixed. It is important to become aware of your thoughts, feelings, and behaviors as they relate to people of your own group.

Some of you, especially those of you from a European-American (White) background, may be saying, "I don't have a culture." Students often say things like,

Whenever we start talking about culture in class I feel left out because I don't really have a culture. Or, I'm boring. I'm just White. My (LAB) response is, Everyone has a culture. First, it is important to realize that the statement "I have no culture" is a very ethnocentric one. It implies that your own culture is the norm and everything else is different, or abnormal. It means you use your own culture as the standard against which all others are measured. Once you do that, you risk the pitfalls described as the "Ds of Difference," such as devaluing other cultures.

European Americans are not the only ones who can benefit from exploring their own culture, as the following story illustrates.

> *I have to admit that I have never heard of Roscoe's House of Chicken and Waffles until the day my friend's family decided to eat there. The very idea of a restaurant that only served chicken with waffles (what I have always considered a breakfast food) immediately disturbed me. I was amazed as I glanced about the eatery: everyone was African American. Being a first-timer at this restaurant, I had no clue it is an African-American owned establishment and I have never eaten in a vicinity where the majority were of the same ethnicity as my own. I can specifically remember the smell because no sooner than I stepped inside, the aroma of southern cooking took me back to the days my Grandmother used to cook for my family during holidays. At that point, my apprehension became excitement because I realized that perhaps chicken and waffles weren't the only foods prepared in this restaurant.*
>
> *The atmosphere was very vibrant. It was about 8 p.m. when we arrived and the place was full to capacity. Music was blasting in the corners playing 80's classics and today's hip-hop. The walls were surrounded by mirrors so everyone had their share of glances at other patrons, giving those who returned the glance a slight nod of recognition, or just to say hello. Everyone was extremely friendly, to the point of familiarity; even customers who had walked in after we had settled down would stop and talk to random customers and comment on the foods they selected. This wasn't the typical family restaurant like Denny's or Coco's; this was a home away from home. Ordering the foods looked simple enough, but being a vegetarian made it harder to choose. Every meal came with either a chicken leg or thigh. The most memorable moment in that night was when I quietly tried to pass over the information to my friend that I was vegetarian. That information got around to everyone else in a matter of seconds and suddenly, 20 pairs of eyes were focused on me in amazement and concern. Apparently, the fact that I don't eat meat was deemed inexcusable, especially in a place like this. The confession leaked out to the waitress, who playfully teased me about my situation; apparently, I was their first African American vegetarian customer in that particular restaurant line. I didn't give in to the chicken leg or chicken thigh, but I did indulge in their famous greens, macaroni and cheese, cornbread and a plate of rice*

*and beans (the plate was so big I had seconds and thirds from my
leftovers the next day). I did, however, observe the main food that gives
the restaurant its name. The chicken was described by my friend's
family as "juicy," "crispy on the outside," "better than any other
chicken you can get around here." The waffles looked so good, I had a
bite. They tasted like regular waffles, but the fact that I was eating them
late at night rather than early in the morning (heaven forbid my mother
caught me eating breakfast food at night) made me feel extremely
devious. I can understand why people stay in Roscoe's so late. The food
is overwhelmingly good and the atmosphere is made so that you don't
need to leave for a long while; sitting and conversing with other people
around the area seemed like their idea of a relaxing time.*

*Towards the end of the night, not all of the customers turned out
to be African American. I saw a few European American and Latino
customers, who brought their children and grandparents. I appreciated
the restaurant even more because I felt like they were giving a piece of
their culture to other people who lived in and around the area. A few
days after my experience at Roscoe's, I reflected on my reactions before
and after my dining there. Arriving at the eatery, I was very petty,
disliking the overall look of the place and the fact it was situated in a
run-down area of L.A. If it was my choice, I wouldn't have even
thought twice about a place like this. Looking back, I had a definite
out-of-the-body experience. I saw myself as a person who looked down
on something that in the long run, did nothing but educate me further
about the traditions of my culture. This is the common food that my
culture eats. And from what I observed, the quality of the structural
design for the building was not their main concern. It was the quantity
of the food, the quality of the service, and the hospitality given that
made me understand why it is our culture names our cooking "soul
food."*

*That night in Roscoe's challenged me to appreciate the ordinary. In
a sense, the restaurant itself was plain and not so attractive on the
outside. But what I appreciated about the restaurant was the way it
communicated to me through its foods. Its simplicity taught me to
enjoy richness in something as trivial as to what some may consider a
hole-in-the-wall restaurant. Exploring my culture through its foods was
the first for me. Even when my Grandmother cooked her southern
Creole foods, I never ate more than a bite. I can understand now how
our food has its own significance, as do foods of other cultures. It
provides comfort and togetherness with people you do not even know.
For that split second, you don't mind enjoying the company of other
people, because there is something in that atmosphere you can relate to.
This is my culture's food, a custom that has been passed down for
centuries and is still holding strong.*

ALICIA, 20+-YEAR-OLD AFRICAN-AMERICAN WOMAN

An important part of multicultural competence is increasing your knowledge about your own group. As mentioned previously, many students feel as if they do not have a culture, or that they know very little about their cultural heritage. For example, we challenge students to find out what it means to be American. American culture also has its own unique beliefs, values, and practices. These are so deeply woven into the fabric of everyday life in our culture that they usually go unnoticed. Examples of some core American values are individualism, materialism, competition, and the Protestant work ethic. Only when something happens to challenge, threaten, or contradict those beliefs, values, and practices are they made explicit.

For example, after the terrorist attacks of September 11, 2001, many people were talking about freedom and religious liberty. Those are two of the values that distinguish American culture, even from other Western cultures. If you were born or raised in the United States, those values are part of your culture and influence your personal beliefs and behaviors. It is important to be aware of this.

How can you learn more about your own culture? Alicia's story above illustrates that even something as simple as exploring the food can be a method for learning about one's culture. Another place to start is with your own family. Interview your parents, grandparents, and other relatives. Ask them to tell you about family stories, traditions, and personalities, and videotape or audiotape the interview. Begin working on a family tree. Take classes that focus on your particular group. Attend cultural events and celebrations. Read books.

My parents did a good job of instilling in me a positive ethnic identity, but your parents can take you only so far. At some point you have to explore for yourself. In high school I was involved in our Black Student Union (BSU) and helped to plan and put on Black History Month programs, but the true meaning of such things didn't really sink in. They never really had much personal significance for me. In fact, deep down I think I had some shame about it. I always had some difficulty reconciling my two worlds—the Black one and the White one. It wasn't until I was in college that I really began to explore my own ethnic identity and have some comfort with and pride about it. My self-exploration was sparked by two courses I took. The first was a sociology course on social problems I took my freshman year. I distinctly remember a film we watched in class one day on the Civil Rights Movement. I remember watching the graphic pictures of the demonstrators being bitten by dogs and being hosed with fire hoses. I felt extreme sadness, but at the same time a great sense of pride. Black people were on the move back then! I was proud of how Black people, MY people, came together to change society. The second course was one I took my junior year on African-American literature. We read 11 books that semester, all by African-American authors. Sad to say, I never knew there were so many books by Black people. I was enthralled as I read through the pages and saw myself, saw my people.

I read about our experiences, our thoughts, our feelings. It was amazingly powerful and sparked an interest I continue to this day. I consider African-American literature a hobby and have a small but growing collection of books. About the time I graduated from college is when Spike Lee's movie She's Gotta Have It *came out. I remember being excited to see Black people up on the big screen and feeling proud and excited when the movie was so successful and received such acclaim. Spike's success led to a sort of renaissance in Black film. I guess Hollywood finally realized that Black people pay money to go to the movies, too. And, not only that, they learned that Black films have cross-over appeal and White people will pay to see them as well. In the following years my friends and I enthusiastically went to see every Black film that came out. After a while there were too many to keep up, which was also nice.*

When I was in graduate school I met a friend who was Black but did not get the same positive foundation about her identity from her family that I did. Soon after we met she said, I want you to teach me about being Black. It was a strange request, but I understood. One of the first things I did was share with her some of my favorite books by African-American authors. We also attended cultural events and celebrations, such as step shows with the Black fraternities and sororities and Martin Luther King Day parades. We threw our own Kwanzaa celebration. We also went to hear speakers who came to our campus, such as Maya Angelou and Kwame Ture (formerly Stokely Carmichael). During Black History Month each week we'd get together at my place and watch Eyes on the Prize *on PBS (a documentary about the Civil Rights Movement). Helping my friend explore her ethnic identity carried me further along on my journey of self-knowledge, a life-long journey I'm sure will never end.*

LaKeisha, 30+-year-old African-American Woman

The strategies used by LaKeisha in her personal identity development are strategies everyone can use. She took classes, read books, watched films and television programs, attended lectures, and attended cultural events and celebrations. Knowledge about your own group provides a springboard for learning about other groups. Knowing yourself gives you the confidence to go out and learn about others who are different from you.

We have spent a large portion of this chapter discussing the first area of multicultural competence—awareness of your own cultural values and biases. That is because self-awareness is arguably the most important part of multicultural competence. Knowing yourself gives you the strength and the confidence to be able to go out and learn about other cultures. It provides you with a foundation upon which to build the other aspects of multicultural competence. Let us turn now to the second part of multicultural competence—understanding other worldviews.

UNDERSTANDING OTHER WORLDVIEWS

Although it is vitally important to know and understand your own culture, it is also important to learn about other cultures. Part of multicultural competence is obtaining basic knowledge about different groups. Although each person within a culture is unique, there are some general facts about each cultural group that are helpful to know, such as the history of the group, current sociopolitical concerns, cultural traditions, family structure, and core values and beliefs. It is important to learn basic information, both about your own culture and about other cultures.

Learning Key Historical Events

Just as it is important to know your own history, it is important to know the key historical events that influenced other groups. For example, to truly understand African-American culture you must study the history of slavery and its continued impact on American culture. As we discussed in chapter 6, the roots of racism in the United States go back to slavery and its aftermath, but African Americans also have a history, going back to Africa, that predates slavery. It is important to know that. It is also important to know what happened after slavery, including the Civil Rights Movement of the 1950s and 1960s, because that had a significant impact on African-American culture as well.

It is important to know the history of the different immigrant groups. As was discussed in chapter 5, there is a difference between groups who immigrate voluntarily, such as those who come looking for a better education and better job opportunities, and refugees who come involuntarily, escaping war or political or religious persecution.

Becoming Aware of Sociopolitical Issues

It is also important to be aware of current sociopolitical issues affecting various cultural groups. For example, in the 1990s several pieces of legislation were passed in the State of California that affected various ethnic minority groups, Latinos in particular. Proposition 187 sought to limit immigration into the state by denying services such as education and health care to undocumented immigrants. Proposition 227 significantly reduced bilingual education in the state, even though literally hundreds of languages are spoken by students in the state public school system. A third piece of legislation, Proposition 209, essentially eliminated all affirmative action programs in the state. As a result, opportunities for ethnic minorities, such as access to higher education, were reduced.

Taken together, these laws reflected an anti-immigrant, anti-minority attitude in the state and created an uncomfortable atmosphere for those groups. Ethnic minority groups interpreted this as the White majority power structure protecting its interests as it saw the numbers of ethnic minorities growing in the state. It was important for individuals working with these groups to be aware of the impact such an atmosphere had on their daily lives. For example, schoolteachers, counselors, and administrators needed to be aware that some students from immigrant families were afraid to come school because, although they might be legal because they were born here, their parents were not. They were afraid their family members might be deported. Doctors, nurses, and other health care professionals needed to be aware that immigrants with health problems delayed going to the doctor because they also were afraid of deportation if their immigrant status became known. People working with high school and college students needed to be sensitive to the fact that funding and other opportunity programs might not be available to students to help them go to school. Students in universities and colleges felt embarrassed because they thought others might look down on them as if they did not deserve to be there, that they were less qualified and there simply because of affirmative action.

These examples illustrate the need to understand how current sociopolitical issues affect individuals from different backgrounds. Other examples include knowledge of the impact of AIDS and HIV on the gay community in the 1980s and 1990s and anti-Arab sentiments following the attacks of September 11, 2001. Such knowledge improves your ability to work effectively with individuals from these groups.

Knowing Basic Values and Beliefs

Aside from factual knowledge about different cultural groups, understanding other worldviews also involves knowing the basic values and beliefs of different cultural groups. In chapter 3 we compared and contrasted the worldviews of different cultural groups. We emphasized that although each individual is unique, there are broad concepts that characterize each group. Knowing something about an individual's culture helps you formulate hypotheses that can be explored in your interactions with that person.

For example, it is helpful to know that Latino culture tends to be patriarchal, with more traditional gender roles. When we work with Latina students on our campus, we recognize that they may have more struggles being in college than other female students because they may not get the same kind of support from their families. They may have more family responsibilities at home, such as taking care of younger siblings, and these may be seen as a higher priority than their studies. One Latina student said, My family is always asking me when I'm going to get married and have babies. However, we cannot assume that this is the case for all Latina students, because it is not. It is a topic that needs further exploration.

Understanding Cultural Practices

It is also helpful to know and understand cultural practices. These are behaviors that may be normal and expected and have a particular meaning in a culture.

In January 2007 I happened to stop by one of the professors' offices, the professor introduced me to a visually impaired young man who was visiting him. We all chatted in the professor's office for approximately forty-five minutes and that was the last time I saw him [that quarter]. This quarter the student happened to be in my class so I thought it was appropriate to say hello; I introduced myself to him in case he did not recognize my voice from our previous meeting. After class we chatted a bit, and then I began to excuse myself because I was headed to the bookstore to buy the textbooks I needed. The student stated that he would like to come with me to the bookstore because he too was headed that way to purchase his books. My first thought was, Oh! What do I do? I did not know him that well; however, the polite thing to say was okay. We walked out of the classroom together and he suddenly stopped in the hallway and proceeded to fold his guiding cane. Suddenly there was no communication between us, I just stood there wondering why he was folding the cane at the same time I was making sure no one was going to bump into him. I looked away for a split second, he touched and grabbed my arm and then he found his way to my elbow, which was an indication that we could start walking now. It took me by surprise, and personally I was a bit uncomfortable because it was as though he was invading my space, so quickly I adjusted my arm away from my body enough to where I was comfortable and we headed out to the bookstore.

After we both purchased our books, we headed across the campus to the Starbucks coffee stand since we both had hours to spare before our next class. During our conversation I found myself not knowing where to look, since I personally like to have eye contact with the person I am conversing with. It seemed strange that these things were going through my mind, but I quickly adjusted my mentality and was able to just enjoy the conversation with this person.

The next day, I looked up on the internet, "the blind or visually impaired culture," hoping it would provide me necessary information on what is acceptable in their culture. I felt the need to know the proper etiquette when assisting or approaching the blind or visually impaired, so that in the future I may be more sensitive or aware of what to do. I found a web page, www.afb.org American Foundation for the Blind, which listed some tips on how to approach or assist blind or visually impaired people, which are listed below.

- *Identify yourself by name before you make physical contact.*
- ***Ask if they would like assistance** and let them tell you how you may assist them. If they say no, don't take it personally.*
- *When guiding them, **let them take your arm**. Do not touch the individual's cane; it is considered part of their personal space.*
- *Let them know when you are leaving.*

If I would have had this knowledge prior to this encounter I may have avoided the awkwardness that I felt.

ANA MARIA, 30+-YEAR-OLD LATINA WOMAN

Ana Maria's experience illustrates the importance of cultural differences and knowing about the values, beliefs, and practices of different groups. Knowing these things increases your level of multicultural competence.

Knowing the Dynamics of Racism, Discrimination, and Stereotyping

A final aspect of understanding other worldviews is knowledge of the dynamics of racism, oppression, discrimination, and stereotyping. We discussed each of those concepts in detail in chapter 6, so it is not necessary to explain them again here. However, it is important to understand how those forces affect people in their everyday lives. One of our former students who was active in the gay/lesbian community on campus said that one of the main factors influencing formation of a gay/lesbian community was their response to the oppression and discrimination experienced by members of their group. They bonded together because they had a common sexual orientation but also because they had a common "enemy" and came together for protection and support.

In chapter 1 we also discussed one of the early studies by Clark and Clark (1939) in which African-American children preferred White dolls to Black dolls. The researchers concluded that Black children had lower self-esteem because of the racism and discrimination experienced by their group and because of the negative portrayals of Blacks in the media. Remember our discussion of identity development in chapter 7? Every individual from an ethnic minority background must resolve his or her status in relation to the dominant culture. Often that involves resolution of racist encounters. These examples illustrate how racism, discrimination, oppression, and stereotypes have an impact on individuals and on their development, personality, and behavior. It is important to understand those forces and their impact on your interactions with others.

DEVELOPMENT OF CULTURALLY APPROPRIATE INTERPERSONAL SKILLS

The first two dimensions of multicultural competence involve awareness—awareness of your own cultural attitudes and awareness of other worldviews. You might be wondering, Once I become aware of all these things, what do I do? It is true that awareness is essential, but it is not enough. You must act on that awareness and take concrete steps toward building positive relationships with people from different backgrounds. That is where part three of multicultural competence comes in—developing culturally appropriate interpersonal skills. (See Table 10.3.)

A *skill* is the ability to do something well, or the ability to do something with accuracy and ease. Skills are developed through training, experience, and practice (Warren, 1995). Multicultural competence is an interpersonal skill. It is the ability to interact effectively with others who are different from you. To achieve this, you must have *education, training, experience,* and *practice* in working with people from different groups. This section describes specific strategies for increasing your level of multicultural competence.

Education and Training

A skill is developed through education and training. Reading this book and taking this class are significant steps toward your multicultural education and training. From them you gained knowledge that can serve as a foundation for developing

TABLE 10.3 Concrete Things to Do to Increase Your
Multicultural Competence

Take more classes and attend lectures, workshops, seminars, and retreats on
   multicultural issues.

Read books, magazines, and journals on multicultural issues.

Watch relevant films and television shows on diverse issues.

Listen to music and attend plays, concerts, and other cultural events and celebrations
   to understand underlying issues.

Reach out and develop relationships with people from diverse backgrounds.

Get involved in cultural organizations.

Develop the ability to say "I don't know" and to ask questions. You cannot possibly
   know everything, so allow others to help you develop your knowledge.

Travel to experience different cultures directly.

Develop a level of comfort discussing difficult issues. This will take some amount
   of courage.

further competence. You can take more classes and attend lectures, workshops, seminars, and retreats that focus on cultural issues. For example, you can take a class that focuses on a specific cultural group, such as a women's studies course or a course on a particular religion. That will allow you to learn in more depth about some of the topics covered in this class. Or, you can take a class to learn another language. Learning how individuals from another culture communicate is a great way to understand the culture better, and knowing another language opens the door to many opportunities.

You can also attend lectures, seminars, and workshops offered on your campus. College and university campuses offer a wealth of opportunities for cultural education. Programs are usually available throughout the year, but a particularly good time is during cultural emphasis months such as Black History Month, Women's Herstory Month, and LGBT Month. We shared stories about some of our experiences with the Cross-Cultural Retreat on our campus, a weekend of experiential exercises and group discussions related to diversity. Perhaps your campus offers something similar. If not, look for organizations in your area that do. For example, the National Conference for Community and Justice (NCCJ, formerly the National Conference for Christians and Jews) has chapters across the country and regularly offers diversity training workshops, lectures, and seminars.

Local museums are another source for cultural education. Museums often host exhibits, lectures, and other programs related to cultural issues. Some museums focus on a particular culture. For example, in Los Angeles we have the African-American Heritage Museum and the Japanese American National Museum.

You can also further your multicultural education by reading books and journals. Literature provides a wonderful window into different worlds. You read the words, private thoughts, and experiences of individuals from different backgrounds.

PICTURE 10.3   Working with others different from oneself can lead to enriching, creative activities. *Photograph by Philip van Huynh*

Other suggestions for multicultural education and training include watching relevant films and television shows, listening to music, and attending plays, concerts, and other cultural events and celebrations.

Experience and Practice

The more *education* and *training* you get in multicultural issues, the more *experience* you accumulate and the more opportunities you have to *practice* your new-found skills. Practice is necessary to perform any new skill with accuracy and ease. You can practice your culturally appropriate interpersonal skills by seeking out opportunities to interact with people who are different from you. Reach out and develop relationships with people from diverse backgrounds. Start a conversation with the person sitting next to you in class. Volunteer to work with him or her on a group project, or invite him or her to study, go to lunch, or have a cup of coffee with you. When you attend cultural events and celebrations, make an effort to meet some of the other people there.

You can also get involved with cultural organizations on your campus. On our campus we have the multicultural centers, one for each of the major cultural groups. We encourage students to get involved with their own, as well as other centers. Each of these centers puts on programs highlighting its cultural heritage, and they all appreciate those of all cultures who are willing to serve on planning committees.

Saying "I Don't Know" and Asking Questions

Two related skills that are important to learn when reaching out to others from different cultures are the ability to say "I don't know" and the ability to ask questions.

It is impossible to learn everything from taking a class or reading a book. Individual people are an invaluable source of information. Do not be afraid to admit when you do not know something about another group. People are often hesitant to admit they do not know something because they do not want to look ignorant, stupid, or insensitive, and they are afraid to ask because they do not want to be offensive. However, it is better to ask a question than to remain ignorant. You run a greater risk of offending someone if you interact with him or her on the basis of assumptions and stereotypes that may be incorrect, as the following story illustrates.

> *I was sitting in my sociology class one day, and the professor began saying something about African Americans. As often happens in classes when you are the only Black person, he turned and made a reference to me. I don't remember exactly what he said, but he implied that my family members were from the South and that I grew up in the ghetto. He was wrong on both accounts. I was offended. He assumed that all Black people come from the same background and we don't. We are all different. Here he was, a university professor, a sociologist, who claimed to know a lot about ethnic minority groups, and he was perpetuating misinformation and stereotypes.*
>
> BEVERLY, 40+-YEAR-OLD AFRICAN-AMERICAN WOMAN

The professor in the story made a mistake based on his assumptions about African Americans. It would have been nice if that professor, instead of making a faulty assumption, had asked Beverly about her background first. That would have set a more positive example for the students and sparked a more interesting and informative class discussion. Most people will not be offended if you ask questions in a respectful and caring manner. It shows them that you are genuinely interested in getting to know them and their culture. Most people will appreciate your interest and effort. Following is a more positive story about reaching out to others.

> *I learned to be culturally sensitive from my family. My father grew up in a small, all-White town in West Virginia. On his side of the family we can trace our roots back to the original settlers and to the Civil War. However, my father was in the military, served in Vietnam, and was stationed in Iran when I was born. I think his experience overseas taught him to appreciate other cultures. My mother's parents immigrated to the United States from Norway. I think growing up the child of immigrants influenced my mother's attitudes. My family returned to the United States from Iran when I was about one year old. My parents always made an effort to reach out to people from other cultures, and watching them taught me to do the same. For example, following the Iran hostage crisis in 1979 my mother made a special effort to talk to people she thought were from Iran. Many were afraid at that time to say where they were from, but my mother always asked*

and told them that we had lived there. That always surprised them and they would ask her questions, such as if she liked it. She always said yes and would tell them positive things about their country. You could tell they appreciated her kindness and openness. I remember there was an Iranian seamstress in our town who did alterations for my mother. Her face always lit up when we came in because we went out of our way to treat her with kindness and love. I learned those things from my parents. I learned we have a particular responsibility, as Americans, to be nice and to reach out to people from other cultures. It's important to be culturally aware and to be nice and welcoming, even if we make mistakes. It makes such a huge difference.

KATHLEEN, 30+-YEAR-OLD WHITE WOMAN

Kathleen's story shows the positive things that can happen when you reach out and build relationships with people from other cultures.

Travel

Another strategy for building culturally appropriate interpersonal skills is travel. Shakespeare wrote, "The world is a book, and the person that stays at home reads but one page." Traveling to other countries opens up the world to you and changes your perspective. When you travel, you interact with people from another culture. You see them in their daily lives, as they work, play, and love. You experience their food, music, language, sights, and sounds.

Travel helps you learn about others as well as yourself. There are lessons learned and skills obtained when you travel that are hard to gain any other way. We cannot overstate the benefits of experiencing another culture firsthand.

I like to travel because I learn about different cultures. I meet different kinds of people and like to see how they live and interact with one another. My travels help me learn more about people and get along with them faster. It helps me work with them more effectively. For example, we hired a guy from India whose name was "Ganesh." I said, "Ganesh! Isn't that like me being named Jesus?" (Ganesh is a Hindu God.) He looked surprised that I would know that and said, "Why, yes." Then I asked him what part of India he was from. He said, "Bombay." I asked him, "What part of Bombay?" Now he looked surprised that I would get so specific and said, "Central Bombay." I responded, "Central Bombay. Then aren't you Zoroastrian?" He almost fell out of his chair. "Why yes. How did you know that?" He was shocked that I knew what that was. That helped us to quickly establish a relationship. From then on he actively sought me out at work.

I also travel a lot for work. When I have the time, I schedule a few extra days to get in some sight-seeing. When I tell the people I'm meeting with that I'll be in town a few extra days to see more of their city or country they are always surprised and impressed. They can't believe I would take the time to learn more about their culture and history. For example, the Japanese executives are amazed when I tell them I've been to Nara and saw the Buddhist temples and Shinto shrines there. It immediately gives me more credibility and improves our working relationship.

CARL, 30+-YEAR-OLD WHITE MAN

Carl's story illustrates many of the benefits of travel. He gains more knowledge about other cultures and learns about the people and their way of life. That knowledge and experience helps him build stronger relationships with colleagues and increases his effectiveness on the job.

You actually don't have to travel far to learn about another culture. Most cities have cultural centers, or neighborhoods where people of one particular culture tend to gather and live. These neighborhoods often have names which reflect that culture, such as Chinatown and Little Tokyo. You can learn a lot about these cultures by visiting these cultural centers, walking the streets, eating at the restaurants, shopping at the stores, visiting the churches, and talking to the residents.

Being an Ally

Another important interpersonal skill is learning to be an ally. (Recall our discussion in chapter 6.) An ally is someone from a privileged group who speaks up for and supports individuals from oppressed minority groups. For example, if you are heterosexual, you can speak up when you hear someone make a negative comment about gays or lesbians. If you are in a class and hear someone make a comment based on stereotypes, you can point that out. Supporting individuals from oppressed minority groups relieves them of some of the burden they carry every day. Often individuals feel the pressure of having to represent their entire race in their classes. If you see that happening in a class you can speak up in support of that person.

In my opinion, the beauty of this class is to help me understand and appreciate the diverse cultures in my surroundings, if not the whole world. Regardless if it is dealing with populations with different ethnic backgrounds, SES, religions, sexual orientations, or disabilities, I have learned to be aware of my biases and to show more respect for other people's worldviews. Although multiculturalism is particularly important in the mental health professions, I truly believe that this issue is so important that everyone needs to be aware of it. After taking this class, I have started to have more discussions with my friends and family regarding this subject. I have become less silent when I hear discriminating comments. I think the respect for people coming from different cultures is the most essential and fundamental principle in interpersonal relationships. I am very lucky to have the opportunity to broaden my narrow worldview and learn this important lesson. This is not merely a lesson in academia, but a lesson for life.

CECILIA, 20+-YEAR-OLD TAIWAN IMMIGRANT WOMAN

It is also important to develop a level of comfort discussing difficult issues, such as racism, sexism, and heterosexism. These are emotional topics and many people are afraid to discuss them. Race, gender, sexual orientation, and religion are all core parts of a person's identity. Because these topics have such high personal relevance, people get very sensitive when they are discussed. People may also have painful experiences related to these parts of their identity, and talking about these topics brings up that pain. Others may react with anger to what they perceive to be the ignorant, insensitive, or offensive remarks of others. Those witnessing such pain or anger may feel uncomfortable or afraid. These are difficult emotions to handle, and it is easy to be overwhelmed by them, but they should not be avoided. Instead, they need to be brought out in the open, acknowledged, validated, and worked through. A highly used film about multicultural issues is *The Color of Fear* (Lee, 1994). At the end of the film, a White man is able to have a breakthrough because everyone in the group took time to work through the difficult emotions experienced during their weekend together. It takes courage and skill to discuss these difficult topics in a meaningful and beneficial manner, but it is necessary in order to build multicultural competence.

Class this last week was interesting, if uncomfortable for me. I think one of the issues affecting White people is the fear of saying something in the wrong way and offending someone unintentionally. It almost paralyzes speech sometimes, at least for me. I have been thinking about this a lot recently, and since this is the forum for it, I will discuss it. I am beginning to think we are damned if we do, and damned if we don't. If we try to be allies, openly discuss issues, and try to lend our hand to a cause, then we are often made fun of as naïve, with a bottomless pit of liberal guilt. If we just attend to our own lives, living in suburbia where we were born and raised, we are out of touch, isolationists. I believe in political correctness as a form of changing people's perception and ideas, of affording people dignity and respect, however, I think it can also paralyze discussion amongst diverse people even when all have the best intentions and hearts.

I believe that as our demographics change in this country these issues will come more and more to the forefront. I wonder what our future looks like. If White people have to pay the price for how things have been, or if over time we can together attempt to create a society where all can be afforded dignity. It will probably be a little of both, which is probably appropriate as it could ultimately make for a better all around understanding between people, just as now I sit squirming in my seat (in my anthro/history/ethnic studies classes) as I listen to the sins of the White past. I want to know the truth of the past; I believe it's the only way to make a better future. I try to keep an open heart, even when it hurts. I do feel helpless, as it was discussed in the book. So I do what I can. I listen; I speak if I feel I can make a coherent point that is important to me. When I am with family, friends, and acquaintances and hear ideas I feel are wrong, I muster my guts and speak up, trying not to be a hypocrite by remaining silent, and I try to be an ally, for myself, even when I feel like I am probably being naïve.

Sharon, 40+-year-old African-American Woman

An Attitude of Discovery and Courage

Perhaps the two most important skills you need to increase your level of multicultural competence are an attitude of discovery and courage. *Discovery* was defined earlier as openness to new experiences, a willingness to step out of your comfort zone. Doing that takes *courage*. As we said, encountering people and situations that are different naturally makes us feel frightened and uncomfortable. Courage is moving forward in spite of such negative feelings. If you do, you will reap the rewards.

Putnam (2007) conducted a series of research studies which show that as communities become more diverse, people become more isolated from one another. Such diversification has the effect of increasing mistrust, even among our own ethnic group, and disrupting prosocial behaviors and community cooperation. Because of these short-term costs, it is difficult for many to see the long-term economic, cultural, and developmental benefits of diversity. However, Putnam feels that these initial obstacles can be overcome with deliberate, organized, concerted efforts on individual, organizational, societal, and cultural levels. Putnam believes the answer lies in creating "shared social identities," or providing opportunities for lines between groups to become blurred, which fosters a sense of shared citizenship. Examples include developing programs that bring groups together at churches, schools, community centers, and athletic fields. Such local programs should receive public, national support.

Thus, Putnam believes society can be advanced if we make conscious efforts to increase meaningful interactions between diverse groups. Reaching out to others who are different from you is a critical step in this process. However, we should warn you. It will not be easy. Anytime you learn a new skill you make mistakes. Remember learning to ride a bike? How many times did you fall down before you learned to stay up? Did you give up? Chances are you kept trying until you were peddling your way freely down the block. And once you learned, you never forgot how. It was automatic.

The same is true of multicultural competence. In the beginning you will have some falls, but just get up and keep trying. The more you practice, the easier it will become, and the more effective you will be at interacting with others who are different from you. After you learned to ride a bike, you probably still had a spill from time to time. The same will be true of your cultural interactions. There will always be the awkward moment, the uncomfortable situation, the statement or action that is misunderstood. Not everyone will be receptive when you reach out. Making mistakes is part of the process. As Kathleen said in her story, we still have a responsibility to reach out. Be willing to admit your mistakes and learn from them. It will only help you farther along the road to multicultural competence.

Anna Deavere Smith (2000) is an actress whose life mission is to "search for American character." She travels around the country interviewing people hoping to "absorb America" and find the "doorway into the soul of a culture" (p. 12). She then turns these interviews into one-woman shows. One of her most famous plays is *Twilight: Los Angeles, 1992* in which she portrays interviews conducted with Los Angeles residents in the wake of the so-called riots that followed the verdict in the Rodney King beating case (mentioned in chapter 1). Anna Deavere Smith is someone who embodies the spirit of discovery and courage. She says:

> *I am constantly in a state of being. . . . It's actually not a bad state to be in. It might just be the best state in which to find oneself during the twenty-first century, as our culture wars continue and identity politics moves into its next phase. At such a time as this, it would be useful, I think, to have at least a cadre of people who were willing to move between cultural lines and across social strata. Globalism will require it, so we might as well practice our moves.*
>
> *I am prepared for difference, live in difference. My pursuit of American character is, basically, pursuit of difference. Character lives in that which is unique. What is unique about America is the extent to which it does, from time to time, pull off being a merged culture. Finding American character is a process of looking at fragments, of looking at the un-merged. One has to do the footwork, one has to move from place to place, one has to stand outside. It's not easy. . . .*
>
> *The most comfortable place to live is inside of what I call one's safe house of identity. I have observed that this is where most people live. Even if they leave a previous identity to enter another identity of choice, they often end up in another safe house, and leave behind any ambiguity that met them as they went from one house to the other. I tend to be more interested in the unsettled part of us.*
>
> *I am continually leaving safe houses of identity. When you leave the house of what is familiar to you—your family, your race, your social class, your nation, your professional area of expertise—it is not likely that you will find another house that will welcome you with open arms. When you leave your safe house, you will end up standing someplace in the road. I would call these places that are without houses crossroads of ambiguity. On the one hand, they are not comfortable places. On the other hand, in them one acquires the freedom to move. In my work I have moved across many cultural boundaries. For this reason I do not suffer culture shock often. I've developed a lot of stamina for being where I don't "belong". . . .*
>
> *The state of separation is what is expected. To move out of your separate place, your safe house of identity, is hard work. You have to be prepared.*
>
> (SMITH, 2000, PP. 23–24, 76)

Multicultural competence involves learning about your own culture as well as other cultures. The strategies described here can be used to learn more about yourself and others. We have given only a few suggestions here for how to develop culturally appropriate interpersonal skills. If you act on these suggestions, you may find that these activities can be fun and enriching as well as important. There are many other things that you can do as well. We hope these get you started.

SUMMARY

In our increasingly diverse and global society, we come in contact with people who are different from us every day. Sometimes that makes us feel uncomfortable. Our natural tendency is to stick to what is familiar because it is easy and helps us feel good about ourselves. However, if we are to truly benefit from all the world has to offer, it is to our advantage to become skilled at interacting with people from different backgrounds. That is multicultural competence.

The three areas of multicultural competence are (1) awareness of your own culture; (2) understanding other worldviews, and (3) development of culturally appropriate interpersonal skills. Development in these three areas will help you learn to interact effectively with others from different cultural backgrounds. These are important skills in today's world.

Following the so-called Los Angeles riots in 1992, Rodney King pleaded with the public to stop the conflict and asked, "Can't we all just get along?" His statement became the rallying cry for intergroup relationships following that event. Many people believe that Rodney King's beating by the four Los Angeles police officers and the violence that followed occurred because of deep misunderstandings and miscommunications between people of different backgrounds. Could those events have been prevented? Could we have used the aftermath of those events to improve relations between groups? Should the goal be, as Mr. King asked, to simply get along?

Some people say the goal is tolerance. Earlier we mentioned a museum in Los Angeles called "The Museum of Tolerance," which is dedicated to reducing racism, discrimination, and oppression. Is tolerance the ultimate goal? When LAB hears the word tolerance, she thinks of things like an annoying relative or co-worker. We really don't like them; we simply put up with them. What would our world be like if we all simply tolerated one another? Tolerance should be the minimum goal, a starting point. Dr. Joseph White (2001) stated that the goal should not be tolerance but "mutual enrichment." Putnam (2007) agrees and says, "Tolerance for difference is but a first step. To strengthen shared identities, we need more opportunities for meanigful interactions across ethnic lines where Americans (new and old) work, learn, recreate, and live" (p. 164). By getting to know, appreciate, and value people of differing backgrounds and perspectives, we enrich our lives.

In short, multicultural competence is about applying the things you have learned in this book to your life, your work, and your interactions with others. The theories, concepts, and research covered in this book should increase your self-awareness, your understanding of how your own cultural background influences you. They should increase your understanding of and empathy for people from other groups. This increased understanding of self and others should ultimately improve your interactions with others, in school, at work, and in your personal life. If you open yourself up to new knowledge and new experiences, if you take the risk and accept the challenge, your life will be enriched. We are all different; no two people are alike. Our lives are enriched when we adopt an attitude of discovery, open our minds and hearts to the experiences of others, and openly share our experiences with them. If each of you reading this book takes what you have learned and apply it to your life, the world will be a better place. We will close with a wonderful reaction from one of our former students:

> *This class has opened my eyes to so many different things. It seems like every single day I run into a situation that brings up things that I have learned in this class. Whether it is a situation that I am involved in or a situation that I am just an observer to, I find myself constantly reflecting on information that I have learned from this class and trying to apply it to the current situation.*
>
> *I found the five D's of difference really interesting. Before reading all of that I had always thought that people of other races really were no different than me or anyone else for that matter. I guess I never really thought about this statement and how it diminishes and devalues the differences that make others the person that they are. I have always been one to embrace my own differences from others but I never really thought of embracing the differences of people of other cultures in the same way. I mean ever since I was little I have always been fascinated with learning about other cultures and the ways they do things differently but I guess I just never consciously thought about it the way the book writes about the Five D's.*
>
> *I found the line by Dr. White, that tolerance is not enough that we need "mutual enrichment," to be very moving. I believe that we all have so much to teach one another and when both parties are willing we can really change one another's lives for the better.*
>
> KERRY, 20+-YEAR-OLD EUROPEAN-AMERICAN WOMAN

Food for Thought

When one of the authors (JSM) went to graduate school, it was the first time he had ever lived for an extended period of time outside his home state. He encountered people from various places of the country in an intensive environment. (Anyone who has gone to graduate school will tell you how intensive that experience really is.) He sees that time as one of the greatest periods of growth in his life. Another one of the authors (LAB) discusses how enriching it is for her to travel outside the United States. The worldviews of other cultures are quite different from the American worldview, and she learns to understand herself and her culture better through the eyes of people from other cultures. Finally, the third author (JT) is herself an immigrant to this country. She lived all the early years of her life in the Philippines, then came to the United States when she was an adolescent. Moreover, her own experience as a biracial individual has led her to have a quite different worldview from that of most people she encounters. Again, she has enjoyed many mutually enriching interactions in her life. Think back to when you have met someone quite different from you. What did you learn from that person? What did that person learn from you? What you learned from one another is what Joe White calls "mutual enrichment." Now think back to all of those who seemed quite different from you. This number may be far beyond what you can recall. However, if you conceptualize each of those interactions as being mutually enriching, you will get a sense of just how enriched your lives have become from those various encounters.

Critical Thinking Questions

Have you ever been to a foreign country and felt out of place? Have you ever been to another part of the country and felt out of place? Have you ever been to a different area of the city you live in that made you feel out of place? How have you handled those situations?

Have you ever found yourself distancing yourself from the uncomfortable situations in the previous question? Have you ever denied that you felt uncomfortable when upon reflection you actually did feel uncomfortable? Did you ever find yourself being defensive about the differences? Did you ever devalue what was different from your areas of comfort? Did you ever discover something about yourself or discover something new and exciting when you were in a situation of difference?

Did you ever go back to situations of comfort because they made your life more simple? Did you find such situations to be more safe? Did these situations make you feel sane?

Has learning about the values and beliefs of others ever made you reexamine your own values and beliefs? Did that make you feel more enriched?

Have you ever advocated for people or groups of different demographic characteristics from yours? What were those experiences like?

Glossary

acceptance—The feeling that one is accepted as an equal in the conversation.

acculturated—LaFramboise and associates' (1993) term for an integrationist. (See also **integrationist**.)

acculturation—Experiences and changes that groups and individuals undergo when they come in contact with different culture.

acculturative stress—The feelings of tension and anxiety caused by the inability to adapt in the new country.

additive bilingualism—The acquisition of a second language that does not replace the native language.

ALANA—Helms's acronym for African Americans, Latinos, Asian Americans, and Native Americans.

allies—Individuals who are on the upside of power and who cross a demographic boundary to advocate for those on the downside of power.

allocentrism—Collectivistic tendencies that reside within an individual. Collectivism refers to the society, whereas allocentrism refers to an individual.

alternation—Competence in both the host culture and one's original culture such that one is able to apply the values and behaviors that are appropriate for the situation.

anorexia nervosa—An eating disorder marked by such a severe restriction of one's diet that the sufferer's weight falls far below what would be expected, given her/his height and age.

appreciation—The stage or status in which a child/adolescent begins to broaden his/her perspective to include the race or ethnicity not initially selected for his/her identity.

assimilationist—An individual who adapts completely to (assimilates into) the host society, taking on the values of that society and rejecting his or her original values.

attribution theory—A theory that attempts to determine the cause of a behavior. Two major dimensions are internal–external and stable–unstable.

authenticity—Being truthful and not trying to be merely "politically correct."

autonomy—The status in which White people are comfortable with their White identity, understand that racism is connected with other forms of oppression, and work to address all forms of oppression.

availability heuristic—A mental shortcut whereby the importance, frequency, or credence of something is exaggerated because it comes to mind easily.

aversive racism—Covert, unintentional discriminatory behavior practiced by individuals who would deny being racist and who would be appalled to realize that they were engaging in racist acts.

awareness of your own cultural attitudes—The part of multicultural competence that involves an individual's being aware that his/her own attitudes may be heavily influenced by his/her own culture and may be different from those of a person with whom he/she is working.

bias in the usage—A bias introduced when a test is used in an inappropriate manner, such as being administered in a language in which the test taker is not fluent.

bias of the user—A bias in the interpretation of a test when the test user has a particular perspective or bias that may disadvantage a person or group.

biological concept of race—The perspective that a race is a group of people who share a specific combination of physical, genetically inherited characteristics that distinguish them from other groups.

biopsychosocial model—A model of human behavior that takes into consideration biological, cognitive-affective, social interpersonal, social institutional, and cultural factors.

bulimia nervosa—An eating disorder marked by the consumption of a large amount of food in one sitting—called a binge—followed by the purging of that food, most typically through vomiting but also through extreme exercise or the use of laxatives.

choice of group categorization—The stage or status in which a child is forced to choose which race or ethnicity he/she should use as the basis of his/her identity.

class-bound values—Core beliefs of one socioeconomic class that relate principally to that class and may be inappropriate for another level of socioeconomic status.

cognitive dissonance theory—A theory that suggests that when two cognitions are in conflict, a person will be motivated to change one of them to reduce the unsettled feelings caused by the discrepancy.

collectivism—A social pattern in which individuals tend to be motivated by the group's or collective's preferences, needs, and rights when they come into conflict with those of the individual.

coming out—The process by which a gay, lesbian, or bisexual individual openly expresses his/her sexual orientation.

conceptual equivalence—Refers to a term or phrase that is a culturally meaningful equivalent of the term being examined.

contact—The status in which White people are uninformed about the realities of racism and privilege.

cooperative principle—A psycholinguistic term that assumes that we strive to communicate with one another sincerely and effectively when we engage in a conversation.

countercultural individuals—Idiocentric people residing in a collectivistic culture, or allocentric people residing in an individualistic culture.

covert, intentional racism—Discriminatory behavior that is intentional but is covered up so that one can deny that one is racist.

covert, unintentional racism—Discriminatory behavior that is unintentional but serves to perpetuate ongoing racist acts or traditions.

cross-cultural psychology—Comparisons across cultures or countries, as opposed to comparisons of groups within one society.

culture contact—Critical incidents in which people from different cultures come into social contact with one another either (a) by living and working with one another on a daily basis, or (b) through visiting other countries on a temporary basis, such as for business, tourism, or study.

culture-bound syndromes—Disorders that tend to occur only in certain cultures.

culture-bound values—Core beliefs of one culture that relate principally to that culture and may be inappropriate for another culture.

defensiveness—Trying to protect oneself from acknowledging the difference between oneself and another to avoid the discomfort created by that difference.

delay of gratification—The ability to wait for a more desirable reward instead of taking a less desirable reward immediately.

denial—Pretending that there is no difference between oneself and another, minimizing its importance, or ignoring the difference altogether.

devaluing—Assessing the difference between oneself and another as deficient or less important.

development of culturally appropriate interpersonal skills—The part of multicultural competence that involves an individual's knowing how to apply his/her knowledge about someone else's worldview to behaviors that appropriately take into account that knowledge, effecting positive change.

Diagnostic and Statistical Manual of Mental Disorders—The primary reference manual used in all mental health fields to classify mental disorders. Published by the American Psychiatric Association, this manual is currently in its fourth edition (1994), with a text revision made in 2000.

direct communication—Blunt communication that is literal and to the point.

discovery—Appreciating the difference between oneself and another and seeing how enriching that difference may be.

discrimination—A negative behavior toward a group or its members based upon their categorization.

disintegration—The status in which White people are in enough contact with ethnic minorities that their naïveté about racism is shattered.

disparity—The condition or fact of being unequal.

distancing—Avoiding situations in which one feels different.

diversity—Differences beyond race, ethnicity, and nationality, such as sexual orientations, religions, and abilities.

emic perspective—An attempt to derive meaningful concepts within one culture.

encounter stage of minority identity development—The stage or status in which one is confronted with the realities of racism or other forms of devaluation of one's cultural group.

enmeshment/denial—The stage or status in which a child feels guilty about choosing one race or ethnicity over the other, because this is an implicit rejection of the parent whose race or ethnicity was not chosen.

ethnical psychology—The study of the minds of "other races and peoples."

ethnicity—A combination of race and culture.

etic perspective—An attempt to build theories of human behavior by examining commonalities across many cultures.

eugenics—A movement that maintains that only "good genes" should be passed from generation to generation and that "undesirable" groups should be dissuaded from passing on "negative or undesirable" genes.

exosystem—A layer of context that includes major societal institutions, such as the media and the government.

face giving/giving face—Extolling the virtues of another person in public. It would be considered boastful and individualistic if the individual did this himself/herself.

face saving—The protection of one's public persona by maintaining one's self-respect and dignity.

functional equivalence—The equating of items on a test or a survey functionally as opposed to literally.

fundamental attribution error—The tendency to overestimate dispositional (internal, stable) causes of behaviors and to underestimate external causes of behaviors.

fusion—The process whereby one's culture is completely dissolved into other cultures, forming a new, homogeneous culture.

goal attainment—The goal of mutual understanding between two conversational partners.

guilt—A prominent negative emotion in individualistic cultures that involves an individual's sense of personal regret for having engaged in a negative behavior.

health—A complete state of physical, mental, and social well-being—not merely the absence of disease or infirmity.

health behaviors—Behaviors undertaken by people to enhance or maintain their well-being.

Health Belief Model—A set of assumptions that suggests that one's health behavior is affected by one's perception of a personal health threat as well as how a particular health practice would be effective in reducing the personal health threat.

health psychology—The study of psychological influences on how people stay healthy, why they become ill, and how they respond when they do get ill.

high-context communication—Communication in which the context conveys much of the meaning.

human activity—The distinction among being, being & in becoming, and doing. Being refers to an individual's being accepted just as he or she is. Being & in becoming refers to an individual's evolving into something different and presumably better. Doing refers to an individual's being valued for the activity in which he or she is engaged.

identity acceptance—The stage or status in which a gay, lesbian, or bisexual individual fully accepts his/her sexual orientation and is about to "come out" to others.

identity comparison—The stage or status in which a gay, lesbian, or bisexual individual recognizes his/her feelings about same-sex individuals.

identity confusion—The stage or status in which a gay, lesbian, or bisexual individual begins to question his/her sexual identity.

identity pride—The stage or status in which a gay, lesbian, or bisexual individual openly expresses his/her sexual orientation and takes pride in that identity.

identity synthesis—The state or status in which a gay, lesbian, or bisexual individual is able to integrate all aspects of his/her identities, such as ethnic minority status and gender.

identity tolerance—The stage or status in which a gay, lesbian, or bisexual individual fully recognizes his/her homosexual feelings but attempts to hide them from others and from himself/herself, by trying to believe, for example, that it is just a "phase" he/she is going through.

idiocentrism—Individualistic tendencies that reside within an individual. Individualism refers to the society, whereas idiocentrism refers to an individual.

illusory correlation—An overestimation of the co-occurrence of two minority events.

immersion/emersion—The status in which White people begin to form a more positive White identity and to focus on changing Whites, not Blacks.

immersion/emersion stage of minority identity development—The stage or status in which one involves oneself completely within one's cultural group to the exclusion of the majority group. One emerges from this stage because one cannot meet all of one's needs if society is truly dominated by the majority group.

immigrants—People who move to another country voluntarily. The decision to move can take weeks, months, or even years, which allows these people to prepare for the move and to begin the acculturation process before the move.

imposed etics—The forcing of one culture's worldview on another culture, assuming that one's own worldviews are universal.

incidence—The number of new disorders diagnosed in a given period of time.

indirect communication—Communication that relies upon context and the receiver's ability to draw inferences.

individualism—A social pattern in which individuals tend to be motivated by their own preferences, needs, and rights when they come into conflict with a group or collective in which the individual is a member.

integration—The stage or status in which a child/adolescent/adult sees the benefits of embracing both races or ethnicities.

integrationist—An individual who holds on to his or her original values while also learning and adopting the values of the host culture.

internalization stage of minority identity development—The stage or status in which one feels comfortable with one's identity. This allows one to express acceptance of other cultures.

introspection—The method that structuralists used to examine the contents of people's minds.

kinesics—Bodily movements in conversations, including hand gestures, facial expressions, and eye contact.

language attrition—Equivalent to subtractive bilingualism. (See also **subtractive bilingualism.**)

language issues—Differences in language (e.g., an English-speaking therapist and a Spanish-speaking client who may have some limited facility with English) or language usage (e.g., Ebonics or Black English).

linguistic equivalence—The translation of a term from one language to another that carries with it similar meaning.

locus of control—The focus of control over outcomes of one's life, be it internal control or external control.

locus of responsibility—The focus of responsibility for one's position in life, be it internal feelings of responsibility or external, societal responsibility.

Logical Positivism—Scientific approach that attempts to measure "truth" or real phenomena through a methodology of numbers and statistical analyses.

loss of face/face saving—Loss of face involves being publicly revealed for negative behavior; face saving involves being able to protect one's public persona.

low-context communication—Language-dependent communication, in which the words carry most of the meaning and context plays a lesser role.

macrosystem—A layer of context that includes the cultural norms and societal rules that determine rules of conduct.

male privilege—The unearned advantages associated with being male, such as knowing that one's opinions will be respected. Women often feel that their opinions are not respected or are attributed to emotion, not sound reasoning.

manner—The maxim that suggests that we are clear in our language and that we pay attention to normal standards of conversation, such as not shouting at someone who is right in front of us.

marginal man—Stonequist's concept of how one feels when one is caught between two worlds.

marginalist—An individual who does not adopt either the host society's values or his or her original values.

masculine–feminine dimension—A continuum of authority from hierarchical (masculine) to egalitarian (feminine).

mesosystem—A layer of context that includes relationships in the immediate area outside the family, such as schools, work, the extended family, and the community in which one lives.

metric equivalence—Numeric scores that are generally equivalent from one culture to another.

microsystem—A layer of context that includes relationships among family members living within one household.

migration period—The period when a group is migrating from the country of origin to the host country. This includes the period immediately before the migration, when the final feelings about moving are experienced, and leave is taken from family and friends from the country of origin.

multicultural competence—The ability to work and be effective with individuals who are of a different culture from yours.

multicultural perspective—The perspective that there are multiple groups within a society and all groups are mutually appreciated.

multicultural psychology—The systematic study of behavior, cognition, and affect in many different cultures.

multiculturalism as the fourth force—The idea that multicultural psychology is so important that it will fundamentally change the direction of the field of psychology, as psychoanalysis, behaviorism, and humanism did.

native bilingualism—The ability to speak two languages from birth, acquired because both languages are spoken in the household.

Negative Cognitive Triad—Beck's label for the negative view depressed individuals tend to have of themselves, the world, and the future.

negative stereotyping—Stereotyping that casts African Americans in a negative light or that limits discussion to "African-American topics," such as athletics and music.

overt racism—Discriminatory behavior in which those in the majority engage in open, hostile acts of aggression against racial minorities consciously and unapologetically.

paradigm shift—A major change in the way people think about a field.

paralanguage—Nonverbal vocal cues in conversation, such as loudness of voice, silences, and rates of speech.

people/nature relationship—How people relate to nature, be it subjugated to nature, in harmony with nature, or mastery over nature.

personal expressiveness—Speaking from the heart and not the head.

personal identity—The stage or status in which a child bases his/her identity on personal factors, such as self-esteem, instead of on race or ethnicity.

postmigration period—The period after settling into the host culture, when the stress of migration continues to be experienced and the adjustment to the new culture takes place.

power dynamics—Powerlessness and assertiveness in conversations with African Americans. Sometimes, African Americans can feel powerless when conversing with White conversational partners. In response, they may "code switch"; that is, they may switch from the mutual conversational rules to African-American rules, such as Black English or the like. In code switching, African Americans can regain a sense of control over the conversation.

pre-encounter stage of minority identity development—The stage or status in which one feels and accepts that the world is organized according to the dominant culture and against one's own cultural group.

prejudice—A negative judgment about a group or its members based upon their categorization.

premigration period—The time period before migration, when the acculturation process can begin to take place.

prevalence—The current rate of a particular disorder at a given point in time.

proxemics—Personal space in conversations.

pseudoindependence—The status in which White people begin to acknowledge the realities of racism but believe that it is Blacks who should change, not Whites.

qualifiers—Words or phrases that soften statements, such as "I may be wrong, but this is good."

quality—The maxim that suggests that we tell each other the truth when we engage in a conversation.

quantity—The maxim that suggests that we contribute an appropriate amount of talk when we engage in a conversation.

Racial and Cultural Identity Development Model (R/CID)—A general model that covers all forms of cultural identity and addresses how one relates to oneself, to others of the same culture, to others of different cultures, and to the dominant cultural group.

racism—Discriminatory behavior that is backed by institutional power.

refugees—People who are forced to move from their homelands because of war or political oppression. The decision to move is almost immediate, taking days, hours, or even minutes, which allows these people neither to prepare for the move nor to begin the acculturation process because they do not usually know in which country they will finally settle.

reintegration—The status in which White people retreat to their comfort zone within their White communities.

relations with conversational partner—The maxim that suggests that we use our previous relationship with our conversational partner so that we do not have to repeat shared experiences.

relevance—The maxim that suggests that our discussion is relevant to the conversation.

rule violations—The maxim that suggests that we signal our conversational partners when we are about to engage in a violation of one of the other maxims.

safe—Things that are similar to us or our values are not a threat because we know how to deal with them and do not have to encounter unsettled feelings of going beyond the familiar to the unknown.

sane—Things that are similar to us or our values help us feel normal because if we are like everyone else, we are not out of step; we are validated or affirmed.

separationist—An individual who refuses to take on any values of the host society, hanging on to his or her original values completely.

shame—A prominent negative emotion in collectivistic cultures that involves an individual's sense of regret for having engaged in a negative behavior that reflects badly upon his or her family and/or upbringing.

simple—Things that are similar to us or our values are easy or comfortable.

social relations—The distinction among lineal, collateral, and individualistic. Lineal is a respect for the hierarchy within one's family. Collateral is essentially the same as collectivism, and individualistic is the same as our earlier discussion.

sociocultural concept of race—The perspective that characteristics, values, and behaviors that have been associated with groups of people who share different physical characteristics serve the social purpose of providing a way for outsiders to view another group and for members of a group to perceive themselves.

somatization—The expression of mental disorders through physical disorders.

stereotype—A generalization about a group or its members based upon their categorization.

stereotype threat—A fear that one will confirm the negative stereotype of a group to which one belongs in an area in which the individual excels.

structuralism—The first formal approach to psychology that attempted to examine the contents of people's minds.

subtractive bilingualism—The acquisition of a second language that replaces the native language.

tag questions—Questions added to a statement of assertion, such as "This is good, don't you think?"

time focus—An orientation that values a particular time perspective. Some cultures value the past, some value the present, and some value the future. Although all cultures value all three, some cultures value one of these perspectives more than do other cultures.

Tripartite Model of Personal Identity—The understanding that our self-perceptions are made up of unique, individual aspects, aspects of groups to which we belong, and universal aspects of human beings.

ultimate attribution error—The tendency to ascribe the cause of a behavior to dispositional characteristics of the group rather than to an individual member.

understanding—The sense that a conversational partner has enough experience to truly understand the African-American experience.

understanding other worldviews—The part of multicultural competence that involves an individual's knowing that other cultures may have ways of seeing and interpreting the world that are markedly different from his/hers.

VREG—Helms's acronym for those who are Visible Racial/Ethnic Groups.

White privilege—The unearned advantages associated with being White in America, such as knowing that Whiteness will be emphasized in the media. Ethnic minorities are not always portrayed in the media, and when they are, they are often portrayed stereotypically rather than as multifaceted individuals.

worldview—A psychological perception of the world that determines how we think, behave, and feel.

References

Abe-Kim, J., Takeuchi, D. T., Hong, S., Zane, N., Sue, S., Spencer, M. S., Appel, H., Nicdao, E., & Alegria, M. (2007). Use of mental health-related services among immigrant and US-born Asian Americans: Results from the National Latino and Asian American Study. *American Journal of Public Health, 97,* 91–98.

Abrams, K. K., Allen, L. R., & Gray, J. J. (1993). Disordered eating attitudes and behaviors, psychological adjustment and ethnic identity: A comparison of Black and White female college students. *International Journal of Eating Disorders, 14,* 49–57.

Acevedo-Polakovich, I. A., Reynaga-Abiko, G., Garriott, P. O., Derefinko, K. J., Winsett, M. K., Gudonis, L. C., & Brown, T. L. (2007). Beyond instrument selection: Cultural considerations in the psychological assessment of U.S. Latinas/os. *Professional Psychology: Research and Practice, 38,* 375–384.

Adembimpe, V. R. (1981). Overview: White norms and psychiatric diagnosis of Black patients. *American Journal of Psychiatry, 138,* 279–285.

Akan, G. E., & Grilo, C. M. (1995). Sociocultural influences on eating attitudes and behaviors, body image, and psychological functioning: A comparison of African-American, Asian-American, and Caucasian college women. *International Journal of Eating Disorders, 18,* 181–187.

Akbar, N. (1989). Nigrescence and identity: Some limitations. *The Counseling Psychologist, 17,* 258–263.

Akerlund, M., & Cheung, M. (2000). Teaching beyond the deficit model: Gay and lesbian issues among African Americans, Latinos, and Asian Americans. *Journal of Social Work Education, 36,* 279–293.

Akutsu, P. D., Tsuru, G. K., & Chu, J. P. (2004). Predictors of non-attendance of intake appointments among five Asian American client groups. *Journal of Consulting and Clinical Psychology, 72,* 891–896.

Albee, G. H. (2003). Confrontations and change. In D. K. Freedheim (Ed.), *History of Psychology, Vol. 1,* in I. B. Weiner (Editor-in-Chief), *Handbook of Psychology* (pp. 483–508). New York: Wiley.

Alegria, M., Mulvaney-Day, N., Torres, M., Polo, A., Zhun, C., & Canino, G. (2007). Prevalence of psychiatric disorders across Latino subgroups in the United States. *American Journal of Public Health, 97,* 68–75.

Alvarado, N., & Jameson, K. A. (2002). The use of modifying terms in the naming and categorization of color appearances in Vietnamese and English. *Journal of Cognition and Emotion, 2,* 53–80.

American Psychiatric Association. (1994). *Diagnostic and statistical manual of mental disorders* (4th ed.). Washington, DC: Author.

American Psychiatric Association. (2000). *Diagnostic and statistical manual of mental disorders* (4th ed., Text Revision). Washington, DC: Author.

American Psychological Association. (2000). Guidelines for psychotherapy with lesbian, gay, and bisexual clients. *American Psychologist, 55,* 1440–1451.

American Psychological Association. (2002). Ethical principles of psychologists and code of conduct. *American Psychologist, 57,* 1060–1073.

American Psychological Association. (2003). Guidelines on multicultural education, training, research, practice, and organizational change for psychologists. *American Psychologist, 58,* 377–402.

American Psychological Association Committee on Accreditation. (2002). *Guidelines and principles for accreditation of programs in professional psychology.* Washington, DC: American Psychological Association. Retrieved July 12, 2004, from http://www.apa.org/ed/G&P2.pdf

Andersen, P. (1999). Cues of culture: The basis of intercultural differences in nonverbal communication. In L. A. Samovar & R. E. Porter (Eds.), *Intercultural communication: A reader* (8th ed., pp. 244–256). Belmont, CA: Wadsworth.

Angier, N. (2000, August 22). Do races differ? Not really, DNA shows. *New York Times,* F1.

Aranda, C. (1977). *Dichos: Proverbs and sayings from the Spanish.* New York: Greenwood.

Argyle, M. (1975). *Bodily communication.* New York: International University Press.

Armour-Thomas, E. (2003). Assessment of psychometric intelligence for racial and ethnic minorities: Some unanswered questions. In G. Bernal, J. E. Trimble, A. K. Burlew, & F. T. L. Leong (Eds.), *Handbook of racial and ethnic minority psychology* (pp. 357–374). Thousand Oaks, CA: Sage.

Aronson, E. (1990, April). *The return of the repressed: Dissonance theory makes a comeback.* Presidential address presented at the 70th Annual Meeting of the Western Psychological Association, Los Angeles, CA.

Arredondo, P., Toporek, R., Brown, S., Jones, J., Locke, D., Sanchez, J., & Stadler, H. A. (1996). Operationalization of multicultural counseling competencies. *Journal of Multicultural Counseling and Development, 24,* 42–78.

Ashton, C. M., Haidet, P., Paterniti, D., Collins, T. C., Gordon, H. S., O'Malley, K. Petersen, L., Sharf, B., Suarez-Almazor, M. E., Wray, N. P., & Street, R. L. (2003). Racial and ethnic disparities in the use of health services—bias, preferences, or poor communication? *Journal of General Internal Medicine, 18,* 146–152.

Atkinson, D. R. (1983). Ethnic similarity in counseling psychology: A review of research. *The Counseling Psychologist, 11,* 79–92.

Atkinson, D. R. (1985). Research on cross-cultural counseling and psychotherapy: A review and update of reviews. In P. B. Pederson (Ed.), *Handbook of cross-cultural counseling and therapy* (pp. 191–197). Westport, CT: Greenwood.

Atkinson, D. R. (2004). *Counseling American minorities* (6th ed.). Boston: McGraw-Hill.

Atkinson, D. R., Furlong, J. J., & Poston, W. C. (1986). Afro-American preferences for counselor characteristics. *Journal of Counseling Psychology, 33,* 326–330.

Atkinson, D. R., Morten, G., & Sue, D. W. (Eds.). (1979). *Counseling American minorities: A cross-cultural perspective.* Dubuque, IA: Brown.

Atkinson, D. R., Morten, G., & Sue, D. W. (1989). A minority identity development model. In D. R. Atkinson, G. Morten, & D. W. Sue (Eds.), *Counseling American minorities: A cross-cultural perspective* (3rd ed., pp. 35–52). Dubuque, IA: Brown.

Atkinson, D. R., Morten, G., & Sue, D. W. (Eds.). (1993). *Counseling American minorities: A cross-cultural perspective* (4th ed.). Dubuque, IA: Brown.

Atkinson, D. R., Morten, G., & Sue, D. W. (Eds.). (1998). *Counseling American minorities: A cross-cultural perspective* (5th ed.). Dubuque, IA: Brown.

Atkinson, D. R., & Schein, S. (1986). Similarity in counseling. *The Counseling Psychologist, 14,* 319–354.

Backenroth, G. (1998). Multiculturalism and the deaf community. Examples given from deaf people working in bicultural groups. In P. Pedersen (Ed.), *Multiculturalism as a fourth force* (pp. 111–146). Philadelphia, PA: Brunner/Mazel.

Baker, D. B. (2003). The challenge of change: Formation of the Association of Black Psychologists. In Freedheim (Ed.), *History of Psychology, Vol. 1,* in I. B. Weiner (Editor-in-Chief), *Handbook of Psychology* (pp. 492–495). New York: Wiley.

Bandura, A. (1977). *Social learning theory.* Englewood Cliffs, NJ: Prentice Hall.

Bandura, A. (1986). *Social foundations of thought and action: A social cognitive theory.* Englewood Cliffs, NJ: Prentice Hall.

Bandura, A. (1997). *Self-efficacy: The exercise of control.* New York: Freeman.

Barker-Hackett, L. (1995). *The real tragedy of O. J.* Unpublished manuscript.

Barker-Hackett, L. (1999, October). Rosy or racist? *Yale Alumni Magazine,* 6–8. New Haven, CT: Yale Alumni Publications, Inc.

Barker-Hackett, L. (2003). African Americans in the new millennium: A continued search for our true identity. In J. S. Mio & G. Y. Iwamasa (Eds.), *Culturally diverse mental health: The challenges of research and resistance* (pp. 121–140). New York: Brunner-Routledge.

Barker-Hackett, L., & Mio, J. S. (2000). Addressing resistance in larger group formats. In J. S. Mio & G. I. Awakuni (Eds.), *Resistance to multiculturalism: Issues and interventions.* Philadelphia: Brunner/Mazel.

Barret, B., & Logan, C. (2002). *Counseling gay men and lesbians: A primer.* Pacific Grove, CA: Brooks/Cole.

Bauder, D. (2007). Bill O'Reilly's comments about Harlem restaurant draw fire. Retrieved November 8, 2007, at http://www.usatoday.com/life/people/2007-09-25-oreilly-restaurant_n.htm

Beals, J., Manson, S. M., Keane, E., & Dick, R. W. (1991). Factorial structure of the Center for Epidemiologic Studies: Depression Scale among American Indian college students. *Psychological Assessment, 3,* 623–627.

Beck, A. T. (1967). *Depression: Causes and treatment.* Philadelphia: University of Pennsylvania Press.

Beck, A. T. (1970). Cognitive therapy: Nature and relation to behavior therapy. *Behavior Therapy, 1,* 184–200.

Becker, A. E. (1995). *Body, self and society: The view from Fiji.* Philadelphia: University of Pennsylvania Press.

Begley, S. (1995, February 13). Three is not enough: Surprising new lessons from the controversial science of race. *Newsweek,* 67–69.

Behrens, J. T. (1997). Does the White Racial Identity Attitude Scale measure racial and ethnic identity? *Journal of Counseling Psychology, 44,* 3–12.

Ben-Ari, A. (1995). Coming out: A dialectic of intimacy and privacy. *Families in Society: The Journal of Contemporary Human Services, 76,* 306–314.

Bennett, S. K., & BigFoot-Sipes, D. S. (1991). American Indian and White college student preference for counselor characteristics. *Journal of Counseling Psychology, 38,* 440–445.

Bernal, M. E., Knight, G. P., Ocampo, K. A., Garza, C. A., & Cota, M. K. (1993). Development of Mexican American identity. In M. E. Bernal & G. P. Knight (Eds.), *Ethnic identity: Formation and transmission among Hispanics and other minorities* (pp. 31–46). Albany: State University of New York Press.

Berry, J. (1988). *Understanding the process of acculturation for primary prevention* (Contract No. 278-85-0024 CH). Minneapolis: University of Minnesota, National Institute of Mental Health Refugee Assistance Program.

Berry, J. (1990). Psychology of acculturation: Understanding individuals moving between cultures. In R. Brislin (Ed.), *Applied cross-cultural psychology* (pp. 232–253). Newbury Park, CA: Sage.

Berry, J. (1997). Preface. In J. Berry, Y. Poortinga, & J. Pandey (Eds.), *Theory and method: Vol. 1. Handbook of cross-cultural psychology* (2nd ed., pp. x–xv). Boston: Allyn & Bacon.

Berry, J. W. (1969). On cross-cultural comparability. *International Journal of Psychology, 4,* 119–128.

Berry, J. W. (1980). Acculturation as varieties of adaptation. In A. Padilla (Ed.), *Acculturation: Theory, models and some new findings.* Boulder, CO: Westview.

Berry, J. W. (1991). Managing the process of acculturation. In U.S. Department of Health and Human Services, *Mental health services for refugees* (DHHS Publication No. ADM

91-1824, pp. 111–122). Rockville, MD: National Institute of Mental Health.

Berry, J. W., Poortinga, Y. H., Segall, M. H., & Dasen, P. R. (1992). *Cross-cultural psychology: Research and applications.* Cambridge: Cambridge University Press.

Betancourt, H., & Lopez, S. R. (1993). The study of culture, ethnicity, and race in American psychology. *American Psychologist, 48,* 629–637.

Binet, A., & Simon, Th. (1905). Méthodes nouvelles pour le diagnostic du niveau intellectuel des anormaux. *Année psychologique, 11,* 191–244.

Black, L. (1996). Families of African origin: An overview. In M. McGoldrick, J. Giordano, & J. K. Pearce (Eds.), *Ethnicity and family therapy* (2nd ed., pp. 57–65). New York: Guilford.

Blair, R. G. (2000). Risk factors associated with PTSD and major depression among Cambodian refugees. *Health and Social Work, 25,* 23–30.

Blank, M. B., & Tetrick, F. L., III. (1994). Racial matching and service utilization among seriously mentally ill consumers in the rural south. *Community Mental Health Journal, 30,* 271–272.

Blumstein, P., & Schwartz, P. (1983). *American couples: Money, work, sex.* New York: Morrow.

Bochner, S. (1999). Cultural diversity within and between societies: Implications for multicultural social systems: In P. Pedersen (Ed.), *Multiculturalism as a Fourth Force.* Philadelphia: Brunner/Mazel.

Bowen, D., Tomoyasu, N., & Cauce, A. M. (1991). The triple threat: A discussion of gender, class, and race differences in weight. *Women and Health, 17,* 123–143.

Boyd-Franklin, N. (1989). *Black families in therapy.* New York: Guilford.

Bramann, J. K. (2001). Multiculturalism and personal identity. Retrieved June 25, 2003, from http://www.frostburg.edu/dept/phil/forum/multicult.htm

Brenner, C. (1982). *The mind in conflict.* New York: International Universities Press.

Brislin, R. W. (1980). Translation and content analysis of oral and written materials. In H. C. Triandis & J. W. Berry (Eds.), *Handbook of cross-cultural psychology: Vol. 2. Methodology* (pp. 389–444). Boston: Allyn & Bacon.

Brislin, R. W. (1986). The wording and translation of research instruments. In W. J. Lonner & J. W. Berry (Eds.), *Field methods in cross-cultural research* (pp. 137–164). Newbury Park, CA: Sage.

Brislin, R. W. (2000). *Understanding culture's influence on behavior* (2nd ed.). Fort Worth, TX: Harcourt College Publishers.

Brislin, R. W., Lonner, W. J., & Thorndike, R. M. (1973). *Cross-cultural research methods.* New York: Wiley.

Bronfenbrenner, U. (1979). *The ecology of human development.* Cambridge, MA: Harvard University Press.

Broverman, I., Broverman, D., Clarkson, F., Rosenkrantz, P., & Vogel, S. (1970). Sex-role stereotypes and clinical judgments of mental health. *Journal of Consulting and Clinical Psychology, 34,* 1–7.

Brown, D. R., Eaton, W. W., & Sussman, L. (1990). Racial differences in prevalence of phobic disorders. *Journal of Nervous and Mental Disease, 178,* 434–441.

Brown, P., & Levinson, S. (1978). Universals in language usage: Politeness phenomena. In E. Goody (Ed.), *Questions and politeness* (pp. 56–289). Cambridge: Cambridge University Press.

Buchwald, D. S., Beals, J., & Manson, S. M. (2000). Use of traditional healing among Native Americans in a primary care setting. *Medical Care, 38,* 1191–1199.

Butcher, J. N., Dahlstrom, W. G., Graham, J. R., Tellegen, A. M., & Kaemmer, B. (1989). *Minnesota Multiphasic Personality Inventory-2 (MMPI-2): Manual for administration and scoring.* Minneapolis: University of Minnesota Press.

Cain, V., & Kington, R. S. (2003). Investigating the role of racial/ethnic bias in health outcomes. *American Journal of Public Health, 93,* 191–193.

Campa, A. L. (1947). Sayings and riddles in New Mexico. *The University of New Mexico Bulletin, 15,* 5–67.

Campbell, D. T., & Stanley, J. C. (1963). *Experimental and quasi-experimental designs for research.* Chicago: Rand McNally College Publishing Company.

Carli, L. (1990). Gender, language, and influence. *Journal of Personality and Social Psychology, 59,* 941–951.

Carter, R. T. (1995). *The influence of race and racial identity in psychotherapy.* New York: Wiley.

Casas, J. M. (1984). Policy, training, and research in counseling psychology: The racial/ethnic minority perspective. In S. D. Brown and R. W. Lent (Eds.), *Handbook of Counseling Psychology* (pp. 785–831). New York: Wiley.

Cass, V. C. (1979). Homosexual identity formation: A theoretical model. *Journal of Homosexuality, 4,* 219–235.

Castellanos, J., & Gloria, A. M. (2007). Research considerations and theoretical application for best practices in higher education: Latina/os achieving success. *Journal of Hispanic Higher Education, 6,* 378–396.

CBS News Video. (1996, October 23). *O. J. in black and white.* New York: CBS News.

Cemy, J. (no date). Three letters from Teddy. Retrieved December 14, 2002, from http://ss.uno.edu/SS/TeachDevel/FeelGood/ThreeLetters.html

Chan, C. (1989). Lesbians, gay men, and their families: Common clinical issues. *Journal of Counseling and Development, 68,* 16–20.

Chan, C. (1992). Cultural considerations in counseling Asian American lesbians and gay men. In S. Dworkin & F. Gutierrez (Eds.), *Counseling gay men and lesbians: Journey to the end of the rainbow* (pp. 115–124). Alexandria, VA: American Association for Counseling and Development.

Chang, D. F. (2002). Understanding the rates and distribution of mental disorders. In D. S. Kurasaki & S. Okazaki (Eds.), *Asian American Mental Health: Assessment, Theories, and Methods* (pp. 9–27). New York: Kluwer Academic/Plenum.

Chao, M. M., Chen, J., Roisman, G. I., & Hong, Y.-Y. (2007). Essentializing race: Implications for bicultural individuals' cognition and physiological reactivity. *Psychological Science, 18,* 341–348.

Cheal (2001). Refugees and immigrants have different experiences. Available at http://www.disastertraining.org/Articles/refu

Chen, S., Sullivan, N.Y., Lu, Y. E., & Shibusawa, T. (2003) Asian Americans and mental health services: a study of utilization patterns in the 1990s. *Journal of Ethnic & Cultural Diversity in Social Work, 12,* 19–42.

Cheung, F. M. (1985). Cross-cultural consideration for the translation and adaptation of the Chinese MMPI in Hong Kong. In J. N. Butcher & C. D. Spielberger (Eds.), *Advances in personality assessment* (Vol. 4, pp. 131–158). Hillsdale, NJ: Erlbaum.

Cheung, R. K., & Snowden, L. R. (1990). Community mental health and ethnic minority populations. *Community Mental Health Journal, 26,* 277–291.

Chin, J. L., Mio, J. S., & Iwamasa, G. Y. (2006). Ethical conduct of research with Asian and Pacific Islander American populations. In J. E. Trimble & C. B. Fisher (Eds.), *The handbook of ethical research with ethnocultural populations & communities* (pp. 117–135). Thousand Oaks, CA: Sage.

Choi, I., Nisbett, R. E., & Norenzayan, A. (1999). Causal attribution across cultures: Variation and universality. *Psychological Bulletin, 125,* 47–63.

Clark, K. B., Chein, I., & Cook, S. W. (2004). The effects of segregation and the consequences of desegregation: A (September 1952) social science statement in the *Brown v. Board of Education of Topeka* Supreme Court Case. *American Psychologist, 59,* 495–501.

Clark, K. B., & Clark, M. P. (1939). The development of consciousness of self and the emergence of racial identification of Negro pre-school children. *Journal of Social Psychology, 10,* 591–599.

Clark, R., Anderson, N. B., Clark, V. R., & Williams, D. R. (1999). Racism as a stressor for African Americans: A biopsychosocial model. *American Psychologist, 54,* 805–816.

Cohen, R. J., & Swerdlik, M. E. (2002). *Psychological testing and assessment: An introduction to test and measurement* (5th ed.). Boston: McGraw-Hill.

Cohen, S., & Herbert, T. B. (1996). Health psychology: Psychological factors and physical disease from the perspective of human psychoneuroimmunology. *Annual Review of Psychology, 47,* 113–142.

Colapinto, J. (2004). Gender gap: What were the real reasons behind David Reimer's suicide? *Slate.* Retrieved June 25, 2004, from http://www.slate.msn.com/id/2101678/

Cole, M., Gay, J., Glick, J., & Sharp, D. W. (1971). *The cultural context of learning and thinking.* New York: Basic Books.

Coleman, H.L.K. (1996). Portfolio assessment of multicultural counseling competency. *The Counseling Psychologist,* 216–229.

Comas-Díaz, L. (1990). Ethnic minority mental health: Contributions and future directions of the American Psychological Association. In F. C. Serafica, A. I. Schwebel, R. K. Russell, P. D. Isaac, & L. B. Myers (Eds.), *Mental health of ethnic minorities* (pp. 275–301). New York: Praeger.

Constantine, M. G., & Ladany, N. (2001). New visions for defining and assessing multicultural counseling competence. In J. G. Ponterotto, J. M. Casas, L. A. Suzuki, & C. M. Alexander (Eds.), *Handbook of multicultural counseling* (2nd ed., pp. 482–498). Thousand Oaks, CA: Sage.

Constantine, M. G., Kindaichi, M., Okazaki, S., Gainor, K. A., & Baden, A. L. (2005). A qualitative investigation of the cultural adjustment experiences of Asian international college women. *Cultural Diversity & Ethnic Minority Psychology, 11,* 162–175.

Cook, D. A., & Helms, J. E. (1988). Visible racial/ethnic group supervisees' satisfaction with cross-cultural supervision as predicted by relationship characters. *Journal of Counseling Psychology, 35,* 268–273.

Cooper-Patrick, L., Gallo, J. J., Powe, N. R., Steinwachs, D. M., Eaton, W. W., & Ford, D. E. (1999). Mental health service utilization by African Americans and Whites: The Baltimore Epidemiologic Catchment Area follow-up. *Medical Care, 37,* 1034–1045.

Cortés, C. E. (2000). *The children are watching: How the media teach about diversity.* New York: Teachers College Press.

Corvin, S., & Wiggins, F. (1989). An antiracism training model for White professionals. *Journal of Multicultural Counseling and Development, 17,* 105–114.

Costello, E. J., Farmer, E.M.Z., & Angold, A. (1999). Same place, different children: White and American Indian children in the Appalachian Mountains. In P. Cohen, C. Slomkowski, & L. N. Robins (Eds.), *Historical and geographical influences on psychopathology* (pp. 279–298). Mahwah, NJ: Erlbaum.

Costello, E. J., Farmer, E.M.Z., Angold, A., Burns, B. J., & Erkanli, A. (1997). Psychiatric disorders among American Indian and White youth in Appalachia: The great Smoky Mountains study. *American Journal of Public Health, 87,* 827–832.

Crago, M., Shisslak, C. J., & Estes, L. S. (1996). Eating disturbances among American Minority groups: A review. *International Journal of Eating Disorders, 19,* 239–248.

Croom, G. (2000). Lesbian, gay, and bisexual People of Color: A challenge to representative sampling in empirical research. In B. Greene & G. Croom (Eds.), *Psychological perspectives on lesbian and gay issues: Vol. 5. Education, research, and practice in lesbian, gay, bisexual, and transgendered psychology: A resource manual* (pp. 263–281). Thousand Oaks, CA: Sage.

Cross, W. E. (1971). The Negro-to-Black conversion experience. *Black World, 20,* 13–27.

Cross, W. E. (1991). *Shades of Black: Diversity in African American identity.* Philadelphia: Temple University Press.

Cross, W. E. (1995). The psychology of nigrescence: Revisiting the Cross model. In J. G. Ponterotto, J. M. Casas, L. A. Suzuki, &

D. M. Alexander (Eds.), *Handbook of multicultural counseling* (pp. 93–122). Thousand Oaks, CA: Sage.

Cross, W. E., Parham, T. A., & Helms, J. E. (1991). The stages of Black identity development: Nigrescence models. In R. L. Jones (Ed.), *Black psychology* (3rd ed., pp. 319–338). Berkeley, CA: Cobb & Henry.

Cushner, K., & Brislin, R. W. (1996). *Intercultural interactions: A practical guide* (2nd ed.). Thousand Oaks, CA: Sage.

Dana, R. H. (1993). *Multicultural assessment perspectives for professional psychology.* Needham Heights, MA: Allyn & Bacon.

D'Andrea, M. (2003). Expanding our understanding of White racism and resistance to change in the fields of counseling and psychology. In J. S. Mio & G. Y. Iwamasa (Eds.), *Culturally diverse mental health: The challenges of research and resistance* (pp. 17–37). New York: Brunner-Routledge.

Darwin, C. (1859). *On the origin of species by means of natural selection.* London: Murray.

David Reimer, 38, subject of the John/Joan case, dies. (2004, May 12). *New York Times.* Retrieved June 25, 2004, from http://www.nytimes.com/2004/05/12/international/americas/12REIM.html

Davis, C., & Yager, J. (1992). Transcultural aspects of eating disorders: A critical literature review: *Culture, Medicine, and Psychiatry, 16,* 377–394.

DeBruyn, L. M., Hymbaugh, K., & Valdez, N. (1988). Helping communities address suicide and violence: The special initiatives team of the Indian Health Service. *American Indian and Alaska Native Mental Health Research, 1,* 56–65.

Dempsey, D., Hillier, L., & Harrison, L. (2001). Gendered explorations among same-sex attracted young people in Australia. *Journal of Adolescence, 24,* 67–81.

Denzin, N. K., & Lincoln, Y. (Eds.). (2007a). *Collecting and interpreting qualitative materials* (3rd ed.). Thousand Oaks, CA: Sage.

Denzin, N. K., & Lincoln, Y. (Eds.). (2007b). *Strategies of qualitative inquiry* (3rd ed.). Thousand Oaks, CA: Sage.

Deters, K. A. (1997). Belonging nowhere and everywhere: Multiracial identity development. *Bulletin of the Menninger Clinic, 61,* 368–385.

Devos, T. (2006). Implicit bicultural identity among Mexican American and Asian American college students. *Cultural Diversity & Ethnic Minority Psychology, 12,* 381–402.

Diala, C., Muntaner, C., Walrath, C., Nickerson, K. J., LaVeist, T. A., & Leaf, P. J. (2000). Racial differences in attitudes toward professional mental health care and in the use of services. *American Journal of Orthopsychiatry, 70,* 455–464.

Diamond, J. (1997). *Guns, germs, and steel: The fates of human societies.* New York: W. W. Norton.

Dolan, B. (1991). Cross-cultural aspects of anorexia nervosa and bulimia: A review. *International Journal of Eating Disorders, 10,* 67–78.

Dolphin, C. Z. (1999). Variables in the use of personal space in intercultural transactions. In L. A. Samovar & R. E. Porter (Eds.), *Intercultural communication: A reader* (8th ed., pp. 266–276). Belmont, CA: Wadsworth.

Dorfman, D. D. (1978). The Cyril Burt question: New findings. *Science, 201,* 1177–1186.

Dovidio, J. F. (2001, January). *Why can't we get along?: Interpersonal biases and interracial distrust.* Invited address delivered at The National Multicultural Conference and Summit II, Santa Barbara, CA.

Dovidio, J. F., & Gaertner, S. L. (2000). Aversive racism and selection decisions: 1989 and 1999. *Psychological Science, 11,* 319–323.

Duckitt, J. H. (1992). Psychology and prejudice: A historical analysis and integrative framework. *American Psychologist, 47,* 1182–1193.

Duran, E. (2006). *Healing the soul wound: Counseling with American Indian and other native peoples.* New York: Teachers College Press.

Dworkin, S. (2000). Individual therapy with lesbian, gay, and bisexual clients. In R. Perez, K. DeBord, & K. Bieschke (Eds.), *Handbook of counseling and psychotherapy with lesbian, gay, and bisexual clients* (pp. 157–181).

Washington, DC: American Psychological Association.

Dworkin, S. (2001). Treating the bisexual client. *Journal of Clinical Psychology, 57,* 671–680.

Edwards, K. (2003). Increasing cultural competence and decreasing disparities in health (an editorial). *Journal of Cultural Diversity, 10,* 111–113.

Edwards, W. V., & Erwin-Johnson, C. (2003). NAACP to focus on minority health disparities. *Crisis (The New), 110,* 54–56.

Ekman, P. (1972). Universal and cultural differences in facial expression of emotion. In J. R. Cole (Ed.), *Nebraska symposium on motivation, 1971* (pp. 207–283). Lincoln: University of Nebraska Press.

Elliot, S., Scott, M. D., Jensen, A. D., & McDonough, M. (1982). Perceptions of reticence: A cross-cultural investigation. In M. Burgoon (Ed.), *Communication yearbook 5* (pp. 591–602). New Brunswick, NJ: Transaction Books.

Elliott, J. (2005). *Using narrative in social research: Qualitative and quantitative approaches.* Thousand Oaks, CA: Sage.

Engel, G. L. (1977). The need for a new medical model: A challenge for biomedicine. *Science, 196,* 129–136.

Enns, C. Z. (1997). *Feminist theories and feminist psychotherapies.* New York: Harrington Park.

Erikson, E. H. (1950/1963). *Childhood and society* (2nd ed.). New York: Norton.

Erikson, E. H. (1964). *Insight and responsibility.* New York: Norton.

Eron, L. D. (2000). A psychological perspective. In V. B. Van Hasselt & M. Hersen (Eds.), *Aggression and violence: An introductory text* (pp. 23–39). Needham Heights, MA: Allyn & Bacon.

Eron, L. D., Huessman, L. R., Lefkowitz, M. M., & Walder, L. O. (1996). Does television violence cause aggression? In D. F. Greenberg (Ed.), *Criminal careers: Vol. 2. The international library of criminology, criminal justice and penology* (pp. 311–321). Brookfield, VT: Dartmouth Publishing.

Eron, L. D., Walder, L. O., & Lefkowitz, M. M. (1971). *The learning of aggression in children.* Boston: Little, Brown.

Falicov, C. J. (1996). Mexican families. In M. McGoldrick, J. Giordano, & J. K. Pearce (Eds.), *Ethnicity and family therapy* (2nd ed., pp. 169–182). New York: Guilford.

Falicov, C. J. (1998). *Latino families in therapy: A guide to multicultural practice.* New York: Guilford.

Fernandez, K., Boccaccini, M. T., & Noland, R. M. (2007). Professionally responsible test selection for Spanish-speaking clients: A four-step approach for identifying and selecting translated tests. *Professional Psychology: Research and Practice, 38,* 363–374.

Festinger, L. (1957). *A theory of cognitive dissonance.* Stanford, CA: Stanford University Press.

Fish, J. M. (2002). A scientific approach to understanding race and intelligence. In J. J. Fish (Ed.), *Race and intelligence: Separating science from myth* (pp. 1–28). Mahwah, NJ: Erlbaum.

Fitzgibbon, M. L., Spring. B., & Avellone, M. E. (1998). Correlates of binge eating in Hispanic, Black, and White women. *International Journal of Eating Disorders, 24,* 43–52.

Flaskerud, J. J., & Hu, L. T. (1992). Relationship of ethnicity to psychiatric diagnosis. *Journal of Nervous and Mental Disease, 180,* 296–303.

Flaskerud, J. J., & Liu, P. Y. (1990). Influence of therapist ethnicity and language on therapy outcome of Southeast Asian clients. *International Journal of Social Psychiatry, 36,* 18–29.

Fortson, R., & Larson, C. (1968). The dynamics of space. An experimental study in proxemic behavior among Latin Americans and North Americans. *Journal of Communication,* 109–116.

Fox, R. (1996). Bisexuality in perspective: A review of theory and research. In B. Firestein (Ed.), *Bisexuality: The psychology and politics of an invisible minority* (pp. 263–291). Thousand Oaks, CA: Sage.

Freedheim, D. K. (Ed.). (2003). *Handbook of psychology: Vol. 1. History of psychology,* in I. B. Weiner (Editor-in-Chief), *Handbook of psychology.* New York: Wiley.

Frequently asked questions about accreditation in psychology. (2004). Washington, DC: American

Psychological Association. Retrieved July 12, 2004, from http://www.apa.org/ed/accreditation/accrfaq.html

Fujino, D. C., Okazaki, S., & Young, K. (1994). Asian-American women in the mental health system: An examination of ethnic and gender match between therapist and client. *Journal of Community Psychology, 22,* 164–176.

Gaertner, S. L., & Dovidio, J. F. (1986). The aversive form of racism. In J. F. Dovidio & S. L. Gaertner (Eds.), *Prejudice, discrimination and racism* (pp. 61–90). Orlando, FL: Academic Press.

Galton, F. (1883). *Inquiries into human faculty and its development.* London: Macmillan.

Garcia-Preto, N. (1996). Latino families: An overview. In M. McGoldrick, J. Giordano, & J. K. Pearce (Eds.), *Ethnicity and family therapy* (2nd ed., pp. 141–154). New York: Guilford.

Gardner, H. (1983). *Frames of mind: The theory of multiple intelligences.* New York: Basic Books.

Gardner, H. (1993). *Multiple intelligences: The theory in practice.* New York: Basic Books.

Gardner, H. (1999). *Intelligence reframed.* New York: Basic Books.

Garfield, J. C., Weiss, S. L., & Pollack, E. A. (1973). Effects of the child's social class on school counselors' decision making. *Journal of Counseling Psychology, 20,* 166–168.

Garwick, A., & Auger, S. (2000). What do providers need to know about American Indian culture? Recommendations from urban Indian family caregivers. *Families, Systems & Health, 18,* 177–190.

Georgaca, E. (2001). Rethinking qualitative methodology in psychology [Review of the book *The quality of qualitative research*]. *Contemporary Psychology: APA Review of Books, 46,* 268–270.

Gillie, D. (1977). The IQ question. *Phi Delta Kappan, 58,* 469.

Gilligan, C. (1982/1993). *In a different voice: Psychological theory and women's development.* Cambridge, MA: Harvard University Press.

Goldman, M. (1980). Effect of eye contact and distance on the verbal reinforcement of attitude. *Journal of Social Psychology, 111,* 73–78.

Goldstein, E. B. (2005). *Cognitive psychology: Connecting mind, research, and everyday experience.* Belmont, CA: Wadsworth.

Gonsiorek, J. (1993). Mental health issues of gay and lesbian adolescents. In L. Garnets & D. Kimmel (Eds.), *Psychological perspectives on lesbian and gay male experiences* (pp. 469–485). New York: Columbia University Press.

Goodgame, D., & Tumulty, K. (2002, December 22). Tripped up by history. G.O.P. leader Trent Lott's remarks on race raise a storm and a hot question: Have Republicans really outgrown their past? *Time,* pp. 22–30.

Gordon, M. M. (1964). *Assimilation in American life.* New York: Oxford University Press.

Gould, S. J. (1996). *The mismeasure of man.* New York: Norton.

Grabois, H. (1999). The convergence of sociocultural theory and cognitive linguistics: Lexical semantics and the L2 acquisition of love, fear and happiness. In G. B. Palmer & D. J. Occhi (Eds.), *Languages of sentiment: Cultural constructions of emotional substrates* (pp. 201–233). Amsterdam: John Benjamins.

Gray, J. J., Ford, K., & Kelly, L. M. (1987). The prevalence of bulimia in a Black college population. *International Journal of Eating Disorders, 6,* 733–740.

Grbich, C. (2007). *Qualitative data analysis: An introduction.* Thousand Oaks, CA: Sage.

Green, R. J. Bettinger, M., & Zacks, E. (1996). Are lesbian couples fused and gay male couples disengaged? Questioning gender straightjackets. In J. Laird & R. J. Green (Eds.), *Lesbians and gays in couples and families* (pp. 185–230). San Francisco: Jossey-Bass.

Greene, B. (1997). Ethnic minority lesbians and gay men: Mental health treatment issues. In B. Greene (Ed.), *Psychological perspectives on lesbian and gay issues: Vol. 3. Ethnic and cultural diversity among lesbians and gay men* (pp. 216–239). Thousand Oaks, CA: Sage.

Greene, B., & Boyd-Franklin, N. (1996). African American lesbian couples: Ethnocultural considerations in psychotherapy. *Women and Therapy, 19. Special Issue. Couples Therapy: Feminist Perspectives,* 49–60.

Greenson, R. R. (1967). *The technique and practice of psychoanalysis,* (Vol. 1). New York: International Universities Press.

Grice, H. P. (1975). Logic and conversation. In P. Cole & J. L. Morgan (Eds.), *Syntax and semantics: Vol. 3. Speech acts* (pp. 41–58). New York: Seminar Press.

Grieco, E. M., & Cassidy, R. C. (2001). *Overview of race and Hispanic origin: 2000.* U.S. Census Bureau. Retrieved October 13, 2003, from www.census.gov/prod/2001pubs/C2kbr01-1.pdf.

Grills, C. (2002). African-centered psychology: Basic principles. In T. A. Parham (Ed.), *Counseling persons of African descent: Raising the bar of practitioner competence* (pp. 10–24). Thousand Oaks, CA: Sage.

Guthrie, R. V. (1998). *Even the rat was white: A historical view of psychology.* Boston: Allyn & Bacon.

Haddon, A. C. (1910). *History of anthropology.* New York: Putnam.

Hall, C.C.I. (1980). *The ethnic identity of racially mixed people: A study of Black-Japanese.* Unpublished doctoral dissertation, University of California, Los Angeles.

Hall, C.C.I. (1992). Please choose one: Ethnic identity choices for biracial individuals. In M.P.P. Root (Ed.), *Racially mixed people in America* (pp. 250–264). Newbury Park, CA: Sage.

Hall, E. T. (1963). A system for the notation of proxemic behavior. *American Anthropologist, 65,* 1003–1026.

Hall, E. T. (1966). *The hidden dimension.* Garden City, NY: Doubleday.

Hall, E. T. (1976). *Beyond culture: Into the cultural unconscious.* New York: Anchor.

Hall, E. T. (1999). Context and meaning. In L. A. Samovar & R. E. Porter (Eds.), *Intercultural communication: A reader* (8th ed., pp. 45–54). Belmont, CA: Wadsworth.

Hall, G.C.N., & Barongan, C. (2002). *Multicultural psychology.* Upper Saddle River, NJ: Prentice Hall.

Hall, G.C.N., & Okazaki, S. (Eds.). (2002). *Asian American psychology: The science of lives in context.* Washington, DC: American Psychological Association.

Halpern, D. F., Benbow, C. P., Geary, D. C., Gur, R. C., Hyde, J. S., & Gernsbacher, M. A. (2007). The science of sex differences in science and mathematics. *Psychological Science in the Public Interest, 8* (whole issue).

Hamilton, D. L. (1981). *Cognitive processes in stereotyping and intergroup behavior.* Hillsdale, NJ: Erlbaum.

Hamilton, D. L., Dugan, P. M., & Trolier, T. K. (1985). The formation of stereotypic beliefs: Further evidence for distinctiveness-based illusory correlations. *Journal of Personality and Social Psychology, 48,* 5–17.

Hamilton, D. L., & Gifford, R. K. (1976). Illusory correlation in interpersonal perception: A cognitive basis of stereotypic judgments. *Journal of Experimental Social Psychology, 12,* 392–407.

Hamilton, D. L., & Rose, T. L. (1980). Illusory correlation and the maintenance of stereotypic beliefs. *Journal of Personality and Social Psychology, 39,* 832–845.

Hamilton, D. L., & Sherman, J. W. (1989). Illusory correlations: Implications for a stereotype theory and research. In D. Bar-Tal, C. F. Graumann, A. W. Kruglanski, & W. Stroebe (Eds.), *Stereotyping and prejudice: Changing conceptions* (pp. 59–82). New York: Springer-Verlag.

Hamilton, D. L., & Sherman, J. W. (1994). Stereotypes. In R. S. Wyer, Jr., & T. K. Srull (Eds.), *Handbook of social cognition* (2nd ed.). Hillsdale, NJ: Erlbaum.

Hamilton, D. L., & Sherman, J. W. (1996). Perceiving persons and groups. *Psychological Review, 103,* 336–355.

Hamilton, D. L., & Trolier, T. K. (1986). Stereotypes and stereotyping: An overview of the cognitive approach. In J. F. Dovidio & S. L. Gaertner (Eds.), *Prejudice, discrimination, and racism* (pp. 127–163). Orlando, FL: Academic Press.

Hancock, K. A. (2003). Lesbian, gay, and bisexual psychology: Past, present, and future directions. In J. S. Mio & G. Y. Iwamasa (Eds.), *Culturally diverse mental health: The challenges of research and resistance* (pp. 289–307). New York: Brunner-Routledge.

Harrell, S. P. (1995, August). *Dynamics of difference: Personal and sociocultural dimensions of Intergroup relations*. Paper presented at the 103rd Annual Convention of the American Psychological Association, New York.

Harris, S. M. (1994). Racial differences in predictors of college women's body image attitudes. *Women and Health, 21,* 89–103.

Hathaway, S. R., & McKinley, J. C. (1967). *MMPI manual* (Rev. ed.). New York: Psychological Corporation.

Hayes, P. A. (1996). Culturally responsive assessment with diverse older clients. *Professional Psychology: Research and Practice, 27,* 188–193.

Heeringa, S. G., Wagner, J., Torres, M., Duan, N., Adams, T., & Berglund, P. (2004). Sample designs and sampling methods for the Collaborative Psychiatric Epidemiology Studies (CPES). *International Journal of Methods in Psychiatric Research, 13,* 221–240.

Helms, J. E. (1984). Toward a theoretical explanation of the effects of race on counseling: A Black and White model. *The Counseling Psychologist, 13,* 695–710.

Helms, J. E. (1985). Cultural identity in the treatment process. In P. Pedersen (Ed.), *Handbook of cross-cultural counseling and therapy* (pp. 239–245). Westport, CT: Greenwood.

Helms, J. E. (1989). Considering some method-ological issues in racial identity research. *The Counseling Psychologist, 17,* 227–252.

Helms, J. E. (1990). *Black and white racial identity: Theory, research, and practice*. Westport, CT: Praeger.

Helms, J. E. (1992). *A race is a nice thing to have: A guide to being a White person or understanding the White persons in your life*. Topeka, KS: Content Communications.

Helms, J. E. (1995a). Why is there no study of cultural equivalence in standardized cognitive ability testing? In N. R. Goldberger & J. B. Veroff (Eds.), *The culture and psychology reader* (pp. 674–719). New York: New York University Press.

Helms, J. E. (1995b). An update of Helms's White and people of color racial identity models. In J. G. Ponterotto, J. M. Casas, L. A. Suzuki, & D. M. Alexander (Eds.), *Handbook of multicultural counseling* (pp. 181–198). Thousand Oaks, CA: Sage.

Helms, J. E. (2001). Life issues. In J. G. Ponterotto, J. M. Casas, L. A. Suzuki, & C. M. Alexander (Eds.), *Handbook of multicultural counseling* (2nd ed., pp. 22–29). Thousand Oaks, CA: Sage.

Helms, J. E., & Cook, D. A. (1999). *Using race and culture in counseling and psychotherapy: Theory and process*. Needham Heights, MA: Allyn & Bacon.

Helms, J. E., & Talleyrand, R. M. (1997). Race is not ethnicity. *American Psychologist, 52,* 1246–1247.

Henkel, K. E., Dovidio, J. F., & Gaertner, S. L. (2006). Institutional discrimination, individual racism, and Hurricane Katrina. *Analyses of Social Issues and Public Policy, 6,* 99–124.

Herek, G. (1995). Psychological heterosexism in the United States. In A. D'Augelli & C. Patterson (Eds.), *Lesbian, gay, and bisexual identities over the life span: Psychological perspectives* (pp. 321–346). New York: Oxford University Press.

Herek, G. (2000). The psychology of sexual prejudice. *Current Directions in Psychological Science, 9,* 19–22.

Hernstein, R., & Murray, C. (1994). *The bell curve: Intelligence and class structure in American life*. New York: Free Press.

Herring, R. D. (1995). Developing biracial ethnic identity: A review of the increasing dilemma. *Journal of Multicultural Counseling & Development, 23,* 29–39.

Herring, R. D. (1999). *Counseling with Native American Indians and Alaska Natives:*

Strategies for helping professionals. Thousand Oaks, CA: Sage.

Hesse-Biber, S. N., & Leavy, P. (Eds.). (2003). *Approaches to qualitative research: A reader on theory and practice.* London: Oxford University Press.

Hesse-Biber, S. N., & Yaiser, M. (Eds.). (2003). *Feminist perspectives on social research.* London: Oxford University Press.

Hill, C. E., Thompson, B. J., & Williams, E. N. (1997). A guide to conducting consensual qualitative research. *The Counseling Psychologist, 25,* 517–572.

Hilliard, K. M., & Iwamasa, G. Y. (2001). Japanese American older adults' conceptualization of anxiety. *Journal of Clinical Geropsychology, 7,* 53–65.

Ho, M. K. (1987). *Family therapy with ethnic minorities.* Newbury Park, CA: Sage.

Hoffman, L. (1981). *Foundations of family therapy.* New York: Basic Books.

Hofstede, G. (1980). *Culture's consequences.* Beverly Hills, CA: Sage.

Holliday, B. G., & Holmes, A. L. (2003). A tale of challenge and change: A history and chronology of ethnic minorities in psychology in the United States. In G. Bernal, J. E. Trimble, A. K. Burlew, and F.T.L. Leong (Eds.), *Handbook of Racial and Ethnic Minority Psychology* (pp. 15–64). Thousand Oaks, CA: Sage Publications.

Hong, G. K. (1989). Application of cultural and environmental issues in family therapy with immigrant Chinese Americans. *Journal of Strategic and Systemic Therapies, 8,* 14–21.

Hong, G. K., & Ham, M. D.-C. (2001). *Psychotherapy and counseling with Asian American clients: A practical guide.* Thousand Oaks, CA: Sage.

Horwitz, A. V. (1987). Help-seeking processes and mental health services. In D. Mechanic (Ed.), *Improving mental health services: What the social sciences can tell us. New Directions for Mental Health Services* (No. 36). San Francisco: Jossey-Bass.

Hoshmand, L.L.T. (1994). *Orientation to inquiry in a reflective professional psychology.* Albany: State University of New York Press.

Hovey, J. D. (2000). Acculturative stress, depression, and suicidal ideation in Mexican immigrants. *Cultural Diversity and Ethnic Minority Psychology, 6,* 134–151.

Hsu, L. K. (1987). Are eating disorders becoming more common among Blacks? *International Journal of Eating Disorders, 6,* 113–124.

http://census.gov/prod/cen2000/dpi/2kh00.pdf. Retrieved September 25, 2004, from Internet.

http://imateacher.itgo/three.htm. Retrieved December 14, 2002, from Internet.

http://www.dof.ca/gov/HTML/DEMOGRAP/E-1table.xls. Retrieved October 6, 2004, from Internet.

http://www.geocities.com/cubscoutpack501/WhyBeALeader.htm. Retrieved December 14, 2002, from Internet.

http://www.hcc.hawaii.edu/intranet.committees/FacDevCom/guidebk/teachtip/m-files/m-3/lette.htm. Retrieved December 14, 2002, from Internet.

http://www.k12.wa.us/conferences/ospi2001/GomezPresentation/tsld001.htm. Retrieved December 14, 2002, from Internet.

Hunt, J. S., Armenta, B. E., & Seifert, A. L. (in press). Katrina in my community. *Psychological Science.*

Hunt, J. S., Seifert, A. L., Armenta, B. E., & Snowden, J. L. (2006). Stereotypes and prejudice as dynamic constructs: Reminders about the nature of intergroup bias from the Hurricane Katrina relief efforts. *Analysis of Social Issues and Public Policy, 6,* 237–253.

Isajiw, W. W. (1990). Ethnic-identity retention. In R. Breton, W. W. Isajiw, W. E. Kalbach, & J. G. Reitz (Eds.), *Ethnic identity and equality* (pp. 34–91). Toronto: University of Toronto Press.

Israel, T. (2004). What counselors need to know about working with sexual minority clients. In D. R. Atkinson & G. Hackett (Eds.), *Counseling diverse populations* (3rd ed., pp. 347–364). Boston: McGraw-Hill.

Iwamasa, G. Y., & Bangi, A. K. (2003). Women's mental health research: History, current status, and future directions. In J. S. Mio & G. Y. Iwamasa (Eds.), *Culturally diverse mental health: The challenges of research and resistance* (pp. 251–268). New York: Brunner-Routledge.

Iwamasa, G. Y., & Sorocco, K. H. (2002). Aging and Asian Americans: Developing culturally appropriate research methodology. In G.C.N. Hall & S. Okazaki (Eds.), *Asian American psychology: The science of lives in context* (pp. 105–130). Washington, DC: American Psychological Association.

Jacobs, J. H. (1992). Identity development in biracial children. In M.P.P. Root (Ed.), *Racially mixed people in America* (pp. 190–206). Newbury Park, CA: Sage.

Jahoda, G. (1982). *Psychology and anthropology: A psychological perspective.* London: Academic Press.

James, S. A. (2003). Confronting the moral economy of US racial/ethnic health disparities. *American Journal of Public Health, 93,* 189.

Jendrek, M. P. (1994). Grandparents who parent their grandchildren: Circumstances and decisions. *The Gerontologist, 34,* 206–216.

Johnson, D. J. (1992). Developmental pathways: Toward an ecological theoretical formulation of race identity in Black-White biracial children. In M.P.P. Root (Ed.), *Racially mixed people in America* (pp. 37–49). Newbury Park, CA: Sage.

Johnson, D. (1994). Stress, depression, substance abuse, and racism. *American Indian and Alaska Native Mental Health Research, 6,* 29–33.

Johnson, E. P. (1995). SNAP! culture: A different kind of "reading." *Text and Performance Quarterly, 15,* 122–143.

Jones, E. E. (1978). Effects of race on psychotherapy process and outcome: An exploratory investigation. *Psychotherapy: Theory, Research, and Practice, 15,* 226–236.

Jones, E. E. (1982). Psychotherapists' impressions of treatment outcome as a function of race. *Clinical Psychology, 38,* 722–731.

Jones, J. (1993). The concept of race in social psychology. In L. Wheler & P. Shaver (Eds.), *Review of personality and social psychology* (Vol. 4, pp. 117–150). Newbury Park, CA: Sage.

Jones, J. M. (1997). *Prejudice and racism* (2nd ed.). New York: McGraw-Hill.

Jones, R. L. (Ed.). (1998). *African American mental health.* Hampton, VA: Cobb & Henry.

Jones, S. E. (1994). *The right touch: Understanding and using the language of physical contact.* Cresskill, NJ: Hampton Press.

Kamin, L. (1974). *The science and politics of IQ.* Potomac, MD: Erlbaum.

Karlsson, R. (2005). Ethnic matching between therapist and patient in psychotherapy: An overview of findings, together with methodological and conceptual issues. *Cultural Diversity & Ethnic Minority Psychology, 11,* 113–129.

Kaslow, F. W. (Ed.). (1996). *Handbook of relational diagnosis and dysfunctional family patterns.* Oxford, England: Wiley.

Katriel, T. (1986). *Talking straight: Dugri speech in Israeli Sabra culture.* Cambridge: Cambridge University Press.

Keefe, S. E. (1982). Help-seeking behavior among foreign-born and native-born Mexican Americans. *Social Science and Medicine, 16,* 1467–1472.

Keel, P. K., & Klump, K. L. (2003). Are eating disorders culture-bound syndromes? Implications for conceptualizing their etiology. *Psychological Bulletin, 129,* 747–770.

Keerdoja, E. (1984, November 19). Children of the rainbow: New parent support groups help interracial kids cope. *Newsweek,* pp. 120–122.

Keller, M. D., Beardslee, W. R., Dorrer, D. J., Lavori, P. W., Samuelson, H., & Klerman, G. R. (1986). Impact of severity and chronicity of parental affective illness on adaptive functioning and psychopathology in children. *Archives of General Psychiatry, 43,* 930–937.

Kelly, H. H. (1967). Attribution theory in social psychology. In D. Levine (Ed.), *Nebraska symposium on motivation* (Vol. 15, pp. 192–240). Lincoln: University of Nebraska Press.

Kelly, H. H. (1973). The process of causal attribution. *American Psychologist, 28,* 107–128.

Kerwin, C., & Ponterotto, J. G. (1995). Biracial identity development: Theory and research. In J. G. Ponterotto, J. M. Casas, L. S. Suzuki, & C. M. Alexander (Eds.), *Handbook of multicultural counseling* (pp. 199–217). Thousand Oaks, CA: Sage.

Kessler, R. C., Berglund, P.A., Zhao, S., Leaf, P. J., Kouzis, A. C., Bruce, M. L., Freidman, R. L., Grosser, R. C., Kennedy, C., Narrow, W. E., Keuhnel, T. G., Laska, E. M., Manderscheid, R. W., Rosenheck, R. A., Santoni, T. W., & Schneier, M. (1996). The 12-month prevalence and correlates of serious mental illness (SMI). In R. W. Manderscheid & M. A. Sonnenschein (Eds.), *Mental health, United States* (Pub. No. [SMA] 96-3098). Rockville, MD: Center for Mental Health Services.

Kessler, R. C., McGonagle, K. A., Swartz, M., Blazer, D. G., & Nelson, C. B. (1993). Sex and depression in the National Comorbidity Survey I: Lifetime prevalence of *DSM-III-R* psychiatric disorders in the United States: Results from the National Comorbidity Survey. *Archives of General Psychiatry, 51,* 8–19.

Kessler, R. C., McGonagle, K. A., Zhao, S., Nelson, C. B., Hughes, M., Eshelman, S., Wittchen, H. U., & Kendler, K. S. (1994). Lifetime and 12-month prevalence of *DSM-III-R* psychiatric disorders in the United States: Results from the National Comorbidity Survey. *Archives of General Psychiatry, 51,* 8–19.

Kich, G. K. (1992). The developmental process of asserting a biracial, bicultural identity. In M.P.P. Root (Ed.), *Racially mixed people in America* (pp. 304–317). Newbury Park, CA: Sage.

Kim, S. C. (1997). Korean American families. In E. Lee (Ed.), *Working with Asians: A guide for clinicians* (pp. 125–135). New York: Guilford.

Kim, U., & Berry, J. W. (1993). *Indigenous psychologies: Experience and research in cultural context.* Newbury Park, CA: Sage.

Kim, U., & Park, Y.-S. (2006). The scientific foundation of indigenous and cultural psychology: The transactional approach. In U. Kim, K.-S. Yang, & K.-K. Hwang (Eds.), *Indigenous and cultural psychology: Understanding people in context* (pp. 27–48). New York: Springer.

Kim, U., Yang, K.-S., & Hwang, K.-K. (2006). Contributions to indigenous and cultural psychology: Understanding people in context. In U. Kim, K.-S. Yang, & K.-K. Hwang (Eds.), *Indigenous and cultural psychology: Understanding people in context* (pp. 3–25). New York: Springer.

Kinzie, D. J., Boehnlein, J. K., Leung, P. K., Moore, L. J., Riley, C., & Smith, D. (1990). The prevalence of posttraumatic stress disorder and its clinical significance among Southeast Asian refugees. *American Journal of Psychiatry, 147,* 913–917.

Kitano, H.H.L. (1982). Mental health in the Japanese American community. In E. E. Jones & S. J. Korchin (Eds.), *Minority mental health* (pp. 149–164). New York: Praeger.

Kitano, H.H.L. (1999). *Race relations* (5th ed.). Upper Saddle River, NJ: Prentice Hall.

Kitayama, S., & Markus, H. R. (1999). Yin and yang of the Japanese self: The cultural psychology of personality coherence. In D. Cervone & Y. Shoda (Eds.), *The coherence of personality: Social-cognitive bases of consistency, variability, and organization* (pp. 242–302). New York: Guilford.

Kitayama, S., & Markus, H. R. (2000). The pursuit of happiness and the realization of sympathy: Cultural patterns of self, social relations, and well-being. In E. Diener & E. M. Suh (Eds.), *Culture and subjective well-being* (pp. 113–161). Cambridge, MA: MIT Press.

Kitayama, S., Markus, H. R., Matsumoto, H., & Norasakkunkit, V. (1997). Individual and collective processes in the construction of the self: Self-enhancement in the United States and self-criticism in Japan. *Journal of Personality and Social Psychology, 72,* 1245–1267.

Kitayama, S., Snibbe, A. C., Markus, H. R., & Suzuki, T. (2004). Is there any "free choice? Self and dissonance in two cultures. *Psychological Science, 15,* 527–533.

Kitayama, S., & Uchida, Y. (2003). Explicit self-criticism and implicit self-regard: Evaluating self and friend in two cultures. *Journal of Experimental Social Psychology, 39,* 476–482.

Kivel, P. (1996). *Uprooting racism: How White people can work for racial justice.* Philadelphia: New Society.

Kliman, J. (2005). Many differences, many voices: Toward social justice in family therapy. In M. Pravder, K. L. Suyemoto, & B. F. Okun (Eds.), *Psychotherapy with women* (pp. 42–63). New York: Guilford.

Kluckhohn, F. R., & Strodtbeck, F. L. (1961). *Variations in value orientations.* Evanston, IL: Row, Patterson, & Co.

Kohlberg, L. (1966). A cognitive developmental analysis of children's sex-role concepts and attitudes. In E. Maccoby (Ed.), *The development of sex differences* (pp. 82–172). Palo Alto, CA: Stanford University Press.

Kohlberg, L. (1968). The child as a moral philosopher. *Psychology Today, 2,* 25–30.

Kohlberg, L. (1976). Moral stage and moralization. In T. Lickona (Ed.), *Moral Development and Behavior* (p. 31–53). New York: Holt.

Korchin, S. J. (1980). Clinical psychology and minority problems. *American Psychologist, 35,* 262–269.

Korman, M. (1974). National conference on levels and patterns of professional training in psychology. *American Psychologist, 29,* 441–449.

Koss, M. P., Goodman, L. A., Browne, A., Fitzgerald, L. F., Keita, G. P., & Russo, N. F. (1994). *No safe haven: Male violence against women at home, at work, and in the community.* Washington, DC: American Psychological Association.

Krashen, S., Long, M., & Scarcella, R. (1982). Age, rate, and eventual attainment in second language acquisition. In S. Krashen, R. Scarcella, & M. Long (Eds.), *Child–adult differences in second language acquisition* (pp. 161–172). Rowley, MA: Newbury Press.

Krate, R., Leventhal, G., & Silverstein, B. (1974). Self-perceived transformation of the Negro-to-Black identity. *Psychological Reports, 35,* 1071–1075.

Kroeber, A. L., & Kluckhohn, C. (1952). *Culture: A critical review of concepts and definitions.* New York: Vintage Books.

Kumanyika, S. K., Morssink, C. B., & Nestle, M. (2001). Minority women and advocacy for women's health. *American Journal of Public Health, 91,* 1383–1389.

Kurdek, L. (1995). Lesbian and gay couples. In A. D'Augelli & C. Patterson (Eds.), *Lesbian, gay, and bisexual identities over the life span: Psychological perspectives* (pp. 243–261). New York: Oxford University Press.

Kwan, K. K.-L. (2001). Models of racial and ethnic identity development: Delineation of practice implications. *Journal of Mental Health Counseling, 23,* 269–278.

Labouvie-Vief, G. (1985). Intelligence and cognition. In J. E. Birren & K. W. Schaie (Eds.), *Handbook of the psychology of aging* (2nd ed., pp. 500–530). New York: Van Nostrand Reinhold.

LaFramboise, T. D., Berman, J. S., & Sohi, B. K. (1994). American Indian women. In L. Comas-Díaz & B. Greene (Eds.), *Women of color: Integrating ethnic and gender identities in psychotherapy* (pp. 30–71). New York: Guilford.

LaFramboise, T. D., Coleman, H.L.K., & Gerton, J. (1993). Psychological impact of biculturalism: Evidence and theory. *Psychological Bulletin, 114,* 395–412.

LaFrance, M., & Mayo, C. (1976). Racial differences in gaze behavior during conversations: Two systematic observational studies. *Journal of Personality and Social Psychology, 33,* 547–552.

Lakoff, R. (1975). Language and women's place. New York: Harper & Row.

Lambert, W. E. (1967). A social psychology of bilingualism. *Journal of Social Issues,* 91–109.

Lambert, W. E. (1977). The effects of bilingualism on the individual: Cognitive and sociocultural consequences. In P. A. Hornby (Ed.), *Bilingualism: Psychological, social and educational implications* (pp. 15–27). New York: Academic Press.

Lambert, W. E. (1980). The social psychology of language: A perspective for the 1980s. In H. Giles, W. Robinson, & P. Smith (Eds.), *Language: Social psychological perspectives* (pp. 415–424). Oxford: Pergamon.

Lambert, W. E., & Anisfeld, E. (1969). A note on the relationship of bilingualism and intelligence. *Canadian Journal of Behavioral Science, 1*, 123–128.

Landrine, H., Klonoff, E. A., & Brown-Collins, A. (1995). Cultural diversity and methodology in feminist psychology: Critique, proposal, empirical example. In H. Landrine (Ed.), *Bringing cultural diversity to feminist psychology: Theory, research, and practice.* (pp. 55–75). Washington, DC: American Psychological Association.

Late, M. (2003). Many Americans unaware of racial, ethnic health disparities. *Nation's Health, 33*, 6–12.

Latter, B. (1980). Genetic differences within and between populations of the major human subgroups. *The American Naturalist, 116*, 220–237.

Lebra, T. S. (1976). *Japanese patterns of behavior.* Honolulu: The University Press of Hawaii.

Lee, E. (Ed.). (1997). *Working with Asian Americans: A guide for clinicians.* New York: Guilford.

Lee, M. W. (Producer and Director). (1994). *The color of fear* [Film]. (Available from Stir-Fry Productions, 1222 Preservation Park Way, Oakland, CA 94612)

Lee, S. (1993). How abnormal is the desire for slimness? A survey of eating attitudes and behavior among Chinese undergraduates in Hong Kong. *Psychological Medicine, 23*, 437–451.

Legal Services for Prisoners with Children. (n.d.). *People of color and the prison industrial complex: Facts and figures at a glance.* Retrieved July 20, 2004, from http://prisonerswithchildren.org/pubs/color.pdf

le Grange, D., Telch, C. F., & Agras, W. S. (1997). Eating and general psychopathology in a sample of Caucasian and ethnic minority subjects. *International Journal of Eating Disorders, 21*, 285–293.

le Grange, D., Telch, C. F., & Tibbs, J. (1998). Race and eating disorders. *Harvard Mental Health Letter, 15*, 6–8.

Leong, F.T.L. (1998). Career development and vocational behaviors. In L. C. Lee & N.W.S. Zane (Eds.), *Handbook of Asian American psychology* (pp. 359–398). Thousand Oaks, CA: Sage.

Leong, F.T.L. (2001). The role of acculturation in the career adjustment of Asian American workers: A test of Leong and Chou's (1994) formulations. *Cultural Diversity and Ethnic Minority Psychology, 7*, 262–273.

Leong, F.T.L., & Santiago-Rivera, A. L. (1999). Climbing the multiculturalism summit: Challenges and pitfalls. In P. Pedersen (Ed.), *Multiculturalism as a Fourth Force.* Philadelphia: Brunner/Mazel.

Lerner, R., Iwawaki, S., Chichara, T., & Sorell, G. (1980). Self-concept, self-esteem, and body attitudes among Japanese male and female adolescents. *Child Development, 51*, 847–855.

Leung, K., & Lind, E. A. (1986). Procedural justice and culture: Effects of culture, gender, and investigator status on procedural preferences. *Journal of Personality and Social Psychology, 50*, 1134–1140.

Levin, J. (1986). Roles for the black pastor in preventive medicine. *Pastoral Psychology, 35*, 94–103.

Lewin, K. (1941). On growing old in America.

Liamputtong, P., & Ezzy, D. (2005). *Qualitative research methods* (2nd ed.). New York: Oxford University Press.

Liddi-Brown, D., Barker-Hackett, L., & Grizzell, J. (2002, April). *Body image and eating disorders in a multicultural sample.* Poster presented at the 82nd Annual Meeting of the Western Psychological Association Annual Convention, Irvine, California.

Lim, T.-S. (1994) Facework and interpersonal relationships. In S. Ting-Toomey (Ed.), *The challenge of facework* (pp. 209–229). Albany: State University of New York Press.

Lin, K. M., & Cheung, F. (1999). Mental health issues for Asian Americans. *Psychiatric Services, 50,* 774–780.

Lonner, W. J. (1979). Issues in cross-cultural psychology. In A. J. Marsella, R. Tharp, & T. Ciborowski (Eds.), *Perspectives on cross-cultural psychology* (pp. 17–45). New York: Halstead Press.

Lopez, E., Blix, G. G., & Blix, A. G. (1995). Body image of Latinas compared to body image of non-Latina White women. *The Journal of Health Behavior, Education, and Promotion, 19,* 3–10.

Lopez, S. R., & Guarnaccia, P. J. (2000). Cultural psychopathology: Uncovering the social world of mental illness. *Annual Review of Psychology, 51,* 571–598.

Lopez, S. R., Lopez, A. A., & Fong, K. T. (1991). Mexican American's initial preference for counselors: The role of ethnic factors. *Journal of Counseling Psychology, 38,* 487–496.

Lopez-Baez, S. I. (1999). *Ataque (de nervios).* In J. S. Mio, J. E. Trimble, P. Arredondo, H. E. Cheatham, & S. Sue (Eds.), *Key words in multicultural interventions: A dictionary* (pp. 24–25). Westport, CT: Greenwood.

Lorion, R. P. (1973). Social class differences in treatment attitudes and expectations. (Doctoral dissertation, University of Rochester, 1973). *Dissertation Abstracts International, 33(12-B),* 6084–6085.

Lucero, K., Hicks, R., Bramlette, J., Brassington, G., & Welter, M. (1992). Frequency of eating problems among Asian and Caucasian college students. *Psychological Reports, 71,* 255–258.

Luria, A. R. (1976). *Cognitive development: Its cultural and social foundations.* Cambridge, MA: Harvard University Press.

Magee, W. J. (1993). *Psychosocial predictors of agoraphobia, simple phobia, and social phobia onset in a U.S. national sample.* Unpublished doctoral dissertation, University of Michigan, Ann Arbor.

Markus, H. R., & Kitayama, S. (1991). Culture and the self: Implications for cognition, emotion, and motivation. *Psychological Review, 98,* 224–253.

Marsella, A. J. (1980). Depressive experience and disorder across cultures. In H. C. Triandis & J. G. Draguns (Eds.), *Handbook of cross-cultural psychology, Vol. 6. Psychopathology* (pp. 237–289). Needham Heights, MA: Allyn & Bacon.

Mathews, C., & Lease, S. (2000). Focus on lesbian, gay, and bisexual families. In R. Perez, K. DeBord, & K. Bieschke (Eds.), *Handbook of counseling and psychotherapy with lesbian, gay, and bisexual clients* (pp. 249–273). Washington, DC: American Psychological Association.

Matsumoto, D. (1991). Cultural influences on facial expressions of emotion. *Southern Communication Journal, 56,* 128–137.

Matsumoto, D. (2000). *Culture and psychology: People around the world* (2nd ed.). Belmont, CA: Wadsworth/Thomson Learning.

Matsumoto, D., Kasri, F., Milligan, E., Singh, U., & The, J. (1997). *Lay conceptions of culture: Do students and researchers understand culture in the same way?* Unpublished paper, San Francisco State University. As cited in D. Matsumoto (2000), *Culture and psychology: People around the world* (2nd ed.). Belmont, CA: Wadsworth/Thomson Learning.

Maxwell, J. A. (2004). *Qualitative research design: An interactive approach* (2nd ed.). Thousand Oaks, CA: Sage.

Mazur, A. (1977). Interpersonal spacing on public benches in contact vs. noncontact cultures. *Journal of Social Psychology,* 53–58.

McCarthy, M. (1990). The thin ideal, depression and eating disorders in women. *Behavior Research & Therapy, 28,* 205–216.

McDonald, J. D., & Chaney, J. M. (2003). Resistance to multiculturalism: The "Indian problem." In J. S. Mio & G. Y. Iwamasa (Eds.), *Culturally diverse mental health: The challenges of research and resistance* (pp. 39–53). New York: Brunner-Routledge.

McGlone, M. S., & Neal, A. (2003, May). *Stereotype threat and the gender gap in political knowledge.* Paper presented at the 83rd Annual Meeting of the Western Psychological Association, Vancouver, BC.

McGoldrick, M. (1982). Ethnicity and family therapy: An overview. In M. McGoldrick, J. K. Pearce, & J. Giordano (Eds.), *Ethnicity & family therapy* (pp. 3–30). New York: Guilford.

McIntosh, P. (1988). *White privilege and male privilege: A personal account of coming to see correspondences through work in women's studies* (Working Paper No. 189). Wellesley, MA: Wellesley College.

McIntosh, P. (1995). White privilege and male privilege: A personal account of coming to see correspondences through work in women's studies. In M. L. Andersen & P. H. Collins (Eds.), *Race, class, and gender: An anthology* (pp. 76–87). Belmont, CA: Wadsworth.

McKay, V. C. (1989). The grandparent–grandchild relationship. In J. F. Nussbaum (Ed.), *Life-span communication: Normative processes* (pp. 257–282). Hillsdale, NJ: Erlbaum.

McKay, V. C. (1993). Making connections: Narrative as the expression of continuity between generations of grandparents and grandchildren. In N. Coupland & J. Nussbaum (Eds.), *Discourse and lifespan identity* (pp. 173–185). London: Sage.

McKay, V. C. (1999). Understanding the co-culture of the elderly. In L. A. Samovar & R. E. Porter (Eds.), *Intercultural communication: A reader* (8th ed., pp. 174–180). Belmont, CA: Wadsworth.

McKay, V. C., & Caverly, R. S. (1995). Relationships in later life: The nature of inter- and intragenerational ties among grandparents, grandchildren, and adult siblings. In J. Nussbaum (Ed.), *Handbook of communication and aging* (pp. 207–225). Hillsdale, NJ: Erlbaum.

Meltzer, M. (1993). *Slavery: A world history* (revised ed.). Cambridge, MA: DaCapo Press.

Mendoza, R. H. (1989). An empirical scale to measure type and degree of acculturation in Mexican-American adolescents and adults. *Hispanic Journal of Behavioral Sciences, 9,* 183–205.

Mestenhauser, J. A. (1983). Learning from sojourners. In D. Landis & R. W. Brislin (Eds.), *Handbook of intercultural training: Vol. 11. Issues in training and methodology* (pp. 153–185). New York: Pergamon.

Mikkelson, D. P., & Mikkelson, B. (2005) Urban legends references pages: Glurge gallery, www.snopes.com/glurge/teddy.htm.

Miller, J., & Garran, A. M. (2008). *Racism in the United States: Implications for the helping professions.* Belmont, CA: Thomson Brooks/Cole.

Mindess, A. (1999). *Reading between the signs.* Yarmouth, ME: Intercultural Press.

Mio, J. S. (2002). Narrative as examplar: In search of culture. [Review of *Culture in psychology,* C. Squire (Ed.). (2000). New York: Routledge.] *Contemporary Psychology: APA Review of Books, 47,* 506–508.

Mio, J. S. (2003). Modern forms of resistance to multiculturalism: Keeping our eyes on the prize. In J. S. Mio & G. Y. Iwamasa (Eds.), *Culturally diverse mental health: The challenges of research and resistance* (pp. 3–16). New York: Brunner-Routledge.

Mio, J. S., & Awakuni, G. I. (2000). *Resistance to multiculturalism: Issues and interventions.* Philadelphia, PA: Brunner/Mazel.

Mio, J. S., & Barker-Hackett, L. (2003). Reaction papers and journal writing as techniques for assessing resistance in multicultural courses. *Journal of Multicultural Counseling and Development, 31,* 12–19.

Mio, J. S., & Iwamasa, G. Y. (1993). To do, or not to do: That is the question for White cross-cultural researchers. *The Counseling Psychologist, 21,* 197–212.

Mio, J. S., Koss, M. P., Harway, M., O'Neil, J. M., Geffner, R., Murphy, B. C., & Ivey, D. C. (2003). Violence against women: A silent pandemic. In J. S. Mio & G. Y. Iwamasa (Eds.), *Culturally diverse mental health: The challenges of research and resistance* (pp. 269–287). New York: Brunner-Routledge.

Mio, J. S., & Morris, D. R. (1990). Cross-cultural issues in psychology training programs: An invitation for discussion. *Professional*

Psychology: Research and Practice, 21, 434–441.

Mio, J. S., & Roades, L. A. (2003). Building bridges in the 21st century: Allies and the power of human connection across demographic divides. In J. S. Mio & G. Y. Iwamasa (Eds.), *Culturally diverse mental health: The challenges of research and resistance* (pp. 105–117). New York: Brunner-Routledge.

Mischel, W. (1958). Preference for delayed reinforcement: An experimental study of a cultural observation. *Journal of Abnormal and Social Psychology, 56,* 57–61.

Mischel, W. (1961). Delay of gratification, need for achievement, and acquiescence in another culture. *Journal of Abnormal and Social Psychology, 62,* 543–552.

Montgomery, G. T., Arnold, B., & Orozco, S. (1990). MMPI supplemental scale performance of Mexican Americans and level of acculturation. *Journal of Personality Assessment, 54,* 328–342.

Moreland, K. L. (1996). Persistent issues in multicultural assessment of social and emotional functioning. In L. A. Suzuki, P. J. Meller, & J. G. Ponterotto (Eds.), *Handbook of multicultural assessment: Clinical, psychological, and educational applications* (pp. 51–76). San Francisco: Jossey-Bass.

Morelli, P.T.T. (2005). Social work practice with Asian Americans. In D. Lum (Ed.), *Cultural competence, practice stages, and client systems: A case study approach.* Belmont, CA: Brooks/Cole.

Morrow, S. L., Rakhsha, G., & Castañeda, C. L. (2001). Qualitative research methods for multicultural counseling. In J. G. Ponterotto, J. M. Casas, L. A. Suzuki, & C. M. Alexander (Eds.), *Handbook of multicultural counseling* (2nd ed., pp. 575–603). Thousand Oaks, CA: Sage.

Murphy, M. C., Steele, C. M., & Gross, J. J. (2007). Signaling threat: How situational cues affect women in math, science, and engineering settings. *Psychological Science, 18,* 879–885.

Myers, D. L. (2008). *Social psychology* (9th ed.). New York: McGraw-Hill.

Myers, G. G. (2002). *Social psychology* (7th ed.). New York: McGraw-Hill.

Myers, H. F. (1986, October). *The biopsychosocial model.* Lecture presented for the first-year clinical psychology graduate students in the Psychology Department, University of California, Los Angeles.

Myers, H. F., Lewis, T. T., & Parker-Dominguez, T. (2003). Stress, coping, and minority health: Biopsychosocial perspective on ethnic health disparities. In G. Bernal, J. E. Trimble, A. K. Burlew, & F.T.L. Leong (Eds.), *Handbook of ethnic & racial minority psychology* (pp. 377–400). Thousand Oaks, CA: Sage.

Nagata, D. K. (1990a). The Japanese American internment: Exploring the transgenerational consequences of traumatic stress. *Journal of Traumatic Stress, 3,* 47–69.

Nagata, D. K. (1990b). *Legacy of injustice.* New York: Plenum.

Nagata, D. K. (1993). *Legacy of silence: Exploring the long-term effects of the Japanese American internment.* New York: Plenum.

Nagata, D. K. (1998). Internment and intergenerational relations. In L. C. Lee & N.W.S. Zane (Eds.), *Handbook of Asian American psychology* (pp. 433–456). Thousand Oaks, CA: Sage.

Nagata, D. K., & Takeshita, Y. J. (1998). Coping and resilience across generations: Japanese Americans and the World War II internment. *Psychoanalytic Review, 85,* 587–613.

Nash, P. T. (1992). Multicultural identity and the death of stereotypes. In M.P.P. Root (Ed.), *Racially mixed people in America* (pp. 330–332). Newbury Park, CA: Sage.

Nasser, M. (1986). Comparative study of the prevalence of abnormal eating attitudes among Arab female students of both London and Cairo universities. *Psychological Medicine, 16,* 621–625.

National Center for Post-Traumatic Stress Disorder & the National Center for American Indian and Alaska Native Mental Health Research. (1996). *Matsunaga Vietnam Veterans Project.* White River Junction, VT: NCPTSD/NCAIANMHR.

National Healthcare Disparities Executive Reports (U.S. Department of Health and Human Services, 2003).

National Institute of Mental Health (1998). *Genetics and mental disorders: Report of The National Institute of Mental Health's Genetics Workgroup.* Rockville, MD: NIMH.

National Institutes of Health. (2004a). *Cystic fibrosis: Genetics home reference.* Retrieved October 29, 2004, from http://ghr.nlm.nih.gov/condition=cysticfibrosis

National Institutes of Health. (2004b). *Estimates of funding for various diseases, conditions, research areas.* Retrieved November 22, 2004, from http://www.nih.gov/news/fundingresearchareas.htm

National Population Projections. (2002). *Projections of the resident population by race, Hispanic origin, and nativity: Middle series.* U.S. Census Bureau, Population Division, Populations Branch. Retrieved October 13, 2003, from www.census.gov/population/projections/nation.html

Neighbors, H. W. (1984). Professional help use among Black Americans: Implications for unmet need. *American Journal of Community Psychology, 12,* 551–566.

Neighbors, H. W. (1985). Seeking professional help for personal problems: Black Americans' use of health and mental health services. *Community Mental Health Journal, 21,* 156–166.

Neighbors, H. W. (1997). The (mis)diagnosis of mental disorder in African Americans. *African American Research Perspectives, 3,* 1–11.

Neighbors, H. W. (1988). The help-seeking behavior of Black Americans: A summary of findings from the National Survey of Black Americans. *Journal of the National Medical Association, 80,* 1009–1012.

Neighbors, H. W., & Jackson, J. S. (1984). The use of informal and formal help: Four patterns of illness behavior in the Black community. *American Journal of Community Psychology, 12,* 629–644.

Nesselroade, J. R., & Labouvie, E. W. (1985). Experimental design in research on aging. In J. E. Birren & K. W. Schaie (Eds.), *Handbook of the psychology of aging* (2nd ed., pp. 35–60). New York: Van Nostrand Reinhold.

Nichols, M. P., & Schwartz, R. C. (1998). *Family therapy: Concepts and methods* (2nd ed.). Boston: Allyn & Bacon.

Nobles, W. W. (1986). *African psychology: Toward its reclamation, reascension, and revitalization.* Oakland, CA: Institute for the Advanced Study of Black Family Life and Culture.

Nobles, W. W. (1989). Psychological nigrescence: An Afrocentric review. *The Counseling Psychologist, 17,* 253–257.

Norman, D. A., & Rummelhart, D. E. (Eds.). (1975). *Explorations in cognition.* San Francisco: Freeman.

Nussbaum, J., & Bettini, L. M. (1994). Shared stories of the grandparent–grandchild relationship. *International Journal of Aging and Human Development, 39,* 67–80.

O'Brien, G. V. (2003). Indigestible food, conquering hordes, and waste materials: Metaphors of immigrants and early immigration restriction debate in the United States. *Metaphor and Symbol, 18,* 33–47.

Ochs, R. (1996). Biphobia: It goes more than two ways. In B. Firestein (Ed.), *Bisexuality: The psychology and politics of an invisible minority* (pp. 217–239). Thousand Oaks, CA: Sage.

Okagaki, L., & Bojczyk, K. E. (2002). Perspectives on Asian American development. In G.C.N. Hall & S. Okazaki (Eds.), *Asian American psychology: The science of lives in context* (pp. 67–104). Washington, DC: American Psychological Association.

Okagaki, L., & Sternberg, R. J. (1991). Cultural and parental influences. In L. Okagaki & R. L. Sternberg (Eds.), *Directors of development: Influences on the development of children's thinking* (pp. 101–120). Hillsdale, NJ: Erlbaum.

Okazaki, S. (2002). Beyond questionnaires: Conceptual and methodological innovations in Asian American psychology. In G.C.N. Hall & S. Okazaki (Eds.), *Asian American psychology: The science of lives in context* (pp. 13–39). Washington, DC: American Psychological Association.

Olson, L. (2001). *Freedom's daughters: The unsung heroines of the civil rights movement from 1830 to 1970*. New York: Scribner.

Oquendo, M., Horwath, E., & Martinez, A. (1989). *Ataque de nervios:* Proposed diagnostic criteria for a culture specific syndrome. *Culture, Medicine and Psychiatry, 16,* 367–376.

Orbe, M. P. (1999). Utilizing an inductive approach to studying African American male communication. In L. A. Samovar & R. E. Porter (Eds.), *Intercultural communication: A reader* (8ᵗʰ ed., pp. 227–234). Belmont, CA: Wadsworth.

Paludi, M. A. (1998). *The psychology of women*. Upper Saddle River, NJ: Prentice Hall.

Paniagua, F. A. (2001). *Diagnosis in a multicultural context* (2ⁿᵈ ed.). Thousand Oaks, CA: Sage.

Parham, T. A. (1989). Cycles of psychological nigrescence. *The Counseling Psychologist, 17,* 187–226.

Parham, T. A. (2001). Psychological nigrescence revisited: A foreword. *Journal of Multicultural Counseling & Development, 29,* 162–164.

Parham, T. A. (Ed.). (2002). *Counseling persons of African descent: Raising the bar of practitioner competence*. Thousand Oaks, CA: Sage.

Parham, T. A., & Helms, J. E. (1981). Influences of Black students' racial identity attitudes on preferences for counselor race. *Journal of Counseling Psychology, 28,* 250–256.

Parham, T. A., & Helms, J. E. (1985a). Attitudes of racial identity and self-esteem of Black students: An exploratory investigation. *Journal of College Student Personnel, 26,* 143–147.

Parham, T. A., & Helms, J. E. (1985b). Relation of racial identity attitudes to self-actualization and affective status of Black students. *Journal of Counseling Psychology, 32,* 431–440.

Parham, T. A., & Parham, W. D. (2002). Understanding African American mental health. In T. A. Parham (Ed.), *Counseling persons of African descent: Raising the bar of practitioner competence* (pp. 25–37). Thousand Oaks, CA: Sage.

Parham, T. A., White, J. L., & Ajamu, A. (1999). *The Psychology of Blacks* (3ʳᵈ ed.). Upper Saddle River, NJ: Prentice Hall.

Parham, T. A., & Williams, P. T. (1993). The relationship of demographic and background factors to racial identity attitudes. *Journal of Black Psychology, 19,* 7–24.

Pate, J. E., Pumariega, A. J., Hester, C., & Garner, D. M. (1992). Cross-cultural patterns in eating disorders: A review. *Journal of the American Academy of Child and Adolescent Psychiatry, 31,* 802–808.

Patterson, C. (1996). Lesbian mothers and their children: The findings from the Bay Area Families Study. In J. Laird & R. Green (Eds.), *Lesbians and gays in couples and families: A handbook for therapists* (pp. 420–437). San Francisco: Jossey-Bass.

Patterson, M. L. (1983). *Nonverbal behavior: A functional perspective*. New York: Springer-Verlag.

Peal, E., & Lambert, W. E. (1962). The relation of bilingualism to intelligence. *Psychological Monographs, 76,* 1–23.

Pedersen, P. (1988). *A handbook for developing multicultural awareness*. Alexandria, VA: American Association for Counseling and Development.

Pedersen, P. (1990). The multicultural perspective as a fourth force in counseling. *Journal of Mental Health Counseling, 12,* 93–95.

Pedersen, P. (1991). Multiculturalism as a generic approach to counseling. *Journal of Counseling Development: Special Issue on Multiculturalism as a Fourth Force, 70,* 6–12.

Pedersen, P. (1999). *Multiculturalism as a fourth force*. Philadelphia: Brunner/Mazel.

Pedersen, P. B., Draguns, J. G., Lonner, W. J., & Trimble, J. E. (Eds.). (2008). *Counseling across cultures* (6ᵗʰ ed.). Thousand Oaks, CA: Sage.

Peifer, K. L., Hu, T. W., & Vega, W. (2000). Help seeking by persons of Mexican origin with functional impairments. *Psychiatric Services, 51,* 1293–1298.

Peplau, L. (1991). Lesbian and gay relationships. In J. Goniorek & J. Weinrich (Eds.), *Homosexuality: Research implication for public policy* (pp. 177–196). Newbury Park, CA: Sage.

Perez, R. M., DeBord, K. A., & Bieschke, K. J. (Eds.). (2000). *Handbook of counseling and psychotherapy with lesbian, gay, and bisexual clients.* Washington, DC: American Psychological Association.

Perloff, L. S. (1983). Perceptions of vulnerability to victimization. *Journal of Social Issues, 39,* 41–61.

Pettigrew, T. F. (1979). The ultimate attribution error: Extending Allport's cognitive analysis of prejudice. *Personality and Social Psychology Bulletin, 55,* 461–476.

Phillon, J., He, M. F., & Connelly, F. M. (2005). *Narrative and experience in multicultural education.* Thousand Oaks, CA: Sage.

Phinney, J. S. (1992). Multigroup ethnic identity measure. *Journal of Adolescent Research, 7,* 156–176.

Phinney, J. S. (1996). When we talk about American ethnic groups, what do we mean? *American Psychologist, 51,* 918–927.

Pickren, W. E. (2004). Fifty years on: *Brown v. Board of Education* and American psychology, 1954–2004: An introduction. *American Psychologist, 59,* 493–494.

Pike, K. L. (1967). *Language in relation to a unified theory of the structure of human behavior.* The Hague: Mouton.

Poniewozik, J. (2003). October 3, 1995: Color us divided. *Time Magazine.* Retrieved July 20, 2004, from http://www.time.com/time/80days/951003.html

Ponterotto, J. G. (1988). Racial consciousness development among White counselor trainees: A stage model. *Journal of Multicultural Counseling and Development, 16,* 146–156.

Pope, M. (2008). Culturally appropriate counseling considerations for lesbian and gay clients. In P. B. Pedersen, J. G. Draguns, W. E. Lonner, & J. E. Trimble (Eds.), *Counseling across cultures* (6th ed., pp. 201–222). Thousand Oaks, CA: Sage.

Pope-Davis, D. B., & Coleman, H.L.K. (Eds.). (1997). *Multicultural counseling competencies: Assessment, education and training, and supervision.* Thousand Oaks, CA: Sage.

Pope-Davis, D. B., Reynolds, A. L., Dings, J. G., & Ottavi, T. M. (1994). Multicultural competencies of doctoral interns at university counseling centers: An exploratory investigation. *Professional Psychology: Research and Practice, 25,* 466–470.

Poston, W.S.C. (1990). The biracial identity development model: A needed addition. *Journal of Counseling & Development, 69,* 152–155.

Prendes-Lintel, M. (2001). A working model in counseling recent refugees. In J. G. Ponterotto, J. M. Casas, L. A. Suzuki, & C. M. Alexander (Eds.), *Handbook of multicultural counseling* (2nd ed., pp. 729–752). Thousand Oaks, CA: Sage.

Price-Williams, D., & Ramirez, M., III. (1977). Divergent thinking, cultural differences, and bilingualism. *Journal of Social Psychology, 103,* 3–11.

Prince, R. H. (2000). Transcultural psychiatry: Personal experiences and Canadian perspectives. *Canadian Journal of Psychiatry, 45,* 431–437.

Putnam, R. C. (2007). *E Pluribus Unum*: Diversity and community in the twenty-first century. The 2006 Johan Skytte Prize Lecture. *Scandinavian Political Studies, 30,* 137–174.

Rand, C. W., & Kuldau, J. M. (1990). The epidemiology of obesity and self-defined weight problems in the general population: Gender, race, age, and social class. *International Journal of Eating Disorders, 9,* 329–343.

Redding, S. G., & Ng, M. (1982). The role of "face" in the organizational perceptions of Chinese managers. *Organization Studies, 3,* 201–219.

Remland, M. S., Jones, T. S., & Brinkman, H. (1991). Proxemic and haptic behavior in three European countries. *Journal of Social Psychology, 135,* 215–232.

Reynolds, A. L. (1999). Etic/emic. In J. S. Mio, J. E. Trimble, P. Arredondo, H. E. Cheatham, & D. Sue (Eds.), *Key words in multicultural interventions: A dictionary* (pp. 115–116). Westport, CT: Greenwood.

Ribeau, S. A., Baldwin, J. R., & Hecht, M. L. (1999). An African American communication perspective. In L. A. Samovar & R. E. Porter (Eds.), *Intercultural communication: A reader* (8th ed., pp. 147–154). Belmont, CA: Wadsworth.

Richardson, E. H. (1981). Cultural and historical perspective in counseling American Indians. Invited chapter in D. W. Sue, *Counseling the culturally different* (pp. 216–255). New York: Wiley.

Ridley, C. R. (1989). Racism in counseling as an adverse behavioral process. In P. B. Pedersen, J. G. Draguns, W. J. Lonner, & J. E. Trimble (Eds.), *Counseling across cultures* (3rd ed., pp. 55–77). Honolulu: University of Hawaii Press.

Ridley, C. R. (1995). *Overcoming unintentional racism in counseling and therapy: A practitioner's guide to intentional intervention.* Thousand Oaks, CA: Sage.

Rissman, C. K. (2007). *Narrative methods for the human sciences.* Thousand Oaks, CA: Sage.

Roach, R. (2003, May 8). History's burden: After decades of neglect, an academic research agenda is being built around health disparities. *Black Issues in Higher Education, 20,* 18–23.

Roades, L. A., & Mio, J. S. (2000). Allies: How are they created and what are their experiences? In J. S. Mio & G. I. Awakuni (Eds.), *Resistance to multiculturalism: Issues and interventions* (pp. 63–82). Philadelphia: Brunner/Mazel.

Robins, L., & Regier, D. A. (1991). *Psychiatric disorders in America: The Epidemiologic Catchment Area Study.* New York: The Free Press.

Rodriguez, R. (2002). *Brown: The last discovery of America.* New York: Penguin Putnam.

Rogler, L. H., Malgady, R. G., & Costantino, G. (1987). What do culturally sensitive mental health services mean? The case of Hispanics. *American Psychologist, 42,* 565–570.

Root, M.P.P. (1990). Resolving "other" status: Identity development of biracial individuals. In L. S. Brown & M.P.P. Root (Eds.), *Diversity and complexity in feminist therapy* (pp. 185–205). New York: Haworth.

Root, M.P.P. (1992). Within, between, and beyond race. In M.P.P. Root (Ed.), *Racially mixed people in America* (pp. 3–11). Newbury Park, CA: Sage.

Root, M.P.P. (1995). Resolving the "other" status: Identity development of biracial individuals. In N. Goldberger & J. B. Veroff (Eds.), *The culture and psychology reader* (575–593). New York: New York University Press.

Root, M.P.P. (1996). The multiracial experience: Racial borders as a significant frontier in race relations. In M.P.P. Root (Ed.), *The multiracial experience: Racial borders as the new frontier* (pp. xiii–xxviii). Thousand Oaks, CA: Sage.

Root, M.P.P. (1998). Facilitating psychotherapy with Asian American clients. In D. R. Atkinson, G. Morten, & D. W. Sue (Eds.), *Counseling American minorities: A cross-cultural perspective* (6th ed., pp. 214–234). Dubuque, IA: Brown.

Root, M.P.P. (2001). *Love's revolution: Interracial marriage.* Philadelphia: Temple University Press.

Root, M.P.P. (2004, August). *Mixed race identities—Theory, research, and practice implications.* Continuing education workshop presented at the 112th Annual Convention of the American Psychological Association, Honolulu, HI.

Rose, L. R. (1996). White identity and counseling White allies about racism. In B. B. Bowser & R. G. Hunt (Eds.), *Impacts of racism on White Americans* (2nd ed., pp. 24–47). Thousand Oaks, CA: Sage.

Rosenfeld, S. (1980). Sex differences in depression: Do women always have higher rates? *Journal of Health and Social Behavior, 21,* 33–42.

Rosenfeld, S. (1984). Race differences in involuntary hospitalization: Psychiatric vs. labeling perspectives. *Journal of Health and Social Behavior, 25,* 14–23.

Rosenfeld, S. (1999). Gender and mental health: Do women have more psychopathology, men more, or both the same (and why)? In A. V. Horwitz & T. L. Scheid (Eds.), *A Handbook for the Study of Mental Health: Social Contexts,*

Theories, and Systems (pp. 348–360). New York: Cambridge University Press.

Rosenthal, R. (1991). Teacher expectancy effects: A brief update 25 years after the Pygmalion experiment. *Journal of Research in Education, 1*, 3–12.

Rosenthal, R. (1994). Interpersonal expectancy effects: A 30-year perspective. *Current Directions in Psychological Science, 3*, 176–179.

Rosenthal, R., & Jacobson, L. (1968). *Pygmalian in the classroom: Teacher expectation and pupils' intellectual development*. New York: Holt, Rinehart & Winston.

Ross, L. (1977). The intuitive psychologist and his shortcomings: Distortions in the attribution process. In L. Berkowitz (Ed.), *Advances in experimental social psychology* (Vol. 10, pp. 174–221). New York: Academic Press.

Rowe, W., Bennett, S. K., & Atkinson, D. R. (1994). White racial identity models: A critique and alternative proposal. *The Counseling Psychologist, 22*, 129–146.

Rucker, C. E., & Cash, T. F. (1992). Body image, body size perceptions, and eating behaviors among African-American and White college women. *International Journal of Eating Disorders, 12*, 291–299.

Ruiz, A. S. (1990). Ethnic identity: Crisis and resolution. *Journal of Multicultural Counseling and Development, 18*, 29–40.

Samuda, R. J. (1998). *Psychological testing of American minorities*. Thousand Oaks, CA: Sage.

Schmidley, D. (2001). *Profile of the foreign-born population in the United States: 2000* (Current Population Reports, Series P23-206). U.S. Census Bureau, Government Printing Office. Retrieved October 13, 2003, from www.census.gov/prod/2002pubs/p23-206.pdf

Schulman, K. A., Berlin, J. A., Harless, W., Kerner, J. F., Sistrunk, S., Gersh, B. J., Dubé, R., Taleghani, C. K., Burke, J. E., Williams, S., Eisenberg, J. M., Escarce, J. J., & Ayres, W. (1999). The effect of race and sex on physicians' recommendation for cardiac catheterization. *New England Journal of Medicine, 340*, 618–626.

Schwartz, G. E. (1982). Testing the biopsychosocial model: The ultimate challenge facing behavioral medicine. *Journal of Consulting and Clinical Psychology, 50*, 1040–1053.

Scileppi, J. A., Teed, E. L., & Torres, R. D. (2000). *Community psychology: A common sense approach to mental health*. Upper Saddle River, NJ: Prentice Hall.

Scott, D. A., & Robinson, T. L. (2001). White male identity development: The key model. *Journal of Counseling & Development, 79, 4*, 415–422.

Seale, C., Gobo, G., Gubrium, J. F., & Silverman, D. (Eds.). (2004). *Qualitative research practice*. Thousand Oaks, CA: Sage.

Sechzer, J. A., Pfafflin, S. M., Denmark, F. L., Griffin, A., & Blumenthal, S. J. (Eds.). (1996). *Women and mental health*. New York: New York Academy of Sciences.

Seligman, M.E.P. (1982). *Helplessness: On depression, development and death*. San Francisco: Freeman.

Seligman, M.E.P., Walker, E. F., & Rosenhan, D. L. (2001). *Abnormal Psychology* (4th ed.). NY: Norton.

Sellers, J. M. (1994). *Folk wisdom of Mexico*. San Francisco: Chronicle Books.

Sellers, R. M., Smith, M. A., Shelton, J. N., Rowley, S.A.J., Chavous, R. M. (1998). Multidimensional model of racial identity: A reconceptualization of African American racial identity. *Personality and Social Psychology Review, 2*, 18–39.

Sherman, J. (2003). Confronting the moral economy of U.S. racial/ethnic health disparities. *American Journal of Public Health, 93*, 189–190.

Shon, S. P., & Ja, D. Y. (1982). Asian families. In M. McGoldrick, J. K. Pearce, & J. Giordano (Eds.), *Ethnicity & family therapy* (pp. 208–228). New York: Guilford.

Shuter, R. (1977). A field study of nonverbal communication in Germany, Italy and the United States. *Journal of Communication, 26*, 298–305.

Silverman, D. (2004). *Qualitative research: Theory, method and practice* (2nd ed.). Thousand Oaks, CA: Sage.

Silverman, D., & Marvasti, A. (2008). *Doing qualitative research* (2nd ed.). Thousand Oaks, CA: Sage.

Simon, R. (1995). Gender, multiple roles, role meaning, and mental health. *Journal of Health and Social Behavior, 36*, 182–194.

Smedley, A. (1999). *Race in North America: Origin and evolution of a worldview* (2nd ed.). Boulder, CO: Westview Press.

Smith, A. D. (2000). *Talk to me: Travels in media and politics*. New York: Random House.

Smith, M. B. (1992). The American Psychological Association and social responsibility. In R. B. Evans, V. S. Sexton, & T. C. Cadwallader (Eds.), *100 Years. The American Psychological Association: A historical perspective* (pp. 327–344). Washington, DC: American Psychological Association.

Smolowe, J. (1993, May 10). Intermarried . . . with children. *Time, 142*, pp. 64–65.

Snow, C. E. (1983). Age differences in second language acquisition: Research findings and folk psychology. In K. Bailey, M. Long, & S. Peck (Eds.), *Second language acquisition studies* (pp. 141–150). Rowley, MA: Newbury House.

Snow, C. E. (1987). Relevance of the notion of a critical period to language acquisition. In M. Bornstein (Ed.), *Sensitive periods in development: An interdisciplinary perspective* (pp. 183–209). Hillsdale, NJ: Erlbaum.

Snow, C. E. (1993). Bilingualism and second language acquisition. In J. B. Gleason & N. B. Ratner (Eds.), *Psycholinguistics* (pp. 391–416). Fort Worth, TX: Harcourt, Brace, Jovanovich.

Snow, C. E., & Hoefnagel-Höhle, M. (1978). Critical period for language acquisition: Evidence from second language learning. *Child Development, 49*, 1263–1279.

Sodowsky, G. R., Lai, E.W.M., & Plake, B. S. (1991). Moderating effects of sociocultural variables on acculturation variables of Hispanics and Asian Americans. *Journal of Counseling and Development, 70*, 194–204.

Sommers, S. R., Apfelbaum, E. P., Dukes, K. N., Toosi, N., & Wang, E. J. (2006). Race and media coverage of Hurricane Katrina: Analysis, implications, and future research questions. *Analysis of Social Issues and Public Policy, 6*, 39–55.

Spearman, C. S. (1904). "General intelligence," objectively determined and measured. *American Journal of Psychology, 15*, 201–293.

Spearman, C. (1927). *The abilities of man*. New York: Macmillan.

Special Populations Task Force of the President's Commission on Mental Health. (1978). *Task panel reports submitted to the President's Commission on Mental Health* (Vol. 3). Washington, DC: U.S. Government Printing Office.

Spickard, P. R. (1989). *Mixed blood: Intermarriage and ethnic identity in twentieth-century America*. Madison: University of Wisconsin Press.

Steele, C. M. (1997). A threat in the air: How stereotypes shape intellectual identity and performance. *American Psychologist, 52*, 613–629.

Steele, C. M. (2001). Institutional climate and stereotype threat: Enhancing educational performance and identification in the face of negative group stereotypes. Keynote address at the Second Biennial National Multicultural Conference and Summit: *The psychology of race/ethnicity, gender, sexual orientation, and disability: Intersections, divergence, and convergence*. Santa Barbara, CA.

Steele, C. M., & Aronson, J. (1995). Stereotype threat and the intellectual test performance of African Americans. *Journal of Personality and Social Psychology, 69*, 797–811.

Sternberg, R. J. (1985). *Beyond IQ: A triarchic theory of human intelligence*. New York: Cambridge University Press.

Sternberg, R. J. (1988). *The triarchic mind*. New York: Cambridge University Press.

Sternberg, R. J. (1995). For whom the bell curves tolls [Review of the book *The Bell Curve*]. *Psychological Science, 6,* 257–261.

Sternberg, R. J. (1997). *Successful intelligence.* New York: Simon & Schuster.

Sternberg, R. J. (1999). The theory of successful intelligence. *Review of General Intelligence, 3,* 292–316.

Sternberg, R. J. (2002). Successful intelligence: A new approach to leadership. In R. E. Riggio, S. E. Murphy, & F. J. Pirozzolo (Eds.), *Multiple intelligences and leadership* (pp. 9–28). Mahwah, NJ: Erlbaum.

Sternberg, R. J. (2003). *Cognitive psychology* (3rd ed.). Belmont, CA: Wadsworth.

Sternberg, R. J., Ferrari, M., Clinkenbeard, P. R., & Grigorenko, E. L. (1996). Identification, instruction, and assessment of gifted children: A construct validation of a triarchic model. *Gifted Child Quarterly, 40,* 129–137.

Sternberg, R. J., Grigorenko, E. L., Ferrari, M., & Clinkenbeard, P. (1999). A triarchic analysis of an aptitude-treatment interaction. *European Journal of Psychological Assessment, 15,* 1–11.

Stonequist, E. V. (1937). *The marginal man.* New York: Scribner.

Stringer, C., & Andrews, P. (1988). Genetic and fossil evidence for the origin of modern humans. *Science, 239,* 1263–1268.

Substance Abuse & Mental Health Services Administration (SAMHSA). (2003, October). *State estimates of substance use from the 2001 National Household Survey on Drug Abuse: Vol. II. Individual state tables and technical appendices.* Available at http://oas.samhsa.gov/NHSDA/2k1State/pdf/2k1SAEv/pdf

Sue, D., Mak, W. S., & Sue, D. W. (1998). Ethnic identity. In L. C. Lee & N.W.S. Zane (Eds.), *Handbook of Asian American psychology* (pp. 289–323). Thousand Oaks, CA: Sage.

Sue, D. W. (1978). Eliminating cultural oppression in counseling: Toward a general theory. *Journal of Counseling Psychology, 25,* 419–428.

Sue, D. W. (1981). *Counseling the culturally different: Theory and practice.* New York: Wiley.

Sue, D. W. (2001). Multidimensional facets of cultural competence. *The Counseling Psychologist, 29,* 790–821.

Sue, D. W., & Arredondo, P. (1992). Multicultural counseling competencies and standards: A call to the profession. *Journal of Multicultural Counseling and Development, 20,* 64–90.

Sue, D. W., Arredondo, P., & McDavis, R. J. (1992). Multicultural competencies/standards: A pressing need. *Journal of Counseling and Development, 70,* 477–486.

Sue, D. W., Bernier, J. E., Durran, A., Feinberg, L., Pedersen, P., Smith, E. J., & Vasquez-Nuttall, E. (1982). Position paper: Cross-cultural counseling competencies. *The Counseling Psychologist, 10,* 45–52.

Sue, D. W., Carter, R. T., Casas, J. M., Fouad, N. A., Ivey, A. E., Jensen, M., LaFromboise, T., Manese, J. E., Ponterotto, J. G., & Vasquez-Nuttal, E. (1998). *Multicultural counseling competencies: Individual and organizational development.* Thousand Oaks, CA: Sage.

Sue, D. W., Ivey, A. E., & Pedersen, P. B. (1996). *A theory of multicultural counseling and therapy.* Pacific Grove, CA: Brooks/Cole.

Sue, D. W., & Sue, D. (1990). *Counseling the culturally different: Theory and practice* (2nd ed.). New York: Wiley.

Sue, D. W., & Sue, D. (1999). *Counseling the culturally different: Theory and practice* (3rd ed.). New York: Wiley.

Sue, D. W., & Sue, D. (2003). *Counseling the culturally diverse: Theory and practice* (4th ed.). New York: Wiley.

Sue, D. W., & Sue, D. (2008). *Counseling the culturally diverse: Theory and practice* (5th ed.). New York: Wiley.

Sue, S. (1977). Community mental health services to minority groups: Some optimism, some pessimism. *American Psychologist, 32,* 616–624.

Sue, S. (1999). Science, ethnicity, and bias: Where have we gone wrong? *American Psychologist, 54,* 1070–1077.

Sue, S., Allen, D., & Conaway, L. (1975). The responsiveness and equality of mental health care to Chicanos and Native Americans.

American Journal of Community Psychology, 45, 111–118.

Sue, S., Fujino, D. C., Hu, L., Takeuchi, D. T., & Zane, N.W.S. (1991). Community mental health services for ethnic minority groups: A test of the cultural responsiveness hypothesis. *Journal of Consulting and Clinical Psychology,* 59, 533–540.

Sue, S., & McKinney, H. (1974). Delivery of community health services to Black and White clients. *Journal of Consulting and Clinical Psychology,* 42, 794–801.

Sue, S., McKinney, H., Allen, D., & Hall, J. (1974). Delivery of community health services to Black and White clients. *Journal of Consulting Psychology,* 42, 794–801.

Sue, S., & Morishima, J. K. (1982). *The mental health of Asian Americans.* San Francisco: Jossey-Bass.

Sue, S., & Sue, D. W. (2000). Conducting psychological research with the Asian American/Pacific Islander population. In Council of National Psychological Associations for the Advancement of Ethnic Minority Interests (Ed.), *Guidelines for research in ethnic minority communities* (pp. 2–4). Washington, DC: American Psychological Association.

Sue, S., Sue, D. W., Sue, L., & Takeuchi, D. T. (1995). Psychopathology among Asian Americans: A model minority? *Cultural Diversity and Mental Health,* 1, 39–51.

Sue, S., & Zane, N. (1987). The role of culture and cultural techniques in psychotherapy: A critique and reformulation. *American Psychologist,* 42, 37–45.

Suinn, R. M., Rickard-Figueroa, K., Lew, S., & Vigil, P. (1987). The Suinn-Lew Self-Identity Acculturation Scale: An initial report. *Educational and Psychological Measurement,* 47, 401–407.

Sullivan, T. J., & Thompson, K. S. (1994). *Introduction to social problems* (3rd ed.). NY: Macmillan.

Sung, K. (1991). Family-centered informal support networks of Korean elderly: The resistance of cultural traditions. *Journal of Cross-Cultural Gerontology,* 6, 431–447.

Sussman, L. K., Robins, L. N., & Earls, F. (1987). Treatment-seeking for depression by Black and White Americans. *Social Science & Medicine,* 24, 187–196.

Sussman, N. M., & Rosenfeld, H. M. (1982). Influence of culture, language and sex on conversation distance. *Journal of Personality and Social Psychology,* 42, 66–74.

Tafoya, N., & Del Vecchio, A. (1996). Back to the future: An examination of the Native American holocaust. In M. McGoldrick, J. Giordano, & J. K. Pearce (Eds.), *Ethnicity & family therapy* (2nd ed., pp. 45–54). New York: Guilford.

Takeuchi, D. T., Uehara, E., & Maramba, G. (1999). Cultural diversity and mental health treatment. In A. V. Horwitz & T. L. Scheid (Eds.), *A handbook for the study of mental health: Social contexts, theories, and systems* (pp. 550–565). New York: Cambridge University Press.

Takeuchi, D. T., Zane, N., Hong, S., Chae, D. H., Gong, F., Gee, G. C., Walton, E., Sue, S., & Alegria, M. (2007). Immigration-related factors and mental disorders among Asian Americans. *American Journal of Public Health,* 97, 84–90.

Tatum, B. D. (1997). *"Why are all the Black kids sitting together in the cafeteria?" and other conversations about race.* New York: Basic Books.

Taylor, S. E. (2003). *Health psychology* (5th ed.). New York: McGraw-Hill.

ten Have, P. (2004). *Understanding qualitative research and ethnomethodology.* Thousand Oaks, CA: Sage.

Terman, L. M. (1916). *The measurement of intelligence.* Boston: Houghton Mifflin.

The Tragedy of Sudan. (2004, October 4). *Time,* 44–61.

Thompson, B. (1994). Food, bodies and growing up female: Childhood lessons about culture race and class. In P. Fallon, M. A. Katzman, & S. C. Wooley (Eds.), *Feminist perspectives on eating disorders* (pp. 355–378). New York: Guilford.

Thorndike, R. L., Hagen, E. P., & Sattler, J. M. (1986). *Technical manual for the Stanford-Binet Intelligence Scale* (4th ed.). Chicago: Riverside.

Ting-Toomey, S. (1994). Face and facework: An introduction. In S. Ting-Toomey (Ed.),

The challenge of facework (pp. 1–14). Albany: State University of New York Press.

Ting-Toomey, S., & Cocroft, B.-A. (1994). Face and facework: Theoretical and research issues. In S. Ting-Toomey (Ed.), *The challenge of facework* (pp. 307–340). Albany: State University of New York Press.

Tracey, T. J., Leong, T. L., & Glidden, C. (1986). Help seeking and problem perception among Asian Americans. *Journal of Counseling Psychology, 33,* 331–336.

Tremblay, P. J. (1995). The homosexuality factor in the youth suicide problem. Retrieved October 11, 2004, from http://www.qrd.org/qrd/www/youth/tremblay/main.html

Triandis, H. C. (1989). The self and social behavior in different cultural contexts. *Psychological Review, 96,* 506–520.

Triandis, H. C. (1995). *Individualism & collectivism.* Boulder, CO: Westview.

Triandis, H. C., Bontempo, R., Betancourt, H., Bond, M., Leung, K., Brenes, A., Georgas, J., Hui, C. H., Marin, G., Setiadi, B., Sinha, J.B.P., Verma, J., Spangenberg, J., Touzard, H., & de Montmollin, G. (1986). The measurement of etic aspects of individualism and collectivism across cultures. *Australian Journal of Psychology, 38,* 257–267.

Triandis, H. C., Bontempo, R., Villareal, M. J., Asai, M., & Lucca, N. (1988). Individualism and collectivism: Cross-cultural perspectives on self-ingroup relationships. *Journal of Personality and Social Psychology, 54,* 323–338.

Triandis, H., Lambert, W., Berry, J., Lonner, W., Heron, A., Brislin, R., & Draguns, J. (Eds.). (1980). *Handbook of cross-cultural psychology* (Vols. 1–6). Boston: Allyn & Bacon.

Trierweiler, S. J., Muroff, J. R., Jackson, J. S., Neighbors, H. W., & Munday, C. (2005). Clinician race, situational attributions, and diagnoses of mood versus schizophrenia disorders. *Cultural diversity and ethnic minority psychology, 11,* 351–364.

Trimble, J. E. (2003). Infusing American Indian and Alaska Native topics into the psychology curriculum. In P. Bronstein and K. Quina

(Eds.), *Teaching gender and multicultural awareness: Resources for the psychology classroom* (pp. 221–236). Washington, DC: American Psychological Association.

Trimble, J. E., & Gonzales, J. (2008). Cultural considerations and perspectives for providing psychological counseling for Native American Indians. In P. B. Pedersen, J. G. Draguns, W. E. Lonner, & J. E. Trimble (Eds.), *Counseling across cultures* (6th ed., pp. 93–111). Thousand Oaks, CA: Sage.

Trimble, J. E., & Mertz, H. K. (1999). Culture-bound syndrome. In J. S. Mio, J. E. Trimble, P. Arredondo, H. E. Cheatham, & S. Sue (Eds.), *Key words in multicultural interventions: A dictionary* (p. 86). Westport, CT: Greenwood.

Tsai, J. L., Ying, Y.-W., & Lee, P. A. (2001). Cultural predictors of self-esteem: A study of Chinese American female and male young adults. *Cultural Diversity and Ethnic Minority Psychology, 7,* 284–297.

Tversky, A., & Kahneman, D. (1973). Availability: A heuristic for judging frequency and probability. *Cognitive Psychology, 5,* 207–302.

Uba. L. (1982). Meeting the mental health needs of Asian Americans: Mainstream vs. segregated services. *Professional Psychology: Research and Practice, 13,* 215–221.

Unger, R. K. (1995). Conclusion: Cultural diversity and the future of feminist psychology. *Bringing cultural diversity to feminist psychology: Theory, research, and practice* (pp. 413–431). Washington, DC: American Psychological Association.

U.S. Census Bureau. (1999). Interracial married couples: 1960 to present. Internet Web site MS-3.

U.S. Census Bureau. (2001). The two-or-more races population: 2000. Retrieved October 11, 2004, from http://www.census.gov/prod/2001pubs/c2kbr01-6.pdf

U.S. Census Bureau. (2004). Annual estimates of the population by race alone or in combination and Hispanic or Latino origin for the United States: July 1, 2003. Retrieved November 23, 2004, from http://www.census.gov/popest/states/asrh/SC-EST2003-04.html

U.S. Department of Energy, Biological and Environmental Research. (2004). *Genetic disease profile: Sickle cell anemia.* Retrieved October 31, 2004, from http://www.ornl.gov/sci/techresources/Human_Genome/posters/chromosome/sca.shtml

U.S. Department of Health and Human Services. (2001). *Mental health: Culture, race, and ethnicity—A supplement to mental health: A report of the Surgeon General.* Rockville, MD: U.S. Department of Health and Human Services, Public Health Service, Office of the Surgeon General.

U.S. Department of Health and Human Services. (2003). National healthcare disparities report: Executive summary. Washington, DC: Author. Retrieved October 8, 2004, from http://www.ahrq.gov/qual/nhdr03/nhdrsum03.htm

U.S. Department of Health and Human Services. (2004). *Health disparities experienced by racial/ethnic minority populations.* Author. Available at http://www.ncadi.samhsa.gov/govpubs/mmwr/vol53/mm5333a1.aspx

U.S. Department of Health and Human Services. (2007). Addressing racial and ethnic disparities in health care fact sheet. Retrieved November 11, 2007, from http://www.ahcpr.gov/research/disparit.htm

U.S. Department of Health, Education, and Welfare. (1979). *The Belmont Report: Ethical principles and guidelines for the protection of human subjects of research.* Washington, DC: Author. Retrieved October 10, 2004, from the Health and Human Services Web site, http://www.hhs.gov/ohrp/humansubjects/guidance/belmont.htm

U.S. General Accounting Office. (2000, March). *U.S. Customs Service: Better targeting of airline passengers for personal searches could produce better results.* Washington, DC: Author.

Utsey, S. O. (1997). Racism and the psychological well being of African American men. *Journal of African American Men, 3,* 69–87.

Utsey, S. O., Bolden, M. A., & Brown, A. L. (2001). Visions of revolution from the spirit of Frantz Fanon: A psychology of liberation for counseling African Americans confronting societal racism and oppression. In J. G. Pontorotto, J. M. Casas, L. A. Suzuki, & C. M. Alexander (Eds.), *Handbook of multicultural counseling* (2nd ed., pp. 311–336). Thousand Oaks, CA: Sage.

Utsey, S. O., & Payne, Y. (2000). Psychological impacts of racism in a clinical versus normal sample of African American men. *Journal of African American Men, 5,* 57–72.

Utsey, S. O., Payne, Y., Jackson, E., & Jones, A. (2002). Racism, quality of life indicators, and life satisfaction, and indicators of psychological and physical health among elderly African Americans. *Cultural Diversity and Ethnic Minority Psychology, 8,* 224–233.

Vasquez, L. (2000). *Culturally competent counseling & therapy, part III: Innovative approaches to counseling Latin/o people.* [Training videotape available from Microtraining Associates, Inc., Box 9641, North Amherst, MA, 01059-9641]

Vasquez, M.J.T. (2001). Reflections on unearned advantages, unearned disadvantages, and empowering experiences. In J. G. Ponterotto, J. M. Casas, L. A. Suzuki, & C. M. Alexander (Eds.), *Handbook of multicultural counseling* (2nd ed., pp. 64–77). Thousand Oaks, CA: Sage.

Vega, W. A., Kolody, B., Aguilar-Gaxiola, S., Alderate, E., Catalana, R., & Carveo-Anduaga, J. (1998). Lifetime prevalence of *DSM-III-R* psychiatric disorders among urban and rural Mexican Americans in California. *Archives of General Psychiatry, 156,* 928–934.

Velasquez, R. J., Callahan, W. J., & Young, R. (1993). Hispanic-White MMPI comparisons: Does psychiatric diagnosis make a difference? *Journal of Clinical Psychology, 49,* 528–534.

Vernon, W. W., & Roberts, R. E. (1982). Prevalence of treated and untreated psychiatric disorders in three ethnic groups. *Social Science and Medicine, 16,* 1575–1582.

Vital Knowledge G.I.F.T.S. (2001, September). Three letters from Teddy. Retrieved December 14, 2002, from http://www.vitalknowledge.com/teachers/archives/newsletter

Wade, C., & Tavris, C. (2003). *Psychology* (7th ed.). Upper Saddle River, NJ: Prentice Hall.

Wagner, R. K. (2000). Practical intelligence. In R. J. Sternberg (Ed.), *Practical intelligence in everyday life.* New York: Cambridge University Press.

Walters, K. L., & Simone, J. M. (1993). Lesbian and gay male group identity attitudes and self-esteem: Implications for counseling. *Journal of Counseling Psychology, 40,* 94–99.

Warren, R. (1995). *The purpose-driven church.* Grand Rapids, MI: Zondervan.

Warren, W. L., & Srole, L. (1946). *The social systems of American ethnic groups* (2nd ed.). New Haven, CT: Yale University Press.

Watson, O. M., & Graves, T. D. (1966). Quantitative research in proxemic behavior. *American Anthropologist, 68,* 971–985.

Wechsler, D. (1991). *Manual for the Wechsler Intelligence Scale for Children–Third Edition.* San Antonio, TX: Psychological Corporation.

Weissman, M. M., Bland, R. C., Canino, G. J., Faravelli, C., Greenwald, S., Hwu, H. G., Joyce, P. R., Karam, E. G., Lee, C. K., Lellouch, J., Lepine, J. P., Newman, S. C., Rubio-Stipec, M., Wells, J. E., Wickramaratne, P. J., Wittchen, H., & Yeh, E. K. (1996). Cross-national epidemiology of major depression and bipolar disorder. *Journal of the American Medical Association, 276,* 293–299.

Weissman, M. M., Bland, R. C., Canino, G. J., Faravelli, C., Greenwald, S., Hwu, H. G., Joyce, P. R., Karam, E. G., Lee, C. K., Lellouch, J., Lepine, J. P., Newman, S. C., Rubio-Stipec, M., Wells, J. E., Wickramaratne, P. J., Wittchen, H., & Yeh, E. K. (1997). The cross-national epidemiology of panic disorder. *Archives of General Psychiatry, 54,* 305–309.

Weissman, M. M., Bland, R. C., Canino, G. J., Greenwald, S., Hwu, H. G., Lee, C. K., Newman, S. C., Oakley-Browne, M. A., Rubio-Stipec, M., Wickramaratne, P. J., et al. (1994). The cross-national epidemiology of obsessive compulsive disorder. The Cross National Collaborative Group. *Journal of Clinical Psychiatry, 55* (Suppl.), 5–10.

Weissman, M. M., Broadhead, W. E., Olfson, M., Sheehan, D. V., Hoven, C., Conolly, P., Fireman, B. H., Farber, L., Blacklow, R. S., Higgins, E. S., & Leon, A. C. (1998). A diagnostic aid for detecting (*DSM-IV*) mental disorders in primary Care. *General Hospital Psychiatry, 20,* 1–11.

White, J. (2001). My story. In D. W. Sue (Chair), *Surviving racism: Lessons we have learned.* Symposium presented at the National Multicultural Conference and Summit II—The psychology of race/ethnicity, gender, sexual orientation, and disability: Intersections, divergence, and convergence, Santa Barbara, CA.

White, J. L. (1970, September). Toward a Black psychology. *Ebony,* 44–45, 48–50, 52.

White, J. L. (1984). *The psychology of Blacks: An Afro-American perspective.* Englewood Cliffs, NJ: Prentice Hall.

White, J. L., & Parham, T. A. (1990). *The psychology of Blacks: An African American perspective* (2nd ed.). Englewood Cliffs, NJ: Prentice Hall.

Whitney, P. (1998). *The psychology of language.* Boston: Houghton Mifflin.

Whitworth, R. H. (1988). Anglo- and Mexican-American performance on the MMPI administered in Spanish or English. *Journal of Clinical Psychology, 44,* 891–897.

Wildes, J. E., & Emery, R. E. (2001). The roles of ethnicity and culture in the development of eating disturbance and body dissatisfaction: A meta-analytic review. *Clinical Psychology Review, 21,* 521–551.

Will, J., Self, P., & Datan, N. (1976). Maternal behavior and perceived sex of infant. *American Journal of Orthopsychiatry, 46,* 135–139.

Williams, D. R., & Harris-Reid, M. (1999). Race and mental health: Emerging patterns and promising approaches. In A. V. Horwitz & T. L. Scheid (Eds.), *A Handbook for the Study of Mental Health: Social contexts, theories, and systems.* New York: Cambridge University Press.

Williams, J. (1987). *Eyes on the prize: America's civil rights years. 1954–1965.* New York: Viking.

Williams, J. E., & Best, D. L. (1982). *Measuring sex stereotypes: A multination study.* Beverly Hills, CA: Sage.

Williams, J. E., & Best, D. L. (1994). Cross-cultural views of woman and men. In W. Lonner & R. Malpass (Eds.), *Psychology and culture* (pp. 191–196). Boston: Allyn & Bacon.

Williams, R. (1974a). A history of the Association of Black Psychologists: Early formation and direction. *Journal of Black Psychology, 1,* 9–24.

Williams, R. L. (1974b). The death of White research in the Black community. *Journal of Non-White Concerns in Personnel and Guidance, 2,* 116–132.

Witko, T. (Ed.). (2005). *No longer forgotten: Addressing the mental health needs of urban Indians.* Washington, DC: American Psychological Association.

Wittchen, H. U., & Kendler, K. S. (1994). Lifetime and 12-month prevalence of *DSM-III-R* disorders in the United States. *Archives of General Psychiatry, 45,* 1085–1092.

Wolfgang, A. (1985). The function and importance of nonverbal behavior in intercultural counseling. In P. B. Pedersen (Ed.), *Handbook of cross-cultural counseling and therapy* (pp. 99–105). Westport, CT: Greenwood.

Wood, J. (1994). *Gendered lives: Communication, gender, and culture.* Belmont, CA: Wadsworth.

Wood, J. T. (1999). Gender, communication, and culture. In L. A. Samovar & R. E. Porter (Eds.), *Intercultural communication: A reader* (8th ed., pp. 164–174). Belmont, CA: Wadsworth.

Woodside, D. B., & Kennedy, S. H. (1995). Gender differences in eating disorders. In M. V. Seeman (Ed.), *Gender and psychopathology* (pp. 253–268). Washington, DC: American Psychiatric Press.

World Health Organization. (1948). *Constitution of the World Health Organization.* Geneva, Switzerland: World Health Organization Basic Documents.

World Health Organization. (1973). *Report of the International Pilot Study on Schizophrenia.* Geneva, Switzerland: WHO.

Yang, K. (1997). Theories and research in Chinese personality: An indigenous approach. In H. S. R. Kao & D. Sinha (Eds.), *Asian perspectives on psychology* (pp. 236–262). Thousand Oaks, CA: Sage.

Yee, A., Fairchild, H., Weizmann, F., & Wyatt, G. (1993). Addressing psychology's problems with race. *American Psychologist, 48,* 1132–1140.

Yeh, C. J. (2003). Age, acculturation, cultural adjustment, and mental health symptoms of Chinese, Korean, and Japanese immigrant youths. *Cultural Diversity and Ethnic Minority Psychology, 9,* 34–48.

Yeh, C. J., & Huang, K. (1996). The collectivistic nature of ethnic identity development among Asian-American college students. *Adolescence, 31,* 645–661.

Yin, R. K. (2004). *The case study anthology.* Thousand Oaks, CA: Sage.

Ying, Y. W., & Hu, L. T. (1994). Public outpatient mental health services: Use and outcome among Asian Americans. *American Journal of Orthopsychiatry, 64,* 448–455.

Yum, J. O. (1999). The impact of Confucianism on interpersonal relationships and communication patterns in East Asia. In L. A. Samovar & R. E. Porter (Eds.), *Intercultural communication: A reader* (8th ed., pp. 78–88). Belmont, CA: Wadsworth.

Zalewski, C., & Greene, R. L. (1996). Multicultural usage of the MMPI-2. In L. A. Suzuki, P. J. Meller, & J. G. Ponterotto (Eds.), *Handbook of multicultural assessment: Clinical, psychological, and educational applications.* (pp. 77–114). San Francisco: Jossey-Bass.

Zane, N., Hatanaka, H., Park, S. S., & Akutsu, P. (1994). Ethnic-specific *mental health* services: Evaluation of the parallel approach for Asian-American clients. *Journal of Community Psychology, 22,* 68–81.

Zea, M. C., Asner-Self, K. K., Birman, D., & Buki, L. P. (2003). The abbreviated multidimensional acculturation scale: Empirical validation with two Latino/Latina samples. *Cultural Diversity and Ethnic Minority Psychology, 9,* 107–126.

Zea, M. C., & Garcia, J. (Eds.). (1997). *Psychological interventions with Latino populations.* Needham Heights, MA: Allyn & Bacon.

Zhang, A. Y., & Snowden, L. R. (1999). Ethnic characteristics of mental disorders in five U.S. communities. *Cultural Diversity and Ethnic Minority Psychology, 5,* 134–146.

Zhang, A. Y., Snowden, L. R., & Sue, S. (1998). Differences between Asian- and White-Americans' help-seeking and utilization patterns in the Los Angeles area. *Journal of Community Psychology, 26,* 317–326.

Zormeier, S. M., & Samovar, L. A. (1999). Language as a mirror of reality: Mexican American proverbs. In L. A. Samovar & R. E. Porter (Eds.), *Intercultural communication: A reader* (8th ed., pp. 235–239). Belmont, CA: Wadsworth.

Zuckerman, M. (1990). Some dubious premises in research and theory on racial differences: Scientific, social, and ethical issues. *American Psychologist, 45,* 1297–1303.

Credits

CHAPTER 1

Table 1.4: Excerpts from "APA Guidelines on multicultural education, training, research, practice, and organizational change for psychologists" from *American Psychologist 58:* 377–402. Copyright © 2003 by the American Psychological Association. Reprinted with permission.

CHAPTER 2

Ch. 2, pp. 34, 37–38: Excerpts from "Science, ethnicity, and bias: Where have we gone wrong?" by Stanley Sue in *American Psychologist, 54:* 1070–1077. Copyright © 1999 by the American Psychological Association. Reprinted with permission.

CHAPTER 3

Table 3.2: "Ho's depiction of value orientation comparison among racial/ethnic groups" from *Family Therapy with Ethnic Minorities* by Man Keung Ho. Copyright © 1987 by Sage Publications, Inc. Reprinted by permission of Sage Publications, Inc.

Figure 3.2: "Worldview Model" from "Eliminating cultural oppression in counseling: Toward a general theory" by Derald Wing Sue in *Journal of Counseling Psychology, 25:* 419–428. Copyright © 1978 by the American Psychological Association. Reprinted with permission.

P. 79: Excerpts from "Coping and resilience across generations: Japanese Americans and the World War II internment" by D. K. Nagata and Y. J. Takeshita in *Psychoanalytic Review, 85:* 587–613. Copyright © 1998. Reprinted by permission of The National Psychological Association for Psychoanalysis.

Pp. 80–81: Excerpts from "Reflections on unearned advantages, unearned disadvantages, and empowering experiences" by Melba J. T. Vasquez from *Handbook of Multicultural Counseling,* 2nd ed., edited by J. G. Ponterotto, J. M. Casas, L. A. Suzuki, and C. M. Alexander. Copyright © 2001 by Sage Publications, Inc. Reprinted by permission of Sage Publications, Inc.

CHAPTER 4

Table 4.2: "Comparison between North American and East Asian Orientations to Communication Patterns" from "The Impact of Confucianism on Interpersonal Relationships and Communication Patterns in East Asia" by June Ock Yum in *Intercultural Communication: A Reader,* 8th ed., edited by Larry A. Samovar and Richard E. Porter. Copyright © 1997 by Wadsworth Publishing Company, a division of International Thomson Publishing Inc. Reprinted by permission of the author.

Table 4.3: "Differences between Feminine and Masculine Speech Communities" from "Gender, Communication, and Culture" by Julia T. Wood in *Intercultural Communication: A Reader,* 8th ed., edited by Larry A. Samovar and Richard E. Porter. Copyright © 1997 by Wadsworth Publishing Company, a division of International Thomson Publishing Inc. Reprinted by permission of the author.

CHAPTER 7

Figure 7.1: "Tripartite Model of Personal Identity" from "Multidimensional facets of cultural competence" by Derald Wing Sue from *The Counseling Psychologist 29:* 790–821. Copyright © 2001 by Sage Publications, Inc. Reprinted by permission of Sage Publications, Inc.

Box 7.1: "Racial Identity Attitude Scale" from *Black & White Racial Identity: Theory, Research, and Practice* edited by Janet E. Helms. Copyright © 1990 by Janet E. Helms. Reproduced with permission of Greenwood Publishing Group, Inc., Westport, CT.

CHAPTER 9

Pp. 266–267, 268: Excerpts from *Counseling the Culturally Different: Theory and Practice,* 3rd ed., by Derald Wing Sue and David Sue. Copyright © 1999 by John Wiley & Sons, Inc. Used by permission of John Wiley & Sons, Inc.

Index